NO
MARGIN
FOR
ERROR

NO
MARGIN
FOR
ERROR

THE MAKING
OF THE ISRAELI
AIR FORCE

Ehud Yonay

PANTHEON BOOKS NEW YORK

All rights reserved under International and Pan-American
Copyright Conventions. Published in the United States by
Pantheon Books, a division of Random House, Inc., New
York, and simultaneously in Canada by Random House of
Canada Limited, Toronto.

Library of Congress Cataloging-in-Publication Data

Yonay, Ehud.
    No margin for error : the making of the Israeli Air
Force / Ehud Yonay.
        p.   cm.
    Includes index.
    ISBN 0-679-41563-7
    1. Israel.   Hel ha-avir—History.   I. Title.
UG635.I75Y66   1992
358.4'0095694—dc20

                                          92-54112

Book design by Judy Christensen

Maps by Eric Elias

Manufactured in the United States of America

First Edition

To Ruth,
my noblest warrior

CONTENTS

Introduction: A Line of Blood and Fire ix

PART ONE: THE RED SQUADRON

    1 Dead Reckoning 3

    2 The New Brunswick Warning . . . 13

    3 The Czech Knives 23

    4 The Banana Grove . . . 36

    5 The Red Squadron 49

    6 Bloodying the RAF . . . 60

PART TWO: THE PRINCE AND THE FARMER

    7 The Prince . . . 75

    8 The Farmer . . . 89

    9 The Blues and the Greens . . . 102

    10 The Black Spitfire . . . 120

    11 French Shuttle . . . 137

    12 Kadesh . . . 155

PART THREE: EZER'S WAR

    13 Mirage . . . 177

    14 Rebels . . . 188

15 *Moked* . . . 202
16 The Frontiersman . . . 214
17 Three Hours in June . . . 228
18 Keep It Simple . . . 245

PART FOUR: THE BLOODYING
19 "Texas" . . . 261
20 Phantoms . . . 276
21 Missiles . . . 292
22 Judgment Day . . . 307
23 *Operatziot* . . . 323
24 Legacies . . . 339

Epilogue: A Foreign Force, but Friendly . . . 357
Author's Notes . . . 371
Notes . . . 377
Sources . . . 391
Maps . . . 397
Index . . . 403

Illustrations appear between pages 240 and 241

INTRODUCTION

A LINE OF BLOOD AND FIRE

On November 29, 1947, with a rare two-thirds majority led by the United States and the Soviet Union, the UN General Assembly voted to partition Palestine between its embattled Arab and Jewish communities. Few decisions before or since have been imbued with such drama and historic imperative. Just half a decade earlier, 6 million Jews perished in Nazi concentration camps. Since World War II, shiploads of Jewish refugees fleeing Europe for a promise of a homeland in Palestine were turned back by British warships and imprisoned behind barbed wire on the island of Cyprus.

Now the civilized world was setting things right by that haunted, homeless minority. The vote was not about a Jewish state alone. Addressing Jewish and Arab national aspirations alike, the partition resolution provided for the establishment of two states—once the British mandate for Palestine expired and His Majesty's troops pulled out in May of 1948—one Arab and one Jewish. Partition seemed equitable and biblically symmetrical. After thousands of years of war, exiles, and retribution, the children of Abraham would formally share that sliver of ancient land between the Jordan River and the Mediterranean.

The Arab side of the equation was a mere formality. Whether

divided as the world now proposed, or left undivided as the Arab League demanded, an Arab state in Palestine was a given. A Jewish state was not. The partition vote was, above all else, a world referendum on whether the Jews would have a country to call their own. Thus to Palestine's Jews and their supporters, the partition was a victory beyond fondest dreams, and they now burst into the streets from New York to Tel Aviv to sing and dance in swirls of *hora* circles. To them, even one half of Palestine* seemed a fulfillment of ancient prophecies of national resurrection.

To the Arabs in Palestine and the surrounding states, partition was a bitter defeat. For them, keeping just one half of Palestine Arab was no more acceptable than having it all become Jewish. Abdul Rahman Azzam Pasha, the Arab League's secretary-general who just four days earlier warned the gathering that "the partition line shall be nothing but a line of fire and blood,"[1] now furiously led his delegation out of the hall. The die had been cast. Instead of sharing their biblical heritage, Jews and Arabs would have to fight for it.

The war began no more than five hours after the vote, when a well-dressed Arab flagged down a bus making its way from the small beach town of Netanya to Jerusalem. When the bus slowed down, the Arab whipped out a submachine gun from under his coat and began to fire, joined by other Arabs lying in ambush by the side of the road. Five Jewish passengers were killed, two men and three women. Half an hour later, the same Arab gang attacked another bus and killed two more Jews.

That same day, the Palestine Arab Higher Committee called for a three-day general protest strike. Massive Arab riots broke out across the country. In a circular handed to British soldiers and policemen, the committee urged them to stand aside. "The Arabs have taken in hand the final solution of the Jewish problem," the leaflet said. "Soon you shall be evacuated from here. Your sisters, wives, lovers, and family members are waiting for you. You have no stake in the Arab war. Why should you get killed?"[2]

---

*It was really less than one half of one half. In 1921, as a reward for helping the British army route the Ottomans out of Egypt, Palestine, and Syria during World War I, Britain lopped off the vast section of Palestine lying east of the Jordan River and handed it over to Emir Feisal, the sharif of Mecca. It was renamed the Kingdom of Trans-Jordan, later Jordan, with Feisal's playboy brother Abdullah as its first king.

The British troops took heed and stood by as Arab mobs sacked and burned the Jewish commercial district of Jerusalem on December 2, killing one Jew and wounding twenty. The violence quickly spread from the cities to the countryside, reaching even behind prison walls, where Arab prisoners rioted and attacked Jewish inmates.

The open reference to a "final solution"—Hitler's code word for the extermination of Europe's Jewry—was not accidental. Haj Amin al-Husseini, the charismatic Grand Mufti of Jerusalem and head of the committee, had spent most of World War II in Berlin, broadcasting Nazi propaganda to the Middle East. Now in Cairo, he had launched a *jihad* for the liberation of Palestine. His Army of Salvation consisted of two armed forces of one thousand soldiers each. One force operated in the Jerusalem area and was headed by his cousin, Abdel Kader al-Husseini. The other force, commanded by German-trained Hassan Salameh, ranged in the flatlands between Tel Aviv and Jerusalem.* In addition, as Arab Palestine's supreme religious leader, his call for a holy war would mobilize every Arab village and hamlet in the land.

Geography, demographics, and logistics were all on the side of the Arabs. Ever since it began in the 1880s, Jewish settlement in Palestine was a target-of-opportunity affair, with villages set up not on the basis of strategy and economics but solely on where land could be bought cheaply and inhabited quickly. By 1947, the state-in-the-making consisted of 600,000 or so Jews living in scattered pockets of villages and small towns, surrounded by close to one million increasingly militant Arabs.

If one were to draw lines on a map to mark off Jewish concentrations—as the United Nations now did to plan the partition of the land between Jews and Arabs—Jewish Palestine would resemble a

---

*Hassan Salameh's son, Ali Hassan Salameh, led the Black September terrorist organization in the 1970s, and was one of the architects of the 1972 massacre of Israeli athletes at the Munich Olympics. He was killed January 22, 1979, in Beirut by an Israeli-placed car bomb. Black September was an arm of al-Fattah, whose head, PLO chairman Yasser Arafat, is a nephew of the Grand Mufti. Abdel Kader al-Husseini's son, Faisal Husseini, is currently one of the leaders of both the *Intifada*, the Palestinian uprising in the Israeli-occupied West Bank and Gaza Strip, and the Palestinian side of the Arab-Israeli peace talks (he is not formally part of the delegation).

crude five-link sausage zigzagging north to south along the thirty-to-sixty-mile-wide land strip between the Mediterranean and the Jordan River, each link connecting to the next with a thread often no wider than a two-lane highway.

The heaviest Jewish population was along the central coast plain, with Tel Aviv as its center. To the north, a narrow road snaked around Mount Carmel to reach the port city of Haifa and the western Galilee hills, which were in turn attached by another narrow pass to the valleys of Yizre'el and Jordan, and to the Upper Galilee mountain country. To the south, a long, exposed highway led to the desert settlements of the Negev. To the east, the winding canyon pass of Bab-el-Wad connected the coastal flatlands with Jerusalem and its satellite villages to the east.

Within days of the United Nations vote, the mufti's army set out to sever the thin threads that held Jewish Palestine together. On the afternoon of December 11, near Bethlehem, Abdel Kader al-Husseini's guerrillas ambushed a small convoy of twenty-six settlers and escorts carrying supplies from Jerusalem to the Ezion Block, a small cluster of Jewish settlements south of Jerusalem. British soldiers and policemen stood and watched as the Jewish defenders fought to their last bullet, and were then shot one by one by the Arabs, including a young woman who was grabbed by the hair and shot in the temple. Ten members of the convoy were killed. Three days later, soldiers of the British-commanded Jordanian Legion joined the fray, ambushing a convoy headed for a small Jewish village in the Judean foothills and killing thirteen of its passengers and escorts.

In January of 1948, Abdel Kader al-Husseini attacked the Ezion Block itself. The attack failed, but the Arabs kept up the siege, cutting the villages off from the rest of the country save for an occasional supply drop by a small Piper Cub. The war of the convoys escalated rapidly through the spring. It climaxed in March, when in just two weeks sixty-four Jews were killed in four convoys near Jerusalem, and forty-six more when a convoy was ambushed on its way to the western Galilee village of Yehi'am.

By April, the Arabs had won the war of the convoys. The entire Negev and Galilee districts were permanently cut off, and Jerusalem for most of the time. Each city had become a battleground, each

Jewish settlement a frontier outpost under siege. In January, too impatient to wait for the British to leave, the neighboring Arab states raised and financed a volunteer Arab Liberation Army and sent it into Palestine to assist the Grand Mufti's Army of Salvation. On April 4, using Syrian-supplied artillery, the one-thousand-strong Army of Liberation forces attacked the Jewish settlement of Mishmar Ha'Emek, which controlled a narrow pass connecting Tel Aviv to Haifa and the northern valleys, while a second force attacked the village of Ramat Yohanan to cut Haifa off from the northern territories. The battles lasted for more than a week before the Arabs retreated back to the West Bank.

But holding off the Arab irregulars was still only a prelude. In May, with the British out of Palestine, the real war would begin as five Arab armies—Egypt, Trans-Jordan, Syria, Iraq, and Lebanon—would roll in with tanks, armored gun carriers, field artillery, and hundreds of antiaircraft and antitank guns. The entire arsenal of the *Haganah*, Jewish Palestine's self-defense underground, included 10,000 rifles of assorted vintages and calibers, 1,900 homemade submachine guns, and a few hundred light machine guns and mortars. Its small solitary old tank was missing its cannon. The *Haganah* had five antique field cannons and two dozen assorted antiaircraft or antitank guns. It could not even give each soldier a rifle and a handful of cartridges.

Most important, the *Haganah*'s handful of light single-engine passenger planes were no match for the Arab air forces. In the south, Egypt had two squadrons of British-built Spitfire fighters and two squadrons of American C-47 Dakotas converted into bombers. In the north, an entire Syrian squadron of fifteen AT-6 Harvard trainers had been equipped with guns and bomb racks and converted into effective dive-bombers. In the east, Iraq had just taken delivery of modern British Hawker Fury fighters. Once war broke out, the Arabs could seize control of the air over the entire country in minutes, sealing its fate.

Jewish Palestine's survival would depend on the success of a single secret operation, launched in November of 1947 to secure tanks, ships, artillery, and aircraft in time to repel the invasion. With hostile Arabs on three sides and a British-patrolled sea on the fourth, the operation appeared doomed from the start. Even if the weapons could be obtained in the face of a worldwide embargo, the odds of getting anything into the country past the British blockade, and getting it in on time, were laughable.

What was needed was a miracle. The *Haganah* knew that. The operation's code name, *Yakum Purkan*, came from a line in the Jewish Sabbath morning prayer, *Yakum purkan min shmaya,* which in ancient Aramaic meant literally "May salvation come from the skies."

PART ONE

THE RED SQUADRON

Chapter 1

DEAD RECKONING

On the morning of May 2, 1948, on an abandoned airfield outside Brindisi, Italy, four anxious young men in rumpled khakis and World War II flight jackets boarded two small planes for what ordinarily would have been an easy getaway. Their war-surplus Noorduyn Norsemans, canvas-over-spruce Canadian bush hoppers, could take off and land on snow, water, or tiny forest clearings while carrying their own weight in cargo. The grass strip, too, was a smuggler's dream, running to the edge of a cliff that grew like a pimple out of the back of the heel of the Italian boot. Once airborne, they'd be over Greek or Albanian waters in minutes, beyond the reach of the *carabinieri*.

But getting up in the air was the problem. Several nights earlier, the planes' interiors had been ripped out and a huge 200-gallon hard-rubber tank jammed tight into each fuselage, taking up the entire space from back of the pilots' seats to the tail. With the rubber tank now filled with 1,200 pounds of gasoline, along with the same amount in the regular tanks, each overweight Norseman had become a giant Molotov cocktail. If it as much as touched down hard the explosion could wipe out a city block.

The four men had not only to get the planes in the air but fly them clear across the Mediterranean. They also had to do it without proper maps or radios, with life rafts that were missing their compressed-gas bottles, and with no assurance that the fuel would last the entire 1,400-mile run to Palestine. If it didn't, there would be no refueling on the way, not with British troops and warships on the lookout for illegal Jewish immigrants and gunrunners.

Three of the young men were Americans, the fourth a South African. All were veterans of the Second World War. Coleman Goldstein was small, with light hair, protruding profile, and explosive temper. Since he had flown B-17s over Europe, their *Haganah* controller made him flight leader and handed him their only map, a bare textbook outline of the Mediterranean. Eddie Cohen, the South African, was appointed Goldstein's copilot. A gentle, dark-eyed flyer with no combat experience, he was the only one of the four who had ever been to Palestine, and ostensibly could recognize Tel Aviv from the air if they ever got there.

Lou Lenart, who would fly the second plane, was a wiry ex-marine Corsair pilot whose dark eyes watched the world with a mix of suspicion and anticipation from deep sockets atop protruding Slavic cheekbones. Milton Rubenfeld, a small, swarthy former USAF pilot, so cocky he seemed to swagger even while sitting down, was his copilot.

It was time to go. Lenart was still fumbling with his gear when Goldstein's plane disappeared beyond the edge of the cliff, and suddenly it was his turn. Glancing quickly to the sides to make sure all was clear, he gunned his single engine, released the brakes, and instinctively leaned back in anticipation of the lurch forward.

Nothing happened. He cast a worried look at his copilot but Rubenfeld only shrugged. Lenart cursed and slammed the throttle forward as far as it would go. The engine's roar increased, and almost imperceptibly, the plane began to roll. There was nothing wrong with the engine. The plane was simply too overloaded with fuel, with a last-minute load of machine guns, and with an unannounced *Haganah* passenger who squeezed in behind them. As furiously as the propeller dug into the morning air, it could not pull the plane any faster.

Lenart looked at his side of the runway. The ground that should have been speeding past was sliding lazily by. He tried moving the wheel, but it waddled limp in his lap—there was not enough rushing air even to engage the tail rudders. As if through a haze, he noticed their *Haganah* controller waving from the side of the runway. In a flush of panic, he realized that he had just passed the halfway mark, and that the crawling bomb he was strapped into could neither take off nor be stopped, not without collapsing its spindly landing gear and crashing on the runway.

There was no turning back now, no jumping out, nothing to do but keep the throttle forward. The runway was almost gone. In stunned disbelief, Lenart and Rubenfeld watched the edge of the cliff come closer, then disappear below the Norseman's stubby nose.

There was a little bump as the wheels climbed the slight embankment that marked the end of the continent, and then the plane ran over the edge.

But the fall never came. The Norseman that couldn't get up simply rolled off the cliff, dipped slightly, and kept going. As the ground below disappeared, it was suddenly airborne by default. Lenart tried the wheel and felt resistance. He pulled slightly and the plane climbed. Farther ahead was Goldstein's plane, and after a while Lenart caught up and fell into formation somewhere over the Ionian Sea.

Sometime in the late afternoon, after they had droned for hours over an endless succession of jewellike Greek isles on their way to Cyprus, Lenart noticed Goldstein's plane veering to the right. He couldn't figure it. The night before, sitting around a wooden table in the deserted hangar, they had plotted a rough flight plan that would take them along the Greek coastline to Turkey, then down the beaches of Syria and Lebanon to Palestine. But now Goldstein was drifting away from the coastline and gesturing for Lenart to follow.

When Lenart understood, the panic returned. Unsure whether they had enough fuel to go all the way around, Goldstein had pointed his nose toward Palestine and was going for it. Dead reckoning. They would make the rest of the way over water with no radio or survival gear, and with no land in sight. If they ran out of fuel there would be no place to even crash-land, no chance for a rescue.

Lou Lenart was born Laszlo Lajos Lenorovits in 1923 in the small Hungarian town of Sátoraljaújhely. In 1930, his family emigrated to the United States and settled in a poor coal-mining neighborhood in Wilkes-Barre, Pennsylvania. "I was a skinny little Jew who spoke no English. I must have been beaten up a hundred times during our first year there because I killed Christ. I didn't even know who Christ was," he would always remember.[1]

In 1940 he Americanized his name and joined the marines. Inside of three years he was a fighter pilot, flying attack and escort missions over Okinawa and the Japanese mainland. He was intense and humorless. Convinced that to become a true American he had to master language and society, he set out to collect new idioms and social connections with the single-mindedness of a pursuit pilot. The former he memorized, the latter he made himself useful to. It was also in the marines that he made the twin discovery that his insatiable sexual urges and his rugged, exotic looks and attentive social grace proved irresistible to a long succession of clinging camp followers.

When the war ended he retired a captain, married a movie starlet he had met at a wartime Hollywood bash that cosmetics king Max Factor threw for Jewish officers, and moved into a small bungalow in Los Angeles. One night in the fall of 1947, he heard a speaker at his local temple describe the fighting in Palestine. He thought of his grandmother, who had remained behind in Hungary and was killed by the Nazis, and of his marriage, of which he was growing tired. That night, he drove to the Ambassador Hotel, where the speaker was staying, and handed him his military résumé.

A few weeks later his telephone rang. "I understand you're interested in flying?" the man on the other side said without introducing himself.

"No," Lenart replied.

"But I have a piece of paper here that says you are," the man persisted.

Lenart suddenly remembered the Ambassador Hotel. The next day, at a downtown Los Angeles rendezvous, he was handed $5,000 in cash, which he took to the Federal Building and used to buy a war-surplus C-46 Curtiss Commando, a huge twin-engine military transport. If anybody asked why he needed it, "I was to say that a few friends and myself were starting a new airline," he says.

Overnight, he was in the thick of Operation *Yakum Purkan*, the secret *Haganah* quest for salvation from the skies. The operation was just then getting started. Days earlier, a stocky, conspiratorial ex-TWA flight engineer named Adolph Schwimmer flew to Los Angeles, checked into the Hollywood Roosevelt Hotel, and immediately drove over the Hollywood Hills to the Lockheed airfield in Burbank. There he set up shop as Schwimmer Aviation, ostensibly a new charter service for ferrying war refugees from Europe to South America, and quickly began to buy planes and recruit flight and maintenance crews. By early spring, in addition to the C-46 that Lenart bought, Al Schwimmer had three Lockheed Constellations and nine more C-46s undergoing repair on the Lockheed tarmac. He was also negotiating to buy three stripped-down B-17 Flying Fortress bombers, and a number of P-51 Mustang fighters. To get around an American embargo on military goods bound for the Middle East, he registered the transports to a mysterious new Panamanian airline, Líneas Aéreas de Panama, Sociedad Anónima, which like Schwimmer Aviation was also a *Haganah* front.

Schwimmer and his lumbering transports were just one part of the operation. At the same time, Yehuda Arazi, the *Haganah*'s star spy and smuggler, was nailing down deals for B-25 bombers and P-47 fighters in Mexico, and for an old aircraft carrier in Norfolk, Virginia. By early April, except for the fact that it was still halfway around the world, Jewish Palestine had the beginnings of an air force. Barring unexpected developments, Schwimmer's transports and Arazi's aircraft carrier, carrying the Mexican fighters on board, would arrive off the coast of Palestine just as the British left, and before the Arabs had a chance to launch their attack.

On April 15, however, the American government tightened its embargo to include even Schwimmer's gunless, bombless, and armorless flying hulks. A day before the new embargo rules went into effect, Schwimmer managed to get one Constellation and nine C-46s airborne and across the border to Tijuana. Everything else had to be left behind, including two Constellations, the B-17s, and the Mustangs. Mexico also decided against selling its old fighters and bombers, and the aircraft carrier deal fell through as well.

The few fighter and bomber pilots that Schwimmer had collected had barely made it out of the country before federal agents could catch up with them with a formal warning about serving under a foreign flag in violation of an American embargo. Like Lenart, they had joined up to prevent another Jewish Holocaust. Coleman Goldstein was a flight school instructor in Philadelphia when he read about Jewish convoys being ambushed in the Judean and Galilee hills. Fuming at the stupidity that must have kept the *Haganah* from supplying those besieged settlements by air, he sought out a recruiter and volunteered to go over and show them how it should be done.[2]

By the end of April, they were stranded in Rome, waiting for Schwimmer's transports to arrive, and getting thrown out of one hotel after another for picking up girls on the Via Veneto, trading them hotel furniture for sex, and sticking their *Haganah* controllers with the bills.

There was no telling how long they would have to wait. Schwimmer's planes had left Burbank so hastily they were overweighed with spare parts and assorted communication gear. As they attempted to hopscotch their way down to Panama and then to Brazil, whence they would cross the Atlantic to Africa, one of the C-46s crashed while taking off from Mexico City, killing its pilot. The *Yakum Purkan* crew pooled their cash, stuffed it in the dead pilot's wallet, and sent it to his widow. They then unloaded the remaining planes and left for Panama virtually empty.

Haganah buyers in Europe did not fare much better. One had managed to buy a covey of Anson light bombers in England and get them to Italy, but when the planes attempted to run the blockade to Palestine, they were seized during a refueling stop at Rhodes, and their crews arrested. Only one deal came through. During a Jewish fund-raising in Roanoke, Virginia, a Mrs. Sol Silverman told the speaker that her brother, a former USAF pilot, was dealing in used aircraft in Paris. The brother helped arrange the purchase of twenty surplus Norsemans, which still carried U.S. registrations. In twos and threes, the Norsemans were smuggled from France to Holland, where friendly KLM crews fitted them with long-distance tanks for the run to Palestine, and then to Italy.

The arrival of the Norsemans caused excitement in the growing pilot community in Rome. "There was an unspoken contest going on about who would be the first to take a plane through the blockade to Palestine," Lenart and Goldstein would recall years later, "but there was never any doubt in our minds that we'd be the ones."

On April 30, the two of them, along with Rubenfeld and Cohen, were called to the Rome airport, to take the first two Norsemans to Brindisi and from there to Palestine. On the way to Brindisi Goldstein became furious when he found out that the new fuel tank connections were leaking fuel. He was almost apoplectic when his *Haganah* controller told him there would be no lights at the Brindisi field, where they'd arrive after dark. He threw a fit until the *Haganah* man let him land at Bari airfield, sixty miles before Brindisi. The pilot of an Anson light bomber who flew with them decided to continue to Brindisi anyhow and crashed on landing.

Disillusioned with their *Haganah* controller, Goldstein decided to stay another day at Brindisi to fix the leaks and test-fly the planes. Even when they finally got going on May 2, their *Haganah* agent procrastinated so long that it was late morning when they finally walked to their planes. His profile thrust angrily forward like a ship's prow, Goldstein took his time and walked around the planes again and again, kicking tires, shaking struts, searching each fuel line connection for leaks.

While Goldstein checked the planes, Lenart strolled over to the side of the field to pick a small bouquet of wildflowers.

"For the first good-looking dame I meet in Tel Aviv," he said, grinning at Rubenfeld as he finally climbed into his plane.

"Yeah, sure," Rubenfeld grunted.

By late afternoon, Goldstein's decision to risk an open-water dash to Palestine seemed more and more ominous. Shortly after they passed Cyprus they ran into a thick cloud bank. Worried that if he stayed above it he'd miss Palestine and end up in Jordan or Syria, Goldstein went down through it, with Lenart following close behind. Once in the clouds, Lenart could not even see Goldstein's plane. They descended through the soup for what seemed like hours. When they finally broke clear they were barely 500 feet above water, sandwiched between gray water and gray clouds. They still had more than 150 miles to go, and it was getting dark. Sheer fright kept them awake. "If that bloody engine coughed once, the plane would be in the water, and we'd be dead. We did not see a single ship in all that time," Lenart would say later.

The day ended with still no land in sight, and they sweated out the remaining miles in gathering darkness. It was past ten at night when the clouds finally lifted and Goldstein noticed a few specks of light in the distance. If his navigation was correct, it was the coast of Palestine, somewhere between Haifa to the north and Tel Aviv to the south, so when he was over the beach, Goldstein banked to the south. But he had no way of telling where he was or where he was going. If he figured wrong, they'd soon be arriving at Gaza, not Tel Aviv.

In a few minutes, however, Eddie Cohen came alive. "Tel Aviv, Tel Aviv," he shouted over the engine, pointing down toward the twin chimneys of an electric power station. If there was a city below, it was blacked out. In the distance Lenart noticed gunfire. Goldstein was searching through the darkness for signs of an airfield but found none. They kept circling, frantic they'd run out of fuel. Twenty minutes or so passed before half a dozen faint lights suddenly came on in a row near the power station.

Thirteen hours after leaving Brindisi, they landed on a freshly graded dirt strip, almost running into a bulldozer parked at the edge of the field. The runway lights turned out to be tin cans filled with sand and kerosene. A small cheering crowd gathered around them. Hands reached out. Teeth gleamed in the darkness. Hoarse voices shouted unintelligible greetings in Hebrew. Lenart scanned the ecstatic, grinning faces and shoved his small bunch of Italian wildflowers at a young woman who turned out to be the air controller of the small field.

Then two young men, one short and one thin and tall, broke through the crowd and took control of the commotion. The short one welcomed them to Palestine in clipped English, introducing himself as Aharon Remez, chief of operations of the *Haganah* Air Service. The tall one, with long blond hair and a scraggly beard, just said "I'm Ezer Weizman" and herded the dazed pilots into a waiting car. After a few minutes of tire-screeching through the city's dark streets, they pulled up in front of a hotel on the Tel Aviv boardwalk, the Air Service's headquarters. Inside, a party was already under way to toast the first blockade runners.

"Who is *that?*" Lenart asked Weizman when he noticed a striking young woman across the room.

"You want her?" Weizman asked.

"Yeah."

Weizman, whom everybody seemed to know, called the young woman over, and soon Lenart made his excuses and walked out with her into the night, and then up to his room.

Goldstein went to sleep alone, and not for long. At four in the morning, he was awakened, told to dress in a hurry, and was driven back to the airfield. During the night, his Norseman had been stripped of its huge rubber tank and loaded with a large assortment of sacks and crates, all tied up with ropes, and padded with rubber tires. "Time to go to work," someone said. Goldstein climbed into the plane with a *Haganah* navigator to point the way. Inside the plane, two young men sat quietly with the packages.

Goldstein was stunned when, just minutes after taking off and turning eastward, his navigator took him on a zigzag course to bypass a succession of Arab towns and British army bases. Even before an Arab invasion, the Arabs were already at Tel Aviv's city limits. When war truly began, Jewish Palestine would be starting it from its own one-yard line.

Goldstein found the scale of the place hard to get used to. Back when he flew B-17s over Europe, he often flew for hours just to reach enemy territory. Now, a mere twenty minutes after leaving Tel Aviv, his navigator pointed to the silhouettes of small buildings atop the Judean ridge just ahead, against a golden-pink sunrise. "Jerusalem," he said. They had already crossed virtually the entire country. Beyond Jerusalem ran the Jordan River, Palestine's eastern boundary, and past it was the Kingdom of Jordan, the enemy.

Shortly before reaching Jerusalem, they turned south, and in a few minutes were hovering over the Ezion Block. Back in the States, reading about its heroic defenders holding off thousands of Arab attackers, Goldstein imagined fortified bunkers and machine-gun towers. Now he saw only a handful of villages scattered over the barren, rocky terrain, each a smattering of corrugated tin roofs and patches of green. As Goldstein took the plane down and began to circle, and the two young men in back opened the side door and tossed out sacks and padded boxes of supplies, unseen Arab guns in the surrounding hills began to fire at the plane, and then at the settlers who scampered to retrieve the packages.

It suddenly occurred to Goldstein that just twelve hours after arriving in Palestine, he was doing precisely that for which he so angrily sought out the *Haganah* recruiters in Philadelphia and New York just two months earlier—supplying the besieged settlements by air.

He then had another thought: What would have happened had the four of them not taken their flying napalm canisters up and across the Mediterranean the day before? Who would have supplied the men and women below, and with what? During World War II, he had crashed his B-17 in the French countryside and wandered with his crew for days before the Resistance got him back to safety. But not once throughout that entire ordeal had Goldstein worried about the war. There were hundreds of B-17s and thousands of pilots to take his place. Whatever it was that had to be done, there were always a thousand ways of doing it, a thousand other men to take one's place.

Not here. Here there was nobody else. It was a strange feeling, Goldstein would recall many years later, to suddenly realize that at that moment, over those besieged villages, he and his Norseman were all there was.

Chapter 2

THE NEW BRUNSWICK WARNING

In the web of myths and inspirational histories surrounding the establishment of the State of Israel, the sorry readiness of the Air Service on the eve of the Arab invasion is usually attributed to lack of money, the British blockade, and the American embargo, in that order. This is only partially true. Surplus military aircraft was dirt cheap in the wake of World War II, and the *Haganah* would have had no trouble lining up a few Jewish donors to purchase a few combat planes. Also, the British blockade would have expired before any Arab-Jewish war could begin, and the American embargo was imposed only in mid-October, 1947.

So why was Al Schwimmer, who first approached the *Haganah* early that summer with the idea of buying surplus transports, fighters, and bombers for the impending showdown with the Arabs, sent home with a mere "Come in again sometime"?[1] Why was it only in November, with war around the corner and the American embargo in full effect, that he was finally told to go ahead and get his planes?

In reality, right down to the wire the *Haganah* did not try to build an air force for the simple reason that it did not want one. To understand its mystifying aversion to air power one must understand the constellation of ideologies, paranoias, and messianic haze that dominated the Jewish return to their ancient homeland after two thousand years of exile.

Theodor Herzl, a Viennese journalist and a secular Jew, founded the modern Zionist movement in the late 1890s in response to widespread European anti-Semitism. Assuming that Jews were hated and persecuted because they had no state of their own, he formed his movement with the aim of providing the world's wandering Jewry with such a place. At one point Herzl even considered a British offer to establish a Jewish state in Uganda, in darkest Africa.

Herzl's followers, however, had far more Jewish education and religious upbringing than he, and for them the new Zion could rise only on the ruins of the old Zion, in Palestine. Herzl was overruled, and Zionism was transformed from a national escape to a national reclamation movement. But agreement on where the new Jewish state should be did not mean unanimity over what it should be like. The movement's Labor Zionist majority, a collection of leftist movements inspired by the Russian Revolution, wanted a socialist Jewish state coexisting with the Arabs anywhere in Palestine. The Revisionist minority—military-nationalist and vaguely anti-Socialist—did not care what kind of state it should be so long as it was Jewish, strong, and took in both sides of the Jordan River.

The Labor Zionists had the numbers, in the form of thousands of young pioneers who flocked to Palestine to settle on the land. By the 1930s, under the leadership of a short and combative former farm worker named David Ben-Gurion, they had not only taken over the Zionist movement but had given Jewish Palestine the accoutrement of a state, with a provisional government (National Assembly) and an underground army (the *Haganah*).

But the *Haganah* was first and foremost the Labor Zionists' army. In fact, its elite force, the *Palmach* (acronym for "shock troops"), was dominated by the left wing of the Labor Zionist alliance, and was so closely patterned on the Soviet Red Army that each company actually had a Soviet-style *polytrouk*, a political officer in charge of indoctrination. As guardians not only of Jewish Palestine's body but also of its soul, the *Haganah* and the *Palmach* fought not only the Arabs and the British occupation forces but also the Revisionists and their underground army, the Irgun Ze'vai

Le'umi (IZL, acronym for National Military Organization). In their Tolstoyan utopia, where farmers-soldiers tilled their fields by day and patrolled them by night, the kind of full-time professional military that Britain had and which the Revisionists longed for was an abomination.

The Second World War aggravated their dilemma. Colonial Britain, which under a 1939 policy "white paper" was cracking down on the *Haganah* and preventing Jewish refugees from fleeing the Nazis to Palestine, was itself fighting the Nazis. With Rommel on the loose in North Africa, Britain alone stood between Jewish Palestine and Hitler's gas chambers. Ben-Gurion, with characteristic pragmatism, vowed to "fight the White Paper as if there is no Hitler, [and] fight Hitler as if there is no White Paper," and ordered the *Haganah* youth to join the British army to help beat Germany. Indeed, thousands of young *Haganah* members fought under the British flag on every front, driving trucks, flying fighters, and commanding field units.

But the *Haganah* leadership lacked Ben-Gurion's genius for reconciling the irreconcilable. While it went along half-heartedly for as long as the war was on, it turned a cold shoulder and a suspicious eye toward more than twenty thousand *Haganah* members who came marching home in British army uniforms. With few exceptions, the returning veterans were not allowed to rejoin their old underground units. Those who distinguished themselves in the war and won officer and NCO ranks were accused of acquiring British habits and outlook, if not loyalties, and were kept out of the very command circles where their war experience would have been most valuable.

Having built a brave but amateurish and ill-equipped underground army because it was the best they could do under the circumstances, the *Haganah* leadership now clung to it as an embodiment of a social vision. So insular did it become in its guerrilla-mindedness that until the United Nations' partition debate *Haganah* planners never even considered the possibility that they might have to face the armies of the neighboring Arab states. Until November of 1947, all *Haganah* plans for defending Palestine pictured Palestine's Arabs as the only enemy, and small-unit guerrilla warfare as the only mode of confrontation. While the *Haganah* had early on established a small air unit of light planes, the *Pal-mach*'s "Flight Platoon," it was mostly to assist the guerrilla forces on the ground by scouting, delivering supplies, and evacuating casualties.

In the *Haganah*'s mindset, the British army veterans and their modern war experience were not only an ideological aberration— they were militarily irrelevant.

Fortunately, one of the returning war veterans was too tenacious and well-born—politically and ideologically—to be driven into the internal exile where so many of the returning veterans were whiling away their time in anger and resignation.

David Remez was a poet and Hebrew teacher who emigrated from Russia to Palestine in 1913. He began as a farm laborer but soon proved a talented political and labor organizer. By 1944 he was chairman of Jewish Palestine's provisional government, and David Ben-Gurion's close ally and confidant. The two even lived next door to each other, on the quiet, tree-lined Keren Kayemet Avenue in Tel Aviv, two blocks from the sea. His son Aharon, born in 1919, grew up well steeped in Labor Zionist ideology and politics. Small and unassuming, with a bemused Irish-pixie face and a surprisingly deep voice, Aharon dutifully trained to become a pioneer-farmer on the frontier when he came of age. At sixteen he entered the *Haganah* as a runner and then a rifleman, and at eighteen joined a frontier *kibbutz* in the upper reaches of the Jordan Valley, below the basalt cliffs of the Golan Heights. In 1939, he was sent to the United States to recruit and train young Jewish pioneers for Palestine.

When World War II broke out he tried to get back, unsuccessfully volunteering for the merchant marine fleet, and then to drive an ambulance in North Africa. In 1942, the Royal Air Force put out a call for volunteers, and Remez reported to an RAF recruiting office in New York. He had just "one condition—I wanted to wait in the Jerusalem pilot pool before I started flight training in Rhodesia. They agreed. I immediately gave away my heavy winter clothing and reported for duty in shirtsleeves and light trousers. Instead of Palestine, they sent me to an RAF training camp in New Brunswick, Canada, where it was already winter," he says.[2]

New Brunswick was cold in other ways. At an RAF screening

committee hearing he was asked if he were a *kibbutz* member, and if he had ever been arrested. Remez figured that whoever knew enough to ask already knew about his two arrests—both in anti-British demonstrations in Palestine—and replied yes on both counts. The questions became tougher—was he a *Haganah* member? Did he know Dov Hoz or Moshe Shertok or David HaCohen (Zionist and *Haganah* leaders)? His fears that his RAF career was over became a certainty that evening when he was told to report back to the committee chairman's office the next day.

The following morning, however, he found the committee chairman alone in his office, and in a talkative mood. A grizzled World War I aviator, he was not only familiar with Palestine and its Jewish leaders, but was "a great admirer of what you people are doing there." He did not bring Remez in to reminisce. "He told me that we were in great danger. He said that there are no personal favors in international relations, and that Britain's interest was to win the Arabs over from the Germans—especially with the military situation in the Western Desert being so bad," Remez would recall many years later. "He told me that if we could not defend ourselves, we would all be killed and there was nobody we could count on for help."

Not knowing what else to say, Remez promised, "We shall do our best to survive."

"That is not enough. I know what you have, and without an air force you cannot possibly survive," the British officer said.

"That's why I am here," said Remez.

His new friend saw Remez through flight school, from which Remez moved on to fighter training, where the trouble began again. "If you received an order to bomb a *kibbutz*, would you obey it?" he was asked during a commissioning board hearing at the end of his training.

"The question is not pertinent. I volunteered to fight the Nazis," Remez replied.

"You did not answer my question."

"Yes, I did."

There was a brief commotion. Remez was asked to step out of the room. Soon two board members came out and proposed a compromise. If Remez apologized to the third board member, the question would not be repeated, and his RAF officer's commission would be assured since he had finished in the top 20 percent of his fighter training class. Remez agreed to apologize "only if he apologizes to me first," and when that proved out of the question he notified the board that he "did not desire to become an officer." He was assigned to a fighter squadron as a sergeant, and came out at the end of the war still a sergeant, in spite of more than one hundred escort and attack missions over Europe to his credit in Spitfires, Hurricanes, and Tempests.

But the New Brunswick warning stayed with him "like a sharp knife stuck at my side, causing me to think more and more about a Jewish air force." He utilized every available moment to study modern air warfare, and on two occasions sent home proposals for the establishment of a Jewish air force. He received no reply, and when his promised home leaves were canceled with no explanation, he concluded that the British authorities had got hold of his letters.

Only at the end of 1946, when he returned to Tel Aviv for the first time in seven years, did he get a chance to discuss his ideas. His father and other Jewish leaders had just been freed from a British prison, having been arrested the previous June in a massive British crackdown on *Haganah* strongholds. At the homecoming celebration at his parents' home, Remez was pulled out to the garden by his next-door neighbor, David Ben-Gurion.

"I've been reading all those fantasies you sent me. Are you serious?" the stocky leader asked in his high, staccato voice.

"Now more than ever," Remez replied.

"Then we must immediately set up an underground air force," Ben-Gurion said. Remez was so taken back that he hesitated momentarily. "All right, if you don't want to do it we'll find someone else," Ben-Gurion snapped impatiently and turned to leave. "No, no, no. It's okay," Remez protested. Ben-Gurion told him to prepare the necessary plans. "Do you think the Arabs are capable of hitting us with a Blitz?" he asked. Remez hedged. He could not tell, not without access to intelligence about enemy strength. Shaking his head sadly, Ben-Gurion walked away.

The *Haganah*, however, showed little interest in Remez's ideas, and he soon returned to his *kibbutz* at the foot of the Golan Heights. It was another year before he was called back. In the spring of 1947, alarmed at the *Haganah*'s refusal to share his fears of an Arab invasion, and growing suspicious of its military competence, Ben-Gurion took over the provisional government's defense portfolio and began a thorough review of *Haganah* readiness. "I saw an urgent need to buy heavy weapons, tanks, troop-carriers, cannons, heavy mortars for the infantry, fighter planes for an air force, torpedo boats, and so on for a navy," he scribbled in his diary, "[but] I was very surprised to find . . . no understanding of the need for heavy arms."[3]

In the summer, when the *Haganah* command refused to upgrade its battle and readiness plans in the face of an inevitable war with the Arab states, Ben-Gurion staged an end run by forming an alternative command of senior British army veterans to organize the defense of Palestine against the Arab invasion. Worried of being stripped of authority altogether, the *Haganah* command reluctantly agreed to upgrade their war planning and admit a few experienced British army veterans into key positions.

On October 23, Remez delivered a comprehensive and ambitious "proposal for the establishment of a Jewish air force." Its first phase, to be put into effect immediately even with the British still in Palestine, called for a survey of available manpower, aircraft and airfield resources; for the purchase of single-engine civilian planes to be jerry-rigged as guerrilla fighters and bombers; and for training and deploying spotters in every settlement village and town to identify and warn against enemy planes. The second phase, which would go into effect as soon as the British moved out, included immediate occupation of all military airfields, and importation of enough war-surplus planes to form three fighter squadrons, two bomber squadrons, and two transport squadrons.

But it was not the scope or the price tag of the plan—2 million English pounds—that caused the *Haganah* to reject it almost out of hand. It was Remez's suggestion that the future air force should be semiautonomous, like the RAF, with its own command under a separate air ministry. In a series of stormy meetings with Remez, *Haganah* leaders insisted that the new air force should not only be under the total command of the *Haganah*, but that its very name should reflect that fact. Remez reluctantly gave in. On November 10, the Air Service was established with Joshua Eshel, an old *Haga-*

nah hand who knew nothing about aviation, as commander. Remez
was appointed chief of operations, and in New York Al Schwimmer
was told to start buying planes and recruiting volunteer air crews.

Remez's survey of his flying stock turned up just eleven single-
engine light planes—three Polish-built RWDs, two small American
Taylorcraft light trainers, two Canadian DH Tiger Moth biplanes,
an English DH Dragon Rapide light transport, and some Piper
Cubs—of advanced age and sorry state of repair. Of the twenty-two
pilots who answered his survey letters, only thirteen had logged
more than 120 hours with the British, South African, or Soviet air
forces (few had actual combat experience), and the rest were mostly
members of the *Palmach*'s "Flight Platoon," with barely enough
flying time to qualify for a civilian license for flying small planes.

Remez was still getting organized when the fighting broke out.
On December 9, the Air Service had to urgently move its planes
from the Lod airport, where the surrounding Arab villages made
getting in and out risky, to Sedeh Dov, a small landing strip at the
north edge of Tel Aviv, built years earlier by the Reading Power
Company to service its generating station. Hastily organized as
Squadron A, the small fleet was soon straining under the load of
keeping desert and mountain villages alive.

The courage and innovation of its pilots seemingly knew no
bounds. When a plane delivering a load of ammunition to the Ezion
Block could not be restarted for the flight back, its pilot hunted
around for a local electrician to replace the ignition assembly—
under constant Arab gunfire—then took off only to come back
down at the edge of the field, denting his landing gear and breaking
one of the propeller tips. He glued the tip back on and the following
day tried again, but the propeller broke and he came back down in
a hail of gunfire from the surrounding hills. He cut off the tip of the
second blade to even them out, and managed to take off, but then
his engine cut out over the Judean Hills and he had to return to the
Ezion Block. Finally, after cannibalizing the wreck of another plane
for a carburetor, he managed to get back to Tel Aviv.

Down in the Negev desert, during an Arab attack on a small
Jewish village, a *Palmach* pilot took the side door off his old Polish-
built plane, strapped a machine gun in its place, and with a local
kibbutznik beside him dived at the attacking Arabs—his passenger

opening fire each time the plane pointed in roughly the right direction—until the attack broke and the Arabs scattered.

But to Yigael Yadin, the *Haganah*'s chief of operations, the Air Service was still no more than a delivery service. A tall, arrogant, balding, second-generation archaeologist, Yadin had an authority grounded more in his piercing intellect than in any military experience, which was confined to biblical campaigns. He had opposed the establishment of the Air Service, as well as plans to purchase military planes in anticipation of the Arab invasion. Now, with the Air Service literally rammed down the *Haganah*'s collective throat, he refused to consult with Remez or even make him privy to planned operations.

On the night of January 15, this lack of coordination resulted in tragedy when a *Haganah* relief platoon sent from Jerusalem to the Ezion Block on foot was ambushed and decimated by Arab villagers before reaching its destination. Remez found out about it only the following morning when told to launch an air search for the lost platoon.

"We could have flown the men in. At the very least, they could have made the trip during daylight with air escort," he insisted furiously, and won a modicum of cooperation, however incomplete and short-lived. On April 3, when Ben-Gurion ordered an all-out drive to clear the road to Jerusalem, the Air Service sent a single-engine Tiger Moth to fly reconnaissance ahead of the advancing forces, and then a couple of Austers to drop a few fifty-pound bombs on enemy concentrations.

In truth, however, the Air Service was still at its best delivering supplies and evacuating casualties. Its contributions to the fighting were minimal and at times comic. On April 10, when an Arab artillery battery was spotted near the Jerusalem road, Remez sent three Austers to bomb it, only to have one come back with engine trouble and the other two miss their target and drop their bombs instead on a few Arab trucks at the entrance to some village. At the end of April, during a Lebanese attack on a strategic Jewish village in the Upper Galilee mountains, the only air support Remez could provide was a single Auster, which dropped two forty-pound bombs on the attackers (although that proved sufficient, since the attackers broke into a wild retreat).

As the deadline for the British pullout and the Arab invasion approached, the *Haganah*'s last-ditch effort to establish more defensive perimeters by dislodging heavy Arab troop concentrations in Galilee and the Judean Hills failed. Remez drew no consolation from the *Haganah*'s belated recognition of the desperate need for modern arms, fighters included.

Everything—the establishment of the Air Service, Schwimmer's hunt for aircraft—was begun too late. The few hastily organized arms-smuggling operations launched the previous fall were falling apart against the impenetrable British and American embargo. Across the Atlantic, Schwimmer's transports were still in Panama, being readied for the long flight to Brazil and then to Africa and Europe. In South Africa, a former combat pilot named Boris Senior had located forty-five P-40 Kittyhawk fighters about to be sold for scrap; he lined up the financing, but export permits proved impossible to get.

Nine years after New Brunswick, the warning Remez received was about to come true. On the night of May 2, even as his pilots celebrated the arrival of the two Norsemans, Remez was alone in his office. One by one, his plans for having a fighter squadron in place before the invasion had come to naught. All but one, that is, and there was no way of knowing how that one would turn out. If the other plans were unrealistic, this one was the kind that worked out only in the movies.

Chapter 3

THE CZECH KNIVES

In the fall of 1947, an attorney approached David Ben-Gurion with an idea. He had just returned from a visit to Czechoslovakia, the country of his birth, where he found some of his former classmates holding high government positions. Since Czechoslovakia was selling arms on the international market—to the Arabs, among others—Otto Felix thought he could swing an arms deal for the *Haganah*. Ben-Gurion promptly sent him back to Czechoslovakia to work it out.

Rotund, severe, and radiating authority, a scaled-down Sydney Greenstreet in black three-piece suit and homburg, Otto Felix did not waste time or words. By December he had closed a deal for 4,300 rifles, 200 machine guns, and a supply of ammunition, and shipped them to Palestine aboard a Yugoslav freighter, hidden under a load of potatoes. Then, in a coded message to Tel Aviv, he reported that Skoda Works, which produced Messerschmitt fighters for the Luftwaffe during World War II and was now making them for Czech use, had twenty-five of the famed World War II Nazi fighters available for immediate sale. Was the *Haganah* interested?

The *Haganah* was not, not with Schwimmer and Arazi spinning deals for fighters, bombers, and an aircraft carrier in the United

States. By April, however, those deals had collapsed, and Felix was asked to pick up ten Messerschmitts. The delay cost the *Haganah* dearly. While a surplus P-51 Mustang could be had for a mere $4,000, the Czechs demanded $44,000 for each stripped-down Messerschmitt, or $180,000 for a fighter complete with guns, ammunition, and bombs. Felix was in no position to haggle. On April 23, he bought ten fighters for $1.8 million, and on his own took an option for fifteen more. In his coded cable exchanges with Tel Aviv, the Messerschmitts became *messers,* Yiddish for knives.

Finally, just three weeks before the invasion, Remez had his fighter squadron. There was only the matter of getting the fighters home. Because of their short range, the Messerschmitts had to be broken down and transported to Palestine inside Schwimmer's C-46s, if those ever got to Europe. Also, his own pilots had to be sent to Czechoslovakia to train on the unfamiliar craft. But when Remez tried to book his pilots for a flight to Europe on a free-lance South African C-47 Dakota, which was flying passengers in and out of Palestine and in between flights was dropping supplies into besieged settlements in Galilee and the Negev for the *Haganah,* Yadin refused to give up the plane. Keeping those settlements supplied, he said, was more important than just about anything.

Remez was frantic. On May 4, with just ten days to go before the British pullout and the Arab invasion, he called Ben-Gurion, who ordered Yadin to release the plane. But it was May 9 before Remez could finally put six pilots aboard the Dakota. Three of the pilots were foreign volunteers—Lou Lenart and Milton Rubenfeld, the Americans, and Eddie Cohen, the South African, who just a week earlier had brought the two Norsemans from Italy. Of the three Palestinian Jews, Ezer Weizman and Modi Alon were blond and blue-eyed RAF Spitfire pilots. The third, Pinya Ben Porat, was a dark and stocky *Palmach* pilot, whose only qualification for flying fighters was that he once broke up an Arab attack in the Negev with a machine gun strapped to the outside of his single-engine Polish plane.

With the exception of Ben Porat, the small group constituted Remez's entire fighter corps. Now, with five days left before the invasion, he was sending them on a secret voyage behind the Iron Curtain, to be trained by Communists, which they hated, on ex-

Nazi fighters that only a few years earlier they would have seen only through their gun sights. There was, of course, no assurance that any of them would ever come back. If the Americans were not snatched by the Communists, they might be arrested by U.S. authorities for going to Eastern Europe without a permit. Likewise, as British subjects and, in the case of Weizman and Alon, RAF veterans, the Palestinian Jews faced a similar threat from the British. Lou Lenart was in the worst predicament—the Czechs might notice his accent, take him for a Hungarian defector, and send him back to Hungary.

So the six sat silent, trying not to draw attention, as the Dakota made brief stops in Cyprus and Rome before dropping them off in Geneva. Making sure they were not followed, they quickly boarded a train to Zurich, where waiting *Haganah* agents rushed them aboard a Czech Airlines DC-3. Several hours later they landed in Prague. As Czech border guards surrounded them with cocked guns, the pale pilots refused to talk or answer questions except with "I am looking for Dr. Felix."[1] It sounded ludicrous. They had never heard of Dr. Felix, had no idea if he even existed. To their amazement, the ranks of the Czech guards parted, and they were allowed out of the terminal with no questions, no searches, not even a look at their documents. Outside the terminal, other *Haganah* operatives whisked them to a once-grand downtown hotel, now shabby and gray, and ordered them to stay put. Two days later they were driven back to the airport and placed aboard a military transport that took them to a small Czech air base near the town of České Budějovice, hard by the Austrian border. They were placed in damp, cold barracks, issued leather Luftwaffe flight jackets, and warned against wandering through the base or talking to anybody.

The invasion was now just two days away.

The Czech Messerschmitts, on which they began training the next morning, turned out to be a far cry from their legendary German namesakes. In September of 1945, a fire destroyed a sugar refinery where the Czechs had kept the Messerschmitts' German-made Daimler-Benz engines. The Czechs switched to old German Heinkel bomber engines, and the heavy, underpowered Heinkels not only made the Messerschmitts sluggish in the air, but so nose-heavy that they would flip over at the slightest pretext.

Worse yet, the Heinkel's huge paddle-blade propeller gave the Czech Messerschmitt a nasty habit that the Czech instructors had trouble explaining in their halting English, and which Lou Lenart, the first to take off in the "Czech Knife," had to learn firsthand, nearly getting killed in the process.

Like many fighter planes of the era, the Messerschmitt had a tiny tail wheel, which made the plane sit nose up on the ground. As Lenart sat strapped down in his cockpit, the only thing he could see in front was the Messerschmitt's huge nose pointing skyward. Until his plane was traveling fast enough so that its tail came up, he had to watch the runway markings on his side, or fix on a distant tree or building for direction.

But the Czech field was only an expanse of gray-green grass blending seamlessly into the gray, dreary countryside. There were no runway markings, no trees in the distance to navigate by. When his instructor jumped off the wing and barked something in Czech that Lenart assumed was an order to take off, he pushed the throttle forward and let go of the brakes. When his speed gauge indicated he was going fast enough, he flicked his stick forward to raise the tail, and got ready to take off.

To his horror, as the Messerschmitt's huge nose came down he suddenly found himself speeding between two huge hangars, heading straight for a tall chain-link fence. He had no idea where he was, or how the buildings suddenly got in front of him. Cursing and pulling hard on the stick, he managed to lift the plane over the fence, but he was not yet going fast enough and the Messerschmitt promptly dropped back down on the other side. Fighting to keep it from cartwheeling or smashing belly-first into the ground, Lenart managed to keep it skimming the grass until it picked up enough speed, and then pulled it up in the air.

When he came back down after completing his prescribed training maneuvers, he found the others subdued—and surprised to see him alive. They had watched him taxi off, then veer sharply to the left and disappear behind the hangars at the side of the field. Since they did not see him clear the fence, they assumed he had crashed.

It was their introduction to the Messerschmitt twist. The huge paddle blades of the Heinkel engines were just too big for the small fighter. As they spun through the air, they torqued the entire plane to the left. Since the Messerschmitt lacked a trim tab, a small blade that most fighters had on their vertical tail fins and which could be set to compensate for a sideways drag, the only way to keep the plane going straight was to shove the right-hand pedal all the way forward. Ben Porat, the *Palmach* pilot, couldn't get the hang of it, and promptly washed out after crash-landing on his first try. For the first few days, the remaining five had their hands full just surviving through the Czech Knives' takeoffs and landings. It could have taken weeks until they could take the planes up with bombs and ammunition, and attempt actual combat maneuvers.

But there was no time left. On May 10, the day after they left Palestine, one of the Norsemans crashed while bombing Arab positions in the Judean Hills, killing its entire crew of six. On May 11, with just six light planes in flyable condition, Remez notified Ben-Gurion he had to stop his flights to the front or he'd have no planes left when the Arabs invaded three days later. On May 12, without waiting for the British to clear out, an Arab Legion force of fifteen hundred attacked the Ezion Block with tanks and artillery. On May 13 one of the villages surrendered, and its defenders were slaughtered by Arab villagers. On the morning of May 14, as British soldiers began boarding ships at Haifa, the Ezion Block fell, giving the Jordanians a clear run to Jerusalem. In the north, the Syrian army had crossed the Jordan River, while in the south an Egyptian expeditionary force began rolling up from the Sinai.

At four in the afternoon on that day, with battles already raging up and down the country, Ben-Gurion mounted a podium at the Diezengoff House in Tel Aviv and declared the formation of the State of Israel. Within hours, the United States and the Soviet Union recognized the new state. As masses of enthusiastic residents began to sing and dance in the streets, however, Ben-Gurion rushed to the Red House, the *Haganah*'s headquarters, to await the Arab response. "I am like a mourner among the merrymakers," he noted in his diary. "Will they bomb Tel Aviv tonight?"[2]

Just before dawn, they did. Ben-Gurion had begun a radio broadcast to the United States when Egyptian Spitfires swept in from the south and began to bomb Tel Aviv and the Air Service's tiny airfield at its north end. Remez, who was awakened by the explosions and rushed to the airfield, found half of his planes destroyed on the ground, and five Air Service men dead. But the soldiers guarding the field had meanwhile found several machine guns that were waiting to be shipped to the front and quickly set them up. When the Spitfires returned for a second attack later that morning, the soldiers shot and forced one of them down on the beach north of Tel Aviv, where its dazed pilot was promptly arrested.

One of the radios tuned to Ben-Gurion's international broadcast that morning was in a Czech Air Force barracks 1,800 miles away. Huddled around it, the five pilots seethed as Ben-Gurion described the Arab bombing of Tel Aviv. "There we were, two Israeli zealots and a handful of Jews who came to build the Third Temple, just sitting around while the Egyptians were bombing our city," Weizman recalled later.[3]

That night, their base commandant dropped in for a drink. He had flown fighters with the Free Czech Air Force out of Britain during World War II, he said, and had no more sympathy for the Communists than he had had for the Nazis. "If I didn't have my family to worry about I'd come with you," he said.[4] They talked air tactics deep into the night, dreaming up impossible schemes for their handful of Messerschmitts to hold back the Arabs' flying armada.

"Fuck them on the ground, before they have a chance to take off," said the Czech commandant, dismissing their suggestions with a contemptuous flick of his hand. "Fuck them on the ground." It was not at all clear that they would have the chance. The coming war, the Arab League's secretary general Azzam Pasha warned on May 16, "will be a war of extermination and a momentous massacre which will be spoken of like the Mongolian massacres and the Crusades." Indeed, the five Arab armies now moved in ferociously. On May 18, the fighting reached the very heart of Tel Aviv, as Egyptian bombers hit the city's central bus depot, killing forty-two civilians.

As soon as they heard the news, the five pilots informed their instructors and *Haganah*—now Israeli government—agents in Prague that they had had enough training, and that they were going home. In vain the instructors pleaded that a few hours of air time were not enough, and that they should at least stay through a few more days of gunnery and bombing practice. On May 19, they were taken to an air base near the town of Žatec, in the Sudetenland near the German border, for the flight back to Israel.

Coming from the dismal gloom of České Budějovice hardly prepared them for Žatec. With Soviet blessing, the Czechs had set aside an entire section of a former Nazi airfield near Žatec for the Israeli arms airlift. Army and police were instructed to let the Israeli transport crews come and go at will, and have the run of Žatec's hotels and nightspots. Žatec was now teeming with Israeli and American pilots, navigators, mechanics, arms buyers, and a host of spies, smugglers, and veterans of countless Zionist undergrounds that had operated in Europe since World War II and were now finally coming up into the light.

Seven months after its beginning in Los Angeles, Operation *Yakum Purkan* was about to deliver its promised salvation. Ten days earlier, five of Schwimmer's nine C-46 Commandos left Panama for Natal, at the eastern edge of Brazil. Two of them broke down, and of the three that began to cross the Atlantic to Africa, one developed engine trouble and had to return. But on May 17, after hopscotching through Casablanca and Sicily, the remaining two C-46s landed in Israel, unloaded their scant cargo of spare parts and a disassembled small BT-13 training airplane, and headed back to Žatec, to join the chartered Dakota and C-54 Skymaster that had already begun the arms shuttle to Israel.

On the morning of May 20, the five fighter pilots squeezed into the C-54 with one disassembled Messerschmitt, a load of bombs and ammunition, and several Czech mechanics. Eleven and a half hours later they landed at Tel Nof, a huge air base fifteen miles south of Tel Aviv, which the Israelis occupied as soon as the British pulled out a week earlier. As cargo and passengers were hastily unloaded and stashed away, the plane was refueled and rushed back out before the Egyptian dawn patrols spotted it and shot it down. At daybreak, the base appeared deserted.

On the next day, May 21, Schwimmer's two C-46s brought in a second dismantled Messerschmitt—one carried the fuselage, the other the wings and propeller—and on May 22 the C-54 brought the third fighter over. By then two more of Schwimmer's C-46s had arrived in Žatec, and on May 23 they ran the fourth Czech Knife to Israel. When they touched down at Tel Nof in a thick fog, however, one of the planes crashed into a low hill, losing its navigator and one half of a $180,000 Czech Messerschmitt.

As the shuttle flights from Žatec continued, and as the Czech mechanics worked to put the fighters together at the north end of the Tel Nof air base, time was running out. In the north, the Syrian army had swept down from the Golan Heights and was charging the Jordan Valley settlements with tanks and infantry. In the center, Jordan's Arab Legion was laying siege to Jerusalem, while three Iraqi infantry and armor brigades had pushed westward from the West Bank to within a few miles of the Israeli coast, threatening to cut Israel in half. In the south, a massive Egyptian invasion force of tanks and infantry moved under air cover from the Sinai in a giant pincer move, one claw climbing up along the coast toward Tel Aviv, while the other swept east with the aim of linking up with Jordan's Arab Legion at the Judean foothills, and cutting off the Negev.

Two weeks after the invasion began, Israel's defenses were giving in. On May 28, the Jewish Quarter of the Old City of Jerusalem surrendered, and the Arab Legion's seizure of the police fortress of Latrun, at the entrance to the Bab-el-Wad canyon pass to Jerusalem, meant that the city was now cut off from the rest of the country. On Friday, May 29, the Egyptian Second Armored Brigade had pushed north of Gaza to the Arab village of Ishdud, just seventeen miles from Tel Aviv. The Egyptians stopped briefly to repair a small bridge that Israeli sappers had blown up the night before, but in a few hours they'd be across the bridge, where only two tired and ill-equipped infantry companies from the Givati Brigade stood between them and Tel Aviv.

That morning, too, the first four Messerschmitts were ready for action.

Remez had known all along where they'd strike first. Two weeks earlier, he had personally interrogated the Egyptian pilot who had been shot down over Tel Aviv, and learned that an Egyptian Spitfire squadron had just moved to the El 'Arīsh airfield, in the western Sinai just fifty miles south of Gaza. Both Tel Aviv and Jerusalem, less than a hundred miles from El 'Arīsh, were in their easy reach. But according to Israeli reconnaissance flights the Egyptians were oblivious to any threat from the air, and kept parking their Spitfires in one straight row on the tarmac.

"From the moment I heard that, I could not think of anything but hitting El 'Arīsh," recalls Remez.[5] With a well-timed surprise attack, even his handful of Messerschmitts could destroy the Spitfires on the ground and instantly seize control of the air over the southern front. Stripped of air cover, the Egyptian column would have to stop its advance on Tel Aviv. It was a rare opportunity, never to be repeated. It could work only as long as the Egyptians did not know that the Messerschmitts existed.

Remez had already ordered the pilots briefed for the attack on El 'Arīsh when an urgent call came from Col. Shimon Avidan, commander of the Givati Brigade. "If you don't attack the Egyptian column right now, I have nothing with which to stop them," Avidan said. Remez refused. An attack on the Egyptian column would tip off the Egyptians to the existence of the Czech Knives. In fact, if they scrambled fast enough the Egyptian Spitfires could ambush the Israeli fighters on their way home from Ishdud.

Avidan called Yadin, then rushed to Tel Nof to personally plead with the pilots to go to Ishdud. Remez, too, had rushed down, but as soon as he reached Tel Nof he was called to the telephone. Yadin was on the other end, and he now ordered Remez to hit the Egyptians at Ishdud. Remez had no choice. Lou Lenart, who earlier that day was appointed mission leader, was handed the new orders.

What the pilots knew but did not say was that it might all have been in vain. None of them had flown a Messerschmitt in combat or even over a gunnery range. And with the Egyptians at Ishdud only ten miles away from Tel Nof, the planes had to be assembled in such secrecy and silence that even testing the engines or guns had been out of the question. There was no telling if the engines would start, if the planes would take off, if the guns would fire, or if the bombs would disengage. The first fighter mission of the Israeli Air Force would be, above all else, an act of faith.

Secrecy was maintained to the last moment. "It was crazy, we had to start our takeoff right from inside the hangar," Lenart would recall. Even so, Egyptian Spitfires suddenly roared over the base as the four sat strapped in their cockpits with their engines started. The pilots barely wriggled out of the cockpits and jumped into the trenches outside when the Arab fighters began to strafe the hangars. Fortunately, they destroyed only a hangar that contained two unassembled Messerschmitts. The hangar with the four fighters was hardly touched.

When the Spitfires left, the shaken pilots climbed back into their cockpits. At 7:45 P.M. they rolled out, Lenart and Modi Alon first, Weizman and Eddie Cohen after them. To avoid being spotted by the Egyptians, they took off to the east, staying low, then began the wide sweep to the west, going out to sea so they would approach their target out of the setting sun. They were heading back toward land when Lenart suddenly realized he had no idea where Ishdud was. He had been in the country only a few days, and could not tell one village from another. Since the Messerschmitts did not have radios that worked, he turned back in the cockpit and gestured his bewilderment to Modi Alon, his wingman. Alon calmly pointed him the right way.

There was no mistaking Ishdud once they arrived over it. The village, clumps of mud houses surrounding a dome and a minaret, swarmed with Egyptian trucks, tanks, and soldiers. The Egyptians were well trained. As soon as the Israeli fighters appeared, the village virtually exploded with fire as gunners and foot soldiers quickly took cover and began shooting at them.

Lenart brought his Messerschmitt right over the village, dived straight at the minaret, and released his bombs at the village square. Not sure whether they went off or not, he pulled his plane back up, swung it around to begin a regulation U.S. Marine Corps cloverleaf attack pattern, and dived back into the heavy fire. This time he picked a large concentration of trucks at the south end of the village, flipped the safety off his guns and began firing. When the guns jammed after firing no more than a dozen shells, he pulled back up, looked around, and when he saw none of the other planes, headed back to base.

Weizman was already there when Lenart landed. His guns had also jammed, he said, and he had no idea if his bombs hit anything. Alon's guns also jammed, and when he landed he blew a tire, which caused his plane to loop over and break a wing tip. Eddie Cohen never returned. Weizman mistakenly thought he saw his plane explode during the attack, but Cohen had in fact radioed to base that he had completed his mission and was heading back home. His plane was subsequently found near Beit Daras, a small airfield farther to the south, where he apparently tried to land by mistake and was shot down by the Egyptians.

In its first mission ever, Israel lost half of its fighter force and one-fifth of its fighter pilots. And as the remaining pilots made clear in their reports, the few small bombs and gun shells they managed to get off barely nicked the massive Egyptian force. Avidan, who waited anxiously for their return, shook his head at their accounts and sadly headed back to prepare his troops for the inevitable Egyptian assault the next morning.

But the attack never came. That night, the commander of the Egyptian column radioed back to his superiors that he had come under heavy enemy air attack and was taking defensive positions. The next morning, according to messages intercepted by Israeli intelligence, he refused to move on and instead ordered his troops to dig in. What the Messerschmitts did not do physically, they accomplished psychologically. The Egyptian Spitfires did not take off after the Israeli fighters. The Egyptian column never crossed the Ishdud bridge. It would never reach Tel Aviv.

Just fifty miles to the north, meanwhile, the Iraqi armored column was outside Tul Karm, with ten miles to go before it reached the coast and completed the envelopment of Tel Aviv. On the next morning, May 30, Remez sent Weizman and Rubenfeld in the two remaining Messerschmitts to stop it. They found the Iraqis strung along the narrow highway that led from Tul Karm directly due west to the sea. It was a sobering sight. That one column alone had more tanks and pieces of artillery than existed in all of Israel at the time. Gun for gun, there did not exist in the whole country a concentration of armor and firepower to stop the Iraqi advance. In less than an hour, they would cross the Haifa–Tel Aviv highway, cut northern Israel from its center, and the envelopment of Tel Aviv would be complete.

With Weizman leading the way, the two swept east toward Tul Karm, then came in from behind the Iraqis and dropped their bombs on the front end of the column. They then pulled up and began to come around to strafe the tanks and trucks as they screeched into a confused stop. They never got the chance. As he was pulling up, Rubenfeld's plane was hit by antiaircraft fire or by fragments from his own bomb and began to fall to the west, thick black smoke trailing behind. A moment later, Weizman had begun to fire his guns when a heavy object smashed through his windshield, splattering him with glass and forcing him to turn back to base.

Rubenfeld, who managed to bail out before his plane crashed at sea, landed in the surf and was wading toward shore when an angry crowd of Israeli farmers came down to the water's edge, waving spades and pitchforks at what they were certain was an Arab pilot. Rubenfeld, who spoke no Hebrew, began waving his arms and yelling the only Yiddish words he could remember at the top of his voice—"*shábes, shábes; gefílte fish, gefílte fish*"—until the farmers caught on and pulled him out of the water.

Weizman had in the meantime landed. "I seem to have been hit," he announced dramatically. Tev Zimmerman, a gruff, diminutive South African mechanic, reached into the cockpit, snickered, then pulled out the small bird that had broken through the window.

As it had at Ishdud the day before, it was the Messerschmitts' sudden appearance rather than their effectiveness that carried the day, because like the Egyptians, the Iraqi column also stopped its advance. But the cost was high. By the next morning, when Remez was urgently asked to take out the Jordanian guns that were preventing the construction of a back access road to Jerusalem, he had just one Messerschmitt and two pilots left.* Lenart and Alon flipped a coin; Alon won, and for the rest of the day attacked the guns again and again until "his Messerschmitt was so full of holes we didn't know how he kept it flying," as one of the mechanics recalls.

Remez now had to make a critical decision. Heavy fighting was raging throughout the country, and urgent pleas for air assistance were coming in constantly. Egyptian Spitfires were bombing villages and strafing Israeli ground troops. Tel Aviv was being bombed with increasing frequency by Egyptian C-47 Dakotas converted into bombers. In Galilee, in the Judean Hills and in the wide expanses of the Negev, scantily defended towns and villages were under attack by tanks, cannons, and heavily armed infantry. If he attempted to respond to even a small fraction of those impending

---

*That morning, as he sped from Tel Aviv to Tel Nof on Modi Alon's motorcycle, Weizman hit a bomb crater, was thrown off, and cracked his arm. He would not be flying for weeks.

disasters, the one badly mauled plane that was left of his small fighter squadron would be destroyed in hours. For as long as it could be kept flying, his remaining Czech Knife had to be placed where it would do the most good.

Remez assigned it to the defense of Tel Aviv. The results could not have been more dramatic. In the late afternoon of June 3, Modi Alon had just begun riding shotgun over the city when two Egyptian Dakotas arrived for their nightly bombing run. Alon calmly headed out to sea, swept back so he came at the Dakotas from out of the setting sun, then shot one down just south of Tel Aviv, and the other as it attempted to escape to the south. The residents of Tel Aviv, who watched the air battle from rooftops and balconies, were electrified. The secret was out. Israel had an air force. The pilots' rooms at the Yarden hotel were filled with flowers and candy. Well-wishers crowded the bars along the waterfront till all hours.

More important, as Lou Lenart and Modi Alon continued their twilight patrols, taking turns in the remaining Czech Knife, the Egyptian bombers stopped coming. The ancient prayer that gave Al Schwimmer's airlift its name, Operation *Yakum Purkan*, was answered. Salvation did come from the skies.

Lenart was flying the lone Czech Knife in the silent skies over Tel Aviv one evening, he recalled many years later, when "I suddenly had the feeling that I was David. I was watching over my people, ready to defend them with my own body. It was such a powerful sensation that tears literally came up in my eyes."

On June 11, Israel and the Arab states agreed to a twenty-eight-day cease-fire arranged by the United Nations. The war, however, had only just begun.

Chapter 4

THE BANANA GROVE

Aaron Finkel was a stocky and cheerful radio component salesman, a former U.S. Air Force fighter pilot whose friends continued to call Red even as his hair began to fade and recede. One night in early May of 1948 he woke up in his small Brooklyn apartment to find a stranger sitting on his bed. "I would like you to go to Palestine to be a fighter pilot. How much would we have to pay you?" the man asked in broken English.[1]

"Of course I knew what was going on in Palestine," Finkel would later recall. "My thinking was that any Jews willing to stand up and fight for their life deserved all the help I could give them. So I told the man—I still don't know who he was, how he found me, or how he got into my apartment—that I'd do it for a bottle of whiskey, cigarettes, and thirty dollars a month."

Within days, he was on a TWA Constellation bound for Rome. He had no idea that the burly young man sitting next to him was headed the same way. Sidney Antin had been visiting his parents in Boston when a girlfriend of his sister told him that the 107 combat missions he had logged in a P-47 Thunderbolt during World War II gave him "exactly the kind of talent the Jews need in Palestine."[2] She also put him in touch with the Israeli recruiters.

In Rome, and then in Czechoslovakia for Messerschmitt training, Finkel and Antin found themselves part of a small but growing crowd of idealists, adventurers, and mercenaries bound for Palestine. What Al Schwimmer's telephone network did not accomplish before the war was now being done by the Arab invaders—in North and South America, Africa, Europe, and Asia, alarmed by the prospects of a second Holocaust, Jewish war veterans by the dozens sought out Israeli recruiting agents, or else Jewish activists sought out the veterans and signed them up. Sid Cohen, a stocky, deep-voiced South African who flew P-40s against Rommel in the western desert, had left medical school to join in the fighting. Rudy Augarten, a lanky and taciturn American P-47 Thunderbolt pilot, cut short his international relations studies at Harvard after listening to a rousing speech by Abba Eban, then a plump, spectacled young member of the Palestinian lobby at the United Nations.

Not only Jews came. To Chris Magee, a tall ex-marine who had shot down four Japanese fighters while flying P-40s off the Solomons in Pappy Boyington's Black Sheep Squadron, Israel was the only place left where one could still fly in anger on the side of righteousness. Leon Nomis, a giant part Native American from Southern California who flew Spitfires with the RAF and accumulated a formidable collection of decorations from several governments, sniffed out the remnants of Al Schwimmer's *Yakum Purkan* crew in Los Angeles and volunteered to fight for Jewish Palestine.

When the first Arab-Israeli truce went into effect on June 11, the pilots began to arrive in Israel, alone or in small groups so as not to draw attention. They were given one orientation flight—Mitchell Flynt, a redheaded former U.S. Navy pilot, recalls getting shot at by Arab gunners just outside Tel Aviv—and told to wait for the next round of fighting.

Some truces are preambles to armistice and peace. The June 11 truce was not one of these. After a month of heavy fighting, Israel still lay within the ludicrous link-sausage boundaries drawn by the architects of the United Nations partition plan. With the Arab Liberation Army in control of the Galilee mountain region, the Jordanians and Iraqis in the West Bank, and the Egyptians reaching up from the Sinai, each Jewish sausage was now either surrounded

by two or three Arab armies, or facing them with its back to the sea.
In the south, the Egyptian pincers had already closed around the
Negev region, severing it from the rest of the country.

As a result, both sides could only gain from a resumption of the
fighting. For the Arabs, whose frontline units now had Jerusalem,
Tel Aviv, and the Mediterranean coast in view, the end of the Jewish
state seemed close at hand. Conversely, having survived and
blocked the initial Arab onslaught, the Israeli command no longer
thought just in terms of defending its sausagelike perimeter, which
would forever invite new Arab aggression, but now had plans to
push back the Arab armies and with them the state's future boundaries. For both sides, the truce came like the sound of the bell in a
boxing match, an opportunity to rest and recuperate briefly before
the next round, to rearm and regroup. Israel's airlift from Czechoslovakia was in full swing. Schwimmer's transports landed daily
with arms and ammunition, and chartered airliners brought scores
of recruits and volunteers.

For a moment, however, it wasn't all that certain that Israel
would survive to begin the next round of fighting. Combat against
Arabs had barely ceased when Jews fell to fighting against one
another with such uncompromising intensity that just one week
into the truce the country was on the brink of civil war. The
detonator was Ben-Gurion's attempt to create a nonpartisan national army by disbanding the heavily politicized former undergrounds of the pre-statehood years, and by having their members
enlist in the new Israeli Defense Forces (IDF) individually.

The *Palmach*, the former elite fighting force of the *Haganah*
underground, rebelled first. During more than a decade of struggle
for independence, the rumpled, idealistic, self-sacrificing, sing-
around-the-campfire *Palmachnicks* embodied the best in the new
state's farmer-warrior generation, the quintessential New Jews.
Politically, however, the *Palmach* was the creature and national
showcase of the small, far-left United Labor Party (Mapam).
Through the *Palmach*, Mapam enjoyed a disproportionate influence in the military arena, an influence that Ben-Gurion clearly
aimed to erode.

Mapam agreed to let the *Palmach* join the IDF, but with its
command, structure, and membership intact. But this would have

effectively placed the IDF's elite unit under the political command of the Mapam Central Committee, not the new Israel Defense Ministry. Ben-Gurion rejected the offer, and Mapam launched a political campaign to remove him as defense minister, instigating a mass resignation of the IDF's entire high command, including the IDF chief of staff Yigael Yadin. At literally the same time, a rebellion erupted on the right when Menachem Begin's right-wing IZL, also known as the *Irgun,* similarly insisted on joining the IDF in toto, and had just brought in a chartered foreign freighter named *Altalena,* loaded with arms and ammunition for the IZL's own use.

Through political maneuvering and threats of resignation, Ben-Gurion managed to put down the putsch from the left, and on June 22, after Begin refused to surrender the *Altalena,* ordered the IDF to fire at the ship, then anchored offshore within view of the Tel Aviv boardwalk. With scores of Israeli civilians and foreign volunteers watching, a mortar shell struck the *Altalena's* cargo hold, blew it up, and set it on fire. At a cost of three IDF and twenty IZL dead, the insurrection on the right also ended.

With only days left before the truce terminated on July 9, the IDF command finally got around to preparing for the fighting ahead, quickly putting together ambitious battle plans to dislodge the Arab Liberation Army from the Central Galilee, push the Arabs back from around Tel Aviv, retake the Latrun fortress and Jerusalem, and break through the Egyptian fortifications that separated the Negev settlements from the rest of the country. Time was of the essence. In New York, a new partition plan was working its way through the United Nations machinery, aimed at giving the Negev to the Arabs and placing Jerusalem under international administration. The new plan would leave Israel with a puny, ax-shaped piece of real estate (with the Galilee hill country constituting the head, the Jordan Valley the blade, and the narrow coastal belt the handle), and with dozens of Jewish settlements stranded in Arab territory. There was just one way of countering the new plan—pushing the Arabs back to create a contiguous stretch of country which by logic and right of possession would remain Jewish.

Much of the success of this new offensive would depend on Remez's lone Messerschmitt squadron, now formally designated Squadron 101 under the command of Modi Alon and, at the start of the truce, still consisting of four pilots, a single flyable Messer-schmitt, and eight more planes in various states of assembly or repair.

The squadron had spent the truce getting the planes out of Tel Nof, out of the range of the Egyptian guns at Ishdud and the Egyptian Spitfires at El 'Arīsh. At Remez's urging, a secret new fighter base was built around a half-mile dirt field running east to west among orange and banana groves outside the town of Herzliyya, ten miles northeast of Tel Aviv. The field was plowed, leveled, and seeded with grass. Work crews cut square sections out of the bordering orange groves and covered them with camouflage netting to serve as makeshift revetments, and erected surplus British army tents to house the ground crews. A twenty-foot concrete water tower was rigged with an air sock, radio, and field telephone to serve as control tower. As soon as it was completed, the Messerschmitts were shuttled in from Tel Nof and hidden in the orange groves. Foreign volunteers were hustled out of Tel Aviv as soon as they arrived and settled at the Falk Pension, a small residential hotel in the village of Kefar Shemaryahu just west of the new airfield.

Secrecy was total. Truce or no truce, one Egyptian air attack could wipe out field, planes, and support facilities, so everything had to be hidden, disguised, and denied. From the air, there was little to distinguish the small grass field from the surrounding farm country. It had none of the telltale signs of a fighter base: criss-crossing runways, hangars, control tower, planes lined up on a concrete tarmac. A low ridge to the west sheltered the field from sea fog and hid it from view of the busy coast road. The two small farming villages that bordered it from north and west kept the secret and watched the narrow dirt roads running to the outside. Once holed up at Herzliyya, the 101 might just as well have been on the moon.

By the time the truce drew to an end, Remez's small band of planes and flyers had acquired enough of the accoutrement of a real air force to insist on a greater role in the fighting ahead. In addition to the Messerschmitt fighter squadron at Herzliyya, there was now a squadron of transports that could double as makeshift bombers at Ramat David, a former RAF air base in the Yizre'el Valley in the north, east of the port city of Haifa and south of the ancient town of Nazareth. Also, Al Schwimmer had finally managed to spirit his three B-17 Flying Fortresses out of the United States; they were now getting outfitted in Czechoslovakia, a few flight hours away. There were also more than a dozen Norsemans and assorted light planes fitted as dive-bombers.

Indeed, the Israeli offensives on both the northern and southern fronts, planned for July 9, were now predicated on surprise air strikes on the evening before the ground attacks began. In the south, the Messerschmitts would hit the El 'Arīsh airfield to destroy the Egyptian Spitfires on the ground, and the Norsemans would drop bombs on the Egyptian fortifications guarding the highway from Tel Aviv to the Negev. In the north, a C-47 Dakota from Ramat David would stage a night bombing run on the Syrian forces east of the Jordan River, to delay or prevent their crossing into Galilee.

Although these missions looked good on paper, not a single one of them was carried out. The small planes that headed south in the gathering darkness did not find their targets. One bombed an Israeli *kibbutz* by mistake, and another got lost and dropped its bombs at sea. In the north, the Dakota crew, made up of foreign volunteers who did not know the terrain, aborted the mission when they could not tell if they were flying over Syrian or Israeli positions.

The 101 squadron did worst of all. With four experienced American pilots assigned to the mission—Lou Lenart as flight leader, and recent arrivals Stanley Andrews, Robert Vickman, and Bi'l Pomeranz—and with El 'Arīsh just twenty minutes away, it seemed a simple matter to sweep in out of the setting sun, demolish the Egyptian fighters on the tarmac, and get back to Herzlyya before supper.

Unfortunately, even working around the clock, the ground crews could not prepare four planes for that evening. It was only late the next morning that the planes were ready, and then, just after Lenart lifted off from the grass field, Andrews's Messerschmitt spun to the left, thrust its right wing into the ground, vaulted over it and landed flat on its back in the middle of the runway. For the next twenty minutes, Lenart circled above, the other two planes waited, and Andrews hung head down in the cockpit while ground crews tried in vain to move the plane. Finally, several Yemenite farmers from the nearby village showed up with long poles, flipped the plane right side up and helped push it off the field.

By the time Vickman and Pomeranz took off and the three planes reached Gaza, Lenart realized that he had spent too much fuel circling and could not make it to El 'Arīsh and back. Ordering his flight to turn around, he spotted an Arab ship unloading what appeared to be troops and military supplies at the Gaza port, and dived at it bombing and strafing with—he would report later—Vickman close behind.

When he pulled back up from the dive, he saw no one around and returned to Herzliyya. His fuel was so low that his propeller stopped just as soon as he touched down. Pomeranz was already there, but Vickman never returned and was never found. The fighting had just begun and the 101 had already lost a fighter and its pilot, damaged another plane, and not even come near its target.

As the fighting now resumed on all fronts, the Egyptians attacked throughout the Negev under heavy air cover, their Spitfires nearly reaching Tel Aviv and Jerusalem without running into Israeli fighters. In the flat desert country Israeli soldiers lay helpless in their trenches, exposed to enemy bombing and strafing. "We simply did not have anything to send up against the Spitfires," Remez would recall. By the second day of the fighting, mechanics got two Messerschmitts ready, and both were dispatched to the north, where the Syrians had begun crossing the Jordan River into Galilee. The two volunteer pilots, a stocky, cockney-accented Briton named Morris Mann and a South African named Lionel Bloch, were strafing the Syrian troops when they were jumped by two Syrian T-6 Harvards. Mann shot one of them down. Bloch chased the other into Syria, where he, too, mysteriously disappeared.

It was only by chance that, on the third day of the fighting, a third pilot avoided a similar fate and in the process discovered a possible explanation for Vickman's and Bloch's disappearances. Sid Cohen, the stocky South African with the booming voice, was on his way to the Syrian front when he swung out to sea to test-fire his guns. Almost immediately, his plane developed a vibration, which Cohen dismissed as another peculiarity of the Czech Knife. Luckily, the mission was uneventful. When he landed he discovered bullet holes running clear through his massive propeller. The plane's two machine guns, mounted above the engine and designed to fire between passes of the propeller blades, had apparently gone out of synchronization. Had he kept firing a bit longer, Cohen would have drilled his propeller clean off, which was probably what Vickman and Bloch had done, literally shooting themselves down.

Only the three B-17 Flying Fortresses did better. On the night of July 16, on their way from Czechoslovakia to Israel, one detoured to the south and dropped two tons of bombs near King Faruk's palace in the middle of Cairo, while the other two bombed Gaza and Rafah in the Gaza Strip. That same night, the Forts went out again and attacked El 'Arīsh, damaging the runway and the Egyptian fighters on the tarmac. In the next two days, before the United Nations imposed a new truce, the B-17s carried out eighty sorties, dropping fifty tons of bombs on the Syrian invasion force at the Jordan River, and on Damascus and its neighboring Al Mazzah airport.

Only on July 18, the last day of the fighting, did the 101 fighter squadron finally regain its stride. That morning, Modi Alon led Sidney Antin and Rudy Augarten, the American P-47 Thunderbolt flyers from Boston and Philadelphia, in a successful fighter strike on an Egyptian armored column in the Negev south of Beersheba. On their way back, Antin, who was flying at Alon's right, spotted four Egyptian Spitfires flying on a parallel course to their left, oblivious to the Israelis' presence. Augarten, who flew on Alon's left, was closest, so he peeled off, rolled in behind one of the Spitfires, and tried to fire. Nothing happened—he had gotten so excited during the strafing, his first combat mission since arriving in Israel, that he used up all of his ammunition. Modi Alon quickly took his place, and in a brief dogfight shot down one of the Spitfires.

Instead of a victory roll, however, their return to Herzliyya was out of the Keystone Kops. Alon's Messerschmitt, spinning to the right as soon as it hit the ground, ran off the runway and nearly flipped over. Antin's plane hit a bump, nosed over, and remained standing tail up on the runway. Augarten nearly ran into both of them as he tried to land into the setting sun; by the time he came around again he was out of fuel.

On the ground as in the air, what became known as the Ten-Day Campaign failed to achieve most of its objectives for either Arabs or Israelis. Having just turned from underground guerrillas into an army, the Israelis were too untrained, inexperienced, and badly equipped to sustain a complex offensive. While they managed to seize some territory in Galilee, as well as the Lod railway junction and international airport, the Arab Liberation Army still held most of Galilee, the Jordanians remained in Latrun and around Jerusalem, and the Egyptian encirclement of the Negev actually got tighter.

Again, Israel entered the second truce, one that would last all summer, with a flurry of accusations and feuding. The Air Force in particular was blamed for delayed and aborted missions, for failing to locate targets, for inefficiency in command and administration. In return, Remez charged that IDF General Staff failed to provide resources for badly needed spare parts, maintenance, and communication gear. He pointed out that with a single telephone line connecting Herzliyya with the outside, by the time an army unit in the Negev got a distress call through and the fighters were scrambled, the enemy had done its damage and departed.

"Things got to a point that one night I was personally chasing all over Tel Aviv, looking for a twenty-four-volt battery without which one of the B-17s could not fly the next day. I don't know how many people we pulled out of bed until we finally found a small junkyard that had such a battery. On that occasion the plane left for its mission the following morning, but we were not always so lucky," Remez would later recall.[3]

The problem was more than a battle for scarce resources. Even though Israel became a state on May 15, 1948, and the *Haganah* underground was ostensibly replaced by a formal armed force, the new IDF command was in reality the same old *Haganah* leadership, only in new uniforms and with new titles. Like the *Haganah* before statehood, the IDF was now commanded by Yigael Yadin and his old cadre of former underground warriors, the same clique who opposed the creation of the independent Air Service the previous fall. "To them we were still a foreign element," says Remez. "Our language was formally English. Our pilots lived in hotels, and they got drunk and wrecked bars in Tel Aviv when everybody else slept in the trenches."

Clearly something had to be done, and it could be done only

by the small, white-maned, combative man who single-handedly
brought the Air Force about in the first place. As the second truce
took hold, at the advice of some of the South African volunteers
Ben-Gurion invited Col. Cecil Margo, a South African Jewish lawyer
who had served as bomber wing commander in the South African
Air Force during World War II, to come and look things over.
Margo arrived on July 21. The next day, after visiting the squadrons
and getting briefed by the local South Africans, he gave Ben-Gurion
a scathing but accurate assessment of the situation. The operational
units were fine, Margo said. His visit to the squadrons revealed
nothing but high morale and battle readiness. The problem was
with the IDF command, which failed to make adequate appropria-
tions for IAF training, maintenance, field organization, communication, and transportation. Although itself ignorant of the proper use
of air power, the IDF kept the IAF command out of the operational
planning loop, which meant that Israel's meager air power was more
often than not wasted on the wrong operations.

The last point was critical, although not new. Yadin's insistence
on personally running the IAF like he did his artillery, as a support
arm for the ground troops, had long drawn opposition from Remez,
but to Ben-Gurion their bickering had seemed like personality
clashes from which he conveniently stayed away. Margo, however,
gave Ben-Gurion a crucial lesson in modern air warfare. The first
and foremost role of the IAF, said Margo, was to defend Israel and
its ground forces from enemy planes. To do that it had to establish
air superiority over the war zone by scaring away, defeating, or
preferably destroying the enemy's fighters and bombers. Since the
IAF was greatly outnumbered by its Arab counterparts, mobilizing
its entire resources first to win the war in the air was crucial. Once
the enemy lost its ability to wage war from above, the IAF could get
around to helping the ground troops or attacking ground targets
behind enemy lines. But not before. In fact, Yadin's constant demands for ground support were sapping the IAF's limited resources
and making the entire country more vulnerable to enemy air attacks, not less.

What Margo gave Ben-Gurion was something the pragmatic
leader could easily grasp—an order of priorities—which the following day Margo elaborated on with a detailed reorganization plan. In

addition to new procedures for target selection and mission planning and control, Margo proposed the formation of two more fighter squadrons and one each of medium and heavy bombers. Finally, he urged Ben-Gurion to appoint Remez as the IAF's supreme commander, and place him on equal footing with the heads of the other armed services so that he'd be answerable only to the IDF chief of staff.

Margo's proposals were not so different from ones that Remez had already made and argued for. But Remez was an RAF sergeant, while Margo was a wartime wing commander. Remez could make suggestions based on his readings, but Margo gave Ben-Gurion a credible air doctrine and a glimpse at the way big-time armies were deploying their air forces. He had precisely the kind of commanding personal authority that the beleaguered prime minister needed to beat down the resistance of his reluctant military commanders. On July 26, he stunned them with an announcement that "from now on the Air Force is an independent branch among the armed forces, answerable only to the IDF chief of staff," and that its primary mission was to achieve and maintain air superiority over the enemy. Three days later, he appointed Remez as commander of the Air Force.*

In mid-August, two weeks after taking command, Remez used the occasion of the formal dedication of the Tel Nof air base to treat Ben-Gurion and his entourage to a modest air show. With Lou Lenart calling the shots with a portable radio—Remez had appointed him head of air-ground operations for the southern region—a formation of Messerschmitts buzzed the field, followed by *Yakum Purkan*'s C-54 Skymaster and three C-46 Commandos, which landed and disgorged an entire infantry company, complete with Jeeps and field artillery. As the transports quickly departed, the soldiers staged a mock ground attack, while additional transports arrived overhead to drop supplies and ammunition for the advancing troops.

It was a good show, particularly the sight of the Messerschmitts overhead. But it was the clumsy transports that Ben-Gurion

*Ben-Gurion first offered the post to Margo, who turned it down and returned to his law practice in South Africa. He ultimately became a justice of the South African Supreme Court.

watched with particular interest. The next day, he called Remez to an emergency meeting at IDF headquarters. The siege of the Negev had reached a crisis stage. Food and supplies could not last for more than a week, and livestock feed for less than four days. Several attempts to break through the Egyptian encirclement with truck convoys failed. With the memory of the air show at Tel Nof fresh in his mind, Ben-Gurion asked Remez if the settlements could be supplied by air.

"We can do it all," Remez said. Uncertain of just what he meant by that, one of the infantry commanders suggested that even if Remez's planes could ferry south "just ten tons of supplies [it] would save the day" for the besieged settlements and their isolated defenders. It was the first time the IDF command considered doing the job by air.

"We'll start with thirty tons each night, and work up to fifty," Remez said, shrugging.

That same day, a senior transport pilot was dispatched in a small plane to the Negev, where he located an old RAF landing strip near the village of Ruhama, and arranged for tractors from nearby settlements to lengthen and grade it to handle the heavy transports. Five days later, on August 23, the first C-46 landed on the makeshift strip in a huge dust cloud, bringing with it goose-neck oil lanterns which were promptly laid down to light the landing strip for additional transports that followed that night. By dawn, twenty-nine tons of cargo had been ferried in above the Egyptian positions, and nearly seventy-five tons on the following night.

By September 9, Operation Dust Bowl logged 170 ferry runs, in which a thousand tons of supplies were brought to the Negev, and the entire exhausted Negev Brigade, which had held off the Egyptian army since the war began four months earlier, was brought back up north to rest (the replacement Yiftach Brigade infiltrated on foot through the Egyptian lines to take their place).

But keeping the Negev alive was no longer enough. On September 16, Count Folke Bernadotte of Sweden, the United Nations mediator for the Arab-Israeli conflict, submitted to the Security Council a settlement proposal that handed the entire Negev region to the Arabs. It was just a plan, but when the next day Bernadotte was assassinated in Jerusalem by three gunmen from the renegade

Stern Gang, "what were recommendations . . . now became a political testament," President Chaim Herzog of Israel would write later.[4]

There was no point debating the plan. As long as it was encircled by the Egyptians, the Negev was not truly a part of Israel. Flying over the Egyptian lines, Israel might keep its settlements alive for months more, but to establish a political claim the IDF had to physically break through the Egyptian noose.

In early October, preparations began for a major southern campaign to lift the Egyptian siege and establish the southern borders of the new state. Its success would depend on whether the few remaining Czech fighters could beat Egypt's numerous and superior Egyptian Spitfires for control of the air over the disputed desert. If they couldn't, the attack would be doomed and the Negev would be lost.

Chapter 5

THE RED SQUADRON

In sheer emotional impact, few air engagements in the 1948 war equaled Modi Alon's June 3 downing of the two Egyptian bombers over Tel Aviv. The citizens of the city would have been happy and grateful no matter who it was who shot down the planes, and for a while they had assumed it was one of the foreign pilots. "Some said it was a Canadian ace, serving with the Israeli Air Force . . . others could prove it was a South African. The Air Force, as usual, kept quiet," Modi Alon's father, a Polish-born schoolteacher, would later write.[1] When word got out a few days later that it was an Israeli who had rescued the city from the dreaded bombers, ecstasy became mixed with pride. The young country had its first air hero.

Quiet and serious, and handsome with large blue eyes and tousled blond hair, the twenty-seven-year-old Modi Alon was so perfectly cast for the role that had he been around half a decade later, when American author Leon Uris came to write his epic novel *Exodus* about the birth of Israel, Uris might have picked him as the model for Ari Ben Canaan, the novel's hero, rather than—supposedly—that other blond and blue-eyed young Israeli hero of the war, Yitzhak Rabin.

A pioneer before he became an aviator, Alon had joined a farm-

ing commune on the Lebanese frontier, where, straight out of high
school, he spent his time in the hills with a huge German shepherd
named Lona, herding sheep and operating a secret *Haganah* trans-
mitter. He enlisted in the RAF in 1940, and flew briefly with a
Spitfire squadron in Europe after the war. But he acquired no
British sympathies, as he proved shortly after returning to Palestine
by punching out a British paratrooper during a British roundup of
Jewish refugees in Haifa.

His appointment as commander of the fighter squadron did not
sit well with all the foreign volunteers. Some resented his compar-
ative youth and lack of combat experience and saw themselves
more fitting for the job. Others were put off by his preachy disap-
proval of their drinking (he spent his evenings at the theater or at
home with his wife, Mina, a *kibbutz*-born nurse), and his refusal
to accept flight reports and correspondence not written in Hebrew. "Truth is, I never really liked him," Red Finkel would
admit later.[2]

The squadron would have been a handful for anyone to handle,
especially as the truce stretched into the summer and there was little
flying to do. Only one enemy plane showed up during the entire
summer, and while it kept coming back again and again it posed
more of a mystery than a threat. It made its first appearance in the
early summer. Flying so high that only its vapor trails were visible,
it swept in from the sea, circled around the Ramat David airfield to
the north, arched south to linger briefly over Herzliyya and Tel Nof,
and then headed back out to sea. Dubbing it *Shuftykeit* (Yiddish-
Arabic for "spy business") and suspecting it to be an Iraqi spy
plane, the Messerschmitt pilots repeatedly tried to intercept it but
never even came close.

Without daily combat, parties and drinking were the bane of the
squadron's existence. Several months into the war, the pilots were
still holed up at the Falk Pension, the small residential hotel in the
village of Kefar Shemaryahu overlooking their landing strip (the
ground crews slept in tents by the runway). Bill Pomeranz, who ran
a New Jersey hamburger stand before volunteering to fly for Jewish
Palestine, had taken over the kitchen, supplementing the meager
food rations with an occasional calf that he bought from the local
farmers, and which he then butchered, dressed, and cooked for the

appreciative crew. "He would leave nothing of the animal which he did not use," recalls Nomis. "He'd start feeding us steaks, and worked his way down until we'd be eating jellied hooves, at which point he'd go get another calf."[3]

At night, a pine board was thrown across two oil drums under the big tree in the hotel courtyard, to serve as a cash bar. "There was one night in August, a full moon night, when everybody had squirted so much beer on each other they all took their clothes off," says Nomis, "and then somebody got Ezer [Weizman] to do his dance of the seven veils. He stripped down to his shorts, so tall and skinny he looked like Mahatma Gandhi, and he started gyrating like a whirling dervish, with everybody howling and laughing and falling off their chairs." Other nights, the South Africans would lead the rest of the international crew in Zulu war dances around the courtyard and through the village streets. Also, Bill Pomeranz, who was so fat he barely fit into a fighter cockpit, had bought a white Arabian horse on which he made his rounds of the village farms in search of beef. One night the pilots hoisted him stark naked atop his horse, and paraded him through the village.

Their occasional forays into the Tel Aviv café district were so destructive they struck fear into any nightclub owner's heart, and the mere appearance of their winged-skull squadron insignia (it was Lou Lenart's idea; Modi Alon had held out for a flying scorpion) and red baseball caps (sent from New York by Red Finkel's sister, resulting in the 101 being nicknamed the Red Squadron) was a good enough reason to call in the MPs.

Yet, surprisingly, Modi Alon held them in check. "I remember one morning, after a particularly bad night in Tel Aviv when we literally ripped the town apart, he called us together and gave us a good talking to," recalls Sid Cohen, the stocky South African with the booming voice. "He said that he associated such behavior with the British army during the mandate rule. He said that he felt let down by our behavior, and he asked us to refrain from such acts in the future. The incredible thing was, we all sat there like little lambs. If anyone with lesser personality had tried to give us hotshots such a talk, I don't know what we would have done, but we took it from him as if he were our equal. He was quite an inspiring guy."[4]

Even in the absence of actual fighting, the 101 squadron still faced death every single day. Not from the Arabs, but from their own murderous Messerschmitts, which constantly developed new deadly quirks. Some were harmless. Red Finkel was about to scramble one day at an unidentified aircraft heading for Tel Aviv when he pulled the starter handle to engage the engine, and the handle came off in his hand. But most were deadly. Nomis was returning from a reconnaissance mission over the southern front one day with no fuel left when just over the field his landing wheels refused to come down. He crash-landed, broke his propeller, and the plane then "took me on a roller coaster ride all over the field. [It] swerved this and that way, and then went straight to the side where all the guys and the fire engine were waiting. All I could do was just sit there" (at the last moment the plane plowed into a mound of dirt just feet away from the fire engine, nosed over, made a perfect headstand for a few seconds and then fell back down).

So frequent had those crack-ups—takeoff and landing accidents—become that "we'd be sitting in the orange grove by the runway, and each time someone came in for a landing we'd lay bets on whether he'd crack up or not," says Finkel. The neighboring Yemenite villagers developed a protective routine. Each time a plane would flip, nose-over, crash, or cartwheel off the runway, they materialized out of their citrus and banana groves, flashing white teeth and chattering in a guttural language nobody understood, to flip it right back up with the long bamboo poles that normally propped up their banana trees. "They should have given a medal of valor to anyone who ever flew one of those Messerschmitts," Nomis would say later.

The Messerschmitts took a heavy toll of pilots, since anyone who cracked up more than once either quit the squadron or was removed to fly smaller and safer planes. Lou Lenart never went near a Messerschmitt again after the ill-fated flight to El 'Arīsh in July, and many more pilots were shipped out after their second crack-up. Others left for less obvious reasons. Chris Magee, the ex-marine with his pirate-style red bandanna, went home rather than be inducted into the Israeli Air Force. Leon Nomis was thrown in a Jaffa jail after beating up a squad of MPs during a rampage on the Tel Aviv waterfront, and was then put on a plane for Europe.

Worse yet, by the end of the summer the squadron had just about run out of planes. No more than six of the original twenty-five Messerschmitts were serviceable, and it was a rare day when more than one or two were actually ready for use. In early July the Czechs sold Israel an additional fifty British-made Spitfires for $23,000 apiece, and the sale could not have been better timed. That month, the American Central Intelligence Agency stumbled on Israel's Czech airlift, and Washington told Czechoslovakia to stop it or face international sanctions. On August 11, Israel was ordered to shut down its Czech operation and get its people out. The Spitfires would have to be crated and shipped by train and by boat. Time, however, was running out. Unless Israel could quickly break through the Egyptian encirclement of the Negev, that entire desert region would be severed from the Jewish state by the United Nations. Without the Czech Spitfires, however, the IAF had little chance of holding out against the Egyptian Air Force.

Once again, Schwimmer's resourceful crew of smugglers and gunrunners came up with a solution. Sam Pomeranz, an American flight engineer who'd been with Schwimmer since the beginning of *Yakum Purkan*, jerry-rigged the Czech Spitfires with extra fuel tanks that boosted their flying range from 600 to 1,400 miles. This was still short of the 1,500 miles separating Israel from Czechoslovakia, but a secret deal was struck for the use of a small airfield in Yugoslavia, near the Albanian border, as a refueling spot. In mid-September, six Spitfires were reported ready, Modi Alon flew over with five pilots, and on September 24 they took off for Israel. Only three fighters made it all the way. One crashed on landing in Yugoslavia, while Modi Alon and Boris Senor, the South African volunteer, ran out of fuel and made an emergency landing on the island of Rhodes, where they were arrested on suspicion of working with Greek Communist rebels and their planes were impounded. On October 12, Alon and Senor were released, but their planes were left behind. Three days after their return, the campaign to break the Egyptian siege of the Negev began.

During the summer, the Egyptian force that came up along the Mediterranean coast from the Sinai had thrust eastward from the seaside town of al-Majdal (today the Israeli city of Ashkelon) toward the Jordanian-held Judean Hills twenty miles to the east. The second Egyptian force drove east from the Sinai south of Beersheba toward the Judean foothills, then north. Finally, just west of an Arab village named Beit Gubrin, the two Egyptian forces met, encircling an area roughly forty miles long and twenty-five wide, with some sixteen small Israeli villages and one town.

By the end of the summer, the Egyptians beefed up their lines into a fortified belt of hilltop bunkers and armed villages three to six miles wide. The two narrow roads to the Negev, one running ten miles east of the coast and the other a few miles east of that, passed below these fortifications and within sight of the British-built Iraq Suedan fort which, like the Latrun fort at the entrance to the Jerusalem road, was virtually impregnable. It was through this massive fortified belt that the Israeli army had to break if the Negev were to rejoin the rest of the Jewish state.

All through the summer-long truce, the Egyptians repeatedly violated its provisions by shooting up Israeli supply convoys to the Negev. At noon on Friday, October 15, when another Israeli convoy with UN observers aboard appeared below the Egyptian fortifications at Khartia along the eastern pass to the Negev, the Egyptians opened fire as usual and the convoy turned back.

Only this time the Egyptian fire was the excuse the IDF needed to begin its southern campaign, code-named Operation Yoav. Remez's IAF opened it that same afternoon with remarkable effectiveness. Just before sunset, two C-46 Commandos from Tel Nof met up with three C-47 Dakotas from Ramat David north of Tel Aviv and headed to sea, where they met three Messerschmitts from Herzliyya under Modi Alon's command. With the fighters flying in front and below the bombers, the small force flew west until the shore was no longer visible in the distance. Alon then turned south, and after a while turned left again so that they came straight out of the setting sun at the heavy Egyptian army concentrations in and around Gaza. At the same time, twelve miles to the north, three B-17s from Ramat David made a similar approach to al-Majdal, headquarters of the Egyptian expeditionary forces, while fifty miles to the south three Czech Spitfires and two recently arrived British Beaufighter dive-bombers were approaching El 'Arīsh.

At 5:40 P.M., all three formations reached their destinations and began to bomb along the entire length of the Egyptian-held coastal belt now known as the Gaza Strip. The Gaza and al-Majdal bombings were not very effective, causing more psychological than military damage, but at El 'Arīsh the Spitfires and Beaufighters shot up four Egyptian Spitfires on the tarmac, demolished the main hangar, and dug enough craters in the runway to slow down if not prevent any Egyptian fighters from taking off.

That night, as the pilots celebrated in their hotels, Israeli ground forces struck at the Egyptian perimeter. In the Gaza area, commandos from the Yiftach and Negev brigades hit highways and the railway line running north-south from Gaza to the Sinai. Several miles inland, the Givati Brigade drove through the eastern end of the Egyptian belt, cutting it off from the Jordanian-held Judean Hills.

Things were going so well that Alon had his wife, Mina, join the pilots for one of Pomeranz's festive Sabbath dinners at the Falk Pension, and then promised her that he would finish his flying early the next day and drive her to the Sea of Galilee, where she would spend the coming *Sukkoth* holiday with her family. The following morning he assigned himself to two early missions, and by noon was ready to call it a day and keep his promise to his wife.

That morning, the Egyptians began to pull out of Ishdud and retreat back into the Sinai. Remez ordered the Red Squadron to keep after them. Around noon, Ezer Weizman had just returned from the Egyptian front. "What do you say we go fly in Hebrew for a change?" Alon suggested.[5] Weizman cheerfully agreed, and in midafternoon, with Mina still waiting for her ride, the two flew south to strafe the retreating enemy convoys south of Ishdud.

They lost contact with each other during the battle, so Alon returned to Herzliyya alone when his landing gear refused to come down. It was a routine problem by then, and Alon began to bump and grind his plane to shake the wheels down. Before he could do that, however, Sid Antin, at the control tower, spotted an unidentified plane skimming the treetops over Herzliyya to the west, and asked Alon to check it out. Alon caught up with the plane, reported it as friendly, and returned to his bumps and grinds.

He had managed to get one wheel down and was working on the

second one when Antin noticed a little smoke trailing behind his Messerschmitt. He called Alon on the radio and asked him to check his temperature gauge. "It's fine," Alon replied calmly. Antin was still uneasy. Alon had both wheels down and was seemingly coming in for a landing, but he was going much too slow and losing altitude much too fast.

"Get it up, get it up," Antin shouted on the radio, but this time there was no answer. With Antin watching, the Messerschmitt zoomed into the ground at the far end of the runway, and exploded in a ball of fire.[6]

At first, nobody realized what had just happened. Sid Cohen and Morris Mann were sitting in their Spitfires at the other end of the field, waiting for the runway to clear. Assuming that "somebody made a belly landing," they taxied out and took off. From the village hotel, Red Finkel could see a plane burning on the field, but had no idea what had happened. Only Ezer Weizman, who made a detour on his way back to buzz the house of his uncle Chaim Weizmann, the president of Israel, realized what had happened as soon as he saw the burning plane. He rushed into the operations tent, where Mina was waiting for her ride north. She knew Alon and Weizman had flown out together, but only when she saw Weizman did she realize who was inside the burning plane. Weizman drove the young, three-months-pregnant widow to her family home in Tel Aviv, then rushed back to the hushed airfield.

He found the squadron in turmoil. Morris Mann, who just minutes earlier had taken off for the Egyptian front, was Alon's second in command, and should now have taken over the squadron. But Mann, too, cracked up on his return from the Negev, and while he walked away unharmed, he was so shaken that he announced he would never fly again. Later that evening, Remez phoned the field and asked Sid Cohen to take command. The deep-voiced South African was experienced, calm, and competent. Operationally, the squadron would not miss a beat.

But the pall cast by Modi Alon's fiery death would not lift for the duration of the war and long afterward. So long as he was there, scowling and insisting that everything be written in Hebrew, the 101 was an Israeli squadron. Through him, like him or not, the foreign volunteers were part of the exhilarating, emotional tidal wave that was Israel's fight for independence. Without him, the Red Squadron was a foreign legion, fighting a foreign war in a foreign language. In the bomber and transport squadrons, foreign pilots flew and worked with Israeli navigators, bomb-tossers, or radio operators, who made them feel a part of the national team. But the fighter pilots lived alone and flew alone. There was only Modi Alon to provide the ideological compass, a noble reason for taking off each morning in planes that shot off their own propellers and would like as not crash on landing. And now he was gone.

"Everybody in the squadron was crying that night," recalls one of the pilots.[7] "In all the wars I've been in, I had never seen anything like that." It would be years before Israeli pilots would fly in Hebrew again.

Operation Yoav proved tough going. Failing to break through to the encircled Negev at the eastern pass, the Israelis moved west and threw everything into the battle for the half-dozen hills that controlled the second highway to the Negev. It took five days and nights of intense, often hand-to-hand fighting, but finally the brigade-sized Egyptian contingent near the Judean foothills was cut off from its command and supply source on the coast, and was now itself surrounded and trapped in a small clump of dry, rolling hills around an Arab village named al-Falluja.

Even this limited success owed a lot to the fact that, for the first time, Margo's air doctrine was now in effect. Instead of having his planes at Yadin's beck and call, Remez held them out of the ground fighting and kept after the Egyptian Air Force. The B-17s hit El 'Arīsh twice on the first night of the fighting and again the next morning, while the C-46s returned to strike at Egyptian army strongholds in the Gaza Strip again and again. The Red Squadron, with five Spitfires and eight flyable Messerschmitts, escorted bombers to their targets, kept Egyptian fighters away from the advancing Israeli troops, and kept the El 'Arīsh airfield closed. Egyptian fighters still showed up on occasion. On October 21, a week into the fighting, Rudy Augarten and Jack Doyle, a recently arrived Canadian flyer, were strafing El 'Arīsh when an Egyptian Fiat fighter came down for a landing, followed by four Egyptian Spitfires. Augarten shot down the Fiat, Doyle downed one of the Spitfires, and they each damaged another Spitfire before the Egyptians left.

(The appearances of the Egyptian fighters mystified the Israelis, since El 'Arīsh was kept unusable and the Egyptian air bases on the Suez Canal were far away. It was weeks later that they discovered a small backup airfield near El 'Arīsh, which the Egyptians were still using.)

On only one occasion did Yadin try to pull the IAF into the ground fighting against Remez's judgment, but then it was by special request. Yadin's problem was Iraq Suedan, the British-built fortress from which the Egyptians controlled traffic on the newly opened Negev road. Dubbed "the monster on the hill," it was one of a series of Tagart police forts that the British had built up and down the country—massive, square compounds with thick walls, watchtowers, underground chambers, and small inner courtyards, all surrounded by mines and barbed wire. As in Latrun, repeated attempts to take Iraq Suedan by infantry and armor failed disastrously. The flat hills around the fort offered no hidden approach routes, and left the attacking forces open to merciless Arab fire as they made their way in through the mines and barbed wire.

On October 18, while planning the next day's ground assault, Yadin asked Remez for a suggestion. Remez was skeptical. Iraq Suedan was protected by antiaircraft gun batteries, and its construction was so massive that "without the right planes and bombs, we might knock off the tower or break into one of the upper-story rooms, but that's all," Remez said.[8] When Yadin persisted, Remez reluctantly suggested that a skilled pilot might manage to lob a couple of napalm bombs into the fort's courtyard, so that the burning fuel might spill into the underground chambers and force the Egyptians to surrender.

It would be a suicide mission, he told Yadin. Was it worth it? "I am not going to order you to do it, but it may save a lot of lives and make a difference in the offensive," Yadin said.

Remez "volunteered" a veteran *Palmach* pilot for the mission, but that night a twenty-five-year-old Canadian volunteer named Leonard Pitchett, who three years earlier had shot down the last German plane of World War II, broke at gunpoint into Remez's room at IAF headquarters at the Hayarkon Hotel. "Your Israeli pilots are brave but inexperienced, and they'll get killed and still won't put the bomb inside the target," he said. "I am the only man here who can do it."

Remez reluctantly agreed to let him try. The following morning, after two waves of Spitfires buzzed and bombed the fort to keep its defenders' heads down, Pitchett dived in alone in a Beaufighter bomber and skillfully hooked his napalm load into the fort's courtyard. He returned safely although one of his engines was hit by antiaircraft fire. "Why would you, a non-Jew, insist on flying such a suicide mission?" Remez asked him during the post-mission debriefing. "Ideals are the only thing man has over beast," Pitchett said. "A man who is not willing to die for his ideals is already dead." But still Iraq Suedan stood, and on October 20 Pitchett repeated his attack. This time he was hit by the Egyptian artillery and forced down in Egyptian-held territory. He, his copilot, and his navigator were captured, tortured, and killed by Arab villagers.

"The monster on the hill" held out for nearly three more weeks, but finally fell to a heavy artillery and infantry assault on November 9. By then the remains of the Arab Liberation Army were driven out of Galilee into Lebanon, and the Syrian army was pushed back east across the Jordan. With only the retreating Egyptian army to worry about, Remez now moved the Red Squadron from Herzliyya to Hazor, a former British fighter base five miles southeast of Ishdud. Until a few days earlier Hazor was too close to the Egyptian guns to be usable, but now the Egyptian forces had retreated toward the Sinai. Operating from Hazor, the fighters would be right there as the Israeli troops began for the final push south that would determine the future boundaries of their state.

Chapter 6

BLOODYING THE RAF

Unlike the Herzliyya airfield, with its surrounding orange groves, red-tiled houses, and concerned Yemenite neighbors, Hazor was one of dozens of spartan fighter bases which the British stamped on flat desert plains up and down the country during World War II, to help keep the Nazis out of the Middle East. It had two concrete runways crossing at an angle, a small control tower south of the crossing, and a clump of old barracks on a low rise to the north. There was no tree-shaded hotel—no trees at all for that matter, and no shade save for occasional tent or camouflage netting stretched over an antiaircraft gun. Flat desert land stretched in all directions, scorched by day and, with winter approaching, freezing at night. Red Finkel once placed three kerosene burners under his bed, dropped the blankets down to the floor to keep in the heat, then climbed into bed wearing every stitch of clothing that he had, including his overcoat. The bed nearly caught fire, but he was still cold.

Instead of fatted calves from neighboring farms, there were stray and skinny Arab cows grazing in the Egyptian mine fields south of the base. They had to be chased or lured to safety and then shot with high-power rifles before Bill Pomeranz could convert them to hamburgers and leathery steaks.

Even if the pilots were still welcome at the Tel Aviv nightclubs, getting there by bus or by occasional army transport was now a tiring all-day affair except for "this army guy, 'hot-wire Zoltan,' who used to work for a collection agency back in the States, and who taught us how to hot-wire cars," recalls Denny Wilson, one of the recently arrived Canadian volunteers. "At one point we had nine cars parked in front of the barracks."[1] To fend off Tel Aviv's military police, Sid Cohen appointed a transportation task force headed by Ezer Weizman, to stash the stolen cars in the ruins of a nearby Arab village, where they were painted over and fitted with stolen license plates.

Unlike their pilots, however, the Czech Messerschmitts never adjusted to the new surroundings. Their delicate landing gear, built for the soft bounce of European grass fields, cringed at the hard touch of Hazor's concrete runways. The temperamental fighters now cracked up at such a frightening rate that when Messerschmitts and Spitfires were scheduled to fly on joint missions, the Spitfires had to take off—and land—first, lest the runway was blocked by the carcasses of smashed Messerschmitts.

By mid-November so few fighters were left—three Spitfires, two of Schwimmer's P-51 Mustangs that arrived in the fall and had only now been uncrated and readied for service, and an occasional Messerschmitt or two—that the 101 pilots took to patrolling the Egyptian front singly. On November 19, Rudy Augarten was flying alone when he ran into three Egyptian Spitfires over the Negev, and shot one of them down before the remaining two left. But the handful of fighters would be useless once Israel resumed its campaign against Egypt, which was the reason for moving to Hazor in the first place.

By the end of 1948, the war had reached its final phase. The Lebanese, Syrians, and Jordanians were virtually out of the fighting, leaving Israel to slug it out with Egypt over the Negev desert. The struggle was not military alone. Even as Israel tightened its hold on the Negev by running supply convoys regularly, and even as Egypt was losing its hold on the remains of the former Palestine mandate, Britain launched a diplomatic drive at the Security Council to push Israel back out of the Negev so it could be turned over to the Arabs.

In what would become the stock scenario for future Arab-Israeli wars, the same United Nations that could not or would not stop the Arabs from starting a war rushed in at the first sign of trouble to keep them from losing it.

What it amounted to was this: While Israel's highway-wide connection with the Negev settlements enabled it to hold the region militarily, to keep it politically it had to push five Egyptian brigades—two in Gaza, one in the near Sinai, one in the Jordanian foothills, and one at al-Falluja—all the way back into the deep Sinai. For once, with the war in the north and east all but over, Israel could concentrate enough troops in one area for the task, and toward the end of the year its crack fighting brigades were moved into position along the entire Egyptian front in preparation for the final push.

Only one element was missing. If the fate of this last campaign would hinge on superiority in the air, the few remaining Israeli fighters were no match for several fresh Egyptian squadrons of Spitfires and G-55 Fiat fighters. It was not that Israel did not have enough fighters—it had the fifty Spitfires it bought from Czechoslovakia early that summer. But except for the six that arrived in October, the fighters were still in Czechoslovakia, and the Czechs wanted Israel to crate and truck them down to the Mediterranean, and put them on a slow boat home. At that rate, it would be months before the fighters arrived—far too late for the critical campaign for the Negev in December.

On November 19, after weeks of pleas and negotiations, the Czechs agreed to let fifteen more Spitfires out by air, and on December 9 the Yugoslavs allowed the use of a small airfield in southern Yugoslavia as a refueling stop. With the onset of the harsh Central European winter, that second Spitfire run from Czechoslovakia to Israel would be the most dangerous and dramatic fighter mission of the entire war.

Its outcome rested on one American volunteer who had yet to fly his first combat mission against the Arabs. Trim and restless, with a lean, oriental look, New York–born George Lichter flew P-47 Thunderbolts and P-51 Mustangs in Europe during World War II, then sold used clothing in war-ravaged China, ferried a C-47 Dakota from Hawaii to the states for Kirk Kerkorian's budding air charter service, then got into the New York textile trade. In the spring of

1948 he heard of "the trouble in Palestine," and by late May was at České Budějovice, learning to fly Messerschmitts with Rudy Augarten and Sid Cohen.

But Lichter did not go with them to Israel. His Czech instructors noted his talent for flight instruction and his unusually fine hand with their killer plane, and asked him to stay behind and help train the volunteers—and the several dozens of young Israelis whom the Czechs accepted for basic flight training. With the exception of an occasional visit to Israel during the summer truce, he remained at České Budějovice for the rest of the year, sleeping on "terrible army cots in a bare room" and surviving on food that was "monstrous, it was so bad [that] many meals were just plain soup."[2]

The Czech instructors, reluctant to risk their lives flying a plane so terrible their own army had already got rid of it, soon had Lichter doing all the training. He was taking off and landing as many as a dozen times each day. "George was the one true hero of the 1948 war," says Red Finkel. "Those planes were so dangerous, I remember seeing him at the end of a day of instruction, and he'd be so shook up he'd head straight for the bar, and couldn't even talk until he had a drink."[3]

In the late summer, when the Czechs ran out of Messerschmitts, Lichter began training the young Israeli pilots on Spitfires. He also test-flew each Spitfire as Sam Pomeranz, the veteran *Yakum Purkan* engineer, "was taking the armor off and putting gas tanks on the wings, and taking out the radio equipment and putting gas tanks where the radios were, and taking the internal armor plating off and putting more gas tanks in." In mid-December, fifteen Spitfires were ready, and ten pilots arrived from Israel to make the run. But even with Lichter and Pomeranz, that still made only twelve, and since hiring Czech or Yugoslav pilots for the job was out of the question, Lichter asked two of his most promising Israeli flight cadets, a shy *kibbutznik* named Moti Hod* and a Haifa dandy named Dani Shapira, to volunteer, although they each had had only a hundred flight hours, seven in a Spitfire. That made fourteen. One of the Spitfires would have to remain behind.

---

*Actually, it was four years later that he changed his last name from Fine to the Hebrew Hod. To avoid confusion, however, Hebrew names are used throughout this book where names have been changed.

The Central European winter arrived while the Israelis were still preparing for the flight. On the morning of December 18, Sam Pomeranz and George Lichter led the first six Spitfires out. The tarmac was covered with thick snow and the landscape with heavy clouds as the six planes rose like gray ghosts through the soup. No pilot could see more than the vague outline of one other fighter in any direction, and if he hung back for just a few seconds, not even that.

At 10,000 feet, with the cloud cover still unbroken, Pomeranz and Lichter, whose planes were the only ones equipped with radios, grew uneasy. The stripped-down fighters carried no oxygen gear, and if they climbed much higher the pilots would be unable to breathe. When the clouds were still there at 14,000 feet, Lichter suggested turning back. Although they did not know it, they had already lost one plane. Bill Pomeranz, the 101 Squadron's butcher-chef, had stayed too far back during the climb up through the clouds, and lost contact with the others. He was now on his way alone, with no map or radio, and with only a vague notion of where Yugoslavia was.

"You take the guys back, I am going on ahead," Sam Pomeranz told Lichter, and in seconds vanished into the clouds. Lichter wiggled his wings to signal the others, and started back down. But back where? They had been flying for nearly half an hour, and he had no way of knowing how far they had gone or how far off course they had drifted in the steady wind. There was just one thing to do, turn 180 degrees, head down, and hope to find the field before they got lost. "God must have been watching over us, because we came out of the clouds right in the center of that airfield that I never thought we'd find," he would say later.[4]

The following morning, the weather broke briefly and Lichter took off again, this time with the remaining twelve Spitfires. Shortly before they left, a radio message arrived that one of the Spitfires had crashed in the mountains the day before. There was no clue as to which Pomeranz was lost—Sam the engineer, who flew on ahead to await them in Yugoslavia and prepare for the next leg of the flight, or Bill the chef, who got lost in the clouds.*

*Sam Pomeranz, who thought up and engineered the long-distance ferry run, crashed into a mountain on his way through the clouds. Bill Pomeranz had made it to northern Yugoslavia, where he crash-landed and spent several days at the hands of the Yugoslav authorities before being shipped on to Tel Aviv.

Shortly after they started out, the clouds closed in again. With only a crude map of Europe and a compass—and no radio contact with his pilots—Lichter faced a tricky navigation job. To reach Yugoslavia to the south, he had to overfly hostile Hungary or Romania, or detour to the west over less hostile Austria. If they were intercepted on either route, the American, Canadian, and British fighter pilots would be court-martialed for operating illegally behind the Iron Curtain—in Yugoslav-marked fighters, at that—and Israel would lose the Spitfires. Gambling that the cloud cover made him invisible, Lichter set course to the southwest, heading clear across Hungary to the headwaters of the Adriatic Sea. It was a long way around, but it was the safest.

His luck held out. After several hours of navigating "strictly by time and distance, dead reckoning," Lichter figured he had gone far enough and started down through the still-unbroken cloud cover. He broke free 300 feet above the dark gray waters of the Adriatic. Turning south, he followed the coastline, turned inland, and came down at the small airfield with all twelve planes. On December 22, leaving behind one plane that developed engine trouble, eleven fighters took off for Israel. Another one turned back with a technical malfunction, but seven hours later the surviving ten Spitfires landed at Tel Nof—ironically just minutes after Egyptian Spitfires attacked the base. The Israeli southern offensive had just begun.

Operation Horev, the last major campaign of the war, was remarkably anticlimactic. An Israeli assault along the Gaza Strip drew out the main Egyptian force, while at the same time the main Israeli armor and infantry force swung down south and drove into the Sinai. By New Year's Eve the Israelis had overrun the main western Sinai Egyptian strongholds of Abu Ageila, El Quseima, and Bir El Hassne, and had come close to encircling and trapping the Egyptians in the Gaza Strip.*

Heavy rains at the start of the fighting kept both Israeli and Arab air forces from taking a hand, but once it cleared up the Israelis

---

*While the rains made much of the desert impassable, at the last minute Israeli archaeologists located the route of an ancient Roman road that ran from Beersheba to the Sinai, and army engineers quickly cleared it of heavy deposits of sand. It enabled the Israeli attack force to not only move right through to the Sinai but to go around the heavy Egyptian fortifications guarding the narrow Beersheba–Sinai highway, and to actually cut them off from the main Egyptian force in the western Sinai.

quickly seized control of the air, especially after discovering two airfields in the Sinai from which the Egyptians ran a few fighters along the front, and shutting them down as they had already done El 'Arīsh. The Egyptians attempted to strike back with a bombing campaign inside Israel, but although their bombers managed to reach several Israeli airfields without getting intercepted, they caused only slight damage.

The Egyptians had lost the war. On January 1, 1949, after Britain threatened to intervene under the 1936 Anglo-Egyptian Treaty, Israel pulled out of the Sinai, and on January 5 Egypt and Israel accepted a United Nations proposal for ending the fighting on Friday afternoon, January 7.

The war did not end quietly. On January 7, powerful windstorms buffeted the desert country, kicking up clouds of sand and fine, yellow desert soil. Early that morning, an Israeli military convoy radioed for help after it was attacked by enemy fighters, and two recently arrived volunteers, John McElroy and Chalmers "Slick" Goodlin,* were scrambled to the scene. According to McElroy, he and Goodlin spotted three columns of smoke from a distance, and reached the Israeli convoy just as four Spitfires were swooping down as if to shoot it up again. McElroy shot one of the attacking fighters from such a close range that when it exploded, McElroy's own plane was damaged by the flying debris. According to McElroy, Goodlin was going after the second Spitfire when he himself turned back and returned to base with his damaged plane.

Goodlin's recollection of the affair is somewhat different. He remembers no columns of smoke, and says that the thick sandstorms that day made it difficult to see anything. As he tells it, they had picked up some unidentified radio chatter, and McElroy said, "We've got some bogies out here." Just then, Goodlin recalls, "we noticed dark shapes ahead of us in the dust. McElroy said, 'I'll take the one on the left and you take the one on the right,' and that's

---

*Goodlin was at the time one of America's leading test pilots. A year earlier he had taken the famed Bell X-1 to the threshold of the sound barrier, and it was only because of a contract disagreement that the U.S. Air Force took over the test-flight program and Chuck Yeager ended up breaking the sound barrier. Goodlin had just left Bell when, in the fall of 1948, Joseph Berg, a Hollywood producer, talked him into volunteering to fly for the Israelis.

what we did."[5] Goodlin says he saw McElroy blow up one of the planes, while he himself followed the second Spitfire up through the blowing sand. When they were out in the clear and the enemy pilot spotted Goodlin behind him, "he peeled off and came back, and I noticed gun smoke starting to roll out underneath his wing," Goodlin recalls.

It was only at that point that Goodlin first realized that the fighter he was up against was a Royal Air Force Spitfire with full insignia. "I remember seeing it and wondering why the hell he was shooting at me, especially since he was firing at the wrong angle and couldn't hit anything," Goodlin would say later. But by then the fight was on, and "I managed to get into position behind him and get off a couple of lucky shots [which] struck his engine." The RAF Spitfire went down through the dust clouds and crashed.

Goodlin's account that he saw no columns of smoke, and that the sandstorm made it impossible to see anything from a distance, is also supported by the fact that when he victory-rolled into Hazor and announced that he and McElroy had just shot down two British fighters, McElroy was as surprised as the rest of the pilots in the squadron. Had the air been clear enough to see the smoke columns, the two would have clearly identified the RAF fighters right from the start. The surprise grew as news reached the squadron that two more British Spitfires were shot down in the same area by Israeli antiaircraft fire.

But what were the RAF fighters doing there in the first place? Did Britain decide to send in the RAF to help Egypt just hours before the cease-fire?

Had Britain notified the Israelis of the presence and mission of its fighters things might have turned out differently,* but there was

---

*According to subsequent testimony by Flying Officer Cooper, the RAF flight leader that morning, his four-fighter formation was on a tactical reconnaissance mission along the Egypt-Israel boundary, with two planes flying low for visual inspection of the combat area, and the other two photographing the terrain from 1,500 feet. When they flew over the Israeli advance route in Nizana, the two low-flying Spitfires were shot down by ground fire (one pilot was killed, and the other bailed out and was captured). Cooper and his wingman were looking for the downed pilots when they were attacked by "Jewish aircraft . . . with British-type camouflage and with red airscrew spinners similar to those of the aircraft of the 208 squadron" (both of them bailed out; Cooper was picked up by Bedouins and returned to Egypt, while his wingman was taken by the Israelis).

no such notification that morning, nor later that afternoon, when four Israeli Spitfires led by Ezer Weizman ran into a second British force of four Spitfire and fifteen Tempest fighters, and one of the American volunteers shot down a British Tempest—the fifth RAF fighter to go down that day.

The ensuing furor—Britain insisted that its fighters were on peaceful reconnaissance missions while Israel accused it of "unprovoked aggression"—was relatively short-lived. It was a matter of record that British and Egyptian Spitfires had been overflying Israeli positions for weeks, and since their paint schemes were similar, the Israelis could not easily tell one enemy plane from another. In London and Washington alike, the British government came under heavy criticism for sending armed fighters into the Arab-Israeli war zone. The RAF made things worse when it claimed that its fighters in the area were not even armed, only to be contradicted by its own pilots' debriefing reports, in which they admitted not only to being armed but to having shot back at the Israelis.

The political firestorm also provided the answer to one of the war's longest-running mysteries. All through the summer and fall, Israeli Messerschmitts and Spitfires kept trying to catch up with the *Shuftykeit*, the mysterious high-flying plane whose contrails, snaking from Haifa and Ramat David to the north all the way to Hazor in the south, were by now a familiar feature of the landscape. In the fall, however, Israeli ground crews finished assembling the two American P-51 Mustangs that Schwimmer had managed to get into Israel, and which could fly high and fast enough to give the mystery plane a good chase. On December 1, as soon as the *Shuftykeit*'s vapor trails appeared over Galilee, a spotter at the Ramat David tower called Hazor, and Wayne Peake, a guitar-strumming North Carolina hillbilly volunteer who flew Mustangs in World War II and had just joined the squadron, immediately took off in one of the Mustangs. With the entire squadron watching from the tarmac below, Peake quickly climbed up to 30,000 feet, the *Shuftykeit*'s estimated cruising altitude, and waited.

He didn't wait long. A few minutes after he had settled into his aerial ambush, the pilots below spotted the vapor trails unfurl toward them from the north. When the plane was almost over the base, Sid Cohen, the squadron commander, ordered Peake to shoot it down. But Peake could not find it. The pilots below stared with fury and disbelief as both the mystery plane and Peake's Mustang kept flying their separate routes.

Then the control officer at the tower suddenly realized what had happened. Peake had simply set up his ambush too high. "He is right below you," he yelled into the radio. Peake rolled down, spotted what he later described as a huge four-engine Lancaster or Halifax bomber, and opened fire. But all four of his guns jammed after squeezing out only a few shells. Seemingly unharmed but aware that it was being attacked, the *Shuftykeit* slowly turned west and headed out to sea. For a while it seemed as if the phantom plane would get away once again. "It was going away, and Peake was cursing like hell on the radio and almost crying because he couldn't fire another shot," says Sid Cohen, "but suddenly I noticed that the vapor trails were getting thicker and thicker, and then I saw fire, and the next thing I knew that thing just disintegrated in the air."[6]

When Rudy Augarten in a Piper Cub and Ezer Weizman in a Seabee flew out to sea to find its remains, they found nothing. The *Shuftykeit* had vanished without leaving a single clue as to what it was or to whom it belonged.

The mystery remained until mid-January, when during the commotion over the downing of the five British Spitfires, Winston Churchill unexpectedly stood up at the House of Commons and demanded an explanation for the downing of a British Mosquito fighter-bomber over Israel's coast a month earlier. The British Air Ministry first explained the episode as an accident, claiming that a Mosquito had drifted off course on a routine training flight, and was actually shot down over the Mediterranean. But under Churchill's persistent questioning of why it was necessary to send an aircraft on a training flight over this "delicate and dangerous area," the Air Ministry finally admitted that the Mosquito that Wayne Peake shot down over Hazor was in fact gathering data for the British government and, supposedly, for the United Nations. In other words, it was precisely what the Israelis thought it was all along, an enemy spy plane, a *Shuftykeit*.*

With the downing of the British planes, the war was effectively

---

*The Mosquito had only two engines, but subsequent examination of the incident suggested that faulty oxygen equipment in his Mustang had, at that high altitude, probably caused Peake to suffer from a mild case of hypoxia (oxygen starvation), one of whose symptoms is double vision.

over. The following day Ben-Gurion noted in his diary: "At 10 A.M. I went down to Tiberias. What a beautiful day. Has the war really ended today?" On February 24, 1949, Israel and Egypt signed an armistice agreement that gave Egypt the Gaza Strip and Israel the entire Negev desert down to the port of Eilat on the Red Sea (which Israel effectively occupied only the following month). The trapped Egyptian contingent in the Falluja "pocket" was returned to Egypt with full military honors from Israel.

Technically, the war went on for months. An armistice agreement with Lebanon was only signed on March 23, with Jordan on April 3, and with Syria on July 20. In reality, the war would go on for decades; it would be thirty years before Anwar Sadat and Menachem Begin would sign a formal peace treaty, the first between Israel and an Arab country, and forty-two years before Syrians and Jordanians would sit down with Israelis to talk peace.

But in practical terms, *that* war was over. The fighting ended. United Nations troops inserted themselves between the warring parties. For the first time since its founding nearly a year earlier, Israel could turn its attention from survival to the more mundane tasks of electing a government, providing jobs and housing for the soldiers returning from the front, and preparing to absorb hundreds of thousands of Jewish refugees that would soon stream in from Europe, Asia, and North Africa.

The end of the fighting almost brought an end to the IAF itself. Six years after a warning from an old RAF officer in New Brunswick led him to advocate and plan a Jewish air force, and less than a year after he assumed its command and organized it into a fighting unit, Remez was suddenly faced with its imminent disintegration. The war gave the IAF the one crucial element that enabled it to win in the air—the foreign volunteers—and now that the fighting was over it was a matter of weeks, months at most, before they went home, leaving behind a few planes with practically no one to fly or maintain them. "We are but a passing phase here," Denny Wilson, one of the Canadian volunteers, told Moti Hod and Dani Shapira, the young Israeli flight cadets who helped ferry the Spitfires from Czechoslovakia to Israel, when they begged to take part in the January 7 confrontation with the RAF. "Any day now we'll be going back where we came from, and it will be you who will remain. You will be the Israel Air Force."[7]

The volunteers began to leave as soon as the fighting ended. In February, George Lichter rushed home to keep from losing his textile business, Sid Cohen grew anxious over his interrupted medical studies in South Africa, and Rudy Augarten started to talk about returning to Harvard. Others looked for jobs with the Air Transport Command, which began as Al Schwimmer's *Yakum Purkan* underground airlift and would soon separate from the IAF to become El Al, Israel's national airline. Lou Lenart, who led the first fighter mission that stopped the Egyptians at Ishdud, and Slick Goodlin, the American test pilot who shot down one of the British Spitfires in the Negev, signed on with a private charter service to ferry Jewish refugees from Iraq to Israel.

It wasn't that Remez had not foreseen all this. One of his first acts at the IAF was to establish an IAF-oriented technical high school near Haifa, to give the IAF a source of technical crews, and even before Israel was declared a state he dispatched some thirty-six young Israelis to Czechoslovakia to train as military pilots. But in the previous fall the Czechs had sent those students back home. Four of them, including Moti Hod and Dani Shapira, were now at Hazor, continuing their flight training under the tutelage of the foreign volunteers, while thirty younger students with even less flying experience were getting rudimentary flight training at an abandoned British airfield on Israel's northern coast. None of them would be ready for operational flying for months.

A few volunteers agreed to stay on long enough to finish training the four Israeli cadets at Hazor. With no training literature available, Rudy Augarten composed from memory "a little syllabus—so many hours takeoffs and landings, so many hours of aerobatics, so many hours of formation flying, cross-country navigation and so on," and with Caesar Dangott, an American ex-navy pilot, worked out a system where "we each trained two guys according to the syllabus, and then we'd switch and test each other's pair."[8]

But that only bought Remez a brief respite. In mid-March, in the same week when, in a simple but dramatic ceremony on the Hazor tarmac, he pinned flyers' wings on these four young Israelis, Sid Cohen was notified that unless he returned to South Africa in two weeks his medical school would not take him back. Remez was in a bind. While Rudy Augarten, Cohen's deputy, was the natural candidate to take his place, he spoke no Hebrew and made no secret of his plans to return to America. An Israeli commander? With Modi Alon gone, the only Israeli candidate for the job was the very young and very wild Ezer Weizman. "Ezer was an excellent pilot, and he had leadership ability, but he was also a terrible billygoat. I was not sure he was mature enough to command the first fighter squadron," Remez would later say.[9]

"All things being equal, I'd make you commander," Remez finally confided in Augarten, "but I also have a consideration for appointing an Israeli." On April 1, in a brief ceremony on the Hazor tarmac, Sid Cohen took off his flight jacket and handed it to Weizman in a symbolic transfer of command. The following morning, after partying for most of the night, a handful of squadron members escorted Cohen to Lod airport, and when he took off four Spitfires escorted his plane out to sea, circling and thrilling the passengers with spectacular aerobatics.

Sid Cohen's departure, and the IAF decision three months later to move the 101 squadron to the northern base of Ramat David where it could police the Syrian and Jordanian borders, formally ended the era of the volunteer. Red Finkel stayed long enough to help move the squadron to Ramat David and then left. Mitchell Flynt and Caesar Dangott, the two American navy pilots, stayed a few days longer, but left in time to visit France on Bastille Day before flying on home. By then half a dozen young Israelis from the second flight-training class had joined the squadron, so it had an Israeli commander and a majority of Israeli pilots.

The squadron still functioned in English, the international language of aviation. Its members still wore the red baseball caps that Red Finkel's sister had sent from New York, and the winged-skull insignia. But the Red Squadron was no longer the same. With the volunteers gone, the entire IAF would have to be reinvented and rebuilt from scratch. For the first time since getting their air force a year earlier, the Israelis were on their own.

PART TWO

THE PRINCE AND THE FARMER

Chapter 7

THE PRINCE

If the fiercely egalitarian, pioneering Israel of the 1940s had a first family at all, the Weizmans of Haifa came closest. Formally, their head was Yechiel Weizman, the youngest of twelve children of a well-to-do family of White Russian Jewish timber merchants. Powerfully built and a strict disciplinarian, he immigrated to Palestine in 1913 with a degree in agronomy, married into an older settler family, and went to work as a forestry inspector for the British Mandate authorities before going into business on his own. In the early 1920s he built a fortress-like stone mansion on the side of Mount Carmel overlooking the harbor town of Haifa, with splendid vistas of the Mediterranean coast and the Galilee mountain country all the way to Lebanon and Syria.

But it was Yechiel's eldest brother, Chaim, the world's foremost Zionist leader at the time, who gave the family its cachet. A world-class chemist, Chaim Weizmann had spent the World War I years in England, where he invented and gave to the British government a process for fermenting grain into acetone, a critical ingredient for manufacturing cordite. According to British Prime Minister Lloyd George, it was in recognition of Weizmann's wartime contributions that on November 2, 1917, Foreign Secretary Lord Arthur James

Balfour issued his landmark declaration "of sympathy with Jewish Zionist aspirations," and pledged His Majesty's Government to "view with favour the establishment in Palestine of a national home for the Jewish people."* When Israel became a state, Chaim Weizmann became its first president.

Affluent, cosmopolitan, multilingual, and well-traveled, the Weizmans stood out from Haifa's population of mostly laborers and shopkeepers. A steady flow of foreign diplomats, British military brass, and Zionist leaders made the stone mansion at 4 Melchett Street a seat of national power. Each time Chaim Weizmann (who actually lived in Rehovot, south of Tel Aviv, where he continued his chemical research in what is now the Weizmann Institute) arrived to celebrate a holiday with his family, crowds would gather along the street to cheer and applaud.

The Weizmann mantle extended to its youngest members. To the children of Haifa, Yechiel's son Ezer—tall, thin, and impetuous, with unruly blond hair and large blue eyes—was "a rich man's son, who lived in a villa on Mount Carmel. Where was he and where was I?" recalls Dani Shapira, whose taxi-driver father had sent him to vocational school to learn a trade, and who by the summer of 1949 was flying Spitfires in Weizman's 101 squadron at Ramat David.[1] But such was his charm that even the privileges that Ezer invoked frequently and unabashedly made him, if anything, even more endearing. "I know you are screwing me, but what can I do, I love you," another Haifa native who became a pilot in the 101 squadron would remember telling Weizman during their childhood years.[2]

While he joined the *Haganah* underground in 1938 at the age of fourteen, the young heir of 4 Melchett Street did not take to the spartan existence of the foot soldier. Running messages and odd

*Lloyd George's claim is flattering to Weizmann but not entirely correct. While both the PM and his foreign secretary Lord Arthur James Balfour had long supported the restoration of the Jews to their ancient homeland as a biblical imperative, the Balfour Declaration's timing and content aimed more at persuading world Jewry that in the postwar division of the Middle East among the victorious Allies, Britain should retain the mandate for administering Palestine, the vital connection between her imperial holdings in Egypt on the Mediterranean and Arabia, Iraq, and India to the east. In fact, Britain had even instigated a meeting between Weizmann and Prince Feisal of Arabia, following which the latter agreed to exclude Palestine from his claims for domination over the Arab Middle East, and to accept the establishment of a Jewish community there.

jobs in the city was one thing, but as Jewish-Arab tensions mounted and the *Haganah* evolved into a rudimentary infantry, Weizman discovered that he hated "running around, getting thorns in the rear . . . crawling in mud and crunching mouthfuls of sand." Quitting was unthinkable, but in 1941 salvation beckoned from the skies. He was sweating through rugged infantry squad commander's training in the barren hills overlooking the Yizre'el Valley, as day after day British fighters from the Ramat David airfield streaked overhead. "Weizman, you idiot," he would recall mumbling to himself, "here you are, lying among the bushes and nibbling leaves, when you should be up there in the clouds."[3]

He had found his destiny. In early 1942 he joined the Haifa Flight Club, a private flight school that was really a *Haganah* front. In early summer, he showed up at the Belgian Consulate in Jerusalem with his new pilot's license, and volunteered to fly in the Congo. When he came out of the building, his furious father was waiting. "If you are going to fight for anyone, you will fight for a Jewish people in a Jewish army," Yechiel told his son as he delivered him to an RAF recruiting office near the Damascus Gate in Old Jerusalem.[4]

He didn't get to do much wartime flying. After more than a year as a driver in the Western Desert, he began flight training in Rhodesia but immediately broke his left hand when a propeller kicked back. It was months before he could fly again, and then his hand hurt so badly he had to contort his lanky six-foot frame in the cockpit so he could operate the flaps with his foot. By the time he received his wings in 1945 the war was over. In 1946, after strutting through Haifa for a while and impressing his childhood friends with "his RAF uniforms and his wings [which] for me was something beyond imagination; just to go over and touch him was a thrill," as Dani Shapira would later recall, he began college studies in London.

He didn't get far there, either. Boris Senior, a young South African fighter pilot at the London School of Economics, recruited him into the anti-British IZL underground (a monumental act of political class betrayal for a Weizman, comparable to a Massachusetts Kennedy joining the John Birch Society). The IZL had just blown up the King David Hotel in Jerusalem, killing ninety-two British, Arabs, and Jews. When Gen. Sir Evelyn Barker, the senior

British officer in Jerusalem, ordered his troops to punish "the Jews in a way the race dislikes . . . by striking at their pockets," the IZL sentenced him to death for anti-Semitism. Since Barker was in England at the time, Senior and Weizman were ordered to smuggle in an IZL hit man and facilitate the killing.

The first part of the operation went smoothly. Senior flew a small plane to France, ostensibly on vacation, and on his way back "landed in a small field where the IZL team waited. Four of them strolled over to the plane as if to take a look, one quickly hopped on, and I took off again," he recalled years later.[5] Once across the Channel, he landed at a farmer's field, where Weizman, necking with a young woman in a waiting car, picked up the passenger and spirited him to London. Before they could find Barker, however, Scotland Yard stumbled on to the plot and ordered Weizman and Senior to leave England. Hiding their IZL connections, the two joined the *Haganah* Air Service, where Weizman spent several months flying small planes in the Negev.

To the puritanical settlers of the desert, Weizman embodied capitalist corruption and decadence. Especially since he flaunted his family lineage and riches, smuggled in Cognac and buckets of ice cream from Tel Aviv, and played the scarf-and-goggles RAF pilot to the hilt. But to the American and British volunteers with whom he flew Messerschmitts for the rest of the war he was only a kid with no combat experience—and according to some who flew with him, no particular aptitude for air combat. As in his school days, he was loved but seldom taken seriously—a skinny, tall clown in shorts and a cowboy straw hat, constantly pulling pranks. The only arena where he held his own against the seasoned foreign volunteers was the Tel Aviv nightlife. "He seemed to know everybody in the country, especially girls. He had a long schlang down to his knees, which he used constantly," recalls Red Finkel. "Still, I always had a feeling that there was a method to his madness. Take the way he always buzzed the President's house; he never let you forget who his uncle was."[6]

It was this childish, spoiled, and reckless prince of 4 Melchett Street who in the early summer of 1949, at just twenty-five and with no command training at all, was put in charge of the country's only fighter squadron, and was sent to a remote outpost in the distant north.

Barren and treeless under the fierce sun, Ramat David was like Hazor a bare-bones RAF fighter base—two intersecting runways, a tower, and a few clumps of corrugated-metal Quonset huts and hangars. On a slight rise at the north end, adjacent to the *kibbutz* of Ramat David, the base's namesake, was a sorry "upper base" of rundown residential bungalows and more Quonset huts. The Galilee and Carmel mountains rimmed the narrow valley a few miles to the north and south, while lush fields of wheat and corn ran east and west, fading into shimmering haze.

To no one's surprise, Weizman and his handful of newly arrived foreign volunteers—a short, temperamental American named Cy Feldman; an Indian Air Force veteran named Joe Cohen; a Russian fighter pilot, Grisha Bar On,* who came during the war but because he spoke no English had until recently flown Norsemans and Harvards on the Dead Sea run; and a dashing South African named Bill Kaiser—promptly set out to resurrect the squadron's wartime halcyon days.† The old RAF officers' bar was reopened and restocked. English reigned supreme as the language of flying and drinking. Stolen cars were the chief mode of transportation. On the day he arrived at Ramat David, Bill Kaiser saw a black Lincoln Continental parked in front of the officers' club. "I had just read in the papers that there was only one such car in the whole country, which a rich American had donated to Foreign Minister Moshe Sharett. I asked Ezer if Sharett was visiting us. When he saw the car he just said 'Oh, shit' and sent someone to drive it back to Haifa and leave it there for the police to find."[7]

Grisha Bar On and Bill Kaiser hit it off particularly well, and had soon perfected a stand-up routine for visiting Jewish-American fund-raising delegations. "Tell me the truth, Grisha, if war ever broke out between Russia and America, which side would you fight on?" Kaiser would ask.

"Russia, of course," Bar On would deadpan.

"How come?"

"Because I'd love to be a prisoner of war in America."

Most of the squadron's pilots, however, were Israeli rookies, and

*Originally Braun.
†On January 13, 1949, at a special command meeting, the IAF reluctantly decided to go on employing foreign mechanics and fighter pilots as volunteers and "mercenaries" until it had enough Israelis to take their place.

Weizman's first and most urgent command task was to train them in basic military flying so that, eventually, they could take over from the foreign volunteers. He failed dismally, piling up an alarming record of fatal and near-fatal accidents. In his 1976 biography, *On Eagles' Wings,* he blamed it on his inability to get training manuals or other helpful information. "The *Haganah* had extensive literature in the form of instruction booklets and detailed lesson outlines . . . [but the Air Force] had no trace of those. Nothing. . . . When I took command of the squadron and the first new Israelis started to arrive . . . I knew what I wanted from them, what I longed to give them, what I wanted to turn them into, but then I had to face the insurmountable question—how? At night I'd compose lesson outlines. During the day I'd try them out on the pilots-students."[8]

The facts, however, are that competent help *was* available. That summer, having put his New York business in order, George Lichter kept the promise he made to Remez at the start of the year and rushed back to Israel to help build the new air force. But although formally assigned to the 101 at Ramat David, to do precisely the kind of training Weizman wanted but was unable to provide, Weizman shuffled him and his new wife off to a rented room in a small village outside the base, gave him no assignments, and only occasionally sent a vehicle to fetch him to the base. Lichter's offers of help to train the Israelis, he would recall years later, were ignored, and when several months after his arrival he was invited to the Weizman family mansion in Haifa, where he was a frequent house guest just a year earlier, he realized that Ezer's parents did not even know he was in the country.[9]

More important, the kind of discipline that was mandatory for effective training had no place in the binge of happy destruction that Weizman and his crew unleashed across the peaceful countryside. When a Haifa women's club invited them to a fund-raising evening for the IAF, Weizman and his pilots showed up drunk and wrecked the place. On the way back to Ramat David they were chased by a military police patrol. "If they catch us, you are going to jail," Weizman yelled at his driver, who kept going even when the MPs began firing in the air. They made it to the base just ahead of their pursuers, and escaped punishment only when—as Weizman glowered at the MPs from behind his desk—his pilots snatched one of the MPs' submachine guns and returned it only after the charges were dropped.[10]

On another occasion, returning from a night in Haifa, a young Israeli pilot careened his Jeep across the two-lane highway, stopped a car coming from the opposite direction, and smashed one of its headlights with a rock. "He forgot to dim his lights," he explained as he got back in the Jeep. "We were kings of the valley," Meir Roof, one of the pilots, still swaggered years later. "Everybody knew who we were. It was like the Wild West out there."[11]

In training, too, "there were no guidelines. . . . No plans. Whoever wanted to fly flew whenever he wanted, and whoever shouted louder got a plane first," recalls one of the pilots.[12] Moti Hod was leading a younger pilot in a "rat race" over the hill country south of the base one day—a tough "do-as-I-do" routine, learned from the American instructors at Hazor, in which the student had to follow and stay behind his instructor through every twist and turn—when the young pilot panicked and froze at the controls, and his Spitfire corkscrewed and crashed into the hills below. "We had never really thought about the problems of air currents, or of flying at low speeds and high angles of attack in low altitudes," Hod would say later. "It was only then that we realized that had we done the exercise at 15,000 feet instead of 10,000, the accident might not have happened."[13]

On yet another occasion, Grisha Bar On, the Russian, took an eight-plane training flight to 23,000 feet over the Carmel mountain range even though none of the planes carried oxygen gear. Fortunately, when Bar On noticed one of his pilots weaving and rolling drunkenly he instantly recognized the telltale signs of hypoxia, or oxygen starvation. "I realized there was no point telling him what to do. He was laughing and giggling like he was drunk. So I just went into a dive and ordered everybody to follow, hoping that his instincts would prevail and he would come along. He did, and once we leveled off at 12,000 feet he was fine."[14]

Young pilots not only were allowed to go flying by themselves but had no rules of behavior to live by. A young pilot was doing aerobatics by himself over the hills southwest of Ramat David when he saw four Spitfires from his squadron flying below. As a practical joke, he dived unnoticed below and behind them, and suddenly shot up in front of the leader. Cy Feldman, the American who led the flight, was so taken by surprise he flicked his gun safety off and fired at the intruder, but fortunately missed. "We didn't know any different. We thought that's how it always was in combat squadrons," one of the young flyers later explained.

Yet even as he seemingly neglected their safety and proper training, Weizman's commitment to his Israeli pilots was total and passionate. If he let George Lichter languish without an assignment, he went to any length to gather and retain what he saw as the nucleus of the new *Israeli* air force. Nowhere was this more evident than when Moti Hod, his favorite young Israeli pilot, was ordered by his *kibbutz* to end his military service and return home to work the fields.

To Weizman, losing Moti Hod was unthinkable. When the "first four" Israeli cadets began training at the 101 in Hazor, "I looked at all of them, and while I knew the other three back from my Haifa days, it was Moti whom I liked best. I liked his Israeliness. He was a natural pilot, the sort of Israeli fighter pilot I thought we should develop," Weizman recalls now.[15] One Friday night, he showed up at the *kibbutz*'s weekly membership meeting to plead for his prize pilot. He instantly perceived that his air force tans won him no friends among the suspicious farmers. "I could sense them looking at me distastefully," he recalled. "I was a stranger, an alien who had never plowed the fields of Israel. I was a hired professional . . . trying to seduce one of their young men . . . off the straight and narrow."[16]

Realizing that stories of the Battle of Britain would not work on this left-leaning, still anti-British audience, Weizman decided to work on their hostility instead. "In this war, we were helped by the foreign volunteers. They are leaving us now, one by one, [and] the ones left are boys like your Moti," he said, stretching to his full six-foot frame and fixing them with his best RAF dead-eye. "If they leave the Israeli Air Force, who will remain? Who? Only characters like me! An air force left to characters like me—is that what you want?"

His gambit worked. Horrified at the notion, the *kibbutzniks* voted to let their native son sign on, and from that point on, as the story got around of how Weizman ventured into that den of social-

ism to keep Moti Hod in his squadron, Israel would have two air
forces. Officially, the Israeli Air Force was headquartered in Tel
Aviv and consisted of a number of air bases throughout the country.
But to the young Israelis coming up through flight school it was in
the far north that the real Israeli air force was taking shape. It was
to the Camelot that Weizman had begun forging at Ramat David
that the best of this new crop of aviators would strive and risk all
to go.

They called it Air Force North.

It was probably fortunate that Weizman's squadron was not required to carry out serious combat operations. The major security
threat to the young state actually came from within, from dozens of
Arab and Druze villages who only months earlier fought to keep the
entire region Arab. Through the Wadi Arah pass that connected the
coast to the Yizre'el Valley, along the edge of what would soon
become known as the West Bank, Arabs were furious to find themselves part of a Jewish state. Since the new state had no formal
borders, only vaguely defined armistice lines, smugglers, thieves,
sheepherders, and nomadic Bedouins roamed in, out, and through
the land at will. "As soon as we arrived in Ramat David, we went
on immediate alert over the Wadi Arah situation, with full loads of
bombs and everything," recalled one of the pilots. Even ordinary
training flights were planned for tactical and strategic effect, which
usually meant roaring down hills and canyons, stampeding goats, or
causing an occasional farmer to flee from his fields.

It was not the sort of activity that could be dictated from Tel
Aviv. The frontier had its own rules, more cowboys and Indians
than regular army business. When word came that the Druze villagers on top of Mount Carmel were growing receptive to Syria's
constant calls to arms, "Ezer's father, who spoke fluent Arabic and
knew practically everybody there, took a few of us to the house of
the Druze chief of Isfiya, the biggest village on the Carmel," recalls
Harry Axelrod, the squadron's American technical officer. "We had
it all planned, so just after the Druze sat us down to a great feast,
six of our Spitfires buzzed his house and did aerobatics overhead.
It looked great, the sort of force gesture those people understood."[17] As Ezer bragged about his boys up there, the Druze got
the message.

On another occasion, Bill Kaiser noticed that the Christian owners of a restaurant in Nazareth, next door to the laundry where the pilots took their wash, were eavesdropping on their conversations. Suspecting espionage, he decided to set a trap. "I asked Harry Axelrod to get sixteen Spitfires ready to take off at one time, and when the planes were ready Grisha and I drove back to Nazareth," he recalls.

"I am tired of those Egyptians. It is high times we blew up the Aswan Dam," he said loudly as the two of them sat down at the restaurant. "I'm going to take the entire wing up, every bloody fighter we have, [and] if Egypt starts anything at all we'll blow up the bloody dam."

"When are we going?" Grisha asked excitedly.

"Any moment now."

The following morning Kaiser took off from Ramat David with sixteen Spitfires and flew south toward the Egyptian border. It was a routine training mission, but shortly after his return, Ramat David's intelligence officer called him over. "We have information here that the Egyptians are worried about us striking at the Aswan Dam. Do you know anything about it?"

Fortunately, the 101 was not called upon to prove itself in actual combat. With the country in economic depression and the IDF starved for funds, ammunition was so scarce that gunnery practice was only simulated—no real bullets were fired. The 101 pilots could fly, but they probably could not hit anything with their guns if they tried. Fortunately, their first actual combat mission, in the spring of 1950, was against targets that could not shoot back.

The previous fall, returning from a memorial ceremony for Modi Alon in Tel Aviv, Weizman and Moti Hod picked up a young woman hitchhiker in their Jeep. A dark-haired beauty whom Weizman fell in love with and began to court, Re'uma Schwartz was the daughter of an old and prominent Jerusalem family. Since her sister Ruth was already married to Moshe Dayan, the rising one-eyed star of the Israeli army, and since the Dayans lived in the village of Nahalal, just outside Ramat David, their house became a convenient rendezvous for the young couple.

One night in the spring of 1950, Weizman arrived at Dayan's house to find him bent over military maps of southern Israel. Bedouins from the Jordanian-controlled Judean Hills south of Jerusalem were straying across the border into Israel with their herds, ravaging fields and damaging orchard plantings. While the terrain in question was officially part of Israel under the armistice agreement with Jordan, it was still open, with no Jewish settlements or military facilities. Israel owned it, but the army had no resources to patrol that vast desert country.

"Hell, we'll chase them out, nothing to it," Weizman offered impulsively.[18] Dayan agreed to try, and through April, under the appropriate code-name of Operation *Shashlik*, Spitfires from Ramat David thundered south daily to search for and chase away Bedouin flocks of sheep. "Two camels killed, Arabs ran away and hid," one of the pilots noted in his logbook on April 19.

"To this day I have memories of this one camel, which I had to make several shooting passes over until he dropped," recalls Grisha Bar On.

Operation *Shashlik*, and the similar Operation *Kebab* that followed shortly afterward, accomplished in days what thousands of ground troops might have taken months to do. More than just chase away a few Arabs and their sheep, Weizman's Spitfires literally defined the borders of the new state. The grateful Dayan sent over an ancient human skull from one of his archaeological digs as a gift, an allusion to the 101's winged-death insignia. It was mounted over the bar at the officers' club.

However modest, the two operations were successful, trouble-free, and played nicely into what was already emerging as Weizman's master plan. It extended well beyond the 101 or even Ramat David. "He once told me that somebody had to be number one, and he was going to be number one," said a veteran airplane mechanic whose association with Weizman went clear back to the first Messerschmitt raid on Ishdud more than two years earlier. Weizman was more specific with Bill Kaiser. The two had shared a house at the edge of the base, "where we used to shoot rats and nearly each other," Kaiser recalls. "It was then, back in 1949, that he told me his plans. He said, 'First, I am going to become general in charge of the Air Force, then I'm going to be general in charge of the army, then I will be minister of transport, then minister of defense, and then I'll be prime minister of Israel.' "[19]

In the early summer of 1950, his plans seemed to be unfolding on schedule and were bolstered by an unplanned incident. On May 17, Grisha Bar On and a young Israeli pilot named Avraham Yoffe were about to stage a bombing demonstration at Ramat David for a visiting delegation from IDF Northern Command when a British seaplane suddenly appeared overhead. Without waiting for orders, Bar On and Yoffe gave chase, caught up with it near Tel Aviv, and forced it down near the Tel Aviv harbor. But it was Weizman, who was at IAF headquarters at the time, who seized the occasion. Rushing to the waterfront, he found the plane's crew furious and confused. They had been flying from Hong Kong to England, they told him, and Israel was not even marked on their maps. "I took them ashore, treated them to a beer, let them chatter a bit and then sent them on their way," Weizman recalls.

His star clearly rising, on June 6, Weizman married Re'uma at Moshe Dayan's house in Nahalal, and a month later became Remez's chief of IAF Operations. He was now one of the two highest-ranking IAF officers besides Remez, and since the other one, Chief of Air Staff Dov Peleg, was an American volunteer and therefore out of the running, Weizman was, at just twenty-six, within reach of the command of the IAF itself. The only incident to mar his meteoric rise was a brief rebellion in his squadron over his attempt to name Moti Hod as squadron commander after his departure. He had been grooming Hod for the post ever since he won that showdown with the *kibbutz* general meeting a year earlier. In early 1950, when Bill Kaiser needed an Israeli pilot to accompany him on a trip to France to inspect a jet fighter that the French offered to sell to Israel, "Ezer said . . . he'd rather I took Moti, because he was grooming him to be his number two. He said he was training him for the future," Kaiser recalls. The *Palmach* pilots in the squadron, however, resented Hod's rise, noting that he did not fight in the 1948 war, and that he seemingly picked up too many of the drinking and carousing ways of the foreign volunteers. Once when Remez visited the base, the *Palmachnicks'* unofficial spokesman, a farmer named Menahem Bar,* demanded that instead of Hod, whom he called "Ezer's playboy," Remez named one of their own as the next squadron commander. The rebellion was brief but

*Formerly Bernstein.

successful. Grisha Bar On was appointed squadron commander, and when he moved up to IAF headquarters the following year, Moti Hod was once more passed over in favor of a veteran *Palmach* pilot named Moshe Peled.*

With Ezer's departure, Ramat David changed. Rudy Augarten, the leading ace of the 1948 war, returned to Israel after completing a year of studies at Harvard, and was appointed base commander. But although fired with desire to whip the Air Force into fighting form—"he would tell me, 'Grisha, we can build the best air force in the world here. Now is the time [but] they are not serious,'" recalls Grisha Bar On—he was severely handicapped by his inability to learn even rudimentary Hebrew. His troubles with the language at times took on pathetic dimensions. One pilot remembers Augarten asking a mess hall waiter for *shloshim* [thirty] sandwiches. "You mean *shlosha* [three], don't you?" the waiter asked. Even after realizing his mistake, Augarten refused to concede. "I said *shloshim* and I mean *shloshim*. When I eat sandwiches, I eat sandwiches," he snapped back.

His inability to communicate with his pilots was compounded by his failure to grasp their inherent informality. He court-martialed Moshe Peled, by then commander of the 101 squadron, for not wearing his hat on base, and on another occasion it took a combined plea of the entire squadron to rescind an order banishing Moti Hod from the base for a similar infraction of his severe code. A lone, brooding man, Augarten felt truly comfortable only with other English speakers. "I would get a message from his adjutant telling me to be ready at seven o'clock, because the commander wanted me to come with him," recalls Harry Barak,† an Australian volunteer who had recently joined the 101. "He'd pick me up in his car . . . drive to Haifa to some hotel, and we'd sit and drink, and drink, and drink and drink, and then we'd go home—all without exchanging one word."[20]

By the fall of 1950, the 101 squadron declined to a point where its very survival was doubtful. Joe Cohen, the Indian Air Force veteran, crashed and died while victory-rolling over the base to

*Formerly Feldman.
†Formerly Krasenstein.

celebrate his promotion to major. Bill Kaiser and Cy Feldman left. Several of the *Palmach* pilots were transferred. Bar On developed ulcers and was reassigned to Air Force headquarters. By the end of the year, the Red Squadron had only three active pilots left.

But it was also that fall that Augarten assigned Menahem Bar, the ex-*Palmachnick* who led the anti-Hod rebellion, to train a new batch of Israeli pilots who had just come out of flight school. At the time, there was little in this routine appointment to warrant attention. Bar was not a spectacular pilot, and running a few rookies through operational training was considered more a chore than a plum.

Yet in retrospect that assignment would become the IAF's equivalent of the biblical story of the creation. In years to come, IAF veterans would divide their history into two eras: before and after Bar took command of that section of the 101 squadron named Operational Training Unit 105. Before Menahem, it would be said, there was nothing.

Chapter 8

THE FARMER

East of the Haifa harbor, a series of three adjoining valleys slash to the southeast through the mountain range that runs like a ridgeback the length of Israel. Creating a broad pass from the Mediterranean coast in the west all the way to the Jordan Valley in the east, these valleys—still carrying the biblical names of Zevulun, Yizre'el, and Bet She'an, respectively—are walled in by the Carmel, Ephraim, and Gilboa mountains to the south, and by the Lower Galilee range to the north.

Though lush and fertile in biblical times, the valleys had been devastated by a thousand years of successive Arab, Crusader, and Turkish conquests. The Turks, who lasted for half a millennium, kept the land wasted and largely barren. In the winter, rains would turn the heavy clay basins into malaria-infested swamps, which the harsh sun in the summer would then bake so dry that deep cracks opened in the soil, wide enough to trap and break a horse's leg. Only a few impoverished Arab mud villages stuck it out, perched tentatively atop shallow mounds.

In the mid-1800s, declining and bankrupt, the Ottoman administration began selling its Palestine lands for ready cash. Several Arab and Turkish businessmen bought vast tracts of land and attempted to build farming empires with thousands of imported Arab share-croppers, but by the late 1890s their projects failed, and as Jewish immigration to Palestine mounted, they gladly sold their unproductive lands to Jewish settlement organizations. At the end of 1926, the Jewish National Fund brought a group of young Eastern European pioneers to the flat mound of Tel Shamam at the west end of the Yizre'el Valley. Five men and one woman moved into a wooden shack that the previous owners had built for their Arab sharecroppers, and on March 3, 1927, the rest of the families arrived and also moved into the shack. Two months later, the new settlers drew lots for farm sites, walked down from the mound, and built huts and farmyards in a lopsided ring around the mound. They called their new village Kfar Yehoshua, the village of Joshua.

Yitzhak and Penny Bernstein built their farm at the south end of the village, and remained at its edge, literally and figuratively, for the rest of their lives. Ascetic and frugal, "ideological vegetarians who did not believe in eating animal flesh," as their son would recall many years later, they worked hard and made their garden a showcase of exotic fruits and vegetables. They raised five children to work hard, live simply, and abhor animal flesh.

Menahem, the eldest of the Bernstein brood (he later changed his family name to the more Hebrew-sounding Bar), grew up wiry and toughened by the elements. "He would run barefoot in the mud all winter. I don't think he was sick a day in his life, not even with teeth trouble," recalls a friend. Like his father, he was withdrawn and humorless, and pursued his interests with single-minded dedication. In 1939, curiosity led him to join the Israel Aviation Club, where gliding and flying soon became his driving passion. He sold a cow to buy an olympic-class glider, joined the *Palmach*'s Flight Platoon at its inception, and by the end of World War II had a private pilot's license. When the 1948 war broke out, he joined the Air Service, where his fanatic devotion to flying became legend. "He once stole my Jeep and drove somewhere to visit his future wife, but he had an accident and had to be hospitalized. When I came to visit him, he began to cry, with actual tears. Not because he was in pain, but because he was missing flights," recalls Moshe Peled, another *Palmach* pilot.[1]

After completing flight school he was assigned to fly Spitfires at

the 101 squadron at Ramat David, near his village of Kfar Yehoshua. He soon discovered a small locked gate at the rear end of the
base, got hold of a key, and while the rest of the pilots lived in
Quonset huts on the base he'd walk or bicycle for two miles on a dirt
road to sleep at home each night. In 1950 he got married, and with
money saved from his meager military pay built himself a house on
the farm, right behind his father's, so he could go on farming. He
was an innocent, "always carrying a bunch of fresh carrots to
munch on. He loved gliding more than flying, because it was more
natural, like the flight of birds. And he played the flute," recalls
Peled.

Steeped in spartan Labor Zionist ethos, Bar abhorred alcohol and
tobacco, and despised the foreigners who used them and the Israelis
who picked up the habits. He hated the 101's drunken escapades,
and often denounced them in biblical terms. While his colleagues
were drinking and womanizing, he "would sit up nights preparing
for flights, and trying to develop tactics for the next day's mission.
He was so intense about flying, that on days when he didn't get to
fly it was almost dangerous to be near him," a friend remembers.
Though hardly what flyers call a natural pilot, he "was good at it
because he was persistent and worked hard at learning." He was
humorless and lacking in social graces. "It would never occur to
him to send a New Year's card or simply to sit down and chat. He
never stuck around at the end of the day," recalls a friend.

But he could also be kind and generous. When a young, elfish
German refugee named Ze'ev Liron* arrived at Ramat David out of
flight school, "perhaps because I didn't have a family—my parents
died in Auschwitz—Menahem took me under his wing socially and
professionally. I visited his home, where we ate salads and
cheeses—his parents sat at the main table, Menahem and his family
at a side table—and talked about farm neighbors, about who bought
a new tractor or whose kids don't want to stay on the farm."[2]

Only once did his single-minded devotion to flying waver. During
the *Shashlik* and *Kebab* operations, his vegetarian and farmer's
conscience rebelled against shooting sheep and cows. "My heart was
not in it. I did not even try to aim right. After all, our purpose was

*Formerly Londoner.

not to kill sheep, just to keep the Arabs from coming back. I remember seeing a boy running. He was running right in his own Garden of Eden. I did not even try to shoot him. I couldn't," he would recall later.[3]

In August of 1950, shortly after Bar led the revolt against Weizman's attempt to make Moti Hod squadron commander, a new batch of rookie flyers arrived from IAF Flight School. It was then that Rudy Augarten, the base commander, established Operational Training Unit (OTU) 105 within the 101 squadron, and put Bar in charge.

That appointment would become a singular milestone in the evolution of the IAF. Bar tackled his assignment with customary intensity. Having no access to foreign instructional material—he could barely read English anyhow—he approached the assignment with the plodding meticulousness of a farmer putting together a crop rotation or an irrigation plan. Using a small grammar school notebook, he drew up a four-month training plan that was so detailed it actually listed and described every single training session, in the air or on the ground, on every single day of those four months. Nothing like that had ever been done—or even suggested—at the 101. "The specific exercises were not new. They were the same ones we had carried out all along. But instead of getting together every morning and trying to figure out what to do that day, we now had a plan for everything that had to be accomplished," he would recall.

His devotion to detail was total. "He took care of everything from lessons to planes. Although it was not really his squadron, he would personally talk to the mechanics to verify each plane's readiness," says Liron. While officially the OTU was part of the 101, Bar ran it so autonomously that he managed to purge from it any trace of the Red Squadron's gunslinging anarchy. "On the first day I arrived at Ramat David," recalls Liron, "I saw a Spitfire flying low, doing aerobatics no more than ten meters above the runway, and then hitting a hangar and exploding on the runway. It was my first impression of the 101 squadron. By contrast, from the first day I saw him, Menahem had a notebook in his hand, in which he wrote down everything because he didn't trust anything to memory."

In December, after the first group of students completed opera-

tional training, Augarten took OTU 105 out of the 101 and made it
into a new squadron, with Bar as commander. Since the two dozen
P-51 Mustangs that Al Schwimmer had bought in the United States
two years earlier were finally assembled and ready for action, the
101 became an all-Mustang squadron, while Bar's Squadron 105
took the remaining Spitfires and moved to another corner of the
base.

Freed of outside controls, Bar began moving at a dizzying pace
and scope. Lacking theoretical grounding in aerial warfare—outside
of a few World War II military books which he read, those that had
been translated into Hebrew—he single-handedly and "in an organized manner [determined] what the air force's missions were, what
our fighter pilots were expected to do, and what sort of training was
needed to get there." The IAF already had a formal doctrine, of
course. As defined by Cecil Margo in the summer of 1948, it was to
defend the nation's airspace, maintain air superiority over enemy
forces, and assist the ground units. To carry out those missions, IAF
fighter pilots had to be proficient in both aerial defense and offense.
They had to be able to carry out escort, support, reconnaissance,
and photography missions, and to train new fighter pilots to do the
same. That was obvious.

But nowhere was it ever specified how those goals were to be
accomplished. In fact, flying and gunnery skills even among the
most experienced 101 fighter pilots were so minimal that any talk
of air superiority or interdiction was wishful at best. It was precisely
into this void that Menahem Bar moved. Filling page after page and
one school notebook after another with a childish scrawl, he
stripped the general doctrine down to its smallest components, and
then "figured out how many air-air exercises were needed to reach
the required level of competence, how many simulated attacks on
airfields, how many interdiction raids, how many gunnery practices,
and so on." More important, instead of alternating between dogfighting one day, air strikes the next day and back again on the
third, he broke down the four-month operational training period
into smaller time segments, each devoted to a single mission. For
ten days or so, as an example, his students would practice nothing
but gunnery or navigation or air combat. Each day, they'd debrief
and critique the day's work, then go up the next day to practice the

same thing again while the lessons were still fresh in their minds.

Bar also systematized performance evaluation by installing a huge plywood "achievement board" in the squadron's ready room, where each pilot's accomplishments and shortcomings became a public record. "We lived by the board. It showed where you stood in these olympics," recalls Aharon Yoeli, one of Bar's early students. "There were columns for air-air combat, air-ground strikes, bombing, and rockets. In gunnery, for example, the scores were entered in percentages—if you fired a hundred shells and had seventeen hits, you scored 17 percent. The average was 15 percent or so. Twenty percent was good. Anything over that was incredible. You knew exactly where you stood."[4] Competition at Ramat David, already a way of life, now became an obsession.

Bar left nothing to chance or discretion. His instructors were handed exercise manuals that detailed precisely "what we would be teaching on every day of the course, and no deviations were tolerated," recalls Liron, one of Bar's first flight instructors in the 105 squadron. He never rested. When not personally flying with his students, he was in the control tower, patiently guiding them through each one of the Spitfire's idiosyncrasies. He arrived first every morning—and washed the floors himself if he tracked any mud in—and was the last to leave at night. "He would bicycle from the farm to the squadron and back summer or winter because he did not want to use squadron vehicles, in case something happened and they were needed," says Liron. If the heavy valley soil got too muddy for his bicycle, he would walk in the mud until he reached a grove at the edge of the village where his father or brother would pick him up with a tractor.

"He had this farmer's attitude," says Moshe Peled, his old *Palmach* comrade, who then commanded the 101. "If you didn't work hard or long you were lazy. If you had a tractor or a mule you had to get the most out of them. And you couldn't keep taking breaks. He instilled that attitude in his students, and then in the entire Air Force." While he expected his pilots to do all the work in the squadron, from gardening to cleaning toilets, "he would never say 'This has to be done,' or even 'Let's do it.' He would simply start working, and those of us sitting on the balcony would soon get embarrassed and join him," says a former 105 pilot.

Bar's single-mindedness may have been mocked next door, at the freewheeling 101, but an unexpected incident on April 5, 1951, proved how right he was. The Israeli Air Force could not shoot its way out of a paper bag.

Just east of the southern tip of the Sea of Galilee, near a point where the borders of Israel, Syria, and Jordan met, a deep canyon ran east to an oasis of hot springs and lush vegetation called El-Hamma, home to a Jewish-run hotel and therapeutic baths. El-Hamma also controlled the southern access to Syria's Golan Heights, and while the United Nations partition and armistice agreements required it to be kept under Israeli rule and demilitarized, the Syrians refused to turn it over to Israel and to pull their troops out. In the two years since the armistice agreements were signed, reluctant to force the issue, the Israeli military settled for sending occasional light patrols—wearing police uniforms to avoid military appearance—into the canyon, where they were routinely stopped and turned back by Syrian roadblocks.

In the spring of 1951, however, when Israel began to drain the swamplike Hula Lake north of the Sea of Galilee in order to farm the rich lake bed, the Syrians beefed up their forces in the demilitarized zone and began firing at Israeli workers. On the afternoon of April 4, Israel responded by sending a heavily armed patrol of twenty-two police-uniformed soldiers in a pickup truck and troop carrier into the El-Hamma Canyon. When the Israelis refused to stop at the Syrian roadblock, the Syrians opened fire. The Israelis were trapped in the narrow canyon. Seven Israelis were killed, one was wounded, and one was taken prisoner.

Reluctant to get bogged down in a ground conflict, IDF chief of staff Yigael Yadin ordered an IAF fighter strike on the Syrian-held El-Hamma police station and nearby bunker. At Ramat David, Rudy Augarten assigned four P-51 Mustangs from Squadron 101 to hit the bunker with rockets, and four Spitfires, flown by Squadron 105 instructors, to bomb the police station. It took some manipulation to put together even this small force. The 101 had been running so short of pilots that Menahem Bar, commander of the Spitfire squadron, had to fly one of the Mustangs, while Augarten, the base commander, replaced him as leader of the Spitfire team.

The attack began at two-thirty that afternoon, and was a success only in the sense that all eight fighters returned safely to base. While an ecstatic Israeli newspaper reporter who watched from across the Sea of Galilee reported the next day that "the planes dived and immediately a column of smoke rose above the target," the fact was that although unhindered by either enemy fighters or antiaircraft fire, the Spitfires missed their target entirely, their bombs falling anywhere from twenty to sixty yards wide. Of the four Mustangs, only one hit the bunker with two rockets. Beni Peled,* a young 101 pilot who monitored the operation from a Harvard trainer circling at 5,000 feet, bitingly reported that the bombs fell "everywhere except on the target."†

A second incident a month later ended more successfully, but by sheer accident. The Syrian aggression along Israel's northern frontier continued to escalate. During the first week of May, Syrian forces moved into the demilitarized zone and occupied three hilltop positions overlooking the Jordan Valley north of the Sea of Galilee, killing six Israeli soldiers in the process. Israeli troops, mostly new immigrants with inadequate training and no command of Hebrew, fought back and the hills changed hands several times. By May 5 the Israelis had run out of food, water, and ammunition. When an Israeli relief force tried to break through to them the following morning, it was hit by both Israeli and Syrian artillery.

This time the IDF had no intention of involving the Air Force in the fighting. At Ramat David, Bar's 105 squadron had just graduated its first OTU class and was getting ready to receive a new batch of the cadets the next day. Early that morning, May 6, Bar took off with Liron for a routine instrument-proficiency session, and after their return Augarten and the 105's three instructors went out in four Spitfires for formation-flying practice.

Shortly after ten they arrived over the Hula Valley, where fire and smoke from the raging battle were clearly visible below. Suddenly a familiar voice broke in on their radios. Yoash Tsiddon,‡ a young 101 Mustang pilot, had been detailed to IDF Northern Command

---

*Formerly Weidenfeld.
†Syria complained to the United Nations Security Council, and was backed by the American press and government. The State Department came down so hard on Israel that Abba Eban, its ambassador to the UN, had to formally apologize to Syria.
‡Formerly Chato.

as air advisor, and was now watching the battle from a Jeep on the high ground, along with a United Nations observer and an IDF intelligence officer. When he saw the Spitfires overhead, Tsiddon switched his radio to IAF frequency and asked Augarten to bomb the Syrians so the Israelis could evacuate their dead and wounded.

Augarten was in a bind. Formally, he could take orders only from IAF Operations, which in turn had to receive them from the IDF command in Tel Aviv. On the other hand, the troops on the ground were in trouble and he could help. According to his subsequent testimony, Augarten ordered the three pilots to fly on ahead, and then dived into the valley and crisscrossed it several times at low altitude to draw the Syrians' attention. When Tsiddon urged him to bring in more planes, Augarten declined. "I told him that I was on a training mission in the area, [and to] call if he needed me again."[5]

Augarten had barely left the area when Tsiddon called him back. The situation was getting worse. Figuring on doing more of the same, "I returned [with the three pilots] and ordered a 'dry' run. I made it clear that under no circumstances was anyone to fire," Augarten says. Two unexpected—and unplanned—events soon chaged the course of the fighting. First, just as the Spitfires dived into the battlefield, IDF Northern Command mortars resumed their shelling of Syrian positions, and "the Syrians had no way of knowing that it wasn't actually us firing at them. What with all the fire and mortar shelling, they were sure they were under heavy air attack, and they began firing back at us," says Liron, whose plane nearly exploded when a 20-mm Syrian shell penetrated his ammunition magazine and squashed three shells that only by chance did not go off.

Almost at the same time, the Syrian gunfire also struck a second Spitfire, flown by Joel Costa, a young immigrant from Europe who spoke only minimal Hebrew. All the while, Tsiddon had been cheering them on, alternately shouting "do not fire" in English, for the benefit of the UN observer, and "it is all right to fire by mistake" in Hebrew. With his plane hit, whether in anger, in confusion, or in response to Tsiddon's urging, Costa briefly fired his guns at the Syrians below. "Excellent, excellent. Do it again," Tsiddon yelled excitedly into the radio.

That was all there was. There was no more shooting after that, and according to Augarten, he made eight more dry runs over the

battle area and then headed back to base. It was not until later that
he learned that Costa's momentary indiscretion had actually decided the course of the battle. As it turned out, his single machine-
gun burst struck the Syrian command post and killed its
commander, and the Syrians promptly beat a hasty retreat. The
entire battlefield "became black with men who got up from among
the rocks and began to run toward the Syrian border," recalls
Tsiddon. By noon the battle was over and Israel was back in control
of the territory.

Remembering El-Hamma, Israel played down the air action, and
omitted it entirely from official reports. Still, on May 19 the UN
Security Council once more condemned Israel for its "air attacks"
on the Syrians, and ordered it to stop drainage work at the Hula
basin. Israel got the message—it would be five years before Israeli
war planes would again be deployed in anger.

In the fall of 1951, after putting a third group of new pilots
through operational training, and making the 105 squadron the
best-organized and best-managed unit in the entire IAF, Menahem
Bar was sent for jet, instrument, and gunnery training in England.
Early that year, the British government allowed Israel to take advantage of several RAF study programs. Remez sent Weizman to an
RAF staff college, and Moti Hod for jet and attack-leader training.
In October of 1951, when Hod returned to—finally—take command of the 101 squadron, Bar flew to England.

He was uncomfortable and alone at the RAF school. For one
thing, there was a language problem. A decade earlier, while still
with the *Palmach* Flight Platoon, he taught himself rudimentary
English by forcing his way through several *Reader's Digests*. A tent
mate who grew tired of his questions introduced him to a dictio-
nary, from which he memorized words with little concern for pro-
nunciation or usage. But his new classmates at the RAF had a hard
time figuring that what he spoke was English. Not that Bar particularly craved their acceptance. "You must remember that all this was
not so long after the British left Palestine. I couldn't just forget
their oppressive behavior then," he would recall.

But he made the most of his year there, especially in aerial
gunnery. "For the first time I saw how you could actually teach
air-to-air and air-to-ground gunnery in an organized way. Our gun-

nery training up until then had been a joke. We had no gun cameras—I don't think we even had aerial targets." He couldn't wait to
get back and start implementing all that he was learning. Until then,
he sat up nights, furiously filling one notebook after another with
scribbles which only he could understand.

Back home, with Moti Hod in command of the 101 squadron,
Ramat David was still the Wild West. The excursions to Haifa
continued, and training flights still lacked direction or planning.
"One Friday afternoon we took off for a ground-attack exercise with
eight planes. There was no plan. We flew toward Haifa, and when
we got near the oil refineries Moti ordered an attack and we dived
at the refineries again and again. Since it was a Friday, we left for
home as soon as we landed back in base, so there was no debriefing," recalls Adam Tsivoni, a young 101 pilot at the time.[6]

To be sure, Bar's methods and organization had begun to spread
to other squadrons. Because of his four-month training series, each
squadron now received new pilots from OTU every four months,
which in turn meant that at the same time senior pilots were moving
up to new postings. Before long, the IAF's entire annual cycle of
assignments, promotions, and operations was swinging to Bar's
four-month beat.

At the 101, however, Bar's innovations were still received more
in form than substance. Deadly crashes were still commonplace. A
young Mustang pilot with just twenty-five hours on the plane
crashed and died during low-flying practice in which his flight
leader kept urging him to fly lower and lower. Another pilot crashed
while attempting a dive-bomb practice from just 8,000 feet. Unsu-
pervised weekend flights, where each pilot could take a plane and
do his thing, were particularly deadly. On one Sabbath morning, a
young pilot named Shalom Rakir decided to "take his plane to
25,000 feet, then go into a power dive to see how fast he could go
and still be able to pull up before hitting the ground," recalls Harry
Barak.[7] Rakir was radioing his progress back to base when suddenly
his comrades heard a blood-curdling scream and then silence. A
search party found the plane rammed several feet into the ground
not far from the base. After attempts to dig out the plane failed, the
pilot's family was granted permission to leave him buried in his
plane right there, and to erect a headstone on the site.

None of those crashes was entirely warranted. In what Hod would later describe as "learning from trial and error," the first crash was followed by a requirement that only pilots with at least forty-five hours of fighter air time could practice low flying; and after the second crash, the deck for dive-bombing practice was raised. Rakir's death was particularly tragic. For some time, 101 pilots had been competing to see who could get his plane closest to the speed of sound. But it was only after Rakir's death that "we went back to the manuals and learned about compressibility," says Barak. It was all there in the manuals. As it approached the speed of sound, the Mustang stopped slicing through the air and instead began to push masses of air ahead of itself like a blanket, accumulating and compressing a turbulent air mass that ultimately immobilized its controls until its pilot could not move his stick or operate his flaps. Compressibility was discussed in the manuals because American fighter pilots had died pulling the same stunts earlier, but "it was only after [Rakir's] crash [that] we bought all the literature we could find on compressibility, and posted notices all over the base about maximum speed and all that."

"The valley is strewn with headstones for pilots who didn't make it," Moti Hod would say many years later. "Each time something happened, we'd debrief and change our training programs accordingly. It was all trial and error."[8]

It was precisely that attitude that Menahem Bar couldn't wait to stamp out when he returned from England in the fall of 1952 and resumed command of his 105 squadron. Even as he began a new round of OTU, he submitted a proposal for setting up a gunnery school at his squadron—an intense four-month session for outstanding pilots from all fighter squadrons, who would later conduct similar training sessions within their own squadrons. He did not wait for his proposal to be approved, immediately beginning to write manuals—sitting up nights to translate RAF material into Hebrew—and to conduct gunnery practice for his own flight instructors. In January of 1953, he opened the IAF's first strike-leaders and gunnery training course at the 105 for eight pilots from other squadrons.

As Bar was in England, these hot young flyers were also stunned to find out that they could not hit a target. Bar helped them change all that. He equipped his Spitfires with gun cameras, and sent his students up two at a time, one to act as a target and the other to "shoot" it down with the camera. Films shot in the morning were developed in the afternoon and viewed and analyzed that night. Next came live-ammunition target practice against a drogue, a giant wind sock that was dragged by one plane while the others took turns firing at it. Each student's bullets were painted a different color, and at the end of the day his score would be computed by counting his spent shells and the bullet holes in the wind sock bearing traces of his special paint.

Naturally the farmer expected his students to follow the debriefings by sitting down and sewing up the holes in the drogue so it would be ready for the next day. "He would be sitting with us, sewing better and faster than anybody," recalls Tsivoni, the course's leading sharpshooter.

On June 7, 1953, Bar had just completed his first gunnery course when he was pulled out of the 105 squadron once again, this time for his most special mission yet. The Israeli Air Force was about to receive its first jet fighters. That meant setting up a new squadron, designing and building new facilities, developing new training routines, preparing ground crews, thinking up new combat doctrines and tactics. It would all have to be done with urgency and with no loss of combat readiness.

There was only one man who could do all that, and Menahem Bar now opened a fresh new grammer-school notebook, and with his childish scrawl began filling page after page with what would become the blueprint for the IAF's advance into the jet age.

Chapter 9

THE BLUES AND THE GREENS

When Menahem Bar was picked to spearhead the IAF's transition from World War II piston-driven planes to jets, it was what script-writers call a plot point, a secondary highlight within an unfolding greater drama, which by the summer of 1953 was being played out fifty-five miles to the south, in Tel Aviv.

That greater drama stemmed and continued directly from the Remez-Yadin feuds of the 1948 war, over the role and significance of the Air Force in the Israeli military scheme. True, on July 29, 1948, following Col. Cecil Margo's recommendations and overriding intense objections by Yadin, the IDF's chief of operations, David Ben-Gurion designated the IAF "a special branch . . . under the command of the chief of staff of the Israeli Defense Forces." But in reality the IAF continued to operate with virtual autonomy through the 1948 war, especially in planning and carrying out operations. Jacob Dori, the IDF chief of staff, was too busy running the war to worry about precise chains of command, and according to military historian Yoav Gelber, "there was no real attempt to force the Air Force into full integration with the Army."[1]

But when the war was over and Ben-Gurion launched an ambitious restructuring of the IDF, the debates flared anew, with Remez reviving his demands for independence for the Air Force. His strongest argument was drawn from Ben-Gurion's own defense doctrine. Since Israel was too small—and after the war, too poor—to sustain a massive standing army, Ben-Gurion was going to base the national defense on a small regular army that would be bolstered in times of emergency by rapid mobilization of massive military reserves. But the new, underdeveloped, and war-wounded country, strung along great distances, was too dependent on a few two-lane highways that connected its disparate regions. These could easily clog up with the rush of soldiers joining their units, vehicles moving from one front to another, and supplies being rushed to the frontiers. Worse yet, the entire mobilization could be paralyzed by an enemy air attack.

What Remez argued was that Ben-Gurion's entire system was workable *only* if the IAF had constant and "total control of Israel's skies. If we were attacked without being able to immediately establish air superiority, there would be no way to mobilize the army."[2] To assure such air superiority, Remez said, the Air Force had to be the exact opposite of the reserves-based ground forces. In order for it to respond instantly, seize the initiative and win the first round of fighting, the Air Force had to be a powerful full-time, state-of-the-art machine on constant alert. It had to be independent of the general staff in such vital areas as supplies, training, and manpower. It had to run its own intelligence, command, and operations. And it *had* to have first claim on the nation's scarce defense budget resources.

"I had no doubt that the Arab states would begin rapid development of their air forces, [and that] our force will not develop in a parallel way if it remained a service branch, not a central arm within the IDF," Remez would recall later.[3]

Led by Yadin, the Greens, as the IAF had come to refer to the ground forces for the color of their uniforms (the Air Force was the Blues), fought back. Through the spring of 1949, a rumpled, haggard Remez dragged himself from one meeting to another trying in vain "to explain to the land-forces representatives the structure and special problems of the Air Force."[4] At the same time, he put his staff to work translating his visions to programs. On June 20, he handed Ben-Gurion an ambitious development plan whose first stage alone called for a fifteen-squadron force at the end of just nine months, at the then-incredible cost of $3.7 million. In October, however, an ailing Jacob Dori retired and Yigael Yadin took his place as IDF chief of staff. Yadin promptly intensified his drive to stamp out the "separatist" tendencies of the Air Force.

Unlike Dori, a British army veteran, Yadin was a self-taught, uncompromising intellectual, whose preoccupation with the big military picture was unencumbered by military training, unless one counted his 1948 war experience, and his academic familiarity with biblical campaigns. Unlike the informal Dori, Yadin was downright arrogant. Where Remez and Dori could disagree and still reach a working accommodation, no such compromise was possible with Dori's successor, especially since Yadin appeared to stake his entire career on resolving the "Air Force problem." As he explained in a newspaper interview some years later, "when I took on the post of [IDF] chief of staff I knew that . . . our problem of problems [was] this: Were we going to make the same mistake as other nations that established independent air, sea, and land forces? Or were we going to establish one general staff for all the forces . . . as befitted a small country, a small force, and short, internal communication routes. It was clear to me that the second way was correct, and that if I could not solve the problem that way I had better resign my post."[5]

On October 27, Ben-Gurion issued an extensive document bearing Yadin's unmistakable imprimatur and setting in detail the IDF's organizational structure and doctrine. Remez did win a few points. The Air Force was allowed to run its own training, supplies and police apparatus, and develop its own operational orders—so long as they were "in accordance with the overall planning of the IDF general staff."[6]

In the key areas of doctrine and implementation, however, Remez was dealt a severe defeat. The new plan was predicated on a "virtual certainty that the land forces will be in the future as in the past the decisive force, and that without them it would be virtually impossible to break the enemy's back." From that perspective, the Air Force was no more than a service arm of the infantry. The following month, Yadin began to implement the plan with Command Order 81, which placed all matters concerning IAF intelligence under the direction and control of the IDF's military intelligence branch. This was far worse than merely placing Remez, as Air Force commander, under Yadin's command. Once the Air Force's various functions, such as communications, supplies, operations, or recruitment, were placed under the authority of the appropriate IDF services, Remez's command would become illusionary. In fact, while Yadin's December 12 memo formally required "the heads of the branches in the IDF general staff [to] consult with the commander of the IAF on orders which concerned the Air Force," Yadin admitted in a separate letter to Ben-Gurion that in reality the IDF branch heads would have the final say.

For Remez, it was the last straw. Noting that Yadin's ruling meant "that the IAF commander will have four or five commanders," which would make running the Air Force "impossible,"[7] Remez threw down the gauntlet in a letter to Ben-Gurion: "After my recent talks with the chief of staff and the heads of the branches, it is clear to me that none of [Yadin's] solutions would enable me to accept responsibility for effectively building up the Air Force. The main problem is not the degree of independence of the Air Force but [its] authority, flexibility, quickness and freedom of action . . . I therefore request that before you accept any of the chief of staff's proposals, you withdraw my appointment as commander of the Air Force."[8]

His ultimatum placed Ben-Gurion in a bind. Not only did he like Remez, but from the very start he had been the Air Force's strongest advocate. But Ben-Gurion also felt unbound admiration for Yadin, the young archaeologist-commander whom he credited with winning the 1948 war. He now backed his chief of staff and accepted Remez's resignation.

"I do not believe in the effectiveness of the chosen system, and I am not prepared to be responsible for its implementation," Remez explained in a lengthy, detailed letter to his father.[9] When Ben-Gurion asked him to stay on until a replacement was selected, Remez agreed only if the new system was left unimplemented until his departure. He stayed on for the rest of the year, continuing in vain to press his case for an autonomous Air Force. But many of the infantrymen in command of the IDF had long ago come to view his campaign as an obsession. In another letter to his father at the end of the year, Remez described one of many meetings in which he tried to make Yadin see that "in the next [war] the decision will fall within days to the side that will . . . establish effective control of the arena's skies," and that aerial superiority was irreversible. Once achieved, there would be "no way of changing the inevitable fate of the war, and the longer the fighting went on, the worse the damage and casualty toll." The response to his assessment, he wrote, "was shocking, a mixture of contempt for my stupidity . . . anger at my *chutzpa* . . . and some pity." On December 14, 1950, he surrendered his command.

"Whom would you like to see as your successor?" Ben-Gurion asked him when they met several days earlier. "What does it matter? You have made up your mind to appoint an infantryman," Remez replied. "Still, if you had your choice, whom would you make commander?" Ben-Gurion persisted.

"You are not going to believe this, but, someday, Ezer Weizman," Remez said.

"What? That billy-goat?" Ben-Gurion exploded and ended the conversation. On December 14, the same day Remez left his post, Yadin telephoned Shlomo Shamir, a veteran infantry commander who had just completed the reorganization of the Israeli navy, and asked him to take over the Air Force. Shamir wore navy whites when he met with the IAF senior staff the following day. His terse introduction speech consisted of just two words, which essentially meant "we shall meet at work." At a command-change ceremony at the Hasharon Hotel, Shamir "said that his purpose was to reduce the Air Force . . . to an arm of the IDF," recalls Yeshayahu "Shaya" Gazit,* one of the "first four" graduates of the first Israeli flight training course after the 1948 war, who then commanded a training squadron at IAF Flight School.[10] When Shamir later visited Gazit's squadron, "he told me the same thing—he intended to turn the IAF into a technical force, like the artillery, whose sole purpose is to assist the infantry." Within days, most senior IAF officers resigned and followed Remez out, plunging the entire force into a deep depression.

Shamir had a private pilot's license and no experience in military flying, but he was an energetic administrator. He moved the IAF

*Formerly Schwartzman.

command from its complex of old Arab stone houses in Jaffa to a small air base in Ramla, a former Arab town just outside Tel Aviv. Instead of hotel rooms, he put his staff in barracks and tents. Utilitarian metal replaced the dark, lacquered wood of the Arab furniture they had been accustomed to. A mere six months after he began, however, in August of 1951, Shamir was hospitalized for exhaustion and relieved of his command. To complete the transformation of the Air Force into "an integral part of the general staff," Yadin reassigned Chaim Laskov, then head of the IDF training command, to command the Air Force. Burly, blunt, and a fierce disciplinarian, Laskov epitomized the professional army man, and seemed the perfect choice for busting the unruly Air Force down to size.

Laskov was born in Russia in 1919, was six when his parents immigrated to Palestine and settled in Haifa, and eleven when his teamster father was killed in a traffic accident. He grew up poor and driven, a tall, brooding and massively built man, with a thick neck and tiny black eyes staring defiantly under a high forehead. A brilliant student and outstanding athlete, he joined the *Haganah* and rose rapidly in the ranks. His only setback at the Re'ali Academy, Haifa's leading high school, was the breakup of his youthful romance with Ezer Weizman's beautiful sister Yael, whose parents disapproved of the poor, unpedigreed suitor and shipped her away to school in Jerusalem.*

At the Re'ali Academy Laskov had come to the attention of its principal, Dr. Biram, a prominent German-born educator who drew him in with fatherly guidance that continued for decades. It was at Biram's office that his rivalry began with Biram's other protégé, Mordechai Makleff, a similarly promising student whose father had been killed by Arab assailants. The Laskov-Makleff rivalry intensified as their career paths crossed again and again. Both had joined the British army during World War II and become battalion commanders in the Jewish Brigade. Both commanded major campaigns

---

*Ezer, on the other hand, idolized Laskov and for years looked up to him as to an older brother. In his autobiography, Weizman recalled that in the fall of 1942, while languishing as a British army driver in Egypt, he wrote to Laskov of his frustrations at not making it to the RAF. "In reply, he sent me a copy of Kipling's poem 'If,' and I never bothered him with the subject again."

during the 1948 war. By the summer of 1951, Makleff was Yadin's deputy chief of staff, and Laskov was head of IDF training command.

Laskov was on a study tour of France and Britain when Yadin ordered him back to take over Shamir's job. He was not eager to accept. "I am not sure it is the right decision," he told Ben-Gurion when he got back. "I never had any dealings with the Air Force."

"I never was a prime minister and defense minister, either," Ben-Gurion said.[11]

It was a surprise appointment. "Laskov showed up at first light in Hazor, where we were deployed for war exercises," recalls Gazit, then acting commander of the 105 squadron during Menahem Bar's studies in England. "He assumed command the night before. I knew him because he was my platoon commander in the *Haganah* in Haifa, but I didn't make the connection. I asked him 'Chaim, what are you doing here?' and he said, 'You'll be surprised. I am the new commander.' "

The next day, the 105's Spitfires took off from Hazor to return to Ramat David, and were near the base when Joel Costa, the deputy squadron commander, reported an engine on fire. Gazit, who led the formation, ordered him to bail out, but Costa continued and only at "2,000 feet he finally turned the plane on its back and bailed out. We saw him separate from the plane, but I believe he became alarmed at seeing the ground so close that he opened his chute too soon, and one of the strings got caught in a tow hook on the Spitfire's tail, [which] dragged him down. We found the plane on its belly, almost undamaged, with Costa lying flat on its wing. He must have died on impact."

Laskov was only three days in command when, over Costa's open grave at the military cemetery in Haifa, he came face to face with the daily violence of Air Force existence. "He was shocked. He hadn't realized such things happened all the time, even at peacetime," says Gazit.

"In all my posts in the past, I could always tell my commands how not to get killed. Here—no," Laskov would say later.[12] The foreignness of his new assignment intensified when he attempted to learn to fly but was grounded for inadequate depth perception. "In all the time I remember him in the force, Laskov kept saying he was a stranger there, that he was only with us temporarily," Gazit says.

What he did not know about flying, however, Laskov more than made up for with a genius for military analysis and organization, and he now moved on the Air Force with a bulldozer-like tenacity. After a furious two-week tour of IAF facilities, he issued a scathing—and deadly accurate—assessment. The command at Ramla was top-heavy and paralyzed "with work channels crossing so often they resemble a maze," he wrote, while field units' "state of readiness is low, and the Air Force's fighting ability does not exceed forty-eight hours."[13] He noted that the only connection between Ramla and Ramat David was a single telephone line that often broke down; that there were no adequate stocks of rockets and napalm; that the handful of serviceable planes had fuel for no more than a few days of fighting; that his flamboyant fighter pilots could fly but their ability to actually fight in the air was dubious.

Much of that dismal state resulted from the battering that the force took during Remez's battles with IDF command. So deprived was it of everything, from hardware to suitable manpower, that Laskov's readiness report for October found "all operational units suffering from deadly shortage in air crews, since most pilots are busy with flight instruction." At Ramat David, most of Squadron 105's Spitfires were grounded for lack of spare parts, and the 101 was losing pilots so fast it had only three left. At Hazor, only one of three B-17s, and three of seven Dakotas, were flyable, and the entire new 109 Mosquito fighter-bomber squadron was grounded with all six of its air crewmen in England for training. Of a total of 130 IAF pilots, only 27 were operational in the squadrons, while 36 served as flight instructors.

Finally, nothing was being done to match the rapid buildup of the Arab air forces, whose conversion to jets had begun as early as March of 1949, when three British-made Vampire jets with Egyptian markings were spotted on a military tarmac in Egypt. By the end of 1950, Britain had provided the Egyptian Air Force with more than forty Meteor and Vampire jet fighters, Syria with fourteen Meteors, and Iraq and Jordan with fifteeen and twelve Vampires, respectively. By comparison, Israel's sole acquisition in 1950 was six Mosquitos, aging, wood-framed World War II fighter-bombers— and that deal was canceled when the first Mosquito crashed en route to Israel and its pilot was killed. On February 17, 1951, France sold Israel sixty-seven Mosquitos, including nineteen equipped for night-fighting and four for photo-reconnaissance, but these, too, quickly began to disintegrate in midair because the glue that laminated their wooden shells gave out in the hot Israeli weather. In July, Sweden sold Israel twenty-five P-51 Mustangs, and the following February the Italians followed with thirty Spitfires, but none of those World War II planes could hold their own in the air against Egypt's new Meteor and Vampire jets.

Still, with no pilots, ground crews, fuel, ammunition, or spare parts, the Israeli Air Force was probably better off sticking to Spitfires and Mustangs, which at least could be cannibalized for spare parts so that a handful could be kept in the air. In fact, Laskov's first annual buildup program, submitted to the IDF General Staff on January of 1952, called for only two Mustang, two Spitfire, and two Mosquito squadrons by the end of 1953. Before he asked for new planes, he told Yadin's staff, he could use four early-warning radar stations, and five hundred more men to operate them and his existing planes.

He did not get them. Yadin, under pressure from Ben-Gurion to cut salaried military personnel by five thousand, told Laskov to look for help among his reserves. "Every man who leaves the Air Force is a resource . . .—pilots, navigators, bombardiers and other such roles [sic]. If they and their call-up method were organized correctly, there is no reason to prevent them from becoming operational in 24 hours."[14]

Even as he fought for additional resources, Laskov worked ceaselessly to whip the Air Force into shape. At headquarters and in all IAF bases and facilities, days began with staff meetings that had to be meticulously prepared, recorded, attended, and followed up. Laskov handed out blocks of square paper pads which staff officers were expected to carry everywhere and scribble everything on. He opened a staff officers' school where "every Wednesday afternoon we'd show up at Ramla to study how to write letters, organize reports, develop mission orders," recalls Gazit, and when Weizman returned from England in the spring of 1952, Laskov had him set up an Air Staff College. Dress codes were enforced to the letter. Laskov even picked a design for the Air Force insignia—two eagle's wings, copied from an ancient Hebrew mosaic, flanking a sword and an olive branch.

He instituted strict procedures for carrying out every task, from requisitioning fuel to the precise sequence of events needed to deploy a squadron from one base to another. Once written down, these procedures had to be followed to the letter. In a simulated field exercise, he quizzed Moti Hod, then commander of the 101 squadron, on how he would deploy his squadron to another base if three of his trucks were destroyed in enemy bombing. "I would send my MPs to the highway, stop the first three trucks, and bring them to base," Hod responded in his best Red Squadron can-do bravado. Laskov was furious. "He said, 'How do you know those trucks were not assigned to move a more important unit?' " Hod recalls.[15]

Laskov also immersed himself in the study of air warfare, particularly "the RAF, how it was built and organized and why. Every RAF veteran was an expert in his eyes: Ezer Weizman, Dan Tolkowsky, and so on," says Gazit. Tolkowsky, an RAF pilot who was Laskov's chief of staff, was struck by his "extraordinary ability to plow through masses of material, read and scribble notes with an almost bull-headed persistence, then emerge with clear and coherent conclusions."[16]

On the surface, Laskov was still the quintessential army man. His military crew cut and creased pants—short khakis in summer, long green wools in winter, both held in place by a broad canvas ammunition belt—were vintage British army, as was the whiskey bottle he kept in his desk drawer. Unlike the largely teetotaling Israelis, "he was a big drinker. In the evening he would take his bottle of whiskey, put it on the table, and say 'Harry, tell me some jokes,' and we'd drink," recalls Harry Barak, the Australian volunteer.[17]

Within months of assuming his command, however, like the sorcerer's apprentice, Laskov got out of hand and began to shock Yadin with views that were supposed to have disappeared with Remez, such as leaving the Air Force alone to run its own affairs.

Laskov did not echo Remez's insistence on an independent RAF-style Air Force. Indeed, he had no real problem remaining under the direct command of the IDF chief of staff. But *within* the general staff, he argued, the Air Force had to run its own supplies, training, selection and acquisition, intelligence and operations. "Laskov thought that the commander of the Air Force had three roles. First, to command the force. Second, to head an air section within the IDF general staff. Third, to be an advisor on air matters to the IDF chief of staff. It was all part of what he called 'integrated command,' with the IDF chief of staff heading it all," says Tolkowsky.

Laskov's ideas had irresistible intellectual symmetry, depth, and military logic. Remez demanded independence outside the IDF, but Laskov's plan gave the Air Force independence *within* the IDF—without challenging Yadin's ultimate authority. In October, while still denying Laskov's budget requests, Yadin was impressed enough by his scheme that he actually incorporated it in Command Order 63, which made Laskov an air advisor to the IDF chief of staff, and a permanent member of the IDF high command.

In December, however, just as a modicum of agreement between the Blues and the Greens seemed finally within reach, Yadin resigned over a budget disagreement with Ben-Gurion, and Mordechai Makleff, Yadin's deputy and Laskov's old rival, took his place. Unlike Yadin, the cunning and pragmatic Makleff had no use for flow charts and organizational philosophies. Instead of implementing Laskov's "integrated command," ' Maklef demoted the Air Force back down to a stature similar to the IDF's three regional commands (Northern, Southern, and Central), two rungs below the general staff. In the critical area of funds allocation, the Air Force was now in direct competition with each of the three infantry field commands.

The inevitable Laskov-Makleff showdown came on February 23, 1953, during a general staff meeting on the Air Force's 1953–54 budget. During the previous summer, Britain agreed to sell Israel eleven F-8 Meteor jet fighters and four trainers. Laskov now asked for funds to train and deploy 200 more pilots, ground crewmen and assorted professionals—a 15 percent increase from the previous year—in order to make use of the new jets. "We cannot build new squadrons in a vacuum," Tolkowsky explained at the meeting. "We ran out of sources from which to pull the necessary personnel."[18] Makleff, however, under pressure to cut salaried personnel by 7,000 and to reduce his budget 40 percent, offered Laskov 250 raw recruits, instead. Moshe Dayan, then chief of IDF operations, added that "there is no point in adding a new squadron if it means eliminating another unit."[19]

Laskov blew up. "I did not buy those planes, [but] I see them as money, not mine or anybody else's here, but as the blood money of the Nation of Israel, money that is now being squandered,"[20] he argued, but it was of no use. The debate continued through the spring, with Makleff pushing for ever more cuts. At one point, he suggested transferring the IAF-operated technical school to private civilian hands. Laskov resisted, infuriating the Greens with Remez-like pronouncements such as "without a strong, high-quality Air Force, the land and sea forces will be useless in times of war."

On April 3, concluding like Remez before him that he had outstayed his usefulness, he requested and was granted a study-leave in Oxford. In the final count, Remez never fully understood the source of his disagreement with the Greens. "You can kill me and I still cannot explain who or what . . . is the 'high command,'" Remez wrote to his father two years earlier about Ben-Gurion's reorganization plan. "According to Yadin's thinking, it is the same lady in three gowns—'high command,' 'general staff,' and 'land-forces command'—with Yadin, of course, as the lady."

Laskov, however, had by the spring of 1953 identified the organizational fallacies which Remez only sensed. It was the incongruous command structure of the IDF itself that was the source of the squabbles, Laskov charged on April 28 in a twenty-page, single-spaced document titled "Command and Staff Structure." That was because its very design was rooted in ignorance and incompetence. The British army veterans who helped design the IDF structure, he wrote, had mistakenly borrowed the British "general staff" concept, which in Britain meant the command of the land forces only, instead of the General Headquarters or Supreme Headquarters entity. As a result, the Israeli general staff, which was designed and built to "deal with land forces only," was now attempting to command and control the Israeli air and sea forces without adequate structures, doctrine, or sense of mission.

It was here, Laskov argued, that the conflict between the Green and the Blues—the general staff's "strange" preoccupation with the Air Force's seeming quest for "independence"—had its origins. While the Greens were so preoccupied with mundane matters of Air

Force "methods of supply and control," the fact was that "from that standpoint even the Royal Air Force was not truly independent, because it receives its supplies from the Ministry of Supplies and its manpower from the Labor Ministry." What was essential for the Air Force was to be "independent in its mission. From a mission aspect, the land, air and sea forces [must be] independent, [and] it is the fulfillment of their missions that brings about the combined fulfillment of the IDF mission itself."

In other words, while the Israeli military could only do its job successfully through "cooperation without subordination, because it is impossible to subordinate the Air Force mission to that of the land forces's mission and vice versa," no such cooperation was possible so long as the IDF's overall command structure was totally dominated by the ground forces. To properly oversee all aspects of the nation's defense, the IDF either had to be placed under a true "high command . . . overseeing three equal-status forces," or else it had to surrender its supremacy and make the land, sea, and air arms "three equal forces with three equal general staffs [linked into] one integral command [where] none is subordinate to the others." The former option was simpler but required staffing an entire new command level with resources that were nonexistent. The latter was Laskov's original "integrated command" structure, which was the basis of Command Order 63 six months earlier.

Laskov's thesis was wasted on Makleff, who saw it as just one more pitch for Air Force autonomy, and promptly shelved it. Like Remez, Laskov left bloodied and filled with a sense of foreboding for the fate of the Air Force. Unlike Remez, however, in parting Laskov won a victory that would prove far more crucial to the future of the force than any budgetary gain. At his recommendation, overriding Makleff's opposition, Ben-Gurion appointed Dan Tolkowsky as his successor. For the first time since Remez's resignation, the Air Force was headed by one of its own.

It was a shaky victory. At first Makleff only accepted Tolkowsky as Laskov's temporary replacement, and delayed his promotion to general for six months. Technically, Laskov was still the IAF's commander, and Tolkowsky only his deputy. "Their feeling was simply that I would not survive, that they would wear me down," Tolkowsky says. As in Laskov's case, however, the Greens would be proved wrong.

Even in the international patchwork quilt that made up the early Israeli Air Force, Tolkowsky was odd man out. Dapper and trim, with large pale-blue eyes, a crisp Oxford accent and aloofness to match, Tolkowsky seemed to belong neither with the native Israelis nor with the World War II veterans, although in fact he was both. Born in 1921 to an old-line Jewish family of citrus ranchers, Tolkowsky was studying engineering at London's Imperial College when World War II broke out. He completed his degree in 1942, joined the RAF and flew Spitfires on the French, Italian, and Greek fronts until the war ended.

Back in London for an engineering job, he joined the *Haganah*'s Air Service in the fall of 1947. In April of 1948, with his arm in a cast from a failed attempt to ferry a small plane to Palestine, he set out with Harry Axelrod to run two small Ansons through the British blockade. They were arrested when they touched down in Rhodes for refueling, spent a month in a Greek jail, and arrived in Tel Aviv three days before war broke out. With his arm still disabled, Tolkowsky served as an operations officer for the duration of the war.

It was a drab post that won him few friends. Both the volunteers and the *Palmach* pilots resented his prissy manners—among them a habitual ascot and dry Oxfordian reserve—and many dismissed him as a non-flyer clerk (he never bothered to mention either his broken arm or his combat record). In his dry, self-deprecating manner, he almost shared their disdain for his competence. "I had no idea what I was doing. I was only a pilot, with no experience in anything else, certainly not in staff work. I didn't even know how to get a letter to several persons without retyping it again and again. I had joined the RAF for fun. I never thought of it all as a career," he would admit later.[21]

His superiors, however, noted his disciplined intellect, and after the war Remez insisted that he stay on as the IAF's training chief. "I had no idea what I was supposed to do. I could only think of getting back to engineering work," he would recall later. When Remez then appointed him to the newly created post of Air Force Inspector General, "I asked him what it entailed; he said 'I have no idea, why don't you take it and find out?' "

He was on the verge of resigning when, in the fall of 1950, the IDF staged a countrywide military exercise, and Remez sent him to represent the IAF on the panel of military evaluators. Chaim Laskov, who as head of IDF Training Command supervised the exercise, was impressed by Tolkowsky's formidable intellect, organized thought, and quiet ability to bring method out of chaos. He was particularly taken by Tolkowsky's post-exercise dissertation on the Air Force mission. "My most important conclusion was that in order to go to war, the reserves must be called, [but] you couldn't call the reserves if the enemy kept strafing them," Tolkowsky recalls. "I explained that the Air Force had to be active from the very first moment to clean up the skies, and that it had to explode into this activity from a state of total relaxation. There was nothing new or original in what I said. It was obvious. But it was the first time that Yigael [Yadin], Motke [Makleff] and Chaim [Laskov] heard it presented like that."

At the end of the year, Laskov organized a five-month brigade-level command course, and asked Tolkowsky to attend. Tolkowsky postponed his retirement to take the course, and as soon as it ended he went looking for an engineering job. But then Yadin phoned and invited him to his office. "He told me that Shamir was sick, so sick he had to give up his post. He said that Chaim Laskov had agreed to take his place, but only if I stayed on as his chief of staff. I was reluctant, but he promised that it would be for only a few months." Two turbulent years later, Laskov left and he was suddenly in command.

The Greens' reservations about "that snob Tolkowsky" proved well founded. Instead of acknowledging his tenuous position by towing Makleff's line, he pushed on with his predecessors' quest for free reins. Three months into his term, he invited Ben-Gurion, Makleff, and the general staff to Ramat David, where he presented an ambitious development plan for fourteen jet squadrons by 1957 (he had only three trained jet pilots then, and not a single jet plane on hand). This time there was no honeymoon, and his plan was promptly rejected. But "that snob Tolkowsky," as he became known, did not give up. Standing up before a seminar for the IDF high commanders, his crease razor sharp and every hair in place, he snapped at Makleff in clipped Oxfordian English that "there is no good, cheap cigar. Either it's good or it's cheap, but you can't have both."

His private war was soon swept by far greater national upheavals.

On October 5, 1953, Ben-Gurion nearly traumatized the entire country by announcing plans to retire to a new *kibbutz* in the Negev, and by appointing Moshe Sharett, a timid moralist with a Charlie Chaplin mustache who was his foreign minister and deputy premier, to succeed him as prime minister. Ben-Gurion also named Pinchas Lavon, his deputy at the defense ministry, as defense minister.

Within a week, Israel's new regime faced a military crisis as, on October 12, an Arab terrorist band entered Israel from the Jordanian-held West Bank and tossed a grenade through a window in the village of Yahud, near Lod Airport, killing a mother and two children. For the first time since Israel became a state, Ben-Gurion stayed out of the deliberations—although he was standing by—as Lavon, Makleff, and Dayan approved a next-day retaliatory strike by the recently founded 101 commando unit, headed by Maj. Ariel Sharon, against the West Bank village of Qibya, where several recent terrorist strikes against Israel had originated. The operation turned into a political disaster. Sharon's commandos entered the village, overcame its defenses, ordered its residents to leave, and then blew up some forty-five houses. But as it turned out, dozens of old men, women, and children had remained hidden inside their houses, and seventy bodies were subsequently pulled out of the wreckage.[22]

By the end of the year, Makleff retired, and Dayan took his place as the IDF chief of staff. But Tolkowsky's hopes that the pragmatic Dayan would be more receptive to the Air Force's interests were dashed as Lavon launched an unprecedented austerity drive, and virtually grounded Tolkowsky's planes for lack of spare parts. Dayan backed Lavon. "Our commandos go out on raids across the border with a cheap knife and perform extraordinary deeds—without hot showers or steaks or high pay," he once snapped at IAF Flight School cadets who suggested that special training and risks entitled combat pilots to special treatment.

Tolkowsky did not accept the Greens' new hard line, but in his own sober, bemused way, he conceded a certain justification for it. With the possible exception of Operation Dust Bowl's airlift, stopping the Egyptians at Ishdud by the first four Czech Knives, reconnaissance, and some air strikes by the light craft, he would say later, the Air Force's overall performance in 1948 had been a mere "flash in the pan. There weren't enough airplanes [to] enable the Air Force to present the ground forces with a sensible, consistent doctrine, or with a body of operational thinking." While the Air Force had been talking in terms of what had been achieved during World War II, "we were never able to project a capability that made sense." If the Greens had no real grasp of air operations, "you couldn't really blame them. From the beginning, we have oversold ourselves."

Tolkowsky now set out to change all that. Although no one asked him to and few paid attention, he began to stress and practice combat readiness. Each time Israeli commandos ventured across the border or a firefight broke out on the frontier, he had his armed Mustangs and Spitfires roll out to the Ramat David runway, his Dakotas readied to ferry paratroopers or supplies, his light planes placed on instant readiness to fly commanders or scouts to the battle zone.

He preached readiness on every occasion. "From the ground forces point of view, we were unfortunate. We were surrounded by enemies on all sides. But from the Air Force point of view it was a terrific advantage. We could offer three hundred and sixty degrees of protection, and . . . Cairo, Aman, Damascus were only minutes away," he says. And since to attack Israel the Egyptians or the Iraqis had to first move their forces across large expanses of open desert, it should have been "obvious for any fool that this was an ideal situation for the use of air power."

He also revised the Air Force doctrine, which until then called for achieving air superiority without specifying how that should be done. Now, assuming that Israel would always be outnumbered and outgunned by its opponents, Tolkowsky began to train, motivate, and prepare his Air Force to surprise and destroy the Arab Air Force on the ground, before they had a chance to scramble their jets and do damage.

Before he could do anything else, however, and as his talks of new jet squadrons and preventive raids on enemy airfields were dismissed as irrelevant by the Greens, he had to stay alive. "I made it my business to learn about political infighting. I even mastered the art of submitting resignation letters when they would do the most good—and when they were least likely to be accepted," he recalls.

"It was a matter of time. If I only stuck it out long enough, I was bound to prevail."

Besides, for the time being, what mattered most took place fifty-five miles to the north, where in the summer of 1953 Menahem Bar's new 117 squadron received its first Meteor jet fighters, and Ezer Weizman had once again taken command of Ramat David.

Chapter 10

THE BLACK SPITFIRE

The Israeli Air Force, veterans often claim, was born in Ramat David. This is true neither semantically nor historically. There were Palestine's early aviators, and the *Haganah*'s underground gliding and aviation clubs, and especially the Flight Platoon of the *Palmach*. Then there were the air forces of the World War II allies, whose veterans helped Israel win its independence, and the Czech Air Force, which provided the planes for that victory and the training of the first generation of Israeli military pilots.

Yet in several key areas this old canard is true. It was at Ramat David, the far-flung base in the Yizre'el Valley farm country, that the IAF developed its *Israeliness*. It was there that its combat spirit and eventually its fighter-based doctrine—to this day, the IAF employs not a single heavy or even medium bomber—were forged, and most of the early innovations that shaped the IAF's character and capabilities.

To understand that birth, and the mythical hold it has on today's Air Force, we must consider the utter loneliness in which it took place. While embattled IAF chiefs, following the 1948 war, acted as lightning rods and shielded their pilots from incessant assaults by the IDF command, their personal limitations also deprived their troops of any meaningful guidance. Remez and Tolkowsky had been ordinary RAF pilots with no command experience, and they had not flown operationally since 1946. Shamir and Laskov never flew. Some staff officers had brief flight experiences during World War II and 1948, but those rapidly became obsolete in the jet era that began in the early 1950s.

As a result, whatever happened at Air Force North happened less by outside design than by imposed neglect. Tolkowsky may have emphasized readiness and battle initiative, but he and his senior staff were too far removed from actual flying to translate doctrine into field capabilities. While he did battles against the Greens from his Ramla command post fifty miles away, events at Ramat David unfolded on their own. Little that happened there could have been envisioned or planned. Only in retrospect would it all seem so inevitable, because once it took place, nothing was ever the same again.

What happened at Ramat David in the summer of 1953 was a sudden implosion. Four years after the 1948 war ended, the two rival subcultures of the IAF—the *Palmach* Flight Platoon on one side, in the person of Menahem Bar, the farmer, and the RAF-Haifa Flight Club on the other, represented by Ezer Weizman, the rich man's son from Haifa—converged in a brilliant flash of consuming, creative synergism. What Bar accomplished while working on the flesh and sinews of the ragtag air militia of the north, and Weizman on its spirit and soul, is what Israelis really mean when they talk about the birth of the Air Force at Ramat David. With Bar in command of Squadron 117, and Weizman of Ramat David itself, Air Force North became Camelot.

The Israeli Air Force had entered the jet age on June 17, 1953, when Ben-Gurion, Makleff, and Tolkowsky took delivery of two Meteor jet trainers that were flown by British test pilots from England to Ramat David. Ben-Gurion christened them *Soufa* ("storm") and *Sa'ar* ("tempest"), which he borrowed from a vengeful phrase in Psalms 83:15: "So persecute them with thy tempest, and make them afraid with thy storm."[1]

But even as their numbers swelled to the fifteen that Britain sold Israel, the Meteors were still greatly outnumbered by the six Meteor and Vampire jet squadrons deployed by the Arab air forces to the north, south, and east. And with no pilots to fly them, the new Meteors were a liability—an invitation for the Arabs to strike at Ramat David and destroy them on the ground before they became operational.

It was to Bar, the tireless farmer-teacher, that the urgent task fell of correcting this. Ten days before the first planes arrived, he formed Squadron 117 with himself in command and with Beni Peled, who had just completed jet training in England, as deputy commander, and tackled his new mission with the single-minded urgency of a farmer rushing hay to barn before the rain. Setting Peled down to translate the necessary manuals from English, he designed and supervised the construction of the new squadron complex on the southeastern corner of the base (it was at his insistence that the briefing room was built underground). By mid-September he had taken Tolkowsky up in a Meteor for an introductory flight, rushed Moti Hod, commander of the 101 squadron, through a refresher jet session, and gave a rush jet-flying course to Avraham Yoffe, a former 101 pilot now at Air Force Operations. With him and Peled, it gave the IAF four jet pilots.

In early September, he opened the IAF's first formal jet training course with four students. Of the four, only one, Dani Shapira, by then the Air Force's most elegant pilot and best aerial shot, could recall Ramat David's Dodge City days. The rest were too young. Joe Alon, slim, lively, with curly black hair and a black mustache, was a young Czech refugee who learned to fly at one of the Czech flight courses in 1948, and had only recently arrived at Air Force North. Aharon Yoeli, a baby-faced *Palmach* fighter who joined the Air Force during the war, had just completed flight school. Brooding Jacob Nevo,* nicknamed Yak, was so young that he had missed the 1948 war altogether.

But they were the best of the new crop of Israeli pilots and, infected by Bar's urgency, they completed basic jet training in less than a month, and were soon in the thick of operational flights— formation flying, gunnery, interception, instrument flying, and air-to-air combat. "It was as if a fire was consuming us on the inside, twenty-four hours a day. We were at the edge of a new frontier, of

*Formerly Milner.

new uncharted regions that we could burst into, uncharted because we had nobody to learn from," says Yoeli.[2]

Since Bar "was not really built for air combat; he was an air-ground man, hard work, no brilliance," it was Beni Peled who "took us on wild explorations of every limit," says Yoeli. With no access to fighter tactic texts from other air forces, instructors and students alike had to learn and reinvent every movement from scratch, as when Beni Peled, on his own, suddenly got the idea to drop his flaps in midair.

It was a significant benchmark in their dogfighting evolution. In air combat, it is often the plane that goes slowest that wins, by getting on its opponent's tail to shoot it down. But a plane can slow down only so far before it stalls and drops like a rock. What Peled did was drop his flaps and let the sudden air drag slow him down— while still gunning his engine so it did not lose power. It was not a new discovery. American air force and navy pilots had done it in Korea. But the Israelis were not privy to American combat data. "We had nobody to learn from," says Yoeli, "so we tried every-thing. If the flight envelope is made up of green lines and red lines, outside which is the danger zone, that was where we flew all the time, right to and beyond the red line. There was nothing we didn't try."

On December 28, the first course ended and Bar led eight jets in formation over the base.[3] The next day, he pulled out a new set of manuals which he had scribbled even while carrying his exhausting work schedule, and rushed his four graduates through a quick flight instructors' course. Because Beni Peled was in Europe, testing new jets that Sweden and France offered to sell to Israel, Bar split the course into shifts so he could conduct every session in the air or on the ground himself. Each morning, shivering as the chill of fall and then winter draped the valley, he climbed into the cockpit to go up with each student on each flight, then remained in the plane "as it was refueled, to go up again and again as each new pilot climbed in—three or four flights each morning with no break," he recalled.[4]

But in four weeks the course was finished, and Bar promptly started a second group of four cadets through jet-training—with the graduates of the first course as his assistant instructors. "If there was no Menahem Bar at that time someone would have had to invent him," Yoeli would later say in awe. On March 4, 1954, the second course ended, which Bar marked by leading twelve jets in formation over Tel Nof and Hazor in the south. In August, a year after he began, he completed his third jet-fighter course. With twelve jet pilots in his squadron, he closed it to new flyers, and set to mold his new squadron into a combat unit.

Actually, he had begun operational training even while still breaking in new pilots. Working to the same four-month training beat he developed at the 105, each group had worked through an elaborate range of aerial chores that Bar had prescribed in yet another set of his hand-scribbled, grammar-school notebooks. Starting from the moment the Meteors arrived in the fall of 1953, the silvery jets could be seen from nearby highways as they whipped with seeming abandon over the valley and the surrounding hills, flying so low they clipped the tops off the lush cornfields below, or corkscrewing themselves into the blue until they literally ran out of air and started falling back, like autumn leaves in a storm.

But the new jets soon ran into an unexpected and sobering predicament. As they tired of dogfighting each other, they thought they found fresh game in the old Mustangs of the 101. Yet no matter how hard they turned, piled on speed, or "put on brakes" Peled-style by dropping their flaps, each time they turned around there were the lowly Mustangs riding their tails. It was more than embarrassing—it made no sense. The Mustang was a nearly obsolete, prop-driven World War II relic. How could it outperform the faster and more powerful jets?

Once again, they learned a critical—though hardly new—lesson all on their own. Simply put—a Meteor was a Meteor and a Mustang a Mustang, and neither could or should have been flown like the other. That was their mistake. Both Mustang and Meteor pilots had learned their dogfighting skills on Spitfires and Mustangs, but the faster Meteor could not twist and turn in the "furball" as tightly as the slower Mustang.

It was an expensive lesson—on June 3, 1954, a Meteor pilot trying to protect his tail against four Mustangs rammed into one of them over the Tel Aviv waterfront, killing its pilot and barely managing to land himself—but once learned it became a critical element of IAF fighter tactics. "If you go against a Mustang, and you try to go down to his speeds where you are not manuevering well but he manuevers excellently, he'll get you every time," recalls Aharon "Yalo" Shavit, a young pilot at the time.[5] Instead, the trick was to exploit one's own strengths, which in the case of the faster and more powerful Meteor meant to sweep in unseen from out of the blue and "catch him when he does not see you," or switch the battle to the "vertical plane—you climb hard and fast, and when your opponent loses his power and starts falling back down, you flip over, come back down hard, and you are right behind him," says Shavit.

Even as his pilots dueled in the air, Bar's mind had already soared far beyond. "I got this idea that our strength should not be measured just by how many planes we had, but by how many sorties we could get out of each plane or crew. The point was to keep the plane as little as possible on the ground, and as long as possible in the air. For example, since a plane is very expensive, why not assign two or three pilots to each plane, and get more out of it?" he says.

This farmer's sensibility—instead of buying a second tractor, run the one you have in two or three shifts, with father and sons taking turns at the wheel—brought Bar to a near-fanatic preoccupation with *sevev*, Hebrew for "turnaround." He scribbled and then had retyped and mimeographed a new manual that meticulously out-lined "what each member of the ground crew should do each min-ute the plane is on the ground," and began driving ground and air crews to implement the *sevev* at greater and greater speeds. The moment a fighter landed and was chocked-in with blocks of wood under its wheels, Bar would snap on his stopwatch, and a mad dash would begin to refuel and rearm, replenish oxygen supplies, strap a new pilot into the cockpit and chock the plane back out. What Bar's achievement board did to his pilots, his stopwatch and loudly announced results did to the ground crews, for whom shaving a few seconds off the chock-in-to-chock-out time became the ultimate challenge.

Sevev was more than just rushing ground crews through their paces. It was a state of mind that, under Bar's relentless drive, guided everything from base construction to purchasing priorities. Even Shimon Peres, then director general of the Defense Depart-ment, was treated to a Bar tirade that "having planes without ladders, armament carts, bausers and everything else that made a plane capable of doing ten sorties each day instead of just one, was like trying to keep milking cows without feeding them."

It was as if, given a squadron and a free hand, Bar single-handedly rethought and redesigned the entire Air Force in his own image. It did not matter, says Beni Peled, that "he was ignorant of anything involving technology [and] did not believe in anything that was not living, organic. Gliding was his thing because it was natural and elementary. He was a hippie in his own way. He even argued that you didn't need radar, or gyro navigation. But within the structures that he developed you could introduce all those things. In organizing and managing and getting things done he was head and shoulders above all his generation, an institution."[6]

He did not stop there. Ben-Gurion was visiting the base one day and, while viewing the Meteors on the tarmac, asked Bar how fast his squadron could switch from a state of peacetime relaxation to a fighting state. "I thought and thought and could not answer him. I was not aware of the importance of this point. After he left I began to think about it," Bar says. Without skipping a beat in his already packed daily schedule, he produced yet a new manual and began running his squadron ragged making "fast transitions from peace to war, [with] armament loads ready ahead of time so that planes could be loaded and put in the air as fast as possible." The ultimate result was *yemei krav*—battle days, which marked the end of each four-month training period with a whole-day war game, first for each squadron, and ultimately for the entire Air Force. Like his *sevev* or four-month rotation cycles, *yemei krav* are to this day a cornerstone of IAF training and war preparations.

Nothing escaped his attention, certainly nothing that had the slightest bearing on *sevev*, or readiness. Like a farmer keeping tabs on each cow and fruit tree, Bar equipped each plane's battle station not only with ammunition, tools, and whatever else it needed to fly off to war, but also with a telephone, which hooked it to the squadron switchboard, which in turn connected into base operations. The instant a plane took off, landed, or was turned around to go out again, base operations knew it. At any given moment, whoever was in command knew not only how many planes he had on hand at Bar's squadron, but precisely which plane was doing what and with which pilot inside.

If Tolkowsky made readiness a cornerstone of IAF doctrine, the farmer made it a way of life.

Ezer Weizman made it an inspiration.

Though somewhat matured by marriage and polished by a stretch of hard work under Laskov, Weizman—a colonel at just twenty-nine—had not lost his fighter-jock swagger. With his well-deserved reputation as a brawler and womanizer, clipped mustache, close-cropped hair and sharply creased tans draped around impossibly long legs, comparisons to Errol Flynn and the *Dawn Patrol* were inevitable, and he did little to discourage them. Only now this dash was focused and purposeful. Better than anyone, he understood—and encouraged—the symbolism of his return to Ramat David. Unlike the Greens, whose decades of pre-statehood underground exploits produced numerous men around whom legends of combat and daring had now grown, role models for young generations of soldiers, the Air Force had none save for Modi Alon, who died too young and long ago, and the foreign volunteers, who were, of course, outsiders and therefore unsuitable for the role.

Weizman now set out to forge a mythology for the IAF. He grasped instinctively that to the young crews, reared on his Wild West legends, his appointment was a validation of the Ramat David promise. His very appearance on the base was electrifying. Under his two predecessors, nonflying administrators both, clerks and stockroom attendants had seemingly taken over Ramat David. "Pilots had to live by the goodwill of the supply officers. If you came back late from night flying, you didn't get breakfast. If you did not show up on time for your laundry, you did not get it," recalls Yitzhak "Tsahik" Yavneh, a veteran *Palmach* pilot who took over the 101 at the time of Weizman's return.[7]

Weizman changed all that. "Suddenly, all an officer had to do was tell the kitchen his pilots were flying at night and won't be back for breakfast, and the kitchen stayed open until they did. And the laundry clerk opened at seven at night if that's when the pilots had time to come."

Even more important, says Yavneh, was Weizman's understanding that "a force with no tradition of fighter operations, with no fighter veterans at the high command, had to give squadron commanders room for initiative." When Yavneh, worried about low battle-readiness, asked to try an unprecedented all-squadron live-ammo gunnery practice, Weizman snapped "fine," and that was that. "I took the squadron to a deserted Arab village north of Yavne'el, where we had set up corrugated-metal targets. Twelve planes came in low, split into three groups, and then came in one after another from three different directions. We scored 12 percent hits on the targets—not bad for a first-time try," says Yavneh. What he did not know until later was that "without telling anybody, [Weizman] invited the IDF Northern Command staff to the show. As we were hitting our targets they were sitting on a hilltop watching. He then had them to the base for lunch, and made it seem as though we were always doing things like that."

Such promotional flare could not have come at a better time. By the summer of 1953, the Air Force had all but disappeared from public consciousness. While the magic name "101" was on every young Israeli's lips, woven in elaborate tales of daring raids across angry borders, it was Ariel Sharon's 101 commando unit, not the Mustang squadron. And the red hats that enticed service-bound high school graduates were those gracing the heads of Battalion 890 paratroopers, not Ramat David fighter pilots.

The Red Squadron had become history. Isolated and powerless on and off base, its pilots had little incentive to stay on past their mandatory thirty-month tour of duty—especially when far more rewarding flying jobs were theirs for the asking with El Al, Israel's new national airline. Flying fighters was fun, but there was no future in it.

Weizman exploded this morass with unbounded energy and supreme faith in a destiny—his own and the Air Force's. The long-dormant officers' bar was brought back to life. "There was drinking, real drinking, with bottles flying, so that if you didn't duck your skull might crack. And singing—in English. 'We are the 101' was the best song," recalls Yalo Shavit. "The pride of belonging to the 101, compared with the poor Spitfires of the 105, was incredible. And then there were war stories, which we young clowns drank up with wide-open eyes and ears. That atmosphere nursed a desire to fly, a love of flying with abandon. That was the thing, flight had to be free of care to be good."

Weizman preached the new Air Force gospel outside the base,

too. He lost no opportunity—as in Yavneh's gunnery practice—to remind the IDF command that his fighter boys were there and ready for action. He seized every opportunity to get in on any bit of military activity, which he then used to drive home his message of invincibility to his own pilots. "When we penetrated and photographed Damascus, I could tell the boys 'Well, where was the Syrian Air Force?' And when we photographed Sinai and El 'Arīsh, I could claim 'Where is that growing, terrible Egyptian Air Force?' . . . the fact that Egyptian fighters never pursued us and we never lost a plane contributed to their morale," he recalls in his autobiography.[8]

Morale was everything. Weizman was infuriated by what he thought was an irrational "hidden fear" that afflicted his pilots and the Israeli public, a fear that caused them to attribute Israel's 1948 victory not to their own strength and bravery, but to "a temporary weakness of our enemies, which . . . will never be repeated." Those fears were fanned by the ascent to power of Gamal Abdel Nasser in Egypt, "the great uniter who would gather [the Arabs] under his flag and lead them by the millions to flood this tiny country. Nasser's claim that the Egyptian Army's failure in 1948 was only due to rotten ammunition and bad arms fell on fertile emotional ground in . . . a bewildered, consumed Israel." Weizman's challenge was "to convince the boys that their fears were groundless . . . that the Israeli fighter—the Israeli *pilot*—of the Fifties was as good as his equivalent was in the Forties, and that if the enemy sought another round we would beat them decisively, again and again, because we were *better.*"[9]

He now set out to break through those self-imposed barriers of space and attitude, among his pilots, at least. He scheduled long flights, boundary-pushing navigation flights ranging far beyond Israel's puny perimeter. "We would take off in Mustangs from Ramat David, fly all around the island of Cyprus, then to the Syrian coast, and after two and a half hours land back at home. Such flights inspired confidence. There were large-formation flights, difficult flights, low-altitude flights, bad-weather flights. . . . I could not forge the hearts of the people of Israel, but in that section of it that was under my command, Nasser's name caused nobody to go weak at the knees."[10]

He also tackled the emotional roots of defeatism in his pilots by talking it out of them. His talks were legend. At gatherings in bars or ready rooms, dining halls or on the porch of his bungalow at Ramat David, he talked endlessly, magically whipping his listeners to frenzy. "Ezer saw a far bigger picture than any of us, and he used to talk to us days and nights," says Shavit. "He would tell us that the Ezion Block was still part of the state of Israel, that one day the West Bank will come back to us. That was before the wars, but he saw the wars coming."

Tall, mercurial, with sparkling eyes and machine-gun, stream-of-consciousness delivery, he cast a spell on new pilots and old comrades alike. They loved hearing him talk of the midgets—midget Arabs, midget politicians, midget headquarters clerks, midgets who failed to see the greatness ahead. "I felt that I must foster the longing to return (to the West Bank) rather than stifle it with the false contention that even a small Israel was an inhabitable place," he would recall. "With the Arabs nestled all those years in their mad dream to destroy the state, a battle-hungry commander, who saw his role as leading his command to war and winning it, was a healthy commander, [so] I sought prey. I searched for enemy planes. When I stood before my troops, I would say just give us the MiGs and we shall rip them apart."[11]

It was through flying, "flying without care," that they would reach their destiny, he told them. In the spring of 1954, two hot young pilots at the 101, Jacob Agasi and Omri Ariav, began practicing aerobatics on their own. When the kinks were out of their routine, they brought it to the skies over Ramat David. It was, of course, a transgression of the highest order, a violation of every safety rule in the book. In Weizman Country, however, "everybody got excited, and Ezer rushed over. He slapped us on the back, shook our hands and got excited like a kid," Agasi recalls.[12]

It was also a violation of standing orders when Yoeli and Yak Nevo hopped in their Meteors on one moonlit night and flew "to see what movies were playing in Damascus. We dropped low and flew around the city, buzzed the theaters until the lights in the city went out, then hightailed it back through the valley before anybody knew who it was," Yoeli says. In July of 1954, Yoeli was scrambled south to intercept an Egyptian Fury that reportedly penetrated Israeli air space. He could not find it, but "I figured he had to land somewhere, so I shut off my radio and flew to El 'Arīsh. I got there just as the plane came for a landing, so I came down after it and buzzed it so low that it ran off the runway and flipped over." Weizman was waiting on the runway to reprimand him on his return, but Weizman had a way of making even a reprimand seem like a medal.[13]

Any flying would do, provided it pushed the limits hard enough. Like using a Piper Cub to hunt jackals—"the poor animal would run and run, but when it couldn't run anymore it would give up and roll over on its back. The trick was to come down and hit it on the belly with your landing wheel," says Yoeli. Or buzzing highways as far north as Beirut, dipping low and giving the finger to passing drivers.

Through Weizman, they became more than just pilots, more than even *Israeli* pilots. Now they were members of a fabled international fraternity, a knightly order of aerial warriors. Weizman once brought H. B. "Mickey" Martin, formerly of the famed 617 "Dam Busters" Lancaster squadron of World War II, and then Britain's air attaché in Israel, to visit Ramat David and trade war stories with his pilots. But it was not his tales of bombing the Ruhr Valley dams that stayed in the feverish memories of the young Israelis, but his rendition of an old RAF bombing game: "He got down on the floor on all fours, not the regular way but facing up. He sidled like a crab to where he had placed a potato on the floor, lowered his butt over the potato, grabbed it between his 'cheeks,' and raced on all fours to the end of the room and then let it drop. Bombs away," recalls Yoeli.

Weizman presided over all this like a Viking king. "He was the top, the supreme leader. He'd call you over, tell you to stand at attention, slap you on the face and tell you to go away. You couldn't hit back. He was the boss," Shavit says. The young pilots were mesmerized. More than charisma or charm, Weizman had "style!!! He was our Pierre Cardin, the ultimate decider of what was in and what was out," says Yoeli. "What he liked was automatically the top. What he didn't was, if not the bottom, definitely second best."

Back in 1945, while training to fly Thunderbolts with the RAF in Egypt, Weizman had watched with envy as one of his British commanders boarded his *personal* Spitfire, painted black with a red nose, and tore up the skies on weekends. Now that the Air Force began phasing out its Spitfires and selling them on the Third World market, Weizman held one back. He stripped it of its guns and had it painted glossy black, with a red nose, a jagged red lightning streak on the side, and red stripes on the tail rudder, the 101's old insignia. As he now began tearing up the skies over Ramat David with his own personal mount, the "Black Spit" became the mascot, indeed the very scepter of Weizman's Camelot.

There was a price of admission to his magic circle. To belong, pilots had to sign on for three years and live on base, in the bosom of his fighter family. Those who didn't were "welcome to fly B-17s, Dakotas or Mosquitos," but not fighters.[14] He enforced his rule ruthlessly. On December 8, 1954, five Israeli soldiers were captured by Syrians on the Golan Heights. On January 13, one body was returned. Tortured for days and fearing he'd give in, the young soldier had hung himself in his cell after hiding a tiny note between his toes: "I did not betray." When the note was found on the returned body, Israel was infuriated and eager to strike back. Several days later, a Syrian airliner was spotted off the Israeli coast, and Yoeli and Joe Alon were dispatched in their Meteors to bring it down in Israel, to use as a bargaining chip for the rest of the prisoners.

As it turned out, the Israeli radar report was erroneous and the airliner was Lebanese. As the two returned to Ramat David, however, with Alon almost all out of fuel, Weizman was in the tower and, microphone in hand, refused to let Alon land unless he promised to sign on for three more years. Alon had no choice. Whether he crashed, bailed out, or landed without permission, his Air Force career would end in disgrace. With only seconds to spare, he gave in. His engines died just seconds after his wheels touched the runway. That, too, was part of Weizman's law—you couldn't leave the magic circle, not unless Weizman himself put you out first.

Those who stayed, however, were immortalized by Weizman's new slogan, which soon spread like wildfire through the Air Force grapevine—"the best to Ramat David." The slogan had an added meaning. By 1953, the IAF had two fighter bases. Ramat David had the hotter Mustangs and Meteors, but Hazor, now dubbed Air Force South, was where the action was. Its two Mosquito squadrons were the Air Force's prime reconnaissance force, and the wooden planes roamed the skies of Syria, Jordan and Egypt daily, reaching as far as Libya to the south and Iraq to the east.

With a fighter pilot's killer instinct, Weizman set out to demolish not only the rival base but the rival plane. "What's the use of a plane you can't turn on its back," he would snort contemptuously each time the subject came up. Anyone "tainted" by ever having flown a Mosquito was barred from the magic circle. In Weizman's book, Ramat David and Hazor were "two different worlds, with different kinds of people. In the north were real fighter pilots. In the south dwelled inferior people," recalls Eli Eyal,* a veteran *Palmach* pilot. "The very fact that I was at Hazor at the time, and had actually flown a Mosquito, was enough to make me not *kosher*— although I was really an Air Force North man. I had flown with the 101, and I founded and commanded the first reserve fighter squadron at Ramat David."[15] Weizman's campaign of derision, coming on top of the Mosquitos' dismal safety and survival record, doomed not only the plane, but for years any attempt to equip the Israeli Air Force with anything but the hottest single-combat fighters available.

Only one section of Ramat David escaped Weizman's rule. At the 117 squadron, Bar "was so strong that even Weizman was afraid to show up there," says Agasi. "Menahem would just look at him and Ezer would turn around and leave. I suspect that Ezer, even when we still thought of Menahem as a great man, already knew his limitations, but Menahem so dominated the squadron that everybody was afraid of him."

Bar had no use for Weizman's hard-drinking, hard-flying rhetoric, especially since "once he became base commander he flew very little. He would come to fly every now and then, but he didn't keep up his flying level. I wouldn't have sent him to battle," Bar would say many years later. This was not entirely true. Although he learned to fly Meteors at the 117, Weizman did most of his flying with his spiritual kin at the 101. Although a reckless flight leader— "Weizman led a flight as if he were flying alone. You had to figure out your place in the formation, and as he went down among the

*Formerly Finegersh.

trees you had to follow," says Shavit—Weizman was the one the
young pilots wanted to fly with.

"From Menahem Bar we learned," says Yoeli, "but it was Ezer
and Moti that we tried to emulate. Menahem was like a draft oxen.
He needed no stimulus to work hard. For him it was all work, like
planting carrots. Ezer, on the other hand, understood the importance of atmosphere, of this knightly element, of showing that being
a fighter pilot was above and beyond ordinary things. If Ezer wanted
to have a party for the pilots, Menahem would say 'What for?'
Menahem also said that sports were unnecessary and morning exercises were enough, but Ezer overruled him and instituted Wednesday afternoon games—soccer, basketball, whatever—which he even
made Menahem attend."

Agasi recalls that when he and Ariav first unveiled their aerobatics routine, Weizman ecstatically asked Bar "why he didn't do
aerobatics at his squadron. Menahem said he had more important
things to do."

In the summer of 1954, the differences between them came to a
head as Bar challenged Weizman's two ultimate rules. One rule, the
requirement that pilots live on base, he had been violating all along
by walking or bicycling to his farm at the end of each day. Since
housing shortages at the base were forcing other pilots to also live
outside the base, Weizman did not make an issue out of it. But Bar
then did the unthinkable—he refused to sign on. His refusal had
nothing to do with his commitment to the IAF. Thirty years after
founding his village in the barren lands of Tel Shamam, his father
had grown sick and crippled with Parkinson's disease. As his grip
on the land weakened, he looked to his eldest son to take over the
farm. "I could not sign on. If I did it would mean that I was not
coming back to the farm, and it would have devastated him," Bar
recalls.

Weizman, however, underestimated the deep loyalties of the
farmer to his land, and of the son to his ailing father. As one who
kept preaching the virtues of Israel's pioneering roots he should
have empathized with Bar's dilemma. Bar was not about to leave the
Air Force for the farm—he only wanted his dying father to go on
thinking that someday he would. Yet Weizman would have none of
that. Farm or no farm, unless Bar signed on for a three-year stretch

he would be out of his squadron, out of flying fighters, out of Ramat David, period.

Bar, however, took his case to another farmer in the neighboring village of Nahalal. Unlike Weizman, Moshe Dayan knew all about aging farmers and their expectations of their sons—his own pioneer-settler father, Shmuel Dayan, was also growing old behind his plow. Dayan asked his brother-in-law to let Bar stay on without a formal three-year commitment. Weizman refused, but Dayan ordered Tolkowsky to let Bar continue his service on a year-to-year basis, and Tolkowsky passed the order back down to Weizman. Bar was the only one to break Weizman's rule and get away with it. For the time being, at least.

There was yet another, darker, dimension to Weizman's rule. That became apparent in the summer of 1954, when a graduating high school class from Haifa visited Ramat David, and Tsahik Yavneh, who had just taken over the 101 and heard about Agasi's and Ariav's aerobatics antics, scheduled them to show off for the visiting kids. It ended in tragedy. Agasi and Ariav had been joined by a third, less experienced pilot who, when the three Mustangs pulled out of a barrel roll, drifted out and, trying to force his Mustang back into formation, rammed into Ariav's plane. The students shrieked in horror as the two planes clashed, locked and tumbled downward together. "I heard a thud and shouted to them to jump, but the two planes planted themselves right in Kfar Yehoshua," says Agasi. Both pilots died on impact.

"Unfortunately, such things happen," Yavneh told his visitors. Then, expressing hope that the accident "did not affect your view of the Air Force," he asked how many still wanted to become pilots. Most of the boys raised their hands. But the students' show of faith was the only kind aspect of the tragedy. Yavneh, Agasi, and Moti Hod, who was in the tower at the time of the accident, were court-martialed. Yavneh was convicted of allowing aerobatics over the base without prior permission from base operations, and was severely reprimanded. Agasi was grounded for four months, then put on military trial for, as the team's leader, responsibility in the two pilots' death. The court ruled that although his squadron commander ordered him to do the show, he should have verified that his superior had an authorization to issue such an order—a verdict so tortuous that the court panel backed off and fined Agasi just one Israeli pound. "It told me I was completely free of blame. Everybody knew I was not to blame," says Agasi.

Only Moti Hod was exonerated after claiming that he had no idea that the air show was to take place, and that by the time it started he had no way of stopping it. Much of his defense was based on Weizman's claim that, as base commander, he had no idea that anybody at Ramat David had ever engaged in aerobatics. Weizman's argument alibied not only himself—he wasn't there at the time—but also Hod, since if Weizman did not know of any aerobatics at the base, Hod certainly had no reason to expect any when he climbed into the tower. In his autobiography some twenty years later, Weizman insisted that when the pilots had first approached him with a proposal for an aerobatics team he turned them down, and that Agasi and the dead pilots had only themselves to blame for the accident because "in secrecy, they decided among themselves that [if] they must choose between aerobatics . . . and the ban imposed by their commander, aerobatics comes first."[16]

It is true that Weizman never formally approved the establishment of an aerobatics team at Ramat David. But it is also true that many Ramat David veterans insist to this day that Agasi's and Ariav's aerobatics displays were common knowledge, and that Weizman, who made it his business to know every little thing that took place in his domain, knew about them even if he never did officially sanction them.

And it is also a fact that at Weizman's Camelot, where "flying without care" was the ultimate high, taking risks was never a transgression (although screwing up was). Moti Hod himself, when later asked if he would have stopped the show if he could, shrugged and answered, "Probably not." What it came down to was this: At Camelot, the king could do no wrong.

Chapter 11

FRENCH SHUTTLE

Like Menahem Bar, his commander at the 117, Beni Peled was not a Camelot regular. Plump, owlish, and argumentative, he had married early, did not drink, and on the whole cared little for Weizman's fraternal rites. At day's end he would rush to his rented apartment in the nearby town of Tiv'on, where he would spend hours plowing through aviation texts, with his Bulgarian-born wife, Bertha, patiently sitting by.

Although fascinated with aviation since childhood, in 1947 he entered the Technion in Haifa to study mechanical engineering, and only because school closed a month later due to mounting Arab-Jewish tensions did he volunteer to the Air Service. With no flight experience, he was rushed through a primitive one-month flight mechanics course, and spent the 1948 war fixing Messerschmitts at the Red Squadron—"an excellent mechanic, but always in hot water because he was never where he was supposed to be," recalls Harry Axelrod, the 101's technical officer.[1]

But his interest was piqued, and at the end of the war he entered flight school. Like the rest of the cadets who did not fly in the 1948 war, he seemed destined to lag behind the *Palmach* fighters and the veterans of the Czech summer courses. But he soon astounded his instructors by becoming "the star of the course, a fantastic pilot," and at the end was shipped to Ramat David, to fly Mustangs with the 101.

Peled did not care for the Red Squadron's helter-skelter style. "You came in the morning and decided that today you do this, and you did it. The next morning you decided to do that and you did that. As far as order and cleanliness and appearances and all that, it was a total mess," he would recall.[2] At the end of 1951, however, he was assigned to the 105 squadron and had his first inkling that things could be different. "He may have been a peasant, and not a great pilot, but he was a serious plantation owner. He knew when to bring the cows in, and when to milk, and when to plant," he would say about Menahem Bar. "He was a strange character, not very bright, very sensitive, not particularly capable, incredibly stubborn, and very modest. But when he was at 105 he decided he couldn't live in such disorder, and he drew up plans . . . in his own crazy way. He was a Jesuit to the point of madness."

In Ramat David, too, Peled stood out quickly, and in 1952 became the third Israeli to be sent to England for RAF jet and flight-leader training, after Moti Hod and Menahem Bar. On his first evening at a British base, the commander rose from the dinner table, ordered the glasses filled, and called for "Mr. Vice" to do his thing. Peled's ears perked up. "Mr. Weiss? I look around, and this young second lieutenant gets up at the far end of the table, stands at attention and says 'Gentlemen, the Queen.' I was sure I found a fellow Jew. An RAF pilot, no less," he recalls.

After dinner, he walked up to the young lieutenant. "Your name is Mr. Weiss?" he half-asked, half-stated. The young RAF officer looked him over. "I beg your pardon?" Peled flashed an impatient smile. "Weiss is a Jewish name, no?" The officer stared blankly for a moment, then patiently explained that it was "Mr. Vice," his official title as vice one thing or another of the evening affair. Peled shrugged and walked away. On another occasion, he launched into an angry tirade when the commander of another base, making small talk, said: "Israel, Israel, isn't it in Jerusalem?"

But it was not such trivialities that dimmed his view of the Royal Air Force. "I had such a glowing image of it from the World War II stories, but the postwar RAF was something else. There was dirt and disorder and political intrigues," he recalls. By the time he returned to Ramat David a year later, however, Britain had sold Israel its first Meteors, and "I decided not to say anything about my disillusionment with the RAF." In early 1954, after helping Bar to shepherd the first Meteor course to completion, he left for Europe once again.

It was a momentous trip.

By 1954, even as the 117 squadron basked in jet glory, the British-made Meteor was nearing obsolescence. Although far superior to World War II–era prop-driven fighters, it had long since been surpassed by the Soviet MiG-15 and American-made F-86 Sabrejet—which was probably why Britain was so willing to sell Israel its Meteors. Israeli arms buyers were after better planes, such as North American Aviation's Sabrejet, the famed MiG-killer of Korea; Sweden's Saab J-29 interceptor; and France's Mystère II, made by Avions Marcel Dassault, in that order. In November 1953, Saab agreed to sell Israel a squadron of J-29s, and in January, while still holding out for an American F-86 deal, an IAF evaluation team flew to Europe to check out the Swedish and French offers, with Beni Peled as its test pilot. Peled took the J-29 up on fifteen separate flights and heartily endorsed it, but the deal soon foundered, ostensibly over credit disagreement.[3] On their way home the Israelis stopped in France to check out the Mystère II.

The French seemingly held nothing back, and Peled took the swept-wing, Sabrejet-look-alike jet past the speed of sound—the first Israeli to go supersonic. This time he issued a scathing report. Not only was the plane sluggish and weak, he wired back to Tolkowsky, but since he spoke French, he had figured out the sudden French willingness to sell the Mystère II to the Israelis. "They were coming out with the Mystère IV, which was going to be far better, and they were trying to unload sixty Mystère IIs on anybody they could because they knew it was no good," he says.

Back in Israel, however, Tolkowsky insisted that the plane was good enough, and with Weizman, Dayan, and Shimon Peres, director general of the Defense Ministry,[4] pushed for a quick French deal. They backed off briefly when on March 13, the Americans promised a "favorable" review of Israel's request for twenty-four F-86s,[5] and when North American Aviation representatives assured

Israel that a "green light" from the State Department was forth-coming. In fact, on May 13 North American authorized Canadair, who produced F-86s in Canada under the North American license, to begin manufacturing the Israeli order. But the "green light" failed to materialize. On July 9, Canada cited American opposition and canceled the deal. A month later, on August 13, Israel signed a contract with France for six Mystère IIs, to be delivered in early 1955.[6]

In spite of his reservations about the plane, Peled was put in charge of getting the Mystères over. He handpicked five of Squadron 117's top pilots, including Dani Shapira and Yak Nevo, put them through a brief but intensive French language course, and on July 3, 1955, arrived at the French Air Force base at Mont-de-Marsan for basic jet training. In early August, after five practice flights on Ouragans, eleven-year-old attack jets which the French were about to phase out, they began flying Mystère IIs.

As soon as he started his plane down the runway for his first takeoff, however, Peled realized that even a year after his original report, the faults he spotted in the earlier-version jet were still there. As he urgently wired to Tolkowsky, the Mystère II was not only sluggish at takeoff and unstable at high speeds, but its short range and limited carrying capability made it useless for the sort of desert warfare Israel had in mind, where the same jet had to fly long distances, drop bombs on ground targets, then dogfight its way home. Besides, Peled noted, the French Air Force itself was not buying any Mystère IIs. He recommended waiting for the Mystère IVs, and in the meantime settling for the Ouragan, which although older and not quite state-of-the-art, "was a superb plane for air-ground as well as air superiority, much better than the Meteor, which was not good for either mission."

This time Tolkowsky came around. On September 11, he wrote to Dayan: "This morning information arrived from France with major implications concerning the Mystère IIs . . . this information concerning the discovery of buffeting . . . below 30,000 feet and at Mach .93. Furthermore, it seems that passing the sound barrier was removed from the Mystère II conversion program for French pilots, apparently on flight safety grounds. These facts, along with the tiresome business of deterioration in operational capabilities . . .

cast doubt on the advisability of the purchase." Tolkowsky suggested buying twenty-four Ouragans, enough to equip a full squadron, while holding out for the newer Mystère IVs when they became
available.[7]

He ran into stiff opposition. "Dayan, Peres, and I—and with us
many others—sided with the Mystère II," recalls Weizman.[8] But
Tolkowsky insisted, and in late September Peres renegotiated the
deal—Israel would take twelve Ouragans now and Mystère IVs
when they became available. On October 4, without planes or pilots,
Ouragan Squadron 113 was opened at Hazor, with Beni Peled, at
just twenty-seven, as its commander. Two days later, with two brief
refueling stops in Rome and Athens, he and his five-member
"French team" flew six Ouragans into Hazor. Rushing right back to
France, they returned on October 10 with six more. While Peled
moved furiously to organize his new squadron and train new pilots,
Meteors from Ramat David were deployed to Air Force South to
prevent the still-helpless French jets from being turned into scrap
metal by a sudden Egyptian raid.

The prospects of just such an attack mounted daily. In the long
months that Peled spent in France, the occasional border skir-
mishes of the early 1950s had escalated to the brink of an all-out
war.

On March 18, 1954, an Israeli passenger bus scaling the serpen-
tine Ma'aleh Akrabim (Scorpions' Grade) in the rugged Judean
desert between Eilat and Beersheba had just rounded a hairpin turn
when it ran into a machine gun and grenade ambush. Eleven passengers were killed, and three wounded and left for dead. Although
tracks led from the murder scene to the Jordanian border, UN
observers on the spot failed to make the connection. Israel clamored
for revenge, but Prime Minister Sharett held back. "A response to
this bloodbath will only erase its horrible impression and put us on
equal footings with the murderers," he wrote in his diary.

But a week later, when infiltrators from Jordan killed a night-
watchman in a village outside Jerusalem, Sharett had no choice but
to approve a commando raid on the village of Nahalein on the
Hebron–Bethlehem road. When the attacks continued, he allowed
Dayan to launch a series of reprisals against military objectives in
Jordan and Egypt. Jordan, for one, cracked down on the Palestinian

terrorist bands that operated across its borders, and its frontier with Israel calmed down for a while.

Egypt, however, was another story. On February 24, 1954, President Mohammed Neguib of Egypt was overthrown in a military coup led by Gamal Abdel Nasser, who promptly vowed "to erase the shame of the Palestine War" and threw his support behind the Palestinian *fedayeens* operating against Israel from the Gaza Strip. But it was Nasser's international agenda that presented the real threat. A staunch Pan-Arabist and anti-colonialist, Nasser immediately moved to mobilize the Arab world against the remains of western colonialism, namely the British-French ownership of the Suez Canal and the French domination of Algeria. For starters, he pressed Britain to evacuate its military bases and airfields in Egypt. On April 22, 1954, Lt. Col. Yuval Ne'eman, the IDF planning chief, warned that once that happened and Egypt moved its fighters and bombers to the former RAF airfields in the Canal area, the Egyptian Air Force could "hit us with a surprise attack without us being able to discover its preparations in time."[9]

Israel's initial response was to launch an inept covert operation aimed at turning British and American public opinion against Egypt. On July 23, after several small and ineffectual fires broke out in western facilities in Cairo, a young Egyptian Jew named Phillip Nathanson was arrested when a small firebomb prematurely went off in his pocket. Twelve of a thirteen-member Israeli network were rounded up,* and on October 19, Britain agreed to evacuate its airfields and radar installation in Egypt by June of 1956.

The fiasco, later dubbed the "Lavon Affair" after an internal investigation failed to clear Defense Minister Pinchas Lavon of having ordered the operation, triggered unprecedented fighting within the ruling Labor establishment (military censorship kept the details out of the Israeli press for years). On February 17, Lavon resigned and Ben-Gurion, tanned and rested after his long desert respite, returned as defense minister.

Ben-Gurion ended Sharett's restraint policy. When an Egyptian

---

*On December 11, after two committed suicide in jail, the remaining ten went on trial before a Cairo military court. On January 27, two were released, six received lengthy prison terms, and two were sentenced to death. On January 31, in spite of widespread international appeals for clemency, the two were hanged in the Cairo prison courtyard.

commando unit killed an Israeli bicycle rider near Rehovot on February 25—it was the twenty-seventh Egyptian penetration of Israeli territory in just six months—he ordered a major retaliatory strike against Egyptian military installations south of Gaza. Carried out the following night by Ariel Sharon's paratroopers,* Operation Black Arrow claimed thirty-eight Egyptian dead to Israel's eight. When Nasser continued his border offensive and formed a joint military front against Israel with Syria and Saudi Arabia, Ben-Gurion—who following the July national elections became once again Israel's prime minister *and* defense minister†—approved a major strike on August 31 against the Khan Yunis police fortress south of Gaza, headquarters of the Egyptian army's Palestinian Brigade. With Squadron 117 Meteors watching for Egyptian fighters overhead, Sharon's raiding force rode to battle in armored trucks under heavy artillery cover, and when they crossed back into Israel at daybreak with only nine wounded, seventy-two enemy dead and fifty-eight wounded were left behind.

At seven the following morning, the fighting spread to the air as the alarm bell went off at Hazor. Aharon Yoeli and Yoash Tsiddon, with their Meteors at Air Force South on air alert duty, scrambled and in minutes spotted two Egyptian Vampires heading south over Israeli territory. With Tsiddon watching his tail, Yoeli swooped out of the rising sun and rolled in behind the lead jet. When he turned to frame the Vampire in his gunsight, however, he discovered that his sight was still at its night setting, which left it too dim to look through.

Without stopping, Yoeli fired virtually from the hip. With only the iridescent glow of his tracer bullets to guide him, he maneuvered his plane until the punctuated streams of light popping out of his four 20-mm guns converged on the target. The Vampire's left wing broke off, the plane began to spin down uncontrollably, and finally crashed and fireballed into an Israeli cornfield. As he pulled up and away, Yoeli noticed that Tsiddon was in a bad shooting position, and he rolled right back down after the second Vampire. This time the Egyptian was ready and "started rolling like crazy to

---

*A year earlier, Dayan disbanded Sharon's Commando Unit 101 and merged it into Paratrooper Battalion 890, with Sharon as new battalion commander.
†Moshe Sharett returned to his old post as foreign minister.

shake me off, but I stayed behind, and just as he finished his rolls, *prrrrt*, straight into his cockpit." The Vampire exploded in the air.[10]

The twin air kills exhilarated the nation.* Like Modi Alon's downing of the two Dakotas over Tel Aviv at the start of the 1948 war, it was the Israeli Air Force's first tangible achievement in years—and it took place over the home front. In fact, Yoeli demolished his second Vampire literally above his own home *kibbutz* of Zikim. As in the wake of Alon's twin kills seven years earlier, the Yoeli family home was soon filled with flowers from well-wishers, and his gun camera film was shown on newsreels in movie theaters.

More important, the commendation Yoeli received from Dayan for "carrying out a combat operation with efficiency and exemplary dispatch" was the first formal recognition of the IAF as a combat force in years. It offered Tolkowsky a brief respite from the constant attrition he suffered in his battles with the Greens. On July 8, 1954, he had threatened to resign when the IDF "borrowed" one of his key men for an indeterminate period, and since then he had been embroiled in constant budgetary battles with Dayan, who wanted him to hold back on new plane acquisitions until Israel could obtain top-of-the-line fighters (it was before France offered Israel the Mystère IIs, which Dayan supported). "I kept telling him that readiness is not something in the future. It meant being ready all the time with the best equipment you could master at the moment," says Tolkowsky.

The trouble was that under Sharett's restraint policy, Tolkowsky had had no opportunity to demonstrate the IAF's true capabilities. While Sharon's paratroopers carried out one raid after another across the Egyptian and Jordanian borders, the IAF's two significant operations at the time involved only Piper Cubs. On March 2, 1954, seven Pipers rescued the crew of an Israeli navy ship that struck a reef on the Saudi coast of the Red Sea,[11] and between June 9 and June 12, 1955, six Pipers helped evacuate six infantry scouts from the Sinai. Both operations were successful—IAF Mos-

---

*While Yoeli's were the first officially recognized jet kills for the Israeli Air Force, two days earlier two other Meteor pilots had jumped four Vampires and damaged one before the Egyptians broke contact. The damaged Egyptian plane was seen spinning down into the clouds, and a day later Egypt's radio reported that one of its jets crashed in an accident.

quitos mapped and surveyed the terrain, and Dakota radio planes relayed radio signals to IAF headquarters—but they did little to establish the IAF as anything more than a support force for the Greens.

The downing of the Vampires changed all that. It proved the Air Force's ability to battle and win in the air, and did it at a time when war with Egypt seemed imminent and unavoidable. On September 12, 1955, Nasser blockaded the Red Sea straits and Sinai's air space to Israeli sea and air traffic, and on September 29 announced a massive arms deal with the Soviet Union, which beefed Egypt's military arsenal with close to 150 MiG-15 and MiG-17 fighters, 70 IL-28 bombers, and massive amounts of artillery, tanks, destroyers, torpedo boats, and submarines.* It made the Egyptian Air Force the biggest in the Middle East. Although on November 4 France responded by letting Israel have twelve more Ouragans, these were still too few, and far inferior to the MiGs.

With great misgivings, Ben-Gurion began to explore the possibility of hitting Egypt before it had a chance to go operational with its new weapons. On October 21, he called Dayan back from a Paris vacation and ordered him to prepare plans for capturing the Red Sea straits and reopening them to Israeli navigation, for occupying the Gaza Strip, and for striking at Egyptian installations in the North Sinai.[12] On November 1, the IDF submitted a plan, code-named Operation Omer, for occupying the Sharm el Sheikh and Ras Nasrani strongholds at the southern Sinai, which controlled the vital Red Sea straits.

A day later, IAF Operations submitted a plan for demolishing most of the Egyptian Air Force on the ground by using every available plane, including Harvard trainers and aging Mustangs, in a massive surprise attack. "Unless we can receive Mystère IVs before July–August [1956], or American or Australian F-86s, then toward the end of this winter the Arab states shall have complete air superiority," Tolkowsky wrote to Dayan on November 19, 1955.

---

*Technically, Egypt was buying the weapons not directly from the Soviet Union but from Czechoslovakia. It was ironic not only because it was Czech arm shipments that helped Israel beat Egypt less than ten years earlier, in the 1948 war, but because the same Avia Works that produced the 101's Czech Knives and Spitfires were now turning out the MiGs for Egypt.

"The MiG-15s are clearly superior to anything in our hands today, [and] without planes like Mystère IVs or F-86s we shall have no practical way of standing up to the Egyptian Air Force. Fifty [Egyptian] MiG-15s are enough for two fighter squadrons, and it seems to me [that] the Egyptians will be able to deploy those squadrons starting in March of 1956." Even if the Soviets resupplied the Egyptians with the same planes after an Israeli strike, "at least we will have gained some time, and perhaps brought about the collapse of the Egyptian regime."[13]

Ben-Gurion approved the plans, and began to prepare Israeli and world opinion for the possibility of war by publicly warning Egypt to stop its "one-sided war" against Israel. On November 9, however, Dwight D. Eisenhower reopened talks about Israel's request for "defensive weapons," and Ben-Gurion told Dayan to put his war plans on ice until the end of January. Dayan and Tolkowsky argued together against any postponement, but Ben-Gurion insisted, and the delay proved worthwhile. While the F-86 talks were fruitless, the January national elections in France brought to power a leftist coalition whose three leaders—Prime Minister Guy Mollet and Foreign Minister Christian Pineau, both of them Socialists, and Defense Minister Maurice Bourgès-Maunoury, a radical—were all staunch supporters of Israel. In early March they approved the sale to Israel of twelve new Mystère IV jets.

On February 15, 1956, with war with Egypt postponed for the time being, Tolkowsky ordered the 101 stripped of its Mustangs and moved down to Hazor to become an all-Mystère squadron. At the same time, he moved Weizman from Ramat David to Hazor. It was a perceptive move. The new Ouragans and Mystères would make Hazor the IAF's premier interceptor base—but only if Weizman could be made to remove the "inferior people" stain he had earlier placed on Air Force South. Indeed, flying his Black Spit to Hazor, Weizman immediately banished his hated Mosquitos from the base and set out to build a second fighter Camelot.

Weizman did not move alone. Moti Hod, for one, gave up his deputy base commander post in Ramat David after Weizman assured him command of a new jet squadron at Hazor. With Peled busy building up his Ouragan squadron, and Menahem Bar getting ready to form a new squadron of Sabrejets at Ramat David if the

Americans ever came through, Hod took it for granted that the Mystère squadron would be his. But Tolkowsky was dazzled by the speed, thoroughness, and technical savvy with which Peled brought in the Ouragans, and he now ordered him back to France to bring the Mystère IVs to Hazor, and to become their commander at the 101. Command of the 113 Ouragan squadron went to Hod. "It was an ugly thing," Hod would say later, "but I had no choice. I knew that if I did not accept command of the Ouragans I would have no chance to command a jet squadron before going on to a staff position."[14]

With Weizman in command of the base, and Hod and Peled, two Ramat David veterans, heading its two front-line squadrons, "Air Force North conquered Air Force South," says Eli Eyal. "The war had gone on for two years, and Air Force North won."[15] In mid-March, Peled and his "French team" returned to France. On April 11, after a brief refueling stop at Brindisi—the same clifftop airfield from which Lou Lenart and Coleman Goldstein took off for Palestine in their flying-bomb Norsemans eight years earlier, almost to the day—they brought six Mystères to Hazor, and then six more. On April 23 France agreed to sell Israel twelve more, which made twenty-four, a full squadron, by the end of May.

By then Weizman had transformed the base, which until his arrival had remained rundown, dilapidated, and largely unchanged since the day in 1948 when Wayne Peake shot down the *Shuftykeit* above it. "We have a place full of mice, and they still speak English," one of the pilots complained after moving there from Ramat David. Instead of waiting for outside crews, Weizman had his troops do the work themselves. "For months, we did nothing there but clean and haul trash, tear down the old carousel toilets, and build new ones," says Joseph Tsuk, one of the 101's new pilots.[16]

The skies over the old base were now alive with the crack of sonic booms and the whine of straining jet engines—Meteors dogfighting against Ouragans, Ouragans against Mystères, Meteors against Mystères and Ouragans against Ouragans. As he did at Ramat David, Weizman beat his warrior's code into the young Hazor crowd. "Don't complain, don't explain," he would warn them in long, exhilarating talks. "Press ahead, regardless." Tenacity and aggressiveness was all. When a group of MPs tried to arrest a handful of

101 pilots on the Ashkelon beach for leaving their base without permission, Weizman's boys beat them up and sabotaged their car before returning to base. The MPs complained and Weizman disciplined his pilots, but he did it in such a way that it seemed less a punishment than decoration for valor.

All the while, however, the beat of war drums mounted from the south. On July 27, 1956, Nasser nationalized the Suez Canal and moved his MiGs to the former British air bases along the waterway. It seemed only a matter of time before the border fighting erupted into an all-out war—a war Israel was in no shape to enter into. Even at full strength and readiness, the Israeli Ouragans and Mystères were vastly outnumbered by twelve MiG squadrons in Egypt and Syria—and they were nowhere near as ready. As late as April, when the first Mystères began to arrive, Meteors from Ramat David still had to be stationed at Hazor to guard the Ouragans and Mystères against Egyptian attacks, and in May the 101 had barely a dozen pilots who could "take off and land in a Mystère IV."[17] Things wouldn't get better for months, since to train new Mystère pilots Peled had to cannibalize Hod's Ouragan squadron, who in turn cannibalized Bar's Meteor squadron, while Bar worked furiously to turn Mustang and Mosquito pilots into jet pilots.

In early summer, however, Israel discovered that it might not have to face Egypt alone. On June 22, determined to do something about Nasser, who not only took over its canal but was supporting the anti-French rebels in Algeria, France concluded a secret military treaty with Israel—$80 million worth of modern arms, including thirty-six additional Mystère IVs, in exchange for Israeli help in an unspecified future military action against Nasser. The only condition was total secrecy. The United States was financing the production of 225 Mystères for the French Air Force (in an effort to encourage France to increase its participation in NATO), and France had no intention of antagonizing the Americans with "irresponsible" moves in the Middle East. At least not until the Americans finished paying for the planes.

France would not begin weapon deliveries until its American deal was completed, and in the meantime many more Mystère pilots had to be trained quickly to ferry the new Mystères over and fly them in battle. But less than a dozen IAF officers knew of the French deal, and Peled was not one of them. He soon grew angry and mystified as he kept getting more and more rookie pilots for training, only to have them yanked back out as soon as they were halfway ready, with more rookies sent in their place. Impatiently, he protested to Shaya Gazit, who was doing the shuffling from his desk at IAF Planning, and then to Tolkowsky. "Tolkowsky would then call me in and in Beni's presence bawl me out and promise that it would never happen again," says Gazit, "but that lasted only until the next morning, when the whole thing would start all over again. Peled had no idea what was going on. Here he had a plane for which no combat tactics existed, because it was new for the French Air Force as well. He had to develop tactics, to train his boys, to create a fighter squadron, and here we were driving him nuts. But there was no way we could tell him what was going on."[18]

At the end of July, the Dassault works completed and delivered the 225 American-financed Mystère IVs to the French Air Force, and France finally felt free to begin moving against Nasser. First, however, Israel had to get its new planes. On Tuesday noon, August 14, all of Hazor's Mystère pilots were urgently called into the 101 briefing room. Visibly excited, Weizman ordered the doors closed, and announced that at France's invitation, they would all be getting gunnery training at a French air base at Bizerte, on the Tunisian coast. They had two days of home leave to pick up summer clothes, sandals, and bathing trunks, and they had to keep the trip "top secret, secret of secrets, number one state secret, [with no] hint at the destination or purpose of the trip," recalled one of the pilots. "We were told that [even] French Government circles not directly connected with it knew nothing of what was to happen."[19]

On Thursday morning, the pilots drifted into Tel Aviv, wearing civilian clothes and carrying suitcases. One group, with Moti Hod in charge, met outside the Tel Aviv zoo, where they were picked up by three unmarked Defense Ministry cars and a pickup truck, and taken to a waiting Constellation at the far end of the Lod airport runway. The second group, headed by Menahem Bar, gathered near the Ha'bima National Theater on Rothschild Boulevard, and was taken to a small IAF airfield outside of the city, where a French-made Nord transport was waiting.

When the two transports had passed Brindisi, their pilots got up

from their cockpit seats, walked back, and handed sealed envelopes
to the group leaders. It was only after Hod and Bar read their
contents, first quietly and then aloud, that the stunned pilots realized that instead of swimming at Bizerte, they would soon be flying
brand-new Mystères clear across the Mediterranean to Israel—
fighters in which most of them had only a few flight hours, and no
practice at all in long-distance navigation.

Peled, who was brought in on the secret only a few days earlier,
was waiting in France and escorted them to Mont-de-Marsan. "Although it was obviously going to be his operation, he was not put
in charge of any of the groups in Israel, because his very presence
would be a tipoff," says Gazit. The following morning, after a
French breakfast of toast, eggs, and black coffee, the pilots walked
onto the tarmac. "The sight was awesome, a long line of Mystères,
some of them already painted with our insignia," recalls one of
them. With no time to spare, they flew a single practice flight each,
and the following morning eighteen Mystères lifted off the French
runway and headed over the Mediterranean for Israel.

It was then that the second and most crucial stage of the operation began. Like the previous Mystère transfers, the jets had to
refuel in Brindisi in order to reach Israel. Unlike the other runs,
however, this one officially did not happen. Any tipoff of a new
French-Israeli arms deal would doom the entire operation, and
bringing the Italians in on the secret was out of the question.

It was Shlomo Lahat,* quarterbacking the entire operation from
his Air Section office at Ramla, who came up with a solution. While
arranging for the refueling stop, he confided to the Italians that
eighteen of the Mystères that Israel had bought earlier were defec-
tive and had to be flown back to France for repair. The Italians
nodded in sympathy, and they did so again when eighteen Mystères
with new Israeli markings landed there on August 18, refueled, and
took off again, ostensibly on their way to France for repairs. With
Weizman himself manning the Brindisi tower to guide his flyers in
and out—in Hebrew—any chance for accidental foul-up was further
eliminated.

As soon as the Mystères arrived in Israel, Lahat and the pilots

*Formerly Landau.

were rushed back to France, where the remaining eighteen Mystères had been repainted with the same serial numbers as the eighteen that left earlier, and Weizman returned to the Brindisi control tower. Explaining good-naturedly to the Italians that the jets had now been repaired, he talked Peled and his crew down for their refueling, then talked them up and on their way home.

Back in Israel, the drive for secrecy reached epic proportions. Hazor had been sealed off. "The gate was locked and the base was declared off bounds because of a polio epidemic. Even the telephone lines were disconnected, so that all calls to and from the base were routed through my office," says Gazit. "Even Ezer could not talk to Tolkowsky without going through me." On the night before the first batch of new Mystères arrived, some of Hazor's Mystères were secretly flown to Ramat David. As they were hidden out of sight, Ramat David, too, was abruptly sealed off with the same mysterious polio outbreak. And just before the second shipment of jets arrived, the previous batch was also shuttled out of Hazor. American spy-plane overflights of either base still showed that Israel had no more than its original twenty-four Mystères.*

The French shuttle tripled Israel's jet fighter force, but added little to its actual military strength. Israel had sixty Mystères but barely enough pilots for twenty-four. By summer's end, its slim fighter rosters were further reduced when America signaled a possible delivery of an F-86 squadron. In late September, three of the Bar's top pilots left Ramat David for Canada to train on the new planes, while Bar himself transferred the 117 to Yoeli and prepared to follow them.

Tolkowsky could probably have accomplished the total conversion of his Air Force to jets in two years or so. Trouble was, he did not have two years, or even a year, or even—as it soon turned out—two months.

Through the summer of 1956, tension escalated along the borders. On the night of September 11, after an Israeli rail line was

---

*In fact, so smoothly did the operation run that the only mishap occurred after the dignitaries who gathered to welcome the planes—Ben-Gurion, Finance Minister Levi Eshkol, Dayan, Peres, and Tolkowsky—got up from a festive lunch at the Hazor mess hall. In the absence of hot water and proper sanitation at the rundown base, some came down with acute food poisoning.

blown up, Israeli paratroopers stormed the Jordanian police fortress of El Rahwa in the southwest corner of the West Bank, killing twenty-nine Jordanian soldiers while losing one of their own. The next day, terrorists operating from Jordan killed three watchmen at an Israeli drilling camp in the Negev, and on the following night Israeli paratroopers struck the Jordanian police fortress of Gharandal, killing sixteen soldiers while losing one of their own. During the third week of September, four archaeologists near Jerusalem, a small girl in a southern village, and a tractor driver in a northern *kibbutz* were killed in Jordanian and *fedayeen* attacks. On the night of September 25, Israeli paratroopers staged a broad offensive against the police fortress of Husan near Bethlehem. This time the Jordanians were waiting, and while thirty-nine of them were killed, ten Israeli paratroopers also died. On the night of October 10, following another string of terror attacks resulting in seven civilian deaths, Dayan ordered a massive assault on the police fort at Qalqiliya, near the West Bank city of Tul Karm. The Jordanian Legion was again ready, and the paratroopers were cut off and had to be rescued with help from Israeli armor and Mustangs from Ramat David.

The reprisal raids were only marginally effective in curbing Palestinian terrorism, but they completely diverted attention—in Israel and abroad—from the French-Israeli war plans, which by early October were undergoing final preparations. On September 18, after Secretary of State John Foster Dulles's last-minute attempt to place control of the Suez Canal in the hands of an international user-state association failed, Bourgès-Maunoury, France's new defense minister, approached Shimon Peres with a suggestion for a joint French-Israeli offensive against Egypt. On October 1, after Peres won Ben-Gurion's support while Bourgès-Maunoury received the backing of the French cabinet, the outline of the operation was hammered out at a secret meeting in Paris. Israel would open the campaign by moving troops into the Sinai, which France—and hopefully Britain—would then use as an excuse to come in in force to protect the Canal. Once inside Egypt, the two powers would topple Nasser and bring about a change of government, while Israel went about its business of reopening the Red Sea straits for navigation.

The main stumbling block was Britain. In reality, France and Britain already had plans for a joint military operation, code-named Musketeer, to retake the Canal and overthrow Nasser. But Britain seemed too hesitant. France was counting on Israel not only for a ruse to justify French intervention in Egypt, but for actual assistance should Britain back out in the last moment.

What neither France nor Israel knew was that one of the reasons for Britain's dawdling was the existence of its own active war plan—against Israel. In the summer of 1955, Britain grew worried over the escalating violence on the Israel-Jordan border. Instead of intervening with King Hussein, with whom Britain had a mutual defense pact, to scale down Palestinian terrorist activities in and from his territory, the British military command instructed the RAF to develop plans for wiping out the Israeli Air Force as a first step toward a full British military intervention on the side of Jordan. By August, the RAF had submitted a list of targets for such an operation and was compiling target files on Ramat David, Tel Nof, Hazor, and scores of lesser targets throughout Israel. In January 1956, the British military command approved plans for an operation that was initially code-named Catapult, then Encounter, and finally Cordage.[20] Britain held to the plan even when, on March 1, Hussein knuckled under to growing pro-Nasserite sentiments and fired General Sir John Bagot Glubb, better known as Glubb Pasha, a British officer who had commanded Jordan's Arab Legion for twenty-six years and made it into the best Arab army in the Middle East. Britain stuck to the plan even when unrest in Jordan reached such a level that the RAF could not count on operating—even against Israel—from Jordanian airfields, and had to draw up contingency plans for operating from Cyprus and from British aircraft carriers.

In early October, however, the French got wind of the British plan and, in ten days of intense mediation, between October 14 and October 24, managed to persuade Anthony Eden's government to give priority to Operation Musketeer against Egypt. It undoubtedly helped when, also on October 14, the Nasserite winner of the Jordanian national elections, Suleiman Nabulsi, canceled the British-Jordanian pact, and when on October 23, the chiefs of military staff of Egypt, Syria, and Jordan gathered in Aman to unify their forces.

Still, Britain conditioned her participation in Musketeer on Ben-Gurion's promise not to attack Jordan (at Ben-Gurion's insistence, however, Britain agreed to stay out if Jordan attacked Israel and Israel fought back). On October 24, in a French villa on the outskirts of Paris, Ben-Gurion, French Foreign Minister Christian Pineau, and British Deputy Foreign Secretary Patrick Dean signed a joint plan for war on Egypt. The Israeli strike into the Sinai, the war's opening move, would begin on October 29, just five days away.

Chapter 12

KADESH

The sound of revving engines on the Tel Nof tarmac had been mounting since before noon. Spilling onto the surrounding countryside, it cascaded over rolling orange groves and small red-roofed villages. Even if no one else did, the farmers tilling the loamy flatlands around the base knew something was up. They were always the first to know.

By 3:00 P.M. the noise was deafening, a mechanical roar unheard since Operation Dust Bowl in the fall of 1948, eight years earlier. The narrow asphalt belts leading from hangars to runways were jam-packed with a hodgepodge of planes—camouflage-painted Dakotas, silvery Meteors, beat-up old Mosquitos and Mustangs. The Dakotas, sixteen of them, loaded with four hundred paratroopers and their combat gear, rolled onto the runway, lifted off, and made a wide turn to the south.

As the last of the Dakotas taxied away, Aharon Yoeli, the elfish, baby-faced new commander of the 117, completed his mission briefing at a makeshift shack. The previous day, he secretly brought his dozen Meteors down from Ramat David. Now he and his pilots walked out across the sun-baked tarmac to get strapped in their cockpits. They then sat, canopies slid back, and waited.

At 4:00, engines screeching, Yoeli pushed his throttle forward and raced down the runway, nine Meteors in tow. Once in the air he turned south and streaked down the length of the Negev. Barely fifty miles north of Eilat, Israel's southernmost spot, he caught up with the Dakotas at the Egyptian border. At 4:30, in total radio silence, the combined force crossed into the Sinai. As they crossed the border, the Meteor pilots tried their guns. Their shells exploded in the air ahead of them in unexpected tiny puffs of smoke. Unused to live ammunition, they tensed up, then relaxed. "I didn't realize what it was at first. I thought it was ground flack," Yoeli recalls.

Just as Meteors and Dakotas crossed into the Sinai, Beni Peled scrambled off the Hazor tarmac with four Mystères, followed by another four formation, headed by Yak Nevo, and still another, this one led by Dani Shapira. Together, they streaked straight for the Suez Canal 150 miles to the southwest. They had barely lifted off when Moti Hod throttled up his Ouragan and with five more in tow lifted off the same runway in pursuit of the Dakotas. The short-ranged Meteors, already half an hour in the air, would soon have to turn back, and without his Ouragans the Dakotas would be defenseless.

Hod was anxious. Early evening fog was creeping into the Sinai. "Visibility was terrible. All I had to help me get where I was going were compass and map, and the direction and speed of the Dakotas." Contacting the Dakotas by radio was out of the question, and flying as low as he did to evade Egyptian radar he could see little around him. "I was so afraid I won't find them that I had a contingency plan to just patrol the whole area if I didn't. It was a real relief to finally spot them in the fog below," he recalls.[1]

The flying armada was well inside Egypt when the Ouragans caught up. At thirty-two planes,* the combined force was the most massive assembly of air power Israel had ever put in the air on business. At 4:59, one minute before schedule, the Dakotas reached their destination, a flat stretch of desert near a crossroad at the eastern approaches to the Mitla Pass, some twenty-four miles from the Canal. The Meteors had departed a few moments earlier, and as

---

*The number was closer to fifty, counting the twelve Mystères and assorted other planes on related missions. To all intents and purposes, the entire IAF was in the air, most of it over the desert a hundred or more miles from home.

the Ouragans began patrolling above, the Dakotas circled. Lt. Col. Rafael Eitan, the gruff farmer who commanded the 890 Paratroopers Battalion, jumped first. His paratroopers followed. The gathering darkness blossomed with silken canopies.

Several miles away, Harry Barak was barreling home in his Mustang when he saw the parachutes open. As deputy commander of the hastily assembled 116 Mustang Squadron at Tel Nof, he had spent the afternoon cutting Egyptian telephone wires in the Mitla area (using his propeller after a special chain he was supposed to use broke off). "I saw the canopies in the distance and I knew that this time it was for real. Until that moment, I did not believe anything was actually going to happen," he would recall.[2]

Overhead in his Ouragan, hands tightly clamped to stick and throttle and eyes peeled for signs of enemy aircraft, Hod was struck by the same thought. "There were so many times when we sat in the planes in real readiness. At times, during the retaliation raids, we even taxied out to the runway. But we were always ordered back. When I saw the parachutes open I remember thinking to myself, 'This cannot be called back.' "

It was not. By nightfall Israeli ground forces attacked along the Egyptian border. Ariel Sharon's 202nd Paratroopers Brigade, sent earlier to the Jordanian border to divert attention from the real offensive, quickly crossed the Negev desert to the Egyptian side— following a deep canyon bed to avoid detection—and thrust hard and deep in the direction of Eitan's stranded battalion.

That battalion now frantically dug into the hard desert floor in preparation for the MiGs that would attack at dawn. Additional supplies—recoilless guns, mortars, and even Jeeps—were airdropped through the night, but as morning neared the supply runs ended and silence once again draped the land. Alone under the desert night skies, a hundred miles inside enemy territory, they waited.

Baby-carrying paratroopers to their drop zone was not the way Tolkowsky had figured on entering the war. For three years, his pilots lived and flew with one thought in mind—swooping out of the blue unexpected and unannounced, to rip Egypt's planes with bullets and rockets while they were still prone on the tarmac. "Each squadron had pictures and maps of the airfields it was to take out. We knew every hangar and every access road in 'our' airfields," recalls a former Mustang pilot. Low-level flying and navigation were drilled until "we knew every rock and every bush" in the country and could find "our airfields" while streaking so low that even tall trees blocked the view.

Intelligence about the airfields was constantly updated. For much of the summer of 1956, Dani Shapira headed a special Mosquito unit that "covered the entire Middle East with photo-recon missions—Baghdad to the east, Tripoli to the north, Egypt's western borders, near Tobruk, Ghardaka in the south, Jordan, Syria." The photo-recon missions began under Laskov and were expanded under Tolkowsky. They were lone and hazardous ordeals. Their crews were as vulnerable to enemy fighters as to the Mosquito's own propensity to breakdown in midflight. "You were on your own, like Gary Powers, all alone at 30,000 feet. . . . I was looking for an Egyptian submarine base at Ghardaka one time when I lost both engines. I figured I'd jump in the Sinai or at sea, but at 10,000 feet they began working again. Another time I flew all the way to Baghdad, but when I came back I discovered that the camera glass was covered with oil. None of the photos came out and I had to do the whole thing over. We called the 109 the Kamikaze Squadron. We had a feeling that every mission was a suicide run," Shapira recalls.[3]

By the fall of 1956, the data gathered by the Mosquitos had filtered down to the squadrons and been integrated into mission plans and tactics. On October 5, when IDF Operations issued its first plan for the Sinai campaign, code-named Kadesh 1, the IAF was assigned to go in first and demolish the Egyptian Air Force on the ground with surprise strikes against the Canal air bases, and against the Cairo West airfield, where the IL-28 bombers were waiting.

Both the Greens and Ben-Gurion, however, doubted Tolkowsky's ability to deliver. Objectively, the massive influx of new fighter jets over the summer months had wreaked havoc in IAF ranks. Without trained mechanics, planes were in poor shape, and ammunition was scarce. "Only a day or two before the operation, a French transport

. . . unloaded eight small crates containing 20,000 30-mm shells,"
recalls Weizman. "We didn't have any bombs for the Mystère, and
scarcely any rockets."[4]

Nor were pilots sufficiently trained. "There were very few air-
ground practice sorties for people who never carried out any air-
ground missions," says Weizman, and according to Joseph Tsuk, a
young Mystère pilot, "only on the Saturday before the war we had
our first air-ground gunnery practice. We had no idea how to do it.
We put the rockets in regular launch pipes, and on the way to the
range some of them fell out."[5] Ran Ronen, then a young Ouragan
pilot, recalls that "we were supposed to have first gunnery practice
before the war broke out, but it was canceled. The first time I fired
my gun was over the Mitla with a bunch of MiGs all around me."[6]

While Israel now had enough Mystères to equip three squadrons,
only one, the 101, was operational, and even that was at the expense
of the Meteor and Ouragan squadrons, which were stripped down
to no more than a dozen pilots each. Some Ouragan flyers, who were
flying Meteors only a few days earlier, had so few hours on the
Ouragan that "when squadron commanders received their first battle briefing two nights before the operation," Shaya Gazit reportedly heard Moti Hod protest to Tolkowsky that "I am not going to
war with these pilots." To assemble his airfield strike force, Tolkowsky had to pull out of mothballs recently decommissioned B-17,
Mustangs, and Mosquitos, and to shut down IAF Flight School so
cadets could fly Harvard and Stearman trainers in action. This still
left the IAF outnumbered two to one in each fighter category.*

---

*On the eve of the war, the IAF had 53 operational jet fighter-bombers with the same
number of pilots, to the Egyptians' 150 and 100, respectively. In comparable catego-
ries, Israel had 24 operational Mystère IVs to Egypt's 55 MiGs, and 21 Ouragans to 50
Vampires. Both had 15 Meteors each, but Israel had no bombers to match Egypt's 30
IL-28s. In fact, the United Arab Republic's frontline presence in the Canal bases alone
was double the entire IAF—15 Egyptian and 25 Syrian MiGs at Abu Suweir, 35
Vampires and 22 Meteors at Fayid, 25 Mig-15 at Kabrit, and 15 Vampires at Qasprit.
Most of the IL-28 bombers, along with 15 more MiGs, were deployed farther back at
Al Mazzah, Inshas, and Cairo West near Cairo, and at Luxor 300 miles farther south.
Egypt's rapid conversion to an all-jet force, however, was accomplished by reducing
flight-training courses from thirty-six to eighteen months, so that air-crew level was
generally inferior to the Israelis'. And while Egyptian cities and airfields were ringed
with massive antiaircraft batteries, including 80 heavy, radar-controlled guns and 500
medium and light flack guns, Israel had just 200 light guns and only one small battery
of heavy antiaircraft weapons.

Ben-Gurion also doubted Tolkowsky's ability to destroy Egypt's frontline air force on the ground and to defend Israel against air attacks by Egyptian bombers from rear airfields up the Nile. Israel's portion of the war against Egypt, after all, was a mere footnote to the massive action assigned to Britain and France, whose assembled forces for that campaign in Malta, Cyprus, and Algeria numbered 80,000 troops, 130 ships (including seven aircraft carriers), and 500 planes.[7] According to the latest plans for Operation Musketeer, Israel's sole role in the campaign was to provide, by landing paratroopers deep in the Sinai and ostensibly threatening the Canal area, an excuse for French and British intervention.

But suppose Israel went in first, and Britain and France then decided to stay out? Ben-Gurion needed guarantees, and during the October 24 negotiations in France he set two conditions. First, France would defend Israel against Egyptian air attacks with French-manned fighter squadrons operating not only from aircraft carriers but from inside Israel. Second, Israel's initial role in the fighting would be limited to dropping paratroopers at the Mitla Pass to provide France and Britain with the excuse they needed to intervene. This still left Israel free to retreat should its allies not come through. It would then claim that the operation was just one more retaliatory raid for Egyptian-sponsored terrorism.

In its latest version then, Musketeer would begin with an Israeli airborne and ground thrust into the Sinai on October 29 to create "a threat to the Suez Canal by capturing military sites north of it." But twenty-four hours later, as Arabs and Israelis began to slug it out in the desert, Britain and France would ask both to stop the fighting and back away from the canal to a distance of ten miles on either side. Once Nasser rejected their demand, British and French bombers would begin their campaign for the "defense" of the waterway by bombing Egypt's airfields, starting on the morning of October 31, followed by a combined airborne and sea assault on Port Said.[8]

That meant, first and foremost, no Israeli air attack. On October 25, IDF Operations replaced its Kadesh 1 operational plan with Kadesh 2, which eliminated the IAF attack on Egypt's airfields. As Dayan informed Tolkowsky the following day, the Air Force would do nothing besides ferrying paratroopers and supplies to the Mitla and ride shotgun over the operation. "Limit air combat as much as possible, while attempting to restrict Egyptian air attacks on our forces and civilian population" was how the plan put it. Until Israel's new allies intervened, Egyptian airfields could be hit only if Israel was attacked from the air first, and Egyptian ground forces could be strafed only if Egyptian planes first attacked Israeli ground troops first.[9]

The possibility of France and Britain backing out at the last moment was not farfetched. Had the United States got wind of the operation in time, neither Britain nor France could stand up to Eisenhower's fury, and certainly Israel wouldn't. Diverting America's attention was the key, and since Britain had been planning for weeks to send an Iraqi division into Jordan to stop its drift into Nasser's camp, Israel now seized on that Iraqi threat as an excuse to mobilize its reserves and amass troops on the Jordanian border. The ruse worked. On October 27, two days before the start of Musketeer, Abba Eban was playing golf at Woodmont Country Club with Martin Agronsky and Congressman Sidney Yates of Illinois, when he was urgently called to the State Department. He remembers finding Dulles "looking hard at a map in the middle of the room [but] the map portrayed the Israeli-Jordan armistice boundary, and nowhere touched Sinai."[10] The United States still had no clue.

On October 24, Gen. Abd el Hakim Amer, Egypt's defense minister and commander-in-chief, left for a visit of Syria and Jordan (he would not return even by the time Israeli paratroopers began jumping at the Mitla). As late as 11:00 on the morning of October 29, Egyptian fighters were still parked in peacetime bliss on tarmacs throughout the Sinai. Still taking no chances, Tolkowsky waited until the last of the Dakotas lifted off and scrambled two Meteors on a diversionary flight down the coast, but the Egyptians seemed so ignorant of the impending invasion that another planned diversion, dropping paratrooper dummies near the Canal, was called off.

Even as the Dakotas circled over the Mitla to discard their cargo, and Beni Peled's Mystères patrolled above the Canal air bases of Kabrit, Qasprit, and Fayid, "the Egyptians did not move. We could have wiped them out were it not for the prohibition against doing anything. Tolkowsky had personally warned us," recalls Yalo Shavit, one of the Mystère pilots. While the cocky 101 pilots would later suggest that fear kept the Egyptians from challenging their "magnificent dozen, you know, twelve Mystères with the Air Force's hottest pilots," it is not clear that the Egyptians even knew they were there.

The Egyptian silence was not entirely accidental. Early on Sunday, October 28, IDF Intelligence learned that General Amer and his entire Egyptian military command were about to leave Damascus for Cairo in a Soviet-built IL-14 transport, ostensibly with plans for joint military operations against Israel. At two in the afternoon, Shlomo Lahat, chief of IAF Air Section, pulled Yoash Tsiddon out of the 117 Meteor squadron, now at Tel Nof in preparation for the next day's campaign, and rushed him to Ramla. Formally, Tsiddon commanded the new 191* squadron, operating out of Ramat David with three just-arrived NF-13 Meteors equipped for night or bad weather operations. But the planes were new, and only one was operational, so the 191 was shut down for the duration of the impending campaign, and Tsiddon was detailed to the 117 as ordinary Meteor pilot. Now, Lahat wanted him to go back to Ramat David, take up his one serviceable NF-13 night fighter, and shoot the Egyptian plane down. His mission was code-named Rooster.

Early that evening, half an hour after the Egyptian plane reportedly left Damascus, Tsiddon took off to the west. It was a pitch-black, moonless night, but the NF-13's radar soon picked up an unidentified plane three miles away. In minutes Tsiddon and his navigator were close enough to see the lights from the Il-14's glowing exhaust pipes. Tsiddon slowed down, moved close to the droning piston-powered plane, and slowly circled it, counting windows and tracing its tail shape against the faint glow of the stars. The plane was definitely an Il-14. Finally, Tsiddon pulled alongside and looked into the lit windows. There was no question about it. "From just a few meters I could see men in military uniforms walking in the aisles. It was difficult to identify those sitting down, but they, too, seemed to be wearing uniforms," he reported later.[11]

"Open fire if you have no doubts," Tolkowsky calmly ordered him on the radio. Carrying it out, however, proved nearly impossible. To begin with, the Il-14's air speed was barely above the NF-13's stall speed, in which the faster jet would start dropping.

---

*Not real squadron number for security reasons.

Then, as Tsiddon slipped behind the Il-14 and began firing, it turned out that his guns were loaded with tracer bullets, whose sudden glow temporarily blinded him so he could not see the target. Finally, his extreme-right gun (out of four) jammed, throwing the barely moving night fighter into a sharp left-handed spin. His brief burst of gunfire only damaged the Egyptian plane's left engine and caused an electrical shortage, but the plane was still flying.

"Finish it off at any cost," Tolkowsky ordered. Tsiddon pulled his plane around again and, dropping his flaps and gunning up his engines, came behind the Il-14 and aimed his guns at the tip of the right wing, so that when his jammed gun spun his plane to the left, he would end up hitting the target itself. He was barely fifty yards behind the Egyptian plane when he opened fire. Flames immediately enveloped the Il-14 and "mushroomed to a huge fireball. Burning chunks flew around me [as the Il-14] began to spin and we, below it now, were also thrown into a left-handed spin. A ball of fire and a darkened plane spun out of control alongside and below each other as in some grotesque dance," he would recall. At just 1,000 feet above water, Tsiddon regained control of his plane and watched the Il-14 hit the water and shatter. He landed at Hazor without fuel, his engines dying while taxiing off the runway.

The next day, Egypt had to go to war without most of its senior military command.*

Even as a footnote in the massive British-French offensive, Israel's task was enormous. Not only was the Sinai bigger than anything the Israeli army had attempted to storm in its entire existence, twice the size of Israel itself, but it was the least inviting of territories. Shaped like a wedge of cheese, the Sinai is a massive, hostile, virtually uninhabitable stretch of desert whose base, 120 miles wide, leans against the Mediterranean coast, and whose rounded tip, 230 miles due south, juts into the Red Sea. The bottom half of the wedge, nestled tightly between the Gulf of Suez to the west and the

---

*General Amer, however, had changed plans at the last moment, and left Damascus later in a C-47 Dakota shortly afterward. The IAF command considered sending Tsiddon out again to shoot him down, too, but the plan was canceled for fear of jeopardizing intelligence sources. The Il-14 was apparently downed before its pilot could report the attack, because Egyptian and British planes searched the Mediterranean for clues to its mysterious disappearance for days with no success.

Gulf of Aqaba to the east, consists of rugged, barren mountains and is impassable in any direction. The upper half, bounded by the Suez Canal to the west and the Egyptian-Israeli border to the east, is no less hostile but flatter, with the exception of a stretch of mountains that runs north-to-south along the Canal for fifty miles, from the swampy sands of the coast between Port Said and El 'Arīsh.

With the exception of a few coastal towns, the refugee-packed Gaza Strip, a few Bedouin tribes, oil drillers, and Egyptian soldiers and their families, nobody actually lived in the Sinai. There were no fields, few towns, no reasons for building side roads. Four highways crossed the Sinai's upper half, the southernmost two snaking through the treacherous Mitla and Giddi passes—so treacherous, in fact, that with the exception of a few fortified positions hard by the Israeli border, the entire length of these routes up to the passes was only scantily defended. A major highway north of the passes ran from Israel to the Canal through flatter terrain, but its entire length was heavily secured by a series of massive fortifications at—east to west—Abu Ageila, Jabal Libni, and Bir Gafgafa. The northernmost coastal highway, from the Gaza Strip to the Canal via El 'Arīsh, was of little military value, since it led from fringe to fringe and was too easily disrupted.

Into this hostile, hardly passable and well-guarded biblical battle-ground the Israeli army thrust on the night of October 29 without artillery or armor support. Jabbing into Egypt's midsection, it then paused and waited.

Egypt, however, hesitated, and thereby lost the war.

Although its military was aware of both the Mitla drop and Sharon's thrust in the Kuntilla area almost from the start, and in fact moved the Fifth and Sixth battalions of the Second Egyptian Brigade across the Canal and toward the Mitla as early as 2:00 A.M., Egypt was slow to deploy its air force. Four Egyptian Vampires flew over the Mitla early on the morning of October 30, but they took no action. At 9:00 A.M. two MiG-15s briefly strafed Eitan's defenseless battalion, but all they did was shoot up a Piper Cub and wound seven soldiers. Between 8:30 and 9:30, two pairs of MiGs also strafed Sharon's 202nd Paratrooper Brigade, which was then fighting its way through Egyptian border fortifications toward the Mitla, but they, too, caused no casualties. When a third pair showed up at

10:00, it was intercepted by the paratroopers' surveillance Piper Cub, who took them on a fifteen-minute "dogfight," weaving and bobbing through desert canyons before being destroyed by a burst of gunfire. By then the MiGs were out of fuel and had to turn back.

So slow were the Egyptians to react that by 10:30, when Dayan responded to the MiG attacks by allowing Tolkowsky to engage the enemy in the air, their only significant achievement was getting an armored force into the western opening of the Mitla, where the Egyptian troops quickly took positions in the caves that honey-combed both walls of the narrow, twisting, nineteen-mile pass. They were awaiting the Israeli paratroopers who would soon start down the canyon. At 11:30, Israeli Mystères, Ouragans, and Meteors hit their vehicles on the road below, but while the Israeli pilots reported the force destroyed, the thirty-seven armored vehicles they shot up were already empty. The mistake would help bring about the bloodiest snafu of the war. Over the next few hours, Israeli Mystères, Ouragans, and Meteors demolished an Egyptian mortar unit that had Eitan's paratroopers in range, and from noon till dark turned the roads between the Canal and the Mitla into a virtual shooting gallery, destroying scores of armored vehicles headed for the fighting.

Only at 2:35 P.M. did the Egyptians take some initiative in the air, when a message from an Israeli monitoring unit reported twenty-four Egyptian fighters heading for the Mitla Pass. "We were all at the squadron and suddenly this little secretary comes screaming 'All the Mystères in the air,' " recalls Tsuk. "We each grabbed a plane and started out, but after eight took off Beni [Peled] stopped the whole thing. Yak [Nevo] and [Yeshayahu] Egozi took off first, and I caught up and joined them."[12]

The message was erroneous. An intercepted Egyptian wire only mentioned four fighters, but a typo in transmission—on the Israeli side—resulted in the twenty-four-fighter alarm. As a result, when two of the eight Mystères peeled off to the Mitla, they found noth-ing. The remaining six headed for the Canal, the first trio arriving over the Kabrit airfield just as four MiGs lifted off the runway. "Yak headed down first, then Egozi, then I," Tsuk recalls. "It was a mess. No tactics, no organization. We just followed Yak down in a single file like a bunch of Indians. At first nobody hit anything. We were going too fast. But then I put my air brakes on, and shot one of the MiGs."

As the second trio reached the area and shot down a second MiG, twelve more MiGs appeared. Twisting and looping, Tsuk was on a MiG's tail and about to open fire when "I saw gunfire passing me, and I realized another MiG was on my own tail and firing. The sky was full of MiGs." He shook off the Egyptian and with "a hole in my wing [and] too little fuel to even get home," disengaged and started back. They were so low of fuel that "my engine cut out just as I landed, and Egozi's as he was taxiing back."

By nightfall, the 101's "magnificent dozen" had kept the MiGs away long enough for Sharon's column to overcome the Kuntilla, Thamad, and Nakhl fortifications and join up with Eitan's besieged battalion at the Mitla.* Farther north, the Thirty-eighth Infantry and Armor Division overcame the border fortifications at Quseima, Auja Masri, and Tarat Um Basis, and was readying to assault the Abu Ageila Hedgehog, a massive complex of fortified hilltops with mine fields, fences, and bunkers.

With that, Israel had completed its assigned mission. At 6:00 P.M., France and Britain, as planned, ordered Egypt and Israel to cease fire and to pull away from the Canal. As if following a script, Israel agreed, while Nasser refused and angrily ordered his First Armored Brigade into the Sinai. Next, according to that same script the British-French forces should have started bombing Egypt's air bases the following morning. Free from air attacks, Israel would then consolidate its hold on the Sinai, and break through to the Strait of Tiran, to reopen its sea-lanes south.

As Israel—Blues, Greens, and civilians—held its breath and waited, a fascinating drama, unplanned and unexpected, suddenly unfolded at, of all places, IAF headquarters in the small former-German air base outside Ramla.

For the past three years, while the struggle for acquiring advanced jets dominated the IAF—and public—minds and imaginations, Laskov and then Tolkowsky had invested no less time and

---

*Sharon nearly lost his life that night when his unit was unexpectedly resupplied from the air by French transports. He had fallen asleep on the desert floor and did not hear the warning shouts of his soldiers as one of the 800-pound packages landed barely a foot away.

effort in developing the critical infrastructure of the IAF, particularly in the areas of communications and command and control. By the time the war in the Sinai began, Tolkowsky had in place a primitive but fairly effective central control system. While on the ground any IAF plane was naturally taking orders and reporting to its squadron and wing command, once it was up in the air it automatically came under the authority of a controller at the IAF's central command and control unit at Ramla, who was on a virtually open channel with the pilot for the duration of a mission. On the eve of the Sinai campaign, because of the distances involved, the system was supplanted by two airborne transmission-relay stations, mounted in two converted IAF Dakota transports that were kept constantly in the air, one near the Mitla Pass and the other near Gaza.

The communications system was more complex than that. Each plane had four radio channels—two for communicating with IAF Control and with the plane's home base, and two for communicating with IDF ground forces through IAF air-ground support officers (AGSO's) attached to brigade-level commanders. Each AGSO on the ground had a portable two-channel VHF radio for communicating with ground units, a ten-channel truck-mounted set for communicating directly with IAF planes in the air, and a third set which enabled him to talk to IAF Control at Ramla, or to the various IDF ground commands. Theoretically, at least, any ground unit in need of air support could, through its AGSO, not only request it directly from Ramla, but once the planes were in the air it could guide them directly to their targets and appraise them of any changes taking place in the battle below. All this was separate from the IDF's own communications system, which ran from IDF headquarters near Tel Aviv to the regional commands and the various field units.

Once the fighting began, however, virtually the entire system broke down. In the first place, communications between the IDF war room near Tel Aviv and the IDF Southern Command bunker in Beersheba broke down (Moshe Dayan, who anticipated this, had right from the start moved to Beersheba to run the campaign). The AGSO network also soon bogged down in intense battle fog and electronic overload.

But the IAF command and control system, particularly the simple controller-pilot radio link, worked perfectly, and once the radio chatter was pumped into a loudspeaker at the IAF bunker, Ramla became the only place in the country where one could get a decent picture of the events on the ground and in the air. It is not entirely clear how it happened, but within hours the Greens, too, discovered Ramla. Col. Mordechai Bar-On, Ben-Gurion's military advisor, first showed up in Tolkowsky's bunker, and "that began a snowball. Everybody started coming," recalls Shaya Gazit. "Within hours of the war's beginning the IDF chief of staff was down there, and the IDF chief of operations. They couldn't get over it. [They] could hear everything that was going on in the battle zone, who was doing what, who was asking for air cover."

The command bunker was hardly set up to accommodate such crowds. One side of the large room was taken up with a huge opaque-glass wall, behind which young women rushed constantly, writing and erasing "who's-in-the-air reports" in inverse script. At the center of the room, other young women moved tiny model planes on a table map of the region. Against the back wall just enough seats were installed in two tiers to accommodate the command and control staff below, Tolkowsky and his operations staff on top. This meager space was now crammed full of thrilled Green invaders. Before long, "tents and mini-command posts were set up for those who moved to the bunker, [like] representatives from the Greens' quartermaster, technical, manpower, medical and even antiaircraft units. We even had the French Air Force liaison officers there," Gazit says.[13]

It was the first day of the fighting, in which the IAF was not even meant to take part. But already Tolkowsky's bunker had become the virtual command post for the entire military campaign.

The following morning, there was still no sign of allied bombers. Instead, just before dawn, an Egyptian destroyer that had worked its way up the coast to the Haifa harbor began shelling the nearby oil refineries. Two Ouragans were scrambled from Hazor and set the destroyer on fire with rockets. As the ship began to smoke heavily— and soon surrendered—a second pair of Ouragans en route to the ship was diverted in midair to the south. It was no ordinary pair. "Ever since the war started, Ezer [Weizman] left a standing order to call him if we were going against a ship. His ambition was to shoot up a ship, I don't know why. So when we got an order for two more Ouragans, I woke him up and the two of us followed the first pair north," recalls Hod. Instead of a ship, however, they shot up an armored convoy heading for El 'Arīsh.

The air action began sooner and more spectacularly than on the previous day. Over the Mitla, Shavit and Egozi ran into four Vampires heading for Eitan's paratroopers. Though low on fuel, Shavit dived after the first pair and fired. One Vampire exploded so unexpectedly that "I was rattled by the awesomeness of this whole thing," he recalls. As he pulled up, Egozi dived after the second pair. Lowering his speed and taking careful aim, he shot both jets down in one pass. No longer content with one kill, Shavit followed "the fourth plane, which I saw running to the west," and caught up with it over Kabrit. "I was so low on fuel I squeezed just one burst of gunfire and headed for home," he says, but the fourth Vampire, too, went down. The entire battle, most of it viewed by cheering paratroopers, took less than two minutes.

By noon, there was still no sign of allied bombers, and the wait was straining nerves and tempers. What Ben-Gurion had sought to avoid was now happening—Israel was slugging it out alone in the Sinai, with the Egyptians throwing massive forces into the fray. Heavy fighting was raging clear across the Sinai. To the north, an infantry-armor divisional task force commanded by Brig. Gen. Chaim Laskov—now back in his element after his stretch at the head of the Air Force—was slugging its way trench-to-trench into the Gaza Strip. At the central section, the Thirty-eighth Division was running into heavy opposition at the Abu Ageila Hedgehog.

The most bitter fighting was at the Mitla. Anxious to push on to the Canal, and relying on Air Force assurances that the passes seemed free of enemy forces, Sharon sent a battalion-strength "reconnaissance patrol" into the pass. The force was caught in heavy crossfire from nearly five Egyptian infantry companies that had been holed up in the cliffs since the previous day, with fourteen medium machine guns, a dozen antitank guns, and forty Czech-made recoilless guns. In midafternoon, four Egyptian Meteors, escorted by six MiGs, also attacked the trapped Israelis with machine guns and rockets, killing seven paratroopers and wounding twenty. Although Israeli Ouragans were strafing Egyptian convoys just west of the Mitla at the time, all attempts to contact them failed. Only in early evening did two paratrooper teams scale the cliffs and, in hand-to-hand combat, demolish the Egyptian force.*

The ground-to-air radio communication failure at the Mitla was not an isolated problem. Distances played havoc with the primitive command links as planes and pilots were stretched to the limit covering all fronts. The Israelis were not only outnumbered but handicapped by the vast Sinai distances. Since it took them twenty minutes just to get to the battle zone from Hazor, and the same time to get back, they were already short of fuel even as they began dogfighting. The Egyptians, freshly fueled and minutes from base, could keep on going seemingly forever.

The Israeli fighters held their own even though each pair of Mystères was now running into four, eight, even fourteen MiGs at a time. That morning, after tangling briefly with seven MiGs, Yak Nevo and Tsuk ran into two more. With Tsuk flying cover, Nevo "fired a short burst from 600 yards. Missed. A second burst from 400 yards. Missed. The third burst I squeezed until I got within 200 yards. The plane was hit"†[14] (in early afternoon, he downed a second MiG near El 'Arīsh).

Israeli attack squadrons, however, were less fortunate, taking merciless antiaircraft fire as they attempted to stop Egyptian reinforcements from reaching the front. Fourteen Mustangs, three Harvards, six Meteors, and six Ouragans were hit, of which seven Mustangs and a Harvard were destroyed completely. Maj. Moshe Melnizki, commander of the 105 Mustang squadron, and Capt. Moshe Eshel, commander of the 104 squadron of Harvard dive-bombers, were both killed, and one Ouragan pilot barely brought his plane for a belly landing at Hazor. Around 10:00 A.M., while strafing Egyptian armor near Bir Gafgafa, Yoeli's wingman had his engine set on fire by flak and belly-landed at Hazor. Yoeli himself, whose guns jammed in mid-dive, had both his left engine and left hand shot by flak. Wrapping a tourniquet around his arm, he reached Tel Nof on one engine only to discover that his left wheel

*Thirty-eight Israelis were killed and 120 wounded in the Mitla battle, compared to 250 Egyptian dead.
†"Yak's MiG" went down at the Sabkhet el Bardawill lagoon and was fished out by the Israelis after the war. It is today on display at Hazor.

was also damaged and wouldn't come down. "I landed safely on a nose wheel and one side wheel [but] the fire crews nearly killed me with their axes, trying to get me out [until] I pulled out my pistol and threatened to shoot anybody who got near."[15] He was rushed to a hospital but escaped three hours later to fly another mission.

By afternoon, the Egyptians were still coming, and the Israelis could hardly keep up. Menahem Bar, flying Mystères at the 101 after the collapse of the Sabrejet deal, "went to Ezer and said that we should hit the Egyptian air bases without waiting, that achieving air superiority through air battles is an ineffective method, compared to striking airfields."[16]

Tolkowsky was more than willing to oblige, especially since IAF Intelligence was warning of impending Egyptian bombing strikes against Israel that night. He ordered his B-17s, Mosquito, and Meteor squadrons to prepare for hitting the IL-28 bomber fleet at Cairo West and the land air bases, and at 7:40 in the evening, unable to reach Dayan, he called Ben-Gurion at his home and demanded an immediate go-ahead.[17]

Just then, after a thirteen-hour delay, British Valiants and Canberras from Malta and Cyprus finally appeared and struck the Cairo East and Inshas airfields near Cairo, as well as Abu Suweir and Kabrit on the Canal. Musketeer was finally on. At daybreak of November 1, French and British fighters began strafing and rocketing after the bombers. By the following morning, over fifty Egyptian planes had been destroyed and forty damaged. That night the Allied offensive expanded to include Egyptian radar, shore-artillery, armored and infantry concentrations. The Egyptian Air Force was destroyed by the time the British-French assault on the airfields ended two days later. "The Kabrit field is in ruins, totally burned," reported a 101 pilot who flew over the Canal.[18]

Free of having to worry about Egyptian MiGs, the IAF could now devote its entire resources to assisting the ground forces. With the Israelis now in control of the main highways, the Egyptians began a massive retreat toward the Canal, under fire from Israeli planes as well as from French fighter squadrons, who heretofore were kept out of the fighting. With no air cover of their own, the retreating Egyptians were helpless as Israeli Ouragans, Mystères, and Meteors swooped down on their columns. The Ouragans' effectiveness in picking off armored vehicles resulted in one of the two lasting images of the war—long rows of charred tanks and armored trucks strung along desert highways (the other image was of sand dunes strewn with army boots, discarded by Egyptians fleeing on foot toward the Canal).

Even with the whole of North Sinai in its hands, Israel's little war was still unfinished. The Tiran Straits, guarding its sea-lanes to the Indian Ocean, were still under Egypt's massive shore guns at Ras Nasrani and Sharm el Sheikh. In the vast scheme of Musketeer, little significance was attached to that remote corner of the Sinai, but taking out the guns and occupying the straits was Israel's primary reason for joining the British-French campaign in the first place.

Now, with its allies pounding Egyptian airfields and armor bases, the IDF began its most remarkable campaign of that footnote war. On the night of October 29, close on the heels of Sharon's 202nd Brigade, a reconnaissance company of the Ninth Infantry Reserve Brigade had moved into the Sinai and seized the police fort at Ras El-Naqb, the gateway south. That same night, the entire Ninth began an impossible journey, slithering along a camel route down the western edge of the Gulf of Aqaba toward the straits, 150 miles away.

Their odyssey was the stuff of legends. Led by Col. Abraham Yoffe,* a burly Galilee farmer, the Ninth's two battalions were made up of farmer-reservists from Yizre'el Valley villages, deemed too old for frontline duty. Their mission was momentous. With two hundred half-trucks and trucks loaded with a week's worth of food and supplies, they had to trudge through craggy canyons, sand dunes, moon-scape mountains, and trackless precipices, mostly on foot, mostly pushing or pulling their trucks along winding passes made for donkeys, not four-wheel vehicles. If and when they emerged out of the scorching, parched land barrier they would still have to face two heavily fortified companies at Ras Nasrani, heavily armed with shore and antiaircraft batteries, and a third company at Sharm el Sheikh.

On November 1, with its Piper Cubs flying ahead of the advanc-

*Cousin of the IAF's Avraham Yoffe.

ing force, the IAF launched a massive air attack on Ras Nasrani and Sharm el Sheikh, with two B-17s, a dozen Mustangs, eight Mosquitos, and eight Mystères pounding the forts with bombs and rockets. The Egyptians responded with devastating antiaircraft fire. Dani Shapira's Mystère was hit, but he made it safely to base. Lt. Jonathan Etkes, a Mustang pilot, was hit, crash-landed, and passed out alongside his plane. He was picked up by Egyptian troops and taken a prisoner of war.

Beni Peled was more fortunate. While diving at the Ras Nasrani fort with a load of rockets, his plane was hit by flak and caught fire. He tried to keep flying, but "the fire got worse and even my eyebrows and arms were getting scorched," and he bailed out. The plane crashed nearby. With his foot damaged in the jump, Peled scampered to the cliffs west of the Egyptian fortress, half running and half being dragged by his windblown parachute, where he planned to hide until the arrival of the Ninth Brigade in a day or two. He was almost discovered by two Egyptian soldiers who followed him to the cliffs, but he hid and the Egyptians passed twenty feet away without noticing him.

As Peled hid among the rocks and watched, Mosquitos, Mustangs, and B-17s kept pounding the coastal compounds through the heavy fire. The Mosquitos, having dropped their bombs first, circled above Peled's hiding place. Just before heading back for lack of fuel, recalls Maj. Yeheskiel Somekh, commander of the 110 Mosquito squadron, "we saw . . . three vehicles approaching the area. We attacked and destroyed them with rockets and guns."[19]

Late in the afternoon, a Piper Cub scouting ahead of the Ninth received a radio message to look for two downed pilots near Ras Nasrani. West of the fort he spotted two figures walking, but as he dived over them they turned out to be Egyptian soldiers. The pilot rose higher and kept looking until, three hundred yards to the south, "I saw a man lying and waving at me with a white strip of cloth. I was not sure. I suspected a trap. I came around again and then I identified Beni," he would later recall. The plane landed two hundred yards away. When its passenger-scout rushed to help Peled up into the plane, however, the two heavy men fell down. Finally the pilot also left his plane, rushed over, and together the two of them loaded Peled into the back of the plane and took off.

With pressure at the UN Security Council mounting for an end
to the fighting, Israel began a pincer move by dropping paratroopers at A-Tur, on the Gulf of Suez just north of Sharm el Sheikh.
With the Ninth advancing down one side and the paratroopers from
the other, both under air cover, the Egyptians pulled out of Ras
Nasrani, which fell to the Ninth on November 4 with no fighting,
and holed up at Sharm el Sheikh. On the following morning, after
heavy artillery and aerial bombardments, Sharm el Sheikh, too, was
taken. The next night, after landing troops at Port Said and Port
Fuad, France and Britain bowed to intense international pressure
and accepted a UN-imposed cease-fire.

The British-French campaign failed to achieve either of its two
goals. The Canal was not recaptured, and Nasser was not overthrown.
But Israel's footnote campaign was a success. Although American
pressure the following year forced Israel to pull out of the Sinai, the
Straits of Tiran remained open to Israeli shipping for the next ten
years. Certainly the price that Israel paid, 172 dead and 4 captured,
was not out of line, certainly not in comparison to the Egyptian toll of
over 1,000 dead and 6,000 taken prisoner, and to the toll that Arab
terror would have taken had the war not dented it.

And while it was hardly the "piece of cake" that Tolkowsky would
describe in later years, the air war portion of that footnote campaign
actually scored two important victories for the IAF. It helped defeat
the Egyptians, and it won belated recognition from the Greens. More
than three decades later, an IAF pilot would recall the thrill he felt
when, on the day after the war ended, "some paratroopers drove by in
a Jeep and they stopped to give me a lift."[20]

More important, two days before the fighting ended, Dayan and
Tolkowsky were flying down to the Strait of Tiran in an IAF Dakota
when Dayan fixed Tolkowsky with his one good eye and announced
that he had "come to a decision—when it comes to budgetary
priorities for the IDF, the way I now see it is first comes the Air
Force, second the Armored Corps, and third the paratroopers."[21]

"He was converted," Tolkowsky says now. "It took a lot of time,
and much blood was spilled in the process, [but] the great thing
about Dayan was it never bothered him to be proven wrong."

PART THREE

EZER'S WAR

Chapter 13

MIRAGE

Shlomo Lahat, chief of IAF Air Section during the Sinai campaign, was an anomaly, having come to the IAF neither from the Royal Air Force, the Haifa Flight Club, or from the *Palmach* Flight Platoon. Born in Vienna in 1924, he arrived in Palestine at the age of seven, a darkly handsome boy who was picked to star in one of Jewish Palestine's early motion pictures. He dropped out of high school at fifteen to become an apprentice electrician, and in 1942, rejected by the RAF, he joined the British army as a truck driver, first in North Africa and then, after a Mediterranean voyage in which his ship was attacked by Nazi fighters and submarines and 143 of the Jewish Palestinian company on board were killed, in Europe, starting with the Salerno landing and trucking all the way up the Italian boot until the war ended. In 1947, a childless uncle offered to finance his college education in the United States. Lahat got as far as New York, but there he ran into Teddy Kollek, then a *Haganah* recruiter, who got him into Eleanor Rudnick's private flight school near Bakersfield, California, part of Al Schwimmer's *Yakum Purkan* network. In June of 1948 he returned to Israel with a private pilot's license and 160 hours of air time, and flew light planes and transports for the rest of the war.

Yet although he never flew fighters until much later, his career path quickly crossed Weizman's, and from that point on the two moved almost in lockstep. When Weizman commanded a fighter squadron in Ramat David, Lahat commanded a transport squadron at Tel Nof. When Weizman moved up to IAF Operations, Lahat became chief of operations at Tel Nof. When Weizman was at an RAF staff school in Britain in 1952, Lahat was at a USAF Air Command Staff School at Maxwell Air Force Base near Montgomery, Alabama. Then, as Weizman was assigned to establish a new IAF staff school, Lahat was given command of Hazor, where Mosquito fighter-bombers were just arriving from France.

At the 1952 Independence Day flyby over Tel Aviv, their rivalry went public when Weizman, leading the flyby with six Mustangs, threw his formation into a dive and buzzed the reviewing stand. Lahat, who came right after him with six Mosquitos, promptly dived even lower; "on the next day we were both court-martialed together," Lahat recalls.[1]

For a while, Lahat was dodged by his transport-pilot image, but in 1953 Tolkowsky brought him to IAF Operations (Weizman was sent north to command Ramat David), and it was there that Lahat proved that he had more than chiseled good looks and a deep voice. One Friday morning, without permission, he took a Mosquito and a navigator and flew deep into the heart of Egypt, where for two hours he circled over Cairo and its surrounding air bases and photographed everything in sight. When the photographs turned out well, Lahat kept the mission secret and repeated it a few days later over Alexandria.

When he finally admitted what he had done, the photos he victoriously spread out before his superiors constituted such an intelligence coup that, instead of getting court-martialed, Lahat became the Greens' favorite Blue. In 1953, Makleff left no doubts that, had he had more staff experience, he would have liked Lahat, not Tolkowsky, to succeed Laskov as commander of the Air Force. In 1954, when Tolkowsky made him chief of IAF Air Section, Dayan personally speeded up his promotion to a full colonel, and on several occasions during the following two years tried to engineer Tolkowsky's resignation so Lahat could take his place.[2]

The Lahat threat may have had something to do with Tolkowsky's asking Dayan, on the eve of the Sinai campaign, to sound

Weizman out about becoming the next head of IAF Air Section. Since the head of IAF Air Section was, to all intents and purposes, deputy-commander of the IAF, it was not as if Weizman was about to turn the offer down. But by going through Dayan, Tolkowsky avoided a showdown with the Greens over Lahat. Weizman, of course, enthusiastically accepted the offer, and on December 1, 1956, after obtaining Tolkowsky's agreement to let his protégé Moti Hod succeed him as commander of Hazor, moved to the crowded Air Section offices in Ramla, while Lahat became commander of Tel Nof, the IAF's biggest base.

This latest shuffle had a certain historic significance beyond Lahat's or Weizman's fortunes. Of the three previous IAF chiefs, Shamir was relieved for health reasons, and both Remez and Laskov had to resign in bitter disputes with the Greens. Tolkowsky himself, whose own appointment began as a temporary compromise following Laskov's angry resignation, had on several occasions come close to resigning and, on the eve of the war, to getting dumped by the Greens.

But the success of the Sinai air campaign changed everything. "That snob Tolkowsky" was now so secure in his post that for the first time an IAF commander could not only pick his successor but define the succession process itself for years to come. One key element of the process was Tolkowsky's grooming of not just one but two qualified candidates, which he methodically rotated through top field and staff posts so that each could step into his shoes without missing a beat (there were a few other candidates, who held senior technical and staff posts and felt certain they had the inside track, but in another key policy decision Tolkowsky determined that the IAF had to be commanded by a frontline flyer, which left only Lahat and Weizman).

To many in and out of the IAF, accustomed to the horse-trading of military promotions, the Lahat-Weizman shuffle seemed a charade. Lahat not only *looked* like an IAF commander should, but to the senior Greens he *was* the Air Force. By comparison, even as wing commander Weizman had seemed childish, impulsive, and spoiled. "Lahat was well-adjusted, quiet, relaxed, balanced [and] a Columbia graduate,* [while] I was haunted by my own reputation

*Weizman errs on this point. At the time, Lahat only had a high-school diploma which he earned while serving with the British army in World War II. Later, however, he entered Columbia and completed an MBA degree in just two years.

of a rascal, light-hearted and light-minded," Weizman would note in his autobiography years later.[3]

Frantically, Weizman stayed in the race but saw conspiracies and plots at every turn. Worried that even "my Air Section appointment was no guarantee that . . . it would lead to command of the IAF," he now complained of having "to prove myself before my candidacy could even be considered." He suspected Tolkowsky, because "as wing commander, I had often disagreed with him" and because Tolkowsky had appointed several former Mosquito pilots—not Mustang jocks—to key positions. He feared that neither his brother-in-law Dayan, nor his sister's former beau Chaim Laskov, who became IDF chief of staff in January 1, 1958, would back his candidacy, and that "Ben-Gurion preferred Lahat [because he was] closer than me to the Labor Movement and its leaders." He fell into deep depression when, at the ceremony when Dayan transferred the IDF command to Laskov, a senior army officer leaned over and whispered that "Laskov will pick [Lahat], one hundred percent."[4]

In reality, several developments had made Weizman's promotion to the IAF command as likely as Lahat's. He was at Tolkowsky's elbow during the massive postwar acquisition and development drive, when the IAF's primitive command and control system was upgraded with modern radio, radar, and data analysis machinery, when air bases were fortified with underground pens, when Defense Department buyers were scampering all over Europe with Tolkowsky's shopping lists. It was with Weizman at his side that Tolkowsky replaced the aging World War II Mosquitos with France's newest supersonic attack jets, Sud Aviation's $750,000 Vautours, and added a squadron of Super-Mystères, France's hottest fighter-interceptors, to counter the MiG-19s which the Soviets had begun supplying to Egypt.

Finally, there was the fact that just one year after the 1956 war, demoralized by low pay and poor living conditions, IAF pilots and mechanics were leaving in droves for airline jobs, studies, and other careers. Out of the hundred and twenty-one pilots who completed training between 1950 and 1954, twenty-six died in combat or training accidents, forty-six had simply left, and of the remaining forty-nine only twenty-nine could fly jets. "In three years the IAF would face an intolerable situation. Over 80 percent of the pilots are thinking of leaving, and I believe that at least half of them think about it very seriously," an alarmed Yak Nevo, then acting commander of the 101 Mystère squadron, wrote to Tolkowsky. Attempts to lure pilots into staying—with housing allowances, study grants, or pay increases—met with little success.

What the IAF needed was a commander who would not only stop that drain but reverse it. It had to be someone whom the pilots would not only accept but feel compelled and inspired to stay with and follow. When it came to this point it was a no contest. However well Lahat could fly a Mosquito, he was never close to the Round Table of the single-seat warriors of Air Force North, where Weizman was King Arthur. Weizman may not have had the confidence of Ben-Gurion or the Greens, but no one before or after him so captured the hearts, minds, and spirit of the IAF fighter corps. The old 1948 foreign volunteers, too, came to their squadron buddy's help. When Ben-Gurion asked Lou Lenart, who was visiting Israel at the time, who should command the Air Force after Tolkowsky, "I said that the Air Force needed a fighting, not an executive, commander. I didn't name names, but it was clear I meant Weizman," Lenart says.[5] Even Weizman's old foe Menahem Bar took it for granted that "Ezer was the natural candidate for the job."[6]

The only one who didn't see it, it seemed, was Weizman himself, whose demons of failure and rejection drove him to start cashing in on his family cachet. "Ezer was the first to engage in personal lobbying for himself. It was very unacceptable. I thought it was a disaster and I was not willing to do it. Actually, I had a personal letter from Ben-Gurion telling me that I was destined to be one of the future IAF commanders [but] it never occurred to me to show it to anybody," Lahat says. "It had never occurred to me to call friends at IDF General Staff, of whom I had many, to promote myself."[7]

By the spring of 1958, Weizman's depression reached such a state that Gideon Elrom, commander of Ramat David at the time, remembers coming into his office for a chat, to be told that "Ezer said he was going to the beach to wait for the decision." Weizman actually sat out that year's Independence Day parade—the first he missed since buzzing Tel Aviv with his Spitfire nine years earlier—

and while he showed up for the IAF ball that night at the Ramat Aviv Hotel, he drank heavily and started throwing tables, chairs, and bookcases from the balcony. An old friend recalls spending an evening with Weizman that week, when he "cried like a child about how they were all against making him commander."

A few weeks later, still keeping his moves secret and his options open, Tolkowsky asked Weizman and Lahat both to his office. "We walked in together, not knowing who would come out the next Air Force commander, and we sat down, each one at one end of the desk facing Dan. We were both equally tense, equally white, equally trembling. The whole thing took seventy seconds," Lahat says.[8] Weizman's paranoia continued even after Tolkowsky told him he would be the next IAF commander. When IDF chief of staff Laskov told him that he was approving his appointment, and sending Lahat to study in the United States, Weizman seized on the last part as proof that Lahat was being kept in reserve, to take over the IAF at the first sign of trouble.

One would think that, having finally won his coveted appointment, Weizman would hunker down to prove himself worthy of the trust. Instead, he promptly pulled off a stunt that nearly ended his command, and came close to drawing Israel into a new war with Egypt. Apparently feeling that a routine inauguration ball or parade was not a fitting enough rite for a knightly warrior, he searched for one that was and finally found it. He would launch his reign with a MiG kill.

Trouble was, the borders had been quiet since the end of the war, and the Egyptians meticulously stayed on their side. To bag a MiG, the IAF would have to go inside Egypt.

Keeping his entire staff in the dark, Weizman went into a huddle with Moti Hod, his old Ramat David sidekick, who was now in command of Hazor, and the two waited for an opportune time. It came on December 20, 1958, a quiet Saturday morning, when Weizman set his play in motion by phoning to Hazor out of the blue to report "MiG activity in the area." As two Mystères were automatically scrambled to the border after the imaginary MiGs, Hod himself miraculously appeared on the flight line and, accompanied by Aharon Yoeli, commander of the 101 squadron at the time, took off in two other Mystères "to cut the MiGs off as they returned to El 'Arīsh."[9]

There were no MiGs, of course, but Hod and Yoeli soon reached El ʻArīsh and began to circle. At 30,000 feet, they were so high that their exhaust jets condensed into thick white contrails that were visible for miles. It was precisely what Weizman and Hod had counted on. Soon two MiG-17s came up to investigate the intrusion. Hod called Yoeli and the two slowly began to move back toward the Israeli border. Yoeli, who was unaware of the scheme, couldn't figure out why he and Hod could not loop back and shoot the MiGs down. He was not aware that Hod's script called for the MiGs to be shot down near the border, and that he and Hod were merely the bait. As they lured the MiGs toward Israel, two other Mystères, one of them flown by Yak Nevo, the 101's champion dogfighter, were closing in behind them.

"I remember thinking that the MiG-17 was faster than the Mystère, and that unless I could sneak unseen into gun position the MiGs would take off and get away," Yak recalls.[10] But Hod's classic sandwich ambush worked. As the MiGs followed Hod and Yoeli, Nevo rolled in behind one of them, fired, and the MiG crashed into the desert floor with its pilot.

Hod's ploy failed in only one respect—Nevo's MiG crashed near Bir Lahfan, forty miles inside Egyptian territory, instead of near the Israeli border. It didn't matter to the pilots—"I had no precise idea where we were, somewhere near the border, [but] I had permission to open fire and I did," says Nevo—but the Mystères had barely landed when a furious Laskov summoned Weizman to his office. Grabbing the largest-scale map of the area he could find, Weizman attempted to convince "a tense and angry" Laskov that the MiGs had actually penetrated Israeli airspace and were being chased back when the battle took place. But Laskov could read maps. "How come it just happened to fall practically at El ʻArīsh," he roared. When Weizman cheerfully suggested that "he must have glided there," Laskov ordered him into his car and, grumbling about international implications, rushed to an emergency meeting with Ben-Gurion.

The white-maned leader, however, seemed unconcerned. "Battle? What battle? Where?" he asked curiously. Weizman rolled out his map and pointed—not with his finger but with his huge palm— "more or less here." Ben-Gurion shrugged. "*Nu*, the public will be happy," he said, and told Laskov to release the story to the press.

It was that night, as Nevo regaled Israeli radio listeners with tales of gunslinging on the high frontier, that the Weizman era at the IAF truly began. When the owner of Herzliyya's beachfront Hasharon Hotel offered a free weekend to any IAF pilot who shot down a MiG, Weizman promptly sent him Nevo and his wingman, a young pilot named Amos Lapidot. The following spring, Weizman picked the same hotel, not an Air Force facility, for the IAF's first Independence Day Air Crews Ball, a gala event that Weizman personally thought up, planned, supplied with top Israeli artists and an expanded Air Force band, and emceed with as much flare and glamor as any of the stars on hand.

As he did the 101 in 1949 and Ramat David in the early 1950s, Weizman now turned the entire Air Force into a personal Camelot. Physically, too. For the past two years, the IDF had been moving its scattered headquarters facilities to an abandoned British army complex on the northeast edge of Tel Aviv, and Tolkowsky had begun building a new IAF headquarters right next to it. But it was Weizman who moved his command from Ramla to Tel Aviv—six Mystères buzzed the compound as he moved in—and then stunned the Greens by stringing a high fence around his domain, flying his own flag over it, and placing his own guards at the gate.

The IAF rank and file were electrified as Weizman warned that anyone attempting to fly "over my bases at less than 40,000 feet will crash into our morale." "Ezer imbued the whole force with the spirit of a . . . gang, with him as the gang leader," says Shaya Gazit. "He drummed tenacity and persistence into us, excellence at all cost . . . it is true that he kept an album with the face of each man in the force, but even without it he knew all his pilots personally, each and every one, and it was one of the reasons he could get such an incredible amount of work out of us."[11]

Weizman now locked the Air Force up tight, ordered his pilots to live on base and sign on for at least three years, and made it clear to their wives that their job was to keep the pilots healthy and undistracted. Later, he had a local developer subdivide a stretch of land near the fashionable suburb of Ramat Ha'Sharon, north of Tel Aviv, and arranged attractive financing so IAF pilots and staff officers—and no one else—could buy or build apartments and homes there, and rent them out until they retired or were assigned to IAF headquarters in nearby Tel Aviv.

Shuttling from base to base in his black Spitfire, Weizman personally kept on top of everything, exhorting, flattering, seducing "my pilots, my planes, my Air Force" into white-heat excitement with improved mess-hall menus, richer club offerings, organized trips and outings. "Every squadron had a club with a billiard table even when Israelis looked at billiards as a sign of decadence," recalls Rachel Shaked, the widow of an IAF flyer. "My father had worked for the British Mandate authorities, and when I was little I occasionally came with him to their camps and saw the British officers sitting in their clubs. When my husband first took me to his club all those distant memories rushed back—it all looked so familiar, so British."[12]

Day and night, Weizman flooded his pilots with concern, total attention, unbounded love. Zehava Gazit, Shaya's wife, recalls getting up from a long illness to attend an IAF Independence Day ball. "Ezer had just got up on stage to open the evening, but when he saw me in the audience—I shall never forget it as long as I live—he stopped his speech, came down and picked me up in the air. That act was so . . . I began to cry, overcome by this incredible sense of belonging. It was not that he did or did not love me personally. He would have done it for any other wife. It was that he *knew* everybody and remembered every celebration or tragedy. He remembered everything."[13]

It was also in that year that Weizman found the plane that would become his trademark, a delta-shaped flying blade that slashed through the air like a strange ninja weapon. Even its name was perfect. It was called Mirage.

In the spring of 1959, even before the French Air Force took possession of the first Mirage, Dassault offered to stage a private demonstration of the new plane for the Israelis, whose massive purchases and successful battle use of Dassault's Ouragans, Mystères, and Super-Mystères made them prize clients. Weizman wired back that he would look at the plane only if Dani Shapira, Weizman's old comrade from the 101 days at Ramat David, who was then attending test-pilot school in France, demonstrated it. "Out of the question," Dassault wired back.

"You tell them that I don't give a damn what some French cockroach says about his plane. I am only interested in what Dani Shapira has to say about it, and if they are not willing to let him fly

I am not coming to the show," Weizman instructed his IAF attachés at the Israeli Embassy in Paris to reply.[14]

He got his way. "Dassault's chief test pilot came to the Israeli Embassy in Paris, introduced himself and told me that the next morning I'd fly the Mirage," recalls Shapira. "I asked if I would be getting any ground school briefing. 'What for? You are a test pilot, no?' he said." The next day, at the Dassault test base outside Paris, Shapira was shown to the plane as matter-of-factly "as if the guy was giving me the keys to his car and telling me to drive off. I closed the canopy, started the engine, took off, flew and landed with no problem whatever," Shapira says. In his second flight he passed 1.5 Mach, pulled 7G turns, did a few loops and fell in love with the small, elegant fighter. For his third flight, Weizman was at the control trailer as Shapira read his speed over the radio—"Mach 1 . . . 1.1 . . . 1.2 . . . 1.3 . . . 2 . . . 2.1." When he came down, Weizman hugged and swung him around, and announced that the Mirage was *the* plane for the IAF.

But he insisted on two critical modifications. Ever since the *Enola Gay* dropped "Little Boy" over Hiroshima on August 6, 1945, and another B-29 dropped "Fat Man" over Nagasaki three days later, military planners everywhere considered the nuclear bomber the weapon of the future, and gave fighters only one reason for surviving into the 1950s—as bomber interceptors. In the following decade, cloistered aviation workshops from the Mikoyan-Gurevich Design Bureau in the Soviet Union to Dassault's in France and North American Aviation and Lockheed in California turned out interceptors that could climb at rocket speed to 40,000 feet and shoot a bomber down before it came close enough to do harm.

Not with guns, either, but with another exotic new weapon of that brave new future—the heat-seeking missile. Guns and dogfighting had become irrelevant. The two leading interceptors of the time, the Soviet MiG-25 Foxbat and the Lockheed F-104 Star Fighter, could climb faster and higher than any other plane in existence, but they couldn't dogfight at all and carried no guns. Dassault's Mirage, which came with an auxiliary rocket engine that launched it up like a missile, also had no guns.

It was therefore nothing short of heresy when Weizman demanded that the French take the rocket engines off *his* Mirages, and put guns back in. Israel, after all, worried less about high-altitude nuclear bombers than about Soviet-built MiG-21s, the hottest dog-fighters of the era, which Egypt was about to receive in great numbers. Also, the 1956 air war proved the deadliness of the French 30-mm DEFA guns against the heaviest enemy tanks.

Putting the guns back on a plane that was designed to fly without them was not simple. At first, "Every time we'd fire the guns, the engines died on us because the gas from the firing disrupted the air flow. We had to design and install special deflectors to keep the gas away from the air inlets, and then things were fine," says Shapira. But even though new problems kept cropping up, Weizman refused to wait and ordered a hundred Mirages for the IAF, the same number ordered by the French Air Force itself. The Greens were stunned by the $1.5 million price tag—per plane—and Laskov rolled Weizman's order back to twenty-four. On January 1, 1961, however, before the deal was finalized, Laskov retired and his successor, a gentle, bespectacled Sorbonne graduate named Zvi Tzur who advocated a massive military buildup, raised it back up to seventy-two Mirages, enough to equip three squadrons.

At the last minute, French Foreign Office objections were personally overruled by Charles de Gaulle, and on April 7, 1962, Dani Shapira and a French pilot ferried the first two Mirages to a Sabbath landing at Ramat David. The IAF now entered its Golden Age.

Chapter 14

REBELS

To understand the white-heat brilliance of the Ezer era at the IAF, it is necessary to recognize the streak of fear and hysteria that ran through it and erupted periodically. As in the summer of 1960, when Shlomo Lahat returned to Israel from Columbia and reported back at IAF headquarters.

For Lahat, the visit to Weizman's office was a formality. After two years away he felt out of place at the IAF, and was ready for a new career. For Weizman, however, his arrival revived the demons of the Greens conspiracy to take away his command, and he now gave Lahat such a cold reception that "I was actually told I could not visit any of the bases," Lahat says.[1] As on the eve of his appointment two years earlier, Weizman was so skittish that when a rumor floated that Laskov "was about to meet with Ben-Gurion and tell him that my two years were up," he called Ben-Gurion in panic, and calmed down only when Ben-Gurion personally "assured me that he was satisfied with my performance and was not about to replace me."[2] Just to make sure, he banished Lahat to El Al to spend what remained of his IAF service as the airline's chief of operations.

Weizman's colleagues could do no more than shake their heads. "By 1960 Ezer was near the peak of his power and popularity. I cannot imagine anyone even thinking about replacing him," says

Shaya Gazit.³ But Weizman's anxiety was a steady state that kept his entire force on permanent edge. He worried endlessly about everybody and everything. Jacob Agasi, then commanding a Vautour squadron at Ramat David, recalls a worried telephone call from Weizman one night after a Vautour pilot on a reconnaissance mission behind Egyptian lines was slightly late reporting his whereabouts. His near-hysterical interference in air battles was legendary, stressing his pilots to a point where some switched off their radios, and others did not report getting into a dogfight for fear of being yanked out too soon.

His seemingly impulsive, capricious manner was misleading. "Ezer operated on gut instincts, and the remarkable thing was how often his instincts were right on the mark," recalls Aharon Yoeli, who served as chief of IAF Operations when Weizman took command. But that same intuitive decision-making, coupled with all-too-real impatience and anxiety, gave his command a sense of jerkiness and impetuosity. His aversion to all things technological, which bordered on know-nothingness, did not help. "Ezer's classic line was 'don't bother me with cosines.' He didn't want to deal with electronics or radar, or any technology that went beyond basic stick-and-throttle flying," recalls Yoash Tsiddon, who headed the IAF's advance research and development program under Weizman.⁴

His decision to spend more than $100 million on seventy-two Mirages—in effect mortgaging his offensive strength for the coming half-decade—was characteristic. However agile a dogfighter the Mirage was, staking everything on a single-seat, single-engine fighter, even one with rudimentary radar and missiles, reversed Tolkowsky's thoughtful reliance on a combination of fighters and twin-engine fighter-bombers, and collided with increased reservations in IAF ranks about the primacy of single-seat fighters. First, there was a matter of economics. In 1960, a new Mirage cost twice as much as a Vautour had two years earlier, and ten times more than a new Super-Mystère four years before that. It was now possible to buy an entire squadron of Super-Mystères or two squadrons of Ouragans for the price of a single Mirage. Scaling the Mirage purchase from three to two squadrons could have given the IAF from twenty to forty more squadrons of attack planes for the same money.

Second, the plane was still new, unproven, and plagued with

problems. In the first place, its guns seemed incapable of hitting anything. They worked well enough against friendly opponents—on July 19, 1963, two Mirage pilots used warning shots to force down an American Martin-built RB-57A spy plane, and then three more, two DC-6s and a B-26, to land at Lod[5]*—but not against MiGs. It took a while to figure out that the French had installed the guns with their shell trajectories spaced so far apart that the bullets actually flew on both sides of the small MiG without hitting. Even after the guns were shimmied closer together they still seemed useless—on August 20, 1963, two Mirages from Ramat David fired at eight Syrian MiG-17s but failed to shoot down a single one, and as late as March 3, 1965, six Mirages in a row tried to shoot down the same two Egyptian MiGs without success. Finally a couple of Mirage guns were removed, mounted on a stand, and fired at stationary ground targets. The problem turned out to be with the French ammunition, whose detonators "exploded several hundredths of a second too late, so the shells were actually going right through the target, and exploding several yards after coming out the other side," recalls Dani Shapira, who supervised the construction and delivery of the seventy-two Mirages.[6] "When we ordered new ammunition with near-instant detonators, the targets were blasted to pieces." Still, the fact is that not a single Mirage could claim a single MiG kill during Weizman's entire eight years in command of the IAF.

Worse yet, no less than seven Mirages crashed in mysterious circumstances during 1963—in each case the plane's engine suddenly died and could not be restarted, forcing the pilot to bail out. The mystery was solved by chance on October 11, when a hot young pilot named Ran Ronen, returning from a sensitive photo-reconnaissance mission over the Nile Delta, was coming in for a landing when his engine died. To avoid letting the plane loose above a

*American spy planes had been spotted over Israel earlier, but always beyond the range of the IAF's older planes. In March of 1959, Joe Alon was scrambled in a Super-Mystère after a high-flying object was reported over Israel. At 50,000 feet, the Super-Mystère's maximum altitude, he radioed that even at that altitude, he was still far below a plane which he described as a "huge glider." Once on the ground, he picked the plane out of a book as a Lockheed-built U-2, registered to the U.S. Weather Service. Only when U-2 pilot Gary Powers was shot down over the USSR a year later was the true nature of the spy plane revealed.

farming village near the base, Ronen stayed with it long enough to steer it to a nearby field, then raised its nose in a landing pose and bailed out at just 800 feet. Incredibly, his plane glided down and settled on the ground intact, its by-now empty long-distance fuel tanks cushioning the fall. The plane was ripped open and the problem turned out to be a weak fuel-pump shaft. "Once it broke under stress, the pump no longer worked, and any attempts to restart the engine were futile," says Dani Shapira. All IAF Mirages were immediately grounded for repair, and the problem vanished.

Yet to Weizman, not only was the plane not a lemon, but its dash and promise far transcended its shortcomings, which only tested the manhood of his knightly warriors. To Weizman, Ronen's rescue of the dead Mirage was no mere technical feat, just as the Mirage was not just a plane. Rather, both were taken as validation of the single-seat, single-combat warrior code. Signed "with appreciation and friendship," he penned and sent Ronen the following poem (wrapped around a whiskey bottle):

> If a Mirage engine dies in the air,
> and the plane is far from home,
> it must be a pilot superb and rare,
> to guide it down by his will alone.
>
> For Ran is a pilot of spirit steadfast,
> who gives all the time, all that he's got,
> to inspire, to guide, to lead to the last,
> even his plane, even after he has bailed out.
>
> In the so many years we've been flying,
> we have seen deeds and feats to no ends,
> but never such wonder, so help me, I'm not lying,
> when a plane without a pilot alone lands.
>
> For when fighter and man are bound so tight,
> it must be amply clear to all,
> that our Air Force pilots have all the guts,
> and the enemy—it has no chance at all.*

Weizman's mercurial rule also affected his relations with his commands. Here, too, he managed to personalize everything, every

*Translated from the Hebrew by the author.

single appointment and activity. Those who incurred his wrath were summarily disciplined, frozen out, or removed (although, as an old IAF comrade once said, "Weizman is the only man I know who can tell you to go to hell in a way that makes you look forward to the journey"). His favorites, on the other hand, received unquestioning backing. While entry to his inner circle was based on merit—at times it was a merit only Weizman's sensitive antennas could identify, which to others smacked of caprice.

Nowhere was this more apparent than in Weizman's total, long-standing, utterly mystifying devotion to Moti Hod. Short of his flying ability and complete loyalty to Weizman, even those closest to them had trouble noticing in Hod any of the brilliant dash that characterized so many others at the Weizman court. Weizman was aware of the criticism, but seemed incapable of countering it rationally. "I thought Moti was an uncut diamond," he would say many years later. "[While] others claimed he was not a diamond but a rock."[7]

In 1961, a near rebellion broke out within his senior command when he brought Hod from Hazor to IAF Operations—in effect giving him the inside track in the race for the next command of the IAF. The appointment was particularly condemned by the three commanders of the IAF's major air bases, Menahem Bar at Ramat David, Moshe Peled at Hazor, and Avraham Yoffe at Tel Nof (ironically, the same three *Palmach* veterans who rebelled against Weizman's attempt to make Hod succeed him in command of the 101 back in 1949). "I myself and several others in top positions did not think Moti Hod should become the next IAF commander," recalls Menahem Bar, who was then at the peak of his authority and power. "None of us base commanders thought Moti was suitable. We had many talks about it. People came all the way to Kfar Yehoshua and sat around my table talking. [I] personally did not think him intelligent enough. I thought him a limited man."[8]

The protest continued in the spring of 1962, when Weizman made Hod head of IAF Air Section—in effect Weizman's deputy. Weizman attempted to calm the base commanders by promoting them to full colonels at the same time he did Hod, but Bar's antennas went up when Weizman floated a plan to "choose and appoint deputies to each one of us. It was clear to me [that] once

Moti Hod had put in a year or two as head of Air Section, Weizman would replace us with our new deputies, get us out of the Air Force, and Moti would have no competition for command of the IAF because the new base commanders would be too young to say anything," says Bar. Weizman solved the problem with a character-istic mix of force and seduction—he made Hod head of IAF Air Section, scrapped his deputies-appointment scheme, and then sig-naled to Bar and Peled that they were next in the line of succession.

Another rebellious colonel, however, proved far harder to handle.

Shaya Gazit was born in 1925 at Zichron Abraham, a ramshackle pioneer outpost atop a small mound in Yizre'el Valley, a few hours' walking distance from what would later become Ramat David. Four years later, however, his father gave up the harsh life on the land, moved to Haifa, and built a successful taxicab fleet. Shaya joined the *Haganah* at thirteen, the Haifa Flight Club a few years later, and in the summer of 1948 began flight training in Czechoslovakia. Bright and energetic, he moved with Dani Shapira and Moti Hod to train on Messerschmitts and then Spitfires, and was deeply hurt when George Lichter passed him over and picked Hod and Shapira to ferry the first Spitfires to Israel. His bitterness was compounded when, after finishing the IAF's first flight course in the spring of 1949, Weizman picked Hod and Shapira to join the 101 squadron but left him a flight instructor.

"He always had a chip on his shoulder. He felt that he was being kept back, that he should be in charge of things," recalls Rudy Augarten, then commander of IAF Flight School.[9] After a few terms as flight instructor, and brief stretches in command of Spit-fire, Mosquito, and B-17 squadrons, Gazit served as head of plan-ning under Lahat before and during the Sinai campaign of 1956. His staff work was masterful, and earned him a citation for managing the Mystère-shuttle operation.

Tolkowsky, however, noticed something else behind Gazit's tem-pestuous manner. "He had the soul of an instructor. He could do other things, but he loved to teach, to work with young men who had to be coached and introduced to things. He also understood the significance of the written aspects of flight, such as manuals, flight procedures, the whats and hows and whys of doing things. This was very important in teaching, since it was imperative that we shaped people in the right mold at flight school," Tolkowsky says.[10] In July 1957, he appointed Gazit chief flight instructor at IAF Flight School. Putting up with Gazit's tantrums seemed a reasonable price to pay. "I was used to him getting into a spin every now and then, but I always thought he'd get out of it. Shlomo [Lahat] and I would help him get out of crisis. Shlomo in particular would sit with him for hours."

IAF Flight School suffered for years from lack of proper staff, resources, and attention. As late as the mid-1950s, it was still a jumble of training approaches and flying doctrines, and training was still conducted in English. The near mythic authority of the RAF hovered over everything, and matters were not helped when the best graduates were automatically sent to fly fighters. As fighter pilots would have rather retired than rotated back for even a brief tour of flight instruction. IAF Flight School became an elephants' burial ground for its instructors. A pilot assigned to "Siberia," as it was now called, knew it was time to call El Al about civilian career opportunities.

It was no wonder, then, that Gazit was infuriated at his new appointment. By 1957 "I had commanded a Spitfire OTU squadron, a Mosquito squadron for three tours, and twice a B-17 squadron. Twice I served as deputy base commander. By right I should have received a first-line squadron, if not a wing, to command," he recalls with bitterness undiminished by the intervening years. Since the IAF was about to receive the first Vautours, he determined to become commander of the first Vautour squadron. When Tolkowsky sent him to IAF Flight School instead, Gazit accused him of breaking a wartime promise to give him command of a fighter squadron, and handed in his resignation.

He was on a predischarge home leave in July when, on the day before his service formally ended, he was asked to be on hand during Tolkowsky's visit to IAF Flight School (formally, he was still chief flight instructor). Close to the end of the visit, Tolkowsky asked Gazit what he thought of the place. "I told him it was a piece of junk, a shell of a school, with instructors who did not want to instruct and morale so low it was lying on the ground," Gazit recalls. When Tolkowsky asked him to stick around, "I thought he was offering me a ride home, since we were neighbors. But then he told me to report to his office the next day, to receive command of the school. I told him I was being discharged the next day and looking forward to it, but he put . . . a guard on me, and started a telephone campaign to get [my wife] Zehava to talk me into staying."

The calls came all through the night, while Gazit stayed on base under guard. "The most touching call was from Chaim Laskov," recalls Zehava. "Chaim was then [IDF] chief of staff. I myself had served as an officer under him. It was Chaim who finally persuaded me to get Shaya to stay on. Remember, in those days we were idealists. The Air Force was our life."[11] The next morning, rumpled and unshaven, Gazit was brought before Tolkowsky, who said "You are now school commander. Do what you want." Gazit accepted.

It was, in retrospect, one of Tolkowsky's most brilliant appointments. It was also one of the riskiest, what with Gazit's explosive temper and the massive chip on his shoulder. While those under him, his commands or cadets, "had his complete loyalty and support," recalls Yoeli, "as far as Shaya was concerned, everyone above him was an idiot or a moron, and he constantly spouted fire and brimstone in their direction." To put Gazit in a position of shaping generations of future IAF pilots was if nothing else a supreme act of faith.

Gazit received his new appointment on a Friday. On Sunday morning, having worked straight through the weekend drafting plans and programs, he swept into Tel Nof, ordered the school closed for the day, and called the entire staff into the officers' club. There he presented them with a crash program for completing no less than eight separate flight courses that had backed up in the school pipeline. Joy rides in the school's Mustangs were over, and instructors had to log at least three flights per day with their cadets (he himself would do the same three flights before starting his routine command duties in the morning). "Whoever cannot stand the pace is out," he announced.

His major task, however, lay outside the school. "We had won the air war over Sinai, but then we lost the war for public opinion, for the hearts and minds of Israeli youth," Gazit says. In the eyes of service-bound young Israelis, the paratroopers were the IDF's true elite. The Air Force ranked so low that the summer 1957 flight course opened with only seventeen cadets (of whom just one received his wings two years later).[12] Gazit now drafted a letter that went out under Tolkowsky's signature to all high school graduates who scored high on their military aptitude tests, personally inviting them to join the IAF. The results were immediate and astounding. The fall 1957 course opened with an unprecedented eighty cadets, of whom equally unprecedented twenty-five became pilots.

That, however, created another problem. "In all of Israel, there were only so many high school graduates with the qualifications for being good officers. If you took all of them to flight school and waited to wash out those who did not measure up, there would be no officers in the Israeli army," Gazit says. To make sure he got first crack at the top candidates, he cut a deal with a former IAF officer at the IDF's manpower bureaucracy, to get "all those who qualified on the condition that those who could not cut it with us were returned to the IDF immediately." The IDF yielded on a second critical point. Until that time, IAF volunteers had to first go through basic IDF training in a catchall program with those designated to become truck drivers, cooks, or supply clerks. If they later washed out from flight training, their dismal basic training would render them unfit for joining any other elite unit. At Gazit's insistence, the new cadets were allowed to undergo basic training right at IAF Flight School at Tel Nof. Within a month, he weeded out half of them and sent them back to the IDF, and shipped out additional washouts four months later, and again after four months of rugged pre-flight training. His training proved so tough that soon elite IDF units began to compete for his rejects.

Less than a year after Gazit had taken command of the school, his cadets became the IAF's premier showcase. At the Independence Day parade of 1958, wearing white shoulder ribbons and hat bands, the flight school contingent won the IDF Chief of Staff Trophy as best marching unit—and they did it again in 1959 and 1960. As Weizman had by then taken command of the IAF and launched his "the best to the Air Force" drive, IAF recruitment rolls swelled.

Getting more cadets was only part of the task. Keeping them was another. "One day I received a letter from a teacher in Haifa, telling me that his son felt broken-hearted and hopeless after being washed out from flight school. Since he was blaming me, I called him up and invited him for a meeting. After I took him around the school, he told me that had he known the difficulties that his son faced he would not have aggravated them by putting additional demands and pressures on him [to succeed]. That gave me an idea. One weekend, I took the same buses that were supposed to take the cadets out for leave, and used them instead to bus their parents in to visit the base. We made a day of it. They toured the school, had lunch at the mess hall, and spent a few hours with their kids at their rooms and classes."

It proved a huge success, and Gazit made the parents part of their sons' training program by holding a regular "parents' day" for each flight-school class. Similarly, after a flight instructor "complained that he couldn't convince his wife where he was spending his nights and why he was so tired all the time . . . I started a similar 'instructor's wife day.' It helped."

Gazit also changed the IAF Flight School's "Siberia" image by refusing to accept new instructors who were not jet fighter pilots. Then, he demanded that two of his crack instructors be included in the new Super-Mystère squadron that Yak Nevo was putting together. The battle lasted for two months. Weizman refused to approve the instructors' change of assignment, but Gazit took up the matter with his old friend Laskov, then chief of IDF staff, and won after threatening to wreck the entire IAF Flight School over it. His victory instantly turned the school from an end-of-the-line assignment to a launching pad for choice frontline assignments.

The confrontation over the Super-Mystère appointments was only one round in a constant battle between Weizman, who demanded absolute obedience, and Gazit, who did not know the meaning of the word. Their first run-in took place in the spring of 1958, when Gazit was a year at Flight School and Weizman was still at IAF Air Section. When Gazit overheard Weizman reminding Laskov of Menahem Bar's overdue promotion to lieutenant colonel, he immediately turned to Tolkowsky and demanded a similar promotion. By the time he received it—before Bar—Weizman was in command of the IAF. He called Gazit in, threw his new rank insignia on the table and dismissed him with "take it, you don't deserve it." Furious, Gazit picked it up and left without thanking him or even saluting.

Their next clash came over a seemingly mundane matter of filing monthly progress reports. Gazit felt it was a waste of time, "especially since nobody was reading the reports," but Weizman insisted. Gazit filed one proper report, but the following month he peppered his report with "tomatoes" for flight cadets, "cucumbers" for riflemen, "onions" for airplanes, and so on. "I sent in the report, and—silence. Just as I thought, nobody was reading those things," he says.

The following month, he sent no report at all. When Weizman called to demand it, insisting that "I need it. I read it regularly," Gazit exploded. "I'll eat my hat if you read last month's report— but you will if you didn't," he shouted into the telephone. "How dare you say that?" Weizman yelled back. "Pull out last month's report, read it and tell me if you had read it already," Gazit said and hung up.

"In fifteen minutes I received a telephone call from Ezer's secretary, ordering me to headquarters. When I got there, she warned me to run away, and as soon as I opened his door he grabbed one of his ashtrays, a heavy thing made of an airplane's engine piston, and threw it at me. I closed the door in time and the piston nearly cracked it," Gazit recalls. Weizman gave in after a brief shouting match, and the report requirement was lifted.

But not for long. In early 1959, the IAF received new Fouga Magister jet trainers from France. Without consulting with any of his superiors, Gazit split the IAF Flight School right down the middle, dividing each course in two. While one half of each course followed the normal training program, the other half went through a drastically revised schedule—thirty-five instead of eighty flight hours in piston-driven Stearman trainers, 120 instead of 140 hours on Harvards, then on to flying jets for the rest of the course. "Until then, we used to train cadets to do aerobatics and night navigation on Stearmans. Shaya said it was nonsense. Nobody had to be a fighter pilot with a Stearman. He pushed, and he was absolutely right, to give only the basics on the Stearman, move quickly to Harvards, and get to jets as soon as was possible," recalls Eliezer "Cheetah" Cohen, one of Gazit's instructors at the time.[13]

At the end of a four-month cycle, the new program proved a major success. While graduates of both groups did equally well flying Meteors at operational training, the second group got to that point with sixty-five fewer flight-training hours. When he presented his findings at a meeting with his two superiors at IAF Training Command and with Avraham Yoffe, Tel Nof's new commander, the three protested that he had no authority to introduce such a change on his own. "It was no secret. By that time two hundred fifty men had already gone through the new program, not to mention instructors, mechanics, and clerks. Everybody knew," Gazit says.

His blunt and offensive manner, however, left his superiors no way of backing out gracefully, and they took up the matter with Weizman in an "either he goes or we go" manner. As Gazit refused to budge, Weizman himself was left no choice. "Shaya was a superb instructor and excellent pilot, [but] he had a few impossible traits. He knew everything better than anybody, and he had this terrible way of quarreling with everybody. Arrogant, too. It reached such a state that I thought he had to be slapped down," recalls Weizman.[14]

The following Thursday was an all-IAF battle day, when all flight instructors left to fly with their assigned combat squadrons. Suddenly, Weizman showed up at Tel Nof and ordered Gazit to gather all the cadets for an announcement. "He told me I was being thrown out. I said that I would gather the cadets, but that he was not going to make any speeches, because if he did I would, too. I said that if he tried to explain to the cadets why he was removing me, I would do my own explaining," says Gazit. When the cadets lined up at attention, Weizman said only that "for reasons I cannot go into" Gazit was ending his term as school commander. That day Gazit cleaned out his desk and went home.

Weizman kept him on ice for more than a year. "For weeks all I did was walk to the beach each morning, swim, walk all the way to IAF headquarters for a 10 A.M. snack, play tennis for an hour, and go home. Ezer had put out the word that whoever dared to even visit me would be kicked out. Those who came did so after dark, and we sat in the dark so they could not be seen from the outside. When I went looking for a civilian job, and was offered the post of chief pilot for Arkiah [Airlines], Ezer refused to release me, and he made the recruiters go away," Gazit says.

After six months a long thaw began. First he was reassigned to IAF Supplies Branch, then to a newly opened IDF computer school, then to Ethiopia as a military advisor. Finally, at the end of the year, Weizman not only brought him back in from the cold but appointed him head of IAF Training Command, which meant that he was now in charge of not just IAF Flight School, but every squadron's training program.

He plunged into his new post with the same furious energy he had brought earlier to IAF Flight School. Getting up before dawn each day, he'd check the weather and check with each base for any problems before allowing the day's training flights to begin. Each month, he gathered all squadron commanders to compare notes— each time at another squadron—and those gatherings raised inter-squadron competition to ever higher levels. Using his recently acquired computer skills, he also computerized the entire training system, down to the smallest detail of the entire career path of every IAF pilot. What Menahem Bar did to his Spitfire squadron ten years earlier with his primitive "performance boards," Gazit now did to the entire IAF with his computer. Here, too, performance was everything. Once a fighter pilot, always a fighter pilot may have been the rule at most other air forces, but at the IAF one was always on probation. High-scoring pilots—and squadrons—won praise and citations. Everyone else was on notice. A Mystère pilot who failed to meet Gazit's training goals was bumped down to fly Ouragans or Meteors—or even transports. There was no substitute for performance.

By the early 1960s, having reined in his rebellious colonels and placed his old Air Force North crowd in most key positions—Moti Hod ran IAF Air Section, Yoash Tsiddon IAF Technical Requirements, Yak Nevo IAF Operations, Ze'ev Liron IAF Intelligence, Menachem Bar was in command of Tel Nof and Beni Peled of Hazor—Weizman turned his attention to the challenge that had haunted him since Israel's forced withdrawal from the Sinai six years earlier, the next war with the Arabs. Although his eight years in command of the IAF would be the longest peaceful stretch in the state's first half century, Weizman was convinced that a war was coming, and that its outcome was entirely in his hands.

In the spring of 1963, he called Yak Nevo, the IAF's chief of operations, to his office and, as Nevo remembered the occasion, instructed him to produce a plan for "achieving air superiority through massive deployment of the IAF," which Nevo took to mean destroying the Arab air forces on the ground.

The idea, on which Weizman did not elaborate, was not new. The Italian air-war visionary general Giulio Douhet had thought it out forty years earlier, and during World War II the Luftwaffe used it with deadly effectiveness on June 22, 1941, destroying much of the Soviet air force on the ground at the opening of Operation Barbarosa. The same idea underlay Aharon Remez's wish to use his Czech Knives to surprise the Egyptian Spitfire squadron on the tarmac at El 'Arīsh, and Tolkowsky's plan to disable the Egyptian Air Force on the eve of the 1956 Sinai campaign.

Appointing Nevo, the IAF's premier single-combat gunfighter, to design what was essentially a massive bombing operation seemed neither logical nor workable. As anybody who had ever flown with him could attest to, the only MiGs Yak Nevo found worthy of his attention were those that came straight at him in the air or, better yet, tried to sneak up on his tail.

Here, too, all Weizman could offer to justify his assignment, aside from the fact that Nevo was in charge of IAF Operations, was a feeling that he was putting the right man in the right place.

Chapter 15

MOKED

Yak Nevo was born into a farming family within sight of Ramat David, when it was still an RAF base, but he never gave flying a thought until an army recruiter in 1950 offhandedly suggested that he try the Air Force. Once in flight school, however, he found his destiny, and when he joined Menahem Bar's Spitfire squadron at Ramat David he proved so outstanding that in spite of his limited experience Bar included him in the handful of pilots that made up the first fighter-jet squadron.

It was shortly after he began to fly Meteors at Bar's 117 squadron that he glimpsed the first of what he would later describe as a series of "portholes," small openings in his awareness which, once poked into, turned into endlessly twisting and turning "tunnels" through which his imagination hurtled on exploration quests. It happened when a squadron member boasted of having pulled an illegal "outside turn" with his Meteor. Nevo had never tried such a turn before, but he now "thought and thought about it, and I decided to carry it all the way through by doing a complete inverted loop." Without telling anyone, "I took a plane up, got it to a speed of 300–400 knots, then flipped it on its back and pushed the stick to go up."[1]

His brief description does not begin to describe the sheer insanity of his attempt. Normally, a pilot who wants to climb up from straight and level flying pulls his stick back, which lowers the plane's tail and raises its nose. As the plane climbs, it traces an arch running forward and upward with—and this is critical—the pilot's head pointing toward the center of the arch. The effect is similar to that of a child being swung by his hands—the centrifugal forces pull his blood away from his brain toward his feet. If the turn is fast or tight enough, the pilot's brain may lose so much blood that he blacks out. The condition, however, is reversible—the moment the turn eases, the blood surges back to the brain and the pilot recovers.

To do his outside curve, however, Nevo started out flying upside down, which meant that in order to go up he had to push his stick forward. While this made his tail point downward and his nose up, this time Nevo's head was on the outside of the curve that his plane traced as it went up. To use the child analogy, he was being swung by his feet, with the centripetal forces causing the blood to rush into his head, not away from it. Indeed, within seconds his eardrums and eyes felt ready to pop out, and his head to burst. He had to stop. "It was terrible. The plane didn't seem to be doing what it was supposed to," he recalls.

Instead of quitting, however, he tried it again and again until he figured a speed-radius combination that allowed him to make a complete loop without passing out. "The trick was to make it to the top of the loop without losing speed, and then to come down to complete it without spinning in. It was a senseless maneuver but that, in a way, was its own sense. I had to try everything." When he made it back to base, his plane's wings had begun to bend under the strain.

More than ordinary fighter pilot aggressiveness, Nevo's penchant for taking chances stemmed from a philosopher's passion for knowledge and order. "Most of [the other pilots] did not even see the porthole, and those who did never looked beyond the opening into the tunnel," Nevo would say later. "But once I was inside a tunnel it immediately became *my* tunnel. I could not leave one inch of it undiscovered and unexplored."

His philosopher's sensibilities were also offended at the way "each pilot guarded his bag of tricks. It was a double sin. First, by keeping quiet you could not explain to yourself what you did so you could do it better. Second, you did not share your experience with the others. It was the coming together of these two limitations, the plane's engineering and the pilot's psyche, that drove me to seek the ultimate truth of fighter flying." Through long nights, pad in hand, he began to plot out the mysteries of dogfighting, drawing "energy curves" and "optimum turns," vertical and horizontal thrusts and barrel rolls. Without access to fighter-tactics texts from other armies, he relied on his uncanny ability to imagine—and remember—lengthy three-dimensional scenarios. He could work out entire air battles in his mind's eye, break them down to their most basic components and write them down, where others could only gesture lamely with their hands.

Slim and pixyish, with a passing resemblance to the American film actor Joel Grey, Nevo was solitary, humorless, and—in the air—relentless. By the time Beni Peled picked him for his "French team" to ferry Ouragans and Mystères to Israel, Nevo had become the IAF's premier theorist and practitioner of the dogfighting arts. His stream-of-consciousness talks about "the rationality of the irrational," or his description of dogfighting as "identifying two elements that have nothing to do with each other and then linking them together," would have been dismissed as senseless ramblings were it not for his awesome ability to make them come deadly real in the air.

Characteristically, he followed his dogfighting "tunnel" to the end. In the fall of 1956, while developing air-combat tactics for the Mystère, Nevo came up with a milestone maneuver that he awkwardly named "to let him pass you," and then edited down to "let him pass." It consisted of two parts. First, with the enemy on one's tail, "you suddenly stop—you brake hard, shut your engine, drop your air brakes, whatever—and in a fraction of a second he overshoots you and you are behind him. The genius has not been born yet who can respond to it in time." Second, to avoid losing sight of his opponent and risking another surprise, Nevo worked out a way of going into a barrel roll that not only let him keep his opponent in view, but neatly brought him right onto his tail.

Although essentially defensive, in Nevo's hands "let him pass" became deadly offensive. Nevo had so perfected the last-resort maneuver that having the enemy on his tail had become his preferred starting point for the dogfight. The maneuver was risky and, in Nevo's aggressive hands, controversial. "Yak was lucky that the pilot behind him was not another Yak," Yoeli would say later.[2] Nevo, however, argued that modern jets were so short of fuel that opposing pilots more often than not simply wasted their entire fuel supply flying in circles around each other without ever getting into a shooting position. "Instead of trying to get on the enemy's tail the long way around, I just let him get on my tail first, technically and psychologically. I could almost feel the guy behind me getting happy as he came closer to my tail and set his gunsights."

The 1956 Sinai war enabled him to put his new maneuver to the test. Although he shot down two Egyptian MiGs, it was a dogfight in which he scored no hits that brought him the most satisfaction. He was flying toward the Mitla Pass when he spotted three MiGs below. Ordering his wingman to cover him from above but to stay out of the fighting, he took on the MiGs by himself. "I didn't shoot anyone, but the thing was, I was totally relaxed. A MiG got on my tail, I let it pass. Another came in, the same thing happened. For something like ten minutes I was down there, no kills but constant easy, smooth escape from one after the other. The maneuver worked."

To those who knew him, the image of Yak Nevo tangling alone with three MiGs in enemy skies and angrily rejecting assistance was characteristic. One could easily imagine him stooped over his controls, his heavy-browed eyes coolly looking back, his heavy farmer's hands deftly manipulating stick and throttle to flick MiGs off his tail with the ease of a horse shaking away flies. "He took more risks in his life than anybody, in an incredible combination of bravery and recklessness," one of his squadron members would say later. Moti Hod would call him the poet of the dogfight.

In early 1957, after Nevo wrote a seventy-seven-page dogfighting manual titled "Air Combat," Tolkowsky sent him to France to evaluate the Super-Mystère. "It was love at first sight," Nevo would later recall. "To put on an afterburner [which] had you at 40,000 feet in four minutes . . . all you could do was just sit there and tell yourself 'This is *the* plane.' " He recommended buying the plane. In fact, he figured that if, contrary to French doctrine, he could rig

the Super-Mystère with large 1,300-liter wing tanks normally used
for ferrying, instead of the small 625-liter combat tanks, "the
Super-Mystère could have an attack-mission range like that of the
Vautour or greater—and it still could strafe and dogfight its way in
and out without fighter escort." When the first Super-Mystères
arrived in 1959, he commanded the new Super-Mystère squadron.
By then, his yellow-bound, mimeographed dogfighting manual had
been published and distributed throughout the IAF, making him at
once the IAF's unchallenged dogfighting theorist and practitioner.[3]
"I didn't have the patience to read through the whole book, so I
asked Yak to just show me what this new doctrine was all about,"
recalls Moti Hod. "We went up in two Super-Mystères, and before
I knew what was happening he nearly put me in a spin. When we
came down I told him that if he could do it to me, then he really
had something there."[4]

While Nevo was exploring his next "tunnel," his persistence
nearly torpedoed his Air Force career. It happened when, in 1960,
he entered IAF Staff College and pursued a research topic that soon
sent shock waves through the force. "All I did was take a good look
at the Air Force's three basic missions. It was obvious right from the
start that two of them—reaching air superiority by destroying
enemy air forces on the ground, and assisting the IDF in the ground
war—were essentially air-ground missions. The third mission, defending the nation's skies, did require actual interception and dogfighting, but it was mostly a peacetime mission, aimed at deterring
the enemy from starting a war. At war, it was the air-ground activity
that mattered most," he would later say.[5]

On November 8, 1961, he completed and circulated through the
IAF high command a paper in which he calculated that "ninety-five
percent of the air activity in any future war . . . would be in tactical
[air-ground] missions—like attacking airfields or providing close
support to the ground forces."[6] On the other hand, "even if the
enemy managed a first strike, dogfighting and interception would
constitute no more than five percent of the Air Force's total activity."

If his diminution of the knightly dogfighting pursuit in the
scheme of things seemed heretic, his next conclusion amounted to
downright treason. Instead of the one hundred Mirages which Weiz-

man was just then pushing for, Nevo argued that the IAF should buy no more than one or two squadrons, and use the rest of its scarce funds to buy hundreds of older and cheaper World War II attack planes. The Martin-built B-26 Marauder, a twin-prop attack bomber, could probably become "the cheapest . . . and most effective plane for this mission, *with no inherent disadvantage compared to the more 'modern' planes"* [emphasis in the original], he wrote.

His reasoning was compelling. Since to carry bombs to a ground target both a Mirage and a B-26 would have to travel at low altitude and at roughly the same 300 to 400 knots, the Mirage's ability to fly at Mach 2 was meaningless and both planes would be equally vulnerable to enemy fighters and ground fire. But while the Mirage would soon run out of fuel, the slower B-26 with its enormous fuel supply could dodge enemy fighters long enough for the MiGs themselves to run out of fuel and head for home—and it would still have enough fuel left to carry out its primary missions.

Weizman was mortified. Nevo's thesis not only challenged his single-seat, single-engine fighter supremacy but played right into the hands of the Greens, who opposed the Mirage deal altogether. But here, too, he seemed unable to dispute Nevo's thesis by arguing to its points. All he could do was personalize the issue by turning on Nevo as ferociously as he had on Mosquito sympathizers back in his Ramat David days. "Yak went off his track," he said recently. "B-26s? It was crazy."[7] In reality, Nevo did seem to overshoot a turn or two in his wild exploration of this new thesis, and just as Weizman felt, carried a reasonable argument to an unreasonable end. Sacrificing one Mirage squadron for ten Super-Mystère squadrons was one thing, but going for large numbers of old prop-driven planes went against the lessons of the 1956 war, in which World War II–era planes were so devastated by Egyptian antiaircraft fire it was obvious they had reached the end of their usefulness. Because of Weizman's inability to put up a counter-thesis, however, the Greens adapted Nevo's thesis *in toto,* and it was only because of Laskov's retirement that Weizman received his three Mirage squadrons.

It was this lone gunfighter—in his air combat manual, Nevo even advocated doing away with the traditional notion of having dogfighting team members cover and watch out for each other in the air, arguing instead that he fights best who fights alone—whom Weizman picked to plan what would become the IAF's most important and complex operational plan to date. Nevo, in turn, picked a junior planner at IAF Operations to help him put his ideas into a form that others could follow. "Yak had trouble making people understand him. Sometimes squadron commanders would come to me to find out what he meant," Rafi Sivron recalls. "He used to complain that in all of the Israeli Air Force, the only two people who understood him were me and Giora Furman, and Furman was then just a Mirage pilot."[8]

Tall and slim, with a striking resemblance to movie actor Akim Tamiroff, Sivron was not even a pilot. Since joining the IAF in 1954 he served as Mosquito navigator and then as assistant helicopter pilot, dropping paratroopers off on clandestine desert-warfare missions, and then picking them up in pitch-darkness. In 1962, he was attending a two-week NATO school on antisubmarine warfare when he met Nevo. "Yak apparently noticed me, because a week after returning to my helicopter squadron I received a telephone call that I was wanted at IAF Operations."

As they started to work on the new plan, Nevo and Sivron quickly discovered that previous airfield strike plans offered little to go on. Generally, all those plans called for squadrons from Ramat David to handle Arab airfields in Syria and Iraq, while the southern bases of Hazor and Tel Nof would dispatch planes against Egypt and Jordan. In all past plans, each squadron had been assigned specific airfields, with some pilots slated to take out control towers, others to strafe airplanes on the tarmac, and still others to blow up supply and ammunition depots. But such Indian-style attacks were more form than substance. There were not enough planes to hit all enemy air bases, and it would take more to put an airfield out of action than blowing up its tower and setting a few planes on fire. So long as their frontline airfields were not actually destroyed, Egypt and Syria could easily bring more planes forward from their rear bases in the Nile Valley or close to the Iraq border.

By 1960, IAF planners had begun to think about destroying the runways first. This would trap undamaged planes on the ground for destruction in a later strike, prevent those that took off from landing, and make it impossible for new planes to be brought in from rear bases. But the broad, massively built concrete runways were not so easy to destroy. Traditional cast-iron bombs would mostly roll or bounce off them. Aharon Yoeli, who preceded Nevo at IAF Operations, had tried using rockets, instead, in the hope that more of them would hit the runways and that "for the enemy, repairing twenty smaller holes would be more difficult than plugging up two big ones."[9] But that scheme, too, failed, as did an attempt to use gunfire (which only pockmarked the concrete strips ineffectually).

Until that problem was solved, there was little Nevo and Sivron could do in the way of planning. Before they could start assembling attack teams and plotting attack routes, they had to first figure out what the attacking planes would do once they got to their targets—what kind of bombs, how big, how many?

Next, there was the matter of getting the bombs to their targets. Could the planes he had make it there? Manufacturers' manuals proved useless in projecting effective ranges. Changing a plane's load from two to six bombs changed the air drag, and therefore the rate at which fuel was guzzled. And since the only way the planes could reach their targets unseen was by slithering close to the desert floor or body-surfing on the Mediterranean's waters, the heavier and denser air close to the surface also increased the drag and fuel consumption. Entire specification charts had to be scrapped and rewritten. For weeks, Ouragans, Mystères, Mirages, and Vautours were loaded to new configurations, then flown and monitored at the same speed, weather, and terrain conditions they would encounter in an actual mission. To duplicate the Sinai's vast distances, Nevo and Sivron had the planes fly low up and down the country at all hours, or out to sea and back and out again, until each plane's new performance data could be gathered, calculated and recalculated, verified and reverified.

At the same time, under a stream of mission specification memos from Nevo at IAF Operations, Shaya Gazit's IAF Training Command moved precision bombing to the top of the squadrons' training schedules. An old gunnery range in the Negco was updated with movable flags substituting for planes and mobile structures. Instead of swooping down Indian-style, guns blasting, pilots learned to zigzag across the field and gun down targets where and when they cropped up.

While Gazit's Training Command was busy issuing training

manuals on hitting ground targets, Israel's entire intelligence machinery was mobilized to accumulate Arab airfield data on a scale never before attempted. Through the early 1960s, Israeli agents and informants penetrated virtually every Arab air base and command post, producing a dizzying flood of data that ranged from the location, direction, and makeup of every single runway and the planes that used it to names and biographies of officers and pilots, their eating habits, even the state of their vehicles. Also, since the Egyptians had honeycombed the Sinai with observation posts, the only way to reach Egypt without notice was over the Mediterranean toward the Nile Delta—but only if Liron's intelligence spooks could determine the power and range of the two Soviet-built radar stations at El 'Arīsh (Weizman refused to send fighters to test the radar's range and response). They did.

Plugging the data into his charts, Sivron could calculate the number of runways that had to be damaged and the points at which each runway had to be hit to render it inoperable. That in turn dictated how many bombs—and therefore how many planes—had to be detailed to each field. The vague outline of a plan was finally taking shape.

"It got to be like an abstract three- or four-dimensional puzzle, a game," recalls Sivron. "For some strange reason, I did not even have the feeling that this plan would ever be carried out. If I did, it would have made me uneasy. Strange as it may sound, I just wanted to build something perfect, to get a grade of 100,000 percent. It was almost an academic exercise."[10]

By late 1964, the puzzle was coming together, and it was in this coming together that Yak Nevo, hurtling alone down his newest "tunnel," came up with an innovation that for the first time since its establishment truly pulled the entire IAF together and turned it from an assembly of flying frontier militias into a modern, coordinated juggernaut. What Nevo's little yellow booklet once did for dogfighting, now his thin, blue-covered airfield-attack master plan did for the entire force. Like the dogfighting manual, the new document was deceptively simple. In fact, its main body was so sparse it was almost useless in itself. One section tersely provided the background scenario—say, an impending war with Egypt (there were several scenarios, including separate or combined wars against

Egypt, Syria, and Jordan, as well as a defensive war in which Israel was attacked by surprise). Another section just as tersely described the mission goal—achieving air superiority by attacking airfields and destroying runways. A third section briefly listed the airfields to be attacked, at what time and with what strength.

"The first and second sections were really of interest only to the defense minister. The third section was for the IDF chief of staff. For those carrying out the mission the meat was in the appendices," recalls Sivron. It was there, in the half-dozen massive appendices, that Nevo's flare for the big picture and Sivron's passion for detail had found their expression. Dealing, in that order, with logistics, air control, forces and missions, intelligence and rescue, the appendices contained everything that could conceivably be required for the operation to succeed. And—this was where Nevo's organizational genius really clicked—each appendix meshed with a corresponding branch of the IAF Air Section. "Forces and Missions" corresponded to Nevo's own IAF Operations, "Intelligence" to Ze'ev Liron's IAF Intelligence, and so on.

This linkage was crucial. Once completed, the attack plan could be locked up in a safe for months or years—and then it had to be put into action within twenty-four hours. By that time, every single assumption on which it was based would have changed—enemy forces were moved, new enemy airfields built, the IAF might have newer planes or squadrons. Certainly radio frequencies or navigational routes might have become unusable. But with each appendix falling within the purview of a specific Air Section branch, each branch could keep it constantly updated. Liron's intelligence staff, for example, would periodically plug new revelations of enemy capabilities or deployment into the proper page. IAF Supplies would make sure that enough fuel, ordnance, and equipment was always on hand for instant deployment.

Through these appendices, the entire IAF was now linked together into one mission plan. At IAF Training Command, training routines and performance levels were updated to ensure the plan's success—precision bombing, low-level navigation, takeoffs and landings in total radio silence. At IAF Operations, Nevo and Sivron designed "battle days" simulating major components of their new plan. At Yoash Tsiddon's IAF Technical Requirements, new bombs that could propel themselves onto a runway before going off were being designed and guided into production.

The plan did not necessarily imply victory. The IAF did not have enough planes and pilots to guarantee that. When Tsiddon ran computer simulations of several versions of the operation on his computers, he concluded that even "without accidents or mistakes—in other words, under far better conditions than can be realistically expected"—a first-wave attack against fourteen designated airfields with three or more runways each had below-average chances of destroying even one-third of the targets. Achieving "a 90 percent certainty of success" required 530 planes—200 more than the IAF had. While the IAF might achieve air superiority in forty-eight hours with its existing force—if it struck first with complete surprise—it would be devastated in the process.[11]

By 1965, Tsiddon's reservations notwithstanding, the new plan was completed, printed up, and circulated to all bases and squadrons. The mission order Weizman handed Nevo two years earlier had been carried out. His entire Air Force was now training, practicing, gathering intelligence, and drafting acquisition plans with just one goal in mind—surprising the enemy on the ground and demolishing its air power before it could respond. Now the plan even had a name, *Moked*, Hebrew for focus, convergence point—or sacrificial fire.

Only one part of the puzzle remained missing—the time of the attack. Considering intelligence, meteorological, and psychological data, Nevo and Sivron had agreed on 8:00 A.M. as the ideal strike time. It would allow IAF planes to take off after the morning fogs lifted from their bases, and to reach their targets at a time when the Arab dawn patrols had returned home and the general alert was relaxed. By that time, too, the winds would stabilize over the targets and reduce the chance of bombs being blown away from their course. But when the draft plan reached Weizman, Sivron says, "it came back to us with this section crossed out hard, and near it written 'first light.' Ezer was still playing the gentlemanly, knightly British pilot. He also opposed us using time-delay bomb detonators because that would be 'dirty pool.' He said the Israeli Air Force always struck at dawn, and he ordered me to change the plan accordingly." Sivron refused, and at the end the plan was completed and printed with the notation "zero hour to be announced separately."*

By the time *Moked* was completed, Weizman had put in seven years as commander of the IAF. He had already held the post longer than any of his predecessors, and pressures were mounting—especially from the Greens—for his replacement. In fact, shortly after becoming IDF chief of staff in 1964, Yitzhak Rabin actually called Weizman's old rival Shlomo Lahat for a private meeting at his home. "He told me he was having problems with Ezer's replacement, and asked me if I would return to active duty in order to take his place," recalls Lahat, who says he advised Rabin that bringing him back after so many years out of service "would be a mistake."[12] While the pressures were nothing like those faced by his predecessors, Laskov and Tolkowsky—Weizman was offered a senior post at the IDF high command once he left the IAF—he could not put the matter off indefinitely. But getting his designated successor in place would turn out to be his longest and toughest battle yet.

---

*Weizman denies ever advocating a dawn strike. "Quite the opposite, I objected to striking at dawn because that meant taking off in the dark and joining up in the dark. . . . As a pilot who did not like to fly at night I was deathly afraid of dawn attacks," he said recently. But Weizman does not remember discussing an 8:00 A.M. strike time except by saying that "the whole world expects us to strike at dawn, so we must look for another H hour." Nevo does not recall the specific discussions, but notes that the 8:00 A.M. time frame was "definitely within the spirit of the plan," while "the convention at the IAF at the time was to attack at first light."

Chapter 16

THE FRONTIERSMAN

David and Dinah Eisenberg were among a dozen families of religious Lithuanian Jews who in 1883 settled in the swampy lowlands of the Hula Valley, between Galilee's limestone hills to the west and the brooding black basalt of the Golan Heights to the east. Plagued by malaria, isolation, and marauding Bedouins, they clung to their land and proliferated. One of their daughters, Yocheved, married her neighbor Chaim-Moshe Fine and moved twenty miles north to the frontier village of Metulla, along what is now the Lebanese border. There, on a reed floor mat in a windowless adobe cabin, with a Lebanese midwife for comfort, she bore her husband thirteen children, eleven of whom lived and, working the land from an early age alongside the local Arabs, grew up dark, rugged, and adventurous.

Joseph, the fourth of Yocheved's brood, curly-haired and powerfully built, left home at seventeen and put his frontier skills and fluent Arabic to use as a mounted ranger guarding the orange groves south of Tel Aviv. In 1924, a group of young settlers asked him to pick up their newest member at a remote railroad stop in the Judean Hills. Menucha, the new settler who had just arrived from Poland, would recall stepping off the train into a lightning storm, pouring rain, and a small crowd of Arab villagers. Suddenly a tall man on horseback rode up, helped her onto a second horse he led behind, then guided her through the dark and mysterious hill country to the safety of her new village. The mountain man and the Socialist immigrant girl soon married, moved back to Galilee and settled at *Kibbutz* Degania, where the Jordan River flows out of the Sea of Galilee. In the summer of 1926, Fine loaded Menucha on a horse cart and drove her to a field hospital in the Bet She'an Valley, where she uneventfully gave birth to a son whom they named Mordechai—Moti for short—and took home by train.

Tall, dark, and possessing all of his father's frontier moxie, Moti joined the British army at seventeen, and when the war ended stayed on in Europe to run Jewish refugees into Palestine. In 1948, after serving a brief jail sentence in Italy for smuggling a planeload of Jewish children out of the country, he talked himself into the IAF's first flight school in Czechoslovakia. George Lichter would remember him as shy and quiet, with flashes of unexpected assurance and perception. At a Czech hotel one evening, Lichter recalls, he admonished the young Israelis for eating non-kosher food. "What kind of Jews are you?" he asked in mock exasperation. "That's the difference between us," Moti replied. "When people ask you what you are, you have to think—'Do they mean me as an individual, or me as a Jew, or me as an American?' I don't have such problems. I am an Israeli. I don't have to prove anything."[1]

He never forgot his frontier roots. In the early 1950s, under pressure to adopt a more Hebrew-sounding family name, he changed it to Hod but continued to sign his name Moti Fine. Even after Weizman talked his *kibbutz* into letting him sign on for a few more years of flying, he still felt that he'd soon be going back to work the land. Neither he nor most of those around him ever thought of him advancing beyond, say, the command of a squadron. He showed none of the brilliant organizational talent of Menahem Bar, the technical mastery of Beni Peled, or the meticulous staff work of Shaya Gazit. "Not bright but very practical. Could not be sidetracked. Could separate substance from trivia," was all Menahem Bar would say about him.[2]

Only Ezer Weizman saw the third-generation frontiersman as the embodiment of the ideal new Israeli airman—steady, bold, infinitely resourceful. Weizman pushed him up through the ranks even as Hod kept talking about returning to the land (Weizman was less successful in running Hod's personal life; when Hod struck up a romance with a vivacious, black-haired and blue-eyed squadron secretary named Pninah, Weizman urged him to hold out for "someone from a better family," but Hod ignored the advice and married the girl).

It was easy to misinterpret the friendship that blossomed between the spoiled heir of Melchett Street and the Galilee frontiersman, so little did they seem to have in common except for being tall and fond of whiskey. They were such an odd and unlikely pair, striding Ramat David's tarmacs like Don Quixote and Sancho Panza, with Hod always bringing up the rear. It seemed natural to dismiss Hod as a political flunky who "just hitched his wagon to a rising star," as a pilot from those days recently commented.

Only few recognized that "there really was between them an incredible harmony, a chemistry. In a very special way, they complemented each other—Ezer with his high-flying ideas and Moti with his down-to-earth solutions, Ezer thinking ahead, while Moti checks his step and keeps him from jumping too far," recalls Aharon Yoeli, one of Ramat David's leading pilots at the time.[3] So large did Weizman loom over Hod that it was only on the rare occasions when they were apart that Hod seemed to come into his own. When he did, many did a double take. "He had hid in Ezer's shadow all those years, [so] he was first revealed to me only when he received command of the Ouragan squadron," recalls Dan Tolkowsky. "He was an excellent squadron commander [with] incredible common sense . . . on the ground or in the air."[4] Tolkowsky was impressed enough to let Hod succeed Weizman as commander of Hazor.

When Weizman took command of the IAF and made Hod his chief of operations, and then second-in-command as head of IAF Air Section, Hod seemed to wilt again into Weizman's shadow. Although Weizman to this day insists that Hod sat in on all his important decisions, the fact is that Weizman's greatest accomplishments in office were achieved with little or no apparent input from Hod. Gazit dealt directly with Weizman while revolutionizing the IAF Training Command. So did Nevo and Sivron while developing the *Moked* strike plan, and Dani Shapira in managing the selection and delivery of the Mirages from France. Although as chief of IAF Air Section, Hod was their superior, few remember him as even being there. On the rare occasions when he did get involved in discussions, the very pragmatism and earthy resourcefulness that was so effective in the field now made him seem shallow, uneducated, and outclassed.

To the IDF brass, too, Weizman's constant promotion of Hod as his only acceptable successor seemed puzzling, if not underhanded. Late in 1963, toward the end of his fifth year in command, Weizman was offered the post of deputy to the IDF chief of staff if he passed the IAF command to a candidate more agreeable to the Greens. He refused "as long as they did not reach an understanding with me about Moti," which led the Greens to suspect him of wanting to make sure he continued to run the IAF even after ostensibly leaving it. Weizman stuck to his guns through no less than six face-to-face meetings with Prime Minister Eshkol, and countless confrontations with the IDF high command, all of whom refused to accept Hod as his successor.

It was the longest and toughest battle of his career, and in retrospect the most important. "My wish to have Moti succeed me is not a caprice and does not stem from any personal debt to him. I think I am entitled to decide what's good for the Air Force, and I know that it would be better if Moti received the command. I do want to become chief of IDF staff someday, but the fortunes of the Air Force after my departure are more important to me than my own personal fortunes," he remembers arguing.[5] When Eshkol suggested that Hod needed more education, Weizman retorted that "he may not be able to quote Bialik or Shakespeare, but he will screw the Arabs in plain Hebrew and without much sophistication."[6]

It took three more years, until April 27, 1966, before Weizman finally got his way. In an emotional ceremony at Tel Nof, he said good-bye to each and every one of the assembled men before formally passing the IAF command to Hod. He then climbed into his Black Spit, did a victory roll over the field, and flew off to his new post at IDF command. The gathered assembly watched his departure with sadness and some trepidation. After eight years at the controls, the tall, long-striding swashbuckler—dubbed "jet pilot" by adoring press and public—personified the dash and glamour of the force. "The best to the Air Force," his recruitment slogan, had fired up Israel's youth until many more candidates were volunteering for IAF flight training every year than could be accepted. To many in and out of the IAF, he was inseparable from what he called "my force, my pilots, my planes." So cataclysmic seemed his departure that Hod appeared to be bobbing helplessly in his wake—unknown, untested, and unimpressive.

No matter, the talk went. Weizman would always be running the IAF, no matter where he was.

So it came as a shock that, after less than four months in command, Hod not only held his own but surpassed his legendary predecessor by the one yardstick that, to a veteran fighter jock like Weizman, truly mattered—killing MiGs.

On the face of it, this was a direct result of Syria's escalation of the northern water wars. Israel's completion in 1964 of a massive aqueduct to carry water from the Sea of Galilee to the arid south gave the Arabs a handy jugular, which Syria and then Lebanon sought to squeeze by diverting the sources of the Jordan River into a new canal that would carry the water south through Syria and dump it back into the Jordan River south of the Sea of Galilee, in Jordanian-held territory. Had the scheme worked, both the Jordan River and the Sea of Galilee would have dried up, and Israel would have been cut off from its only significant water source.

For two years, the IDF held them off by slowing and disrupting the Syrian works with limited tank and artillery fire. In the fall of 1965, however, the Syrians moved the diversion route deeper into their territory, beyond the range of the Israeli artillery. It was a calculated political gamble. To keep disrupting the work, Israel would have to call in the IAF. But the use of air power would turn what was formally only a minor border dispute into a fighting war, which Syria did not think was a risk Israel would take. On July 14, 1966, however, when the Syrians escalated both their water-diversion efforts and their shelling of Israeli settlements along the border, the IAF was called in. For an entire afternoon, Israeli Mystères, Super-Mystères, and Vautours bombed Syrian positions along the Golan Heights. It was during the bombing that a 101 squadron pilot named Yoram Agmon spotted two MiG-21s heading toward the Sea of Galilee, rolled his Mirage in after one of them and shot off its right wing. The MiG went into a spin and crashed into the ground.

The aerial strike, the first for the IAF in many years, and the air kill—the first downing of a MiG-21 by a Mirage—were just the start. A month later, when an Israeli navy boat was attacked in the Sea of Galilee by Syrian artillery and aircraft, Israeli planes again demolished Syrian gun positions in the area, and an Israeli Mirage shot down a second Syrian MiG-21. Three months later, during a massive IDF operation against Palestinian terrorists in the West Bank area, Squadron 191's commander Ran Ronen downed a Jordanian Hunter in a dramatic eight-minute battle. Two weeks after that, another Mirage pilot shot down two Egyptian MiG-17s in one pass, one from 2,000 yards with a missile, the other from 400 yards with guns.

This made five MiG kills before Hod's first year on the job was out. "You could hear Weizman's groans and wails all the way to Hazor," recalls an ex-pilot. "Suddenly he was not needed anymore."

What made all this significant was that the MiG kills did not simply take place *while* Moti Hod was in command, but *because* of it. In the small, centralized and intimate IAF of those days, the IAF commander personally ran each operation from the IAF bunker. While technically it was an air controller whose voice the pilot heard through his radio set, most often it was the IAF commander himself who was telling the controller what to say and do. Even if the commander did not actually cut into the radio loop to talk directly to the pilot, which he could do at the flick of a switch, a pilot had no trouble telling whose orders the controller was transmitting.

It was here that Hod finally and ultimately broke out from under Weizman's shadow. Nowhere was the difference between the two more pronounced—or more crucial—than in the way they ran fighter operations. However bold he had been as a young pilot, as a commander Weizman was too cautious and erratic for comfort. In his fears for his pilots' safety—and of political flak—he was constantly second-guessing their dogfighting decisions, interfering in the way they fought their battles, hastily ordering them out of the fighting after just one or two turns with the enemy. "Ezer's hysterical tendency to make you break off too soon was dangerous. His jerkiness was his danger, because sometimes you must let a pilot play his hand to the end without bothering him," said Yak Nevo, the IAF's premier authority on air combat.[7]

Moti Hod, however, was something else again. For one thing, he had none of Weizman's political hangups. "I was not excited about borders. Things were heating up, a plane was running away, and I was much too young and insensitive to things political to worry about how far past the border we shot it down," he recalled many years later.[8] More important, he was cool, patient, and had faith in the judgment of the pilot on the scene.

Above all, Moti Hod had an uncanny ability to conjure, with only the air controllers' sketchy reports in his earphones, a remarkably accurate mental picture of the unfolding air battle many miles away. Quietly sucking his pipe and keeping his eyes on his stopwatch—he would switch it on as soon as his pilots went into afterburner, so it gave him a constant picture of their fuel supply situation—he conducted the battle as accurately and sensibly as if he were over-flying the arena and actually watching things as they happened. "Weizman would keep putting a question here, a question there. A comment here, a comment there. It introduced static into the battle. It was precisely that sort of static that Hod avoided," says Yoram Agmon.[9]*

Ran Ronen's air battle with the Jordanian Hunter could have taken place only with Hod in command. Early on the morning of November 13, a day after three Israeli paratroopers were killed and six wounded when their Jeep struck a mine near the Jordanian

---

*Moti Hod was also lucky that it was on his watch, on August 16, 1966, that one of Israel's *Mossad*'s most spectacular coups, instigated by Weizman three years earlier, came to completion when an Iraqi defector landed a MiG-21 in perfect working order on the Hazor tarmac and surrendered to the startled pilots and ground crews. "Several times we had chased MIGs and hit them, but they didn't fall. We didn't really know their capabilities, their strengths and weaknesses," says Dani Shapira, who, as the IAF's chief test pilot, for the next months took the MiG through every nook and cranny of its flight envelope. "We found out, for example, that at high speeds it had trouble maneuvering as well as the Mirage, which meant that we had to try to get it into tight turns at high speeds. Also, at slow speeds it had a tendency to spin out, and at tight turns at low altitudes it would snap and flick into the ground." After complet-ing his test series and writing a book on the MiG-21, Shapira began flying it alongside and against the Mirages. By the end of the year, each Mirage squadron was thoroughly familiar with every aspect of what was heretofore the world's most mysterious and formidable fighter.

border, Israeli tanks, paratroopers, and artillery crossed into Jordan for a massive daytime attack on the heavily defended village of Sammū, in the Judean Hills south of Hebron. When four Jordanian Hunter jets showed up, a pair of Mirages under Ronen's command were scrambled from Tel Nof to head them off.

The British-made Hunters were no easy prey. Although slower and less powerful than the Mirages, they were far more agile at low speeds and altitudes, and Jordan's British-trained pilots were far superior to any in Egypt or Syria. Indeed, Ronen had barely arrived on the scene when he found one of the Hunters on his tail. While he promptly executed a classic "let him pass" maneuver that Yak Nevo had drilled into his pilots at the 101 ten years earlier, breaking into a barrel roll and letting the Hunter shoot on ahead so that in seconds he himself was behind the Hunter and ready to fire, the battle had just begun. Refusing to stay in the Mirage's line of fire, the Hunter [dived] "like a madman straight for the ground, he then flew into a deep canyon and followed it close to the bottom, heading east," recalls Ronen.[10]

For the next several minutes, eternity in dogfighting terms, Ronen chased the Jordanian as if trying to catch a jackrabbit with a Jeep. "Each time I got close enough to fire he'd break hard, and because he could turn better I had to leave him and come around again in a big circle." Finally, while slithering eastward along the canyon bottom, the Jordanian rose to clear a low mound and pulled up just enough to present Ronen with an opening. "I got in just below him and let go with a burst of twenty-five shells. The Hunter rolled 90 degrees on its side. The pilot ejected straight into the canyon wall and died."

At over eight minutes, it was by far the longest dogfight ever for the IAF, twice as long as the average aerial encounter. With Ronen's wingman flying cover overhead, there was little chance Ronen could not be reached on his radio at almost any point during the long chase. There was also little chance—had the battle taken place a year earlier—that Weizman would have let his protégé remain in danger's eye so long without ordering him to stop fighting and return home.

Hod's MiG-killing spree seemed to climax in the spring of 1967. The year had begun with mounting terrorist strikes from Jordan and Syria, and with daily Syrian artillery and tank shellings of Israeli villages, tractors, and patrols below the Golan Heights. Israeli attempts to respond in kind were rendered ineffectual by the terrain—the Syrians' artillery positions on the Golan Heights were not only 4,000 feet above the Jordan Valley floor, where the Israeli forces were stationed, but were placed just far enough behind the edge of the cliffs to make them invulnerable to Israeli fire. On Friday morning, April 7, a particularly bad day on the Syrian front, IDF chief of staff Yitzhak Rabin reluctantly agreed to call in the IAF.

It was not an easy decision, and it would not have taken place had the IAF not taken a hand in bringing it about. "Rabin was a ground forces man. He had never been exposed to Air Force capabilities or thinking. It was not that he was hostile—he simply did not understand it," says Rafi Harlev, then chief of IAF Operations.[11] Eager to participate in the action, Harlev sent Shabtai Gilboa, Ramat David's deputy commander, to the IDF frontline command post, where Rabin was running the fighting, His job, Gilboa remembers, was to make sure that the air option was presented credibly and forcefully. "What I had to do was talk the IDF command into bringing the Air Force into the action," he says.[12]

It was late morning and the fighting was going badly. "The Syrians had a system. Their tanks would roll forward to the edge of the cliff, fire, then roll right back into their shelters, so it was almost impossible to hit them. We did manage to set one on fire, but it wasn't much," Gilboa recalls. Talking the Greens into asking for air support, however, proved difficult. The entire IDF hierarchy was at the command post—Maj. Gen. David "Dado" Elazar, chief of IDF Northern Command, Maj. Gen. Israel "Talik" Tal, commander of IDF Armored Corps, as well as IDF chief of staff Rabin himself. Gilboa was not only a junior officer by comparison, but his persistent suggestions "that only the Air Force had the capability to end all this" irritated the command team by rubbing in their failure to resolve the situation on the ground.

It was only around noon that Rabin finally called Prime Minister Eshkol and received permission to deploy the IAF. Now he needed an excuse. All through the morning, Israeli armor-plated tractors kept trying to plow the fields below the Syrian-held heights, only to be driven back time and again by shelling from above. "We are sending the tractor into the field one last time. The first Syrian shell that comes down, you guys can have the southern sector to your-selves," Rabin told Gilboa, who was sitting on a communications Jeep above the IDF bunker, with an open radio channel to Rafi Harlev at IAF Operations. At 1:30, the tractor reached the field, a Syrian shell traced a steep trajectory downward from the heights, and "Rabin motioned to me to go ahead. I called Harlev and said 'launch,' and the party began," says Gilboa.

Within minutes, Vautours and Mystères from nearby Ramat David were pounding the Syrian fortifications on the southern slopes of the heights behind the Sea of Galilee. Black columns of smoke rose along the rim of the cliffs as artillery and tank positions were demolished. From their hilltop bunker, the Israeli field com-manders had a clear view of the awesome light-and-sound display on the heights across the Jordan rift. Rabin was overcome by the show, and when new Syrian fire was reported to the north, he ordered the IAF to move up to the heights' Central Sector, and then all the way north.

The bombings were just the beginning. At the same time Hod scrambled the Vautours, he ordered his Mirages to the scene with unprecedented "permission to open fire at any identified enemy plane." Half an hour into the bombings, two Israeli Mirages ran into four Syrian MiG-21s over the Golan Heights, chased them deep into Syrian territory, and shot two of them down near Damascus. Two hours later, a third MiG was shot down, also near the Syrian capital. For a few moments the area fell silent, but when Rabin climbed out of the bunker for a stretch and a smoke, Gilboa warned that Syrian MiGs and Mirages from Ramat David were converging on the area. Rabin had barely turned to look when the planes—from that dis-tance, no more than silvery dots—met in full view, one instantly exploding in a huge fireball.

"What's that?" a startled Rabin asked. "It's a MiG," Gilboa called down after checking with IAF Operations. Rabin was mulling it over when another fireball appeared above the heights—"I am worried, tell them to stop," Rabin began to say,—and then a third, followed by the delayed thunder of the explosions.

As rapidly as it began, the battle was over. In just seconds, three

MiGs had been shot down, raising the day's toll to six, with the IAF suffering no casualties. Back at IAF headquarters, Harlev felt that the show still needed an appropriate finale. "Sir, the pilots of the Israel Air Force want to salute you," Gilboa called down from his Jeep. As Rabin looked up, four Mirages buzzed the command bunker, their thunder shaking the heavily fortified compound. Rabin was ecstatic. Rushing up to Gilboa's Jeep, "he grabbed me, picked me up in the air, and yelled 'What an air force!' "

The scope and success of the air operation, in which Weizman took no part, completed Hod's emergence from under his predecessor's shadow. The MiG kills in particular carried his signature. More than words or written documents, the free hand he gave his fighter pilots to shoot down enemy planes where and when they appeared, without first asking either Eshkol or Rabin for approval, articulated the new fighter doctrine that would characterize his tenure in command of the IAF. Israel's political and military hierarchy had the authority to order the IAF into action and set its goals, but it would be an airman, not a politician or a foot soldier, who would decide how it should be carried out.

The bottom line, of course, which the pragmatic frontiersman instinctively understood, was not only winning but making his superiors look good. He had done just that. Indeed, as the spring of 1967 inched toward summer, turning Judea and then Galilee into a blooming rage of narcissus, anemones, and cyclamen, and then red poppies and orange ranunculus, a new sense of invincible calm blanketed Israel. While Israelis were uneasy the previous fall when, in an interview to an Israeli army magazine, Rabin threatened Syria with heavy retaliation should its shelling of Israeli settlements continue, the downing of the MiGs and Syria's subsequent silence proved him right. With Syria licking its wounds and Egypt bogged down in a third year of a hopeless war in Yemen, IDF analysts foresaw "no direct Arab offensive against Israel [before] 1968–70," and Rabin emerged as the embodiment of a new policy of peace through strength.

It was in such heady and unprecedented confidence and nonchalance that, on the night of May 14, Israel began to celebrate its twenty-fifth anniversary. That evening, in his traditional Independence Day message, Rabin repeated his stern warning to Syria, and assured the nation of a long period of quiet ahead. Eshkol, too, boldly announced that continued Arab terrorism and sabotage would leave Israel "no other choice but to adopt suitable counter-measures against the focal points of sabotage."

Yet even as Rabin's deep and resonant voice rolled from radio sets throughout the country, a war that he had not foreseen, wanted, or prepared for had already begun. As Rabin talked, two Egyptian mechanized divisions were roaring with full fanfare through the streets of Cairo on their way to the Sinai, where only one Israeli tank battalion was watching the entire frontier.*

IDF Intelligence analysts were still insisting that Egypt was merely rattling its sabers when, on May 17, Nasser ordered the UN Emergency Force in the Gaza Strip to pull its troops away from the Egyptian-Israeli front, where they had been stationed since the Israeli pullback from the Sinai in 1957. United Nations secretary-general U Thant attempted to call Nasser's bluff by warning that he would evacuate either none of his troops or all of them, but it turned into one of the worst miscalculations in history as Nasser called his bluff and ordered all United Nations troops out of the area. On May 19, U Thant compounded his mistake by pulling out his forces. The UN-built bunkers along the perimeter of the Gaza Strip were immediately occupied by the Egyptian-commanded Palestine Liberation Army, while Egyptian forces took positions along the entire Israeli frontier.

Nasser kept tightening the noose. On May 20, an Egyptian commando battalion parachuted at Sharm el Sheikh, seizing control of the Straits of Tiran, which connected the Gulf of Aqaba with the Red Sea. On the night of May 22, while visiting Egyptian combat pilots at the Bir Gafgafa airfield in the Sinai, Nasser ordered the closure of the straits to Israeli shipping. "If the Jews threaten to

---

*Egypt was ostensibly helping Syria avert a nonexistent Israeli attack. On April 12, seeking to exploit Arab unrest in the wake of the downing of the Syrian MiGs the previous week, a Soviet intelligence official in Cairo told his Egyptian colleagues that Israel was amassing troops along the Syrian border. The following day in Moscow, Soviet president Nicolai Podgorny repeated the warning to visiting Syrian defense minister Hafez al-Assad, and offered help to fight Israel. The Israelis dismissed the Soviet reports as ludicrous. Eshkol even invited Soviet ambassador Dmitri Chuvakhin to visit the borders and see for himself that no mobilization was taking place. But the Soviet declined on grounds that his job was to communicate Soviet truths, not to test them, and the Soviet Big Lie stood.

make war," he told the cheering crowd, "I reply *ahalan wa saha-lan*, Welcome, we are ready for war." The Arab world was electrified. Nasser's popularity, sagging for years because of his fighting with fellow Arabs in South Yemen, shot up overnight. One by one, the Arab states caught war fever and volunteered their support. Jordan and Iraq rushed to sign joint-defense treaties with Egypt.

The die was now cast. Ever since its withdrawal from the Sinai in 1957, Israel had made its open southern sea routes a cornerstone of its military policy. Successive Israeli governments had declared time and again that any Arab attempt to close the straits would constitute *casus belli*, cause for war. Ignoring Nasser's action now would surrender not only a vital sea link but the very policy of military deterrence that Israel had cultivated over the previous decade.

Nasser's sudden and unexpected challenge, however, seemed to shock Israel into utter paralysis. Just a week after celebrating its most confident Independence Day in years, Israelis woke up to find six combat-ready Egyptian divisions—over one hundred thousand men and more than a thousand tanks—facing them in the Sinai, with Jordan and Syria quickly closing in from east and north. Surrounded, undermanned, and undergunned, Israel was also—as its envoys in Europe and the United States now reported—without friends or chance of outside military support. Its sense of impending doom fed on newsreels and press photos of massive Arab war rallies calling for the destruction of the Jewish state. Rumors that the *Chevra Kadisha*, the national religious burial authority, was digging ten thousand graves in the parks of Tel Aviv in preparation for the bloodbath ahead only deepened the gloom. Most alarming was the seeming sudden collapse of the leaders who only a few weeks earlier radiated strength and resolve. Rabin was nowhere to be seen, while an attempt by Prime Minister Eshkol to reassure the nation in a radio broadcast backfired when, unable to decipher last-minute corrections in his script, Eshkol stuttered so badly he panicked the entire nation.

Only one enclave in the entire country seemed to escape the fright, indecision, and finger-pointing that swept Israel's political and military commands. On May 15, as soon as Egyptian forces crossed into the Sinai, Moti Hod called his operations and intelli-

gence chiefs to his third-story office at the IAF compound in Tel
Aviv and ordered them to prepare for war. As soon as the meeting
was over, Rafi Harlev returned to his office one floor below, opened
his safe, pulled out a thin blue-covered file, and opened it on his
desk. It was titled "Operation Plan *Moked*."

"Nobody had to explain our mission to us," Hod would say later.
"It was clear to me that we were going to war, and that the Air Force
had to fulfill its ultimate destiny—achieving air superiority and
destroying the enemy air power. Everything else was incidental. We
had lived with this knowledge since 1948. It was the reason we
trained to fly low, to take off in radio silence even in large formations, to navigate at low altitudes. We knew we would need it
someday."[13]

A week after the first Egyptian tanks rolled into the Sinai, oblivious
to government and IDF paralysis, the IAF was ready.

Chapter 17

THREE HOURS
IN JUNE

Since taking command as IDF chief of staff on January 1, 1964, Yitzhak Rabin had enjoyed public popularity equaled by few predecessors. Blond, handsome, with a vibrant deep voice and a boyishly taciturn manner, Rabin was the quintessential new Israeli hero. Born in Jerusalem in 1922 into a left-wing Zionist family, he graduated from the legendary Kadouri Agricultural School, began the 1948 war in command of a *Palmach* brigade on the Jerusalem front, married his *Palmach* sweetheart, and ended the fighting as deputy commander of the key southern front. Following the war he represented the IDF at the Israeli-Egyptian armistice talks at Rhodes, and in the 1950s quickly moved up the IDF command ladder.

While he was chief of staff, his warnings to Syria in the fall of 1966, and the IAF strike he ordered on the Golan Heights the following spring, in which six Syrian MiGs were shot down, established him as Israel's credible and resolute defender. When the Sinai front began to heat up in early 1967, he alone seemed to stand unshaken among Israel's leaders.

Publicly, that is. In reality, recalls Weizman, who as IDF chief of operations was Rabin's second in command, "from the moment the tension invaded our lives, I felt that Rabin's condition and stability were growing shakier. This was evident through changing decisions, expressions of worry over anticipated developments, and inability to decide. Rabin inspired uncertainty."[1] Outwardly confident and bullish, Rabin was in reality cracking under two separate strains. The first, as a "very tense, chain-smoking" Rabin confided to Foreign Minister Abba Eban on May 21, was his own sense of failure to prepare the IDF for the task at hand. "Israel's military preparedness for ten years . . . related to the northern and eastern fronts, with little attention to the south," he told Eban. As a result the IDF could not simply turn around to face the Egyptians unless it had considerably more time to prepare and redeploy.[2]

The second strain was political. "In its perplexity, the [Eshkol] cabinet expected me not only to present and analyze the military options [but to tell] it which option to adopt. Needless to say, that made me feel very lonely," he would write later in his memoirs.[3] But it might have been his own uncertainty that contributed to Eshkol's seeming reluctance to engage the Egyptians. On May 22, still desperate for a comforting word after his talk with Eban, Rabin sought guidance and encouragement from David Ben-Gurion and Moshe Dayan—both of them out of power at the time, and both sworn opponents of Eshkol.

He received neither. Isolated and embittered in his political exile, Ben-Gurion lashed into Rabin, berating him and Eshkol for calling in the reserves and for forcing Nasser's hand. Rabin left the meeting "doubly despondent. I now felt the entire burden was resting on my shoulders. Many days were to pass before his words stopped ringing in my ears: 'You have led the state into a grave situation. You bear the responsibility.' "[4]

Later that evening, at his walled-in and antique-filled house in Zahala, Dayan was equally unsparing in his assessment of the government's behavior, although he complimented Rabin for the way he prepared and trained the IDF. "At least no one could accuse me of failing to prepare the IDF for the grave test in store for it," Rabin would gratefully write later.[5] Dayan, however, also was alarmed by Rabin's state. "Yitzhak seemed not only tired—a natural thing—but also ill-at-ease, uncertain, nervous (he smoked constantly, cigarette after cigarette) and definitely not eager to do battle," Dayan noted in his diary.[6]

It was into this gathering gloom that, after only a few hours of sleep, Rabin was awakened at 3:45 A.M. with the news that Nasser had just closed the Tiran Straits. Instead of clarifying his thinking, the news only made Rabin more despondent. Later that morning, pressed from one side by his senior command, which urged an immediate strike against Egypt, and from the other side by Eshkol's desire to hold back while the Johnson administration attempted to resolve matters peacefully, Rabin once again sought assurance, this time from Interior Minister Moshe Chaim Shapira, the highly respected National Religious Party leader, only to have Shapira accuse him of dragging the nation into a hopeless war.

That night, under "mental and physical exhaustion [and] enormous amounts of cigarette smoke" as well as a sense of having "failed in my duty as the prime minister's chief military advisor," Rabin collapsed.[7] Weizman, whom Rabin called to his house at 8:00 P.M., found him "sitting alone in the large room of his flat. Everything was quiet. He seemed broken and depressed. We sat by ourselves, he at the edge of the sofa, I alongside." Rabin was ready to throw in the towel. Weakly insisting that "whoever erred must go," he asked Weizman to administer a coup de grâce of sorts. "I erred. Will you now take the post of chief of staff?" Weizman remembers him asking.*[8]

Weizman would not hear of his resignation. Assuring Rabin of a "great victory" ahead, he urged him to rest (after he left, Rabin's wife called a physician who gave him a sedative that kept him out of action for thirty-six hours) and rushed out to order all military and intelligence dispatches directed "temporarily" to him. The following morning, in a meeting with the IDF's senior operations and intelligence staff, and with the commanders of the southern front and the armored corps, he canceled Rabin's previous plan for a timid strike at the Gaza Strip, and instead approved a broad and deep thrust into the Sinai all the way to the Suez Canal. Ready to attack the next day, Weizman called Hod and ordered him to prepare to strike at Egypt's airfields the following morning.†

---

*Rabin, in his own memoirs, remembers only asking Weizman "Am I to blame? Should I relinquish my post?" He denies actually offering Weizman the post which was not his to "bequeath . . . to him or anyone else."

†Although Rabin now claims he felt better the following evening, May 24, Weizman

The next day, however, even as a fresh and visibly more confident Rabin returned to his post, the military command crisis was followed by a political disaster. While Rabin's real physical incapacitation was brief and, for the most part, kept secret, Eshkol's unfortunate radio address and seeming collapse was public and irreversible. Three days of massive public demonstrations and political attacks followed, forcing him to surrender his defense ministry portfolio to Moshe Dayan, and his party rule to a wall-to-wall government that included his—and Ben-Gurion's—archenemy, Menachem Begin.

Dayan's appointment revived not only the public but the military. "[Dayan] came just in time to fortify our hearts and dissipate any doubts," Weizman would write a decade later. "He gave a surge of our will to fight, [to] go for the total destruction of the Egyptian Army."[9] While Rabin's timid response to Nasser's challenge was a limited plan to occupy the Gaza Strip and use it to bargain for the reopening of the straits, even Weizman's more ambitious plan to seize Gaza and Eastern Sinai, with a thrust toward the Suez Canal, still skirted the matter of the blocked Red Sea straits. Dayan announced from the outset that his goal was "the defeat and destruction of the Egyptian Army in . . . Sinai."

The moment he stepped into his new post, all remaining doubts about the inevitability of war vanished. The only question that remained was—when?

Moti Hod provided the answer.

For the past two weeks, his staff had been tinkering with *Moked* and readying it for action. So remarkably had Nevo and Sivron designed it that the bulk of the plan—the thick supplements detailing attack methods, approach routes, ordnance, and takeoff procedures—hardly needed to be touched. Only a few revisions were required in the "forces and missions" chart—which gave each formation its specific targets, ordnance, approach routes, takeoff and arrival time—and even those were so easy that Harlev, like Sivron before him, actually had fun playing the complex three-dimensional puzzle. "Say some MiGs were moved from deep inside Egypt to the

recalls that when he returned to Rabin's apartment the morning after the collapse, Rabin once again offered him the IDF command, which he again rejected. Both agree that Rabin was effectively incapacitated until the morning of May 25.

Sinai. Originally, you had designated your long-range fighter-bombers to hit them, but now there was no need to waste long-range planes on a nearby target," he would later recall. "So you moved short-range planes from a Canal-area target—where they were at their range limits anyway—to the new Sinai site, and switched the longer-range formation to the Canal, where they could do more good. The whole chart simply changed over," he recalls.[10]

Only one problem remained. To work, *Moked* had to be activated well in advance of all other military moves. To Rabin, this meant a triple gamble which risked the very survival of the state. In the first place, launching *Moked* with the necessary secrecy meant delaying the ground offensive until the IAF aircraft reached their targets. The slightest troop movement anywhere along the border before that moment would put the Egyptians on alert and doom the air strike. But what if the IAF went in first and failed, forcing the ground forces to move against an alert and waiting enemy backed by its own air offensive?

Second, with barely 200 fighter-bombers at his disposal, Hod had no way of striking at once at all three air forces poised along Israel's borders—Egypt, Jordan, and Syria. Hod's decision to leave Syria and Jordan alone for the time being, and concentrate on "catching the Egyptian Air Force by surprise and destroying it on the ground . . . before anything else was done," would leave Israel open for attacks from north and east. As he patiently "explained to [Rabin], we shouldn't bother with Jordan, and we could leave the Syrians alone because by the time they got around to doing anything, we'd be back from Egypt and ready for them. I remember his reaction—he did not think it was possible."[11]

The third risk involved Hod's decision to leave behind only twelve Mirages—four in the air and eight on the ground—to defend Israel should the Arabs strike while the rest of the IAF was heading for its targets. The risk was less military—planes could be called back from the Egyptian front in minutes should any significant scrambling of Arab air units take place—than political. Israel's jittery leaders were in no mood to approve a plan that left the country virtually undefended against Arab bombers for even one minute.

Finally, Rabin and the Israeli government had to do all this risk-taking on faith. *Moked* may have looked good on paper, but it had never been tried. "Until that time, in 1967, the IAF had just one serious operational experience to its credit, and that was the Sinai campaign more than ten years earlier. We were the crazy ones. We believed we could do anything. But it was difficult to convince anybody else of that," says Harlev. Even Weizman, who had initiated and presided over the preparation of *Moked*, could not help Rabin overcome his doubts. "To convince the government that we must attack first . . . the IDF chief of staff first had to *believe* [in the plan]. Rabin did not believe. He had constant doubts," Weizman wrote later.[12]

Hod's penchant for secrecy did not help. Hauled by Rabin and Weizman to one government briefing after another, he delivered sober and precise assessments of enemy strength and intentions, but refused to say anything about his own plan except that it would work. Pressed for more, he relented only so far as to present a single sheet of cardboard "with no arrows, no maps, no time of attack— only a list of targets and the number of aircraft formations allocated to each one. I remember their response—they said that if such was the plan with which the IAF was going to war, then we were in very bad shape," Hod says.

Dayan, however, "was the first person to grasp the plan besides Ezer," says Hod. "I showed him the board, told him briefly what the plan was, [and] that was that. It was forty-eight hours before the war. Rabin had no choice. He did not have another air force." On Sunday, June 4, conceding that the United States was unable to resolve the crisis, the Israeli cabinet approved Dayan's proposal for "a military action to break Israel out of the siege and to prevent the impending attack by the forces of the unified Arab command."[13] Dayan and Rabin scheduled the attack for the next day, June 5, but allowed Hod to pick the precise time. Hod timed the first strike wave to arrive over its targets at 7:45 A.M.. It wasn't just because, as Sivron argued two years earlier, by that time the fogs would have lifted, the winds stabilized, and the Egyptian dawn patrols returned to base. Because of the time-zone difference, it would actually be 8:45 A.M. in Egypt when the attack began. Egypt's senior command would still be fighting traffic on the way to office. It was, literally, a window of opportunity. As risky as the operation was, at that precise time, the odds would be momentarily on Israel's side.

Late in the afternoon, Harlev completed the last update of

Moked's "forces and missions" chart. With no time to print it up, he hand-scribbled the new columns of data on a sheet of cardboard. Starting from the top of the page, he began each line with the code number of a single formation. Then, moving from right to left, he quickly filled in the bare essentials of that formation's mission— type of bombs, amount of fuel, target location, approach and escape routes. Every two or three formations, although coming at different times from different airfields, shared the same target—the first arriving at 7:45 A.M., the second at 8:00 A.M., and so on. Only a few formations, mostly Vautours heading for distant targets deep in Egypt, were assigned later arrival times (they could not be sent out too early for fear of tipping off the Egyptians).

Having completed his cardboard chart, Harlev then made two identical copies, carried all three to the briefing room, and personally gave one to each of the three base commanders, whom he had earlier called in for an urgent and secret briefing. "The name of the game is reaching the Egyptian coast without being spotted," he added at the conclusion of his briefing. "To accomplish that, your pilots will have to fly as low as they know how, and keep their mouths shut no matter what happens."

One of the commanders wondered what would happen if a pilot encountered an emergency on the way. Harlev stared him down with deep, penetrating dark eyes, and spelled out the unthinkable. "Turn back if he can," he said. "Crash at sea if he cannot."

That night, the base commanders briefed their deputies and squadron commanders. Secrecy was so tight that not until early the next morning, just before takeoff, were the pilots themselves told of the coming war. As he turned in for the night, Ramat David's deputy commander, Shabtai Gilboa, contrived an elaborate ruse to arrange for a wake-up without disclosing the true reason. "I told the guard at the gate to wake me up for a security spot check, and I told base operations to wake me up so I could check up on the guards. I also set my own alarm clock. At the end, I woke up before any of them. I remember walking out at dawn. The birds were beginning to chirp and I was thinking to myself 'If those birds only knew what's about to happen here.' "[14]

At 7:14 on the morning of June 5, four Ouragans zipped off the Hazor tarmac, stayed low over the surrounding fields, and quickly disappeared over the mist-draped rolling land to the west. A minute later and sixty miles to the north, eight Mirages from Ramat David streaked low over the golden wheat fields of the Yizre'el Valley, passed over Haifa Bay and then vanished from sight over the Mediterranean. A minute later, four more Ouragans left Hazor for the desert. At 7:17 and again at 7:25, small formations of Vautours lumbered up from Ramat David and droned out to sea. To early-morning bathers on Israel's white-sand beaches, the sight was eerie—their entire air force was streaking west toward Cyprus and Europe, bugging out.

At Ramat David, Hazor, and Tel Nof, the noise was deafening. Carpets of steel draped the tarmacs, rippling and swarming as one by one, moving wing tip to wing tip with no radio sound and only hand signals, bomb-laden Mirages, Mystères, Ouragans, Super-Mystères, and Vautours taxied out, lifted heavily, and headed west. Just that morning, each formation leader was given the numbers of the two planes that would take off before him. It was his responsibility to keep them in sight and, when he saw them move out, to be ready to take off himself (he also received the numbers of the two planes that would follow him, just in case his missed his first cue). If he rolled out in time to the head of the runway, he would see his formation code number on a huge card attached to what seemed like an oversized Rolodex. If no last-minute changes appeared on the card, he'd gun his engine and take off. There would be no call signs, no radio instructions, no dialogues with the tower.

So tricky was this improvised send-off system that as he became momentarily mesmerized by the spectacle of the departing armada, Ran Ronen was suddenly stunned to see two Vautours that were scheduled to take off after him getting ready to lift off. He had missed his cue. Five minutes late and flushed with embarrassment, he slammed his throttle into afterburn and shot out to the runway, ahead of the Vautours, with his formation members scrambling to keep up. Once in the air, he slowed down briefly off the Gaza coast, let them catch up, then gunned his engine once more, dashing out to sea so low and fast that sea foam literally was sucked up to mix with the angry vapors of his fully open exhaust pipe. As if his

mission was not intricate enough, he now had to make up for lost
time without fouling anyone else's timetable, without colliding with
another formation, without overcompensating and arriving at his
target too soon.

Worried Israelis who watched the planes disappear in the west
had no way of knowing that each formation, after flying out for
precisely 18 minutes, rolled left and barreled south on a new heading. Instead of a sheet of paper, Rafi Sivron's three-dimensional
puzzle was finally being played out with actual planes, with the
entire southeastern Mediterranean as a game board. Although leaving at different times and heading in different directions for different destinations over different distances, all the planes had to arrive
at the identical time over their targets—Egypt's eleven major air
bases in Sinai and along the Canal.

By 7:30, all across the region, small formations of Ouragans,
Meteors, Mystères, Mirages, Super-Mystères, Vautours—anything
the Israelis could get up in the air with a load of bombs—were
thundering south. The Ouragans that left Hazor at 7:14 were heading for the Bir Gafgafa fighter airstrip in the Sinai. The Mirages
from Ramat David were bound for the Fayid and Abu Suweir
airfields across the Suez lakes, south of Ismailia. The Ouragans that
departed at 7:16 would 29 minutes later be over Bir El Tamade, a
small fighter airstrip in the Central Sinai. The Vautours would at
the same time reach the Cairo West airfield near Cairo.

It was, to veteran and rookie pilots alike, the hardest and most
critical mission ever. At no time before or after did the survival of
Israel depend so completely on the success of a single mission.
Flying so low over sea and desert, the pilots could barely see enough
of the terrain to be sure they were on the right course. Instead, they
kept their eyes glued to their speed and direction indicators and to
their watches. Like preprogrammed missiles, if they stuck to speed,
time, and direction, they would be over their targets at precisely
7:45.

It had all been figured out ahead of time. Now all they had to do
was hold on and not mess it up.

Having impatiently counted his 18 minutes out at sea, Ronen
swung left and pushed up his speed from 360 to 420 knots. He
regained three minutes by the time his formation crossed into the

Sinai. He still had to make up two more before reaching his target, but he could not be sure. The bleak, undifferentiated desert offered no sense of direction or whereabouts, only "roads, highways, rail lines, power poles, villages and small towns, each looking like the others," he would write later.[15] Several miles away, leading a Mirage formation from Hazor to Cairo West, Capt. Oded Marom also tried "in vain to find my location by the map and the villages on the way. All fields look alike, like rice kernels. All the villages have the same shape."[16]

The desert was uncooperative in other ways. Ground-level air currents played havoc with time-and-direction navigation. Capt. Amichai Gal,* commander of the 117 out of Ramat David, expected to cross into Egypt just west of Port Said, where the Suez Canal ran into the Mediterranean. From there, his plan was to turn south and, with the Canal on his left, continue straight due south until he reached the Abu Suweir airfield at precisely 7:45. Now, however, as the blue watery expanses below him suddenly changed into land, it looked all wrong. Instead of Buheirat el Manzala with its sheltering and sheltered islands, surrounded by the lush greenery of the Nile Delta, "everything around me was yellow flats. I did not know where I was. It was a terrible feeling, to lead a formation, to command a squadron and not to know where you are."[17] Flushed with embarrassment and frustrated by his inability to discuss his predicament with his formation members, he continued on his course, frantically searching the bleak desert terrain for clues. It was already past 7:40. He had just minutes to get to his target, and he still had not the vaguest notion of where he was. The feeling was eerie, especially when suddenly, rising above the yellow desert flat ahead, "I saw antennas and ship's sails. I thought it was a desert mirage, but almost immediately I saw masts, and then decks, and I realized I was coming to the Canal from the east." Grabbing his map, he frantically pinpointed his location, made a course correction, and rushed toward his target.

The radio silence was nerve-racking. Normally full of chatter, the air waves were as unruffled as the land below. Skimming the waves with three inexperienced Mystère pilots in tow on the way to Fayid,

*Not his real name.

a young pilot named Avihu Ben-Nun watched helplessly as one of
his pilots began weaving up and down, seemingly about to crash
into the rushing waters. A minute later, "I look and there is just one
plane to my right. We began on a left foot. One is already gone,"
he wrote later.[18] Not far away, as they turned at the same time to
cross into the Sinai, one slightly early and one slightly late, two
formations found themselves on a collision course. Unable to communicate and fearful to move up higher where they could be spotted by the Egyptian radar, each tried to squeeze below the other as
in a deadly game of "chicken." At the last minute, one flight leader
pulled his formation up a hair, averting disaster.

Nowhere was the silence more thunderous, the tension more
oppressive than in the IAF's underground command bunker. "You
just sit in the 'Hole' and watch the clock. You get phone updates
from the bases as each formation takes off, and the girls run on the
big table to put little model airplanes on the set routes, but you have
no way of knowing if they are really there or not because you hear
nothing. Nobody is talking. There is no radar, no radio, nothing,"
Harlev would later recall. "You sit and look at your watch and
tell yourself 'Now they must be here, or here.' The tension is un-
bearable."[19]

The tiny IAF war room was packed. Hod sat motionless in the
front row of the small gallery, flanked by Harlev, chief of IAF
Intelligence Yeshayahu Bareket, and chief of IAF Control Shmuel
Kislev, each glued to a private telephone headset connected to his
own staff just outside the room. Behind Hod, Dayan had been
sitting since 7:30. And Yigael Yadin, the IDF commander during
the 1948 war and now Eshkol's military advisor. For most of the
morning, so was Rabin, jumping nervously every few minutes to
check with his staff, then returning to his seat, to watch and wait.
Moving about restlessly was Ezer Weizman, feeling left out and
useless just as the fulfillment of his greatest creation was about to
happen. For years "I talked about just that operation. I explained,
weaved and dreamt it. I assembled it link by link. I trained my men
to carry it out," he would write later.[20] Now, there was nothing he
could do but wait.

All along the Egyptian border, Israeli infantry and tank brigades
sat coiled in silence. Not a single gun would fire, not a single engine

turn, not one tank move before Rabin issued his command—and he wouldn't until the planes arrived over their targets and dropped their bombs. For now, the entire war was in the hands of one man. Moti Hod seemed oblivious to the tension that gripped everyone in the underground room. "Incredibly quiet and relaxed," Weizman would later describe him in a rambling, stream-of-consciousness recollection of the morning. "No one in the world can tell what is happening inside him. Instead of smoking he is burning water. Like a huge radiator. There is a giant jar of water near him, which he picks up with both hands, lifts up, brings to his lips and flips it over. You hear a long gurgle and . . . it's empty. You wonder what will blow up first, a few hundred Egyptian planes on the ground, or this human radiator."[21]

Dayan, too, was struck by Hod's calm. Watching him "drinking water and worrying about his pilots who are just now diving over airfields in Egypt, I remember the image of his father, standing on a hill on the northern frontier [twenty-five years earlier], waiting at dawn for my return from Syria," he later wrote in his diary.[22]

At precisely 7:40 A.M., from their seats around Hod, Harlev, Bareket, and Kislev quietly squeezed each other's hands and whispered "We've done it." For the past half hour, they were glued through their telephone lines to Israel's army of spies in the Arab world, where all was still quiet.

At the same moment that the three were shaking hands at the IAF bunker, Ronen's formation crossed the Canal between Port Said and El Qantara, on course and—having made up for its five-minute delay—on time. Five minutes later, over the tiny town of Fâqûs, Ronen kicked in his afterburner and pulled the stick hard into his stomach, throwing his Mirage into a steep climb. As he shot up he looked down along the side of the Mirage's slick nose. For the first time since he had left Tel Nof half an hour earlier, the desert vista opened up so he could see where he actually was.

Up until that instant, when they suddenly pulled up to get into their bombing dives all across the Sinai and Egypt, neither Ronen nor any of the other flight leaders could be sure just what would appear below them. It was a risk inherent in the *Hataf* attack tactic the IAF had developed and was now gambling everything on. Flying low could get you to your target undetected by radar, but at the same time you could never be sure you were at the right place at the right time. You never really *found* your target. You flew fast and low in the right direction, and after the right passage of time you pulled up, rolled on your back, and if everything worked out right you found yourself above the target, about to begin your bombing dive.

But you had no way of *knowing*. Suddenly you were up there, hanging upside down against the sky like a fat duck in a shooting gallery, fair game to enemy radar and antiaircraft gunners, and you had just seconds to figure out where you were, to locate and identify your target, to spot any changes and mistakes and to figure out exactly what you were going to do.

Ronen was lucky. As he reached the top of the climb and rolled over, the runways of Inshas appeared below, running in precisely the way he had expected. There were MIGs everywhere. Idle MiGs were parked in rows and in clumps. Armed MiG-21 interceptors sat in readiness at the edge of runways. As Ronen came down fast and hard, aiming his bombs at precisely one-third the length of his runway, he noticed the startled faces of the MiG pilots as they looked up. At 2,000 feet and thirty-five degrees, the Mirages dropped their bombs at one-third and two-thirds the length of the runways. As they disappeared past the edge of the air base, the bombs exploded, opening deep craters that severed the runways and made them useless.

At the same moment, Amichai Gal completed his own course correction and took his Mirage formation into a climb over what should have been Abu Suweir. As he looked down, however, he could see nothing. Clouds draped the terrain as far as he could see. Having lost his way once, he could not be sure he was even near, let alone over his target. The cloud cover spread pristine and virginal in all directions. Gal shrugged, rolled his plane over and dove through the clouds anyway. He was halfway down to the ground, still uncertain of what awaited below, when the clouds suddenly parted, Abu Suweir's runways appeared right where they were supposed to be, and Gal reached for his bomb release.

Everywhere in the Sinai and across the Canal, Israeli formations were diving at Egypt's airfield network. At Cairo West, four Mirages led by Amos Lapidot, commander of the 101 squadron,

A Czech Knife at an Israeli air base during the 1948 war. It is a Czech version (Avia S-199) of the World War II German ME-109 Messerschmitt fighter. *(Collection of Lou Lenart)*

Prime Minister David Ben-Gurion *(front, right)* visiting the 101 squadron during the 1948 war. Squadron commander Modi Alon (in sunglasses) is showing him around. Between them (with mustache) is South African volunteer Sid Cohen, who took command of the squadron after Alon's death. *(Collection of Lou Lenart)*

Ezer Weizman during the 1948 war. *(Collection of Ezer Weizman)*

Lou Lenart in a Messerschmitt cockpit during the 1948 war. *(Collection of Lou Lenart)*

Rudy Augarten, leading ace of the 1948 war and later commander of IAF Wing 1, at Ramat David. *(Collection of Lou Lenart)*

One of the two dozen Mustangs Al Schwimmer bought in the United States in 1948. *(Collection of Lon Nordeen)*

Yigael Yadin (*left*) and Aharon Remez. Dan Tolkowsky is in the second row on the left. (*Collection of Ezer Weizman*)

This Mystère IVA fighter has the identification stripes that marked all IAF aircraft engaged in the 1956 conflict. *(Collection of Lon Nordeen)*

"The first Israelis"—graduates of the first IAF Flight School class. *Left to right:* Yeshayahu "Shaya" Gazit, Moti Hod, Danny Shapira, Tibi Ben-Shahar. *(Collection of Moti Hod)*

The first jet fighters—Squadron 117 (Meteors) in 1954. *Standing, second, fifth, sixth, and seventh from left:* Danny Shapira, Ezer Weizman, Beni Peled, and Aharon Yoeli. *Sitting, first and fourth from left:* Menahem Bar and Yak Nevo. *(Collection of Menahem Bar)*

The Dassault Super-Mystère B2, which was first delivered to Israel in 1959. *(Collection of Lon Nordeen)*

Conferring on the Hazor tarmac are *(left to right)* Prime Minister David Ben-Gurion, National Security Advisor Israel Galili, IAF Commander Dan Tolkowsky, and IDF Chief of Staff Chaim Laskov. *(Collection of Dan Tolkowsky)*

Jacob "Yak" Nevo, author of the IAF's fighter doctrine and of the *Moked* strike plan, which resulted in the destruction of the Arab air forces in just three hours during the 1967 Six-Day War. *(Collection of Iftach Spector)*

In 1961 Ezer Weizman ordered seventy-two Mirages from France, enough to equip three squadrons. The delta-shaped plane became Weizman's trademark. *(Collection of Lon Nordeen)*

Ezer Weizman as IAF commander. *(Collection of Ezer Weizman)*

A Mirage pilot marking a kill. *(Collection of Lon Nordeen)*

Moti Hod as chief of IAF. *(Collection of Moti Hod)*

Ezer Weizman *(left)* transferring command of the IAF to Moti Hod. In the background the "Black Spit." *(Collection of Moti Hod)*

Ran Ronen at his squadron ready room during the 1967 war. *(Collection of Ran Ronen)*

Iftach Spector playing an Israeli fighter pilot in the 1967 Israeli film *Sinaia*. *(Collection of Iftach Spector)*

Oded Marom. *(Collection of Oded Marom)*

Squadron 101 (Mirage) gunslingers during the War of Attrition. *Standing, first and second from left:* Eitan Ben Eliahu and Oded Marom. *Sitting, first from left,* is the flyer identified in this book as Gad Eldar. Yigael Shochar is the fourth from the left. *(Collection of Oded Marom)*

The first Phantom team during training in the United States. *Standing, left to right:* Ehud Henkin, Shaul Levi, David Yair, Rami Harpaz, Shmuel Hetz, Eyal Ahikar, Avihu Ben-Nun, Menachem Eini, Yitzhak Pier, Yoram Agmon. *Kneeling:* The American trainers. *(Collection of Yair David)*

The Skyhawk A-4 was the first new American-built aircraft to serve with the IAF. *(Collection of Lon Nordeen)*

The first four F-4 Phantom fighter-bombers arrived from the United States in September 1970. *(Collection of Lon Nordeen)*

Beni Peled as IAF commander. *(Collection of Beni Peled)*

Iftach Spector (*right*) briefing air crews of his Phantom squadron before a mission during the 1973 Yom Kippur War. *(Collection of Iftach Spector)*

A somber moment in Ramat David during a celebration of the successful 1981 bombing of the Iraqi nuclear reactor near Bagdad. *Left to right:* Iftach Spector (Commander Wing 1, Ramat David), Lt. Gen. Rafael Eitan (IDF chief of staff), Menachem Begin (Israeli prime minister), General David Ivri (IAF commander). *(Collection of Iftach Spector)*

The Kfir, Israel's ultimate version of the Mirage. *(Collection of Lon Nordeen)*

dropped five of their six bombs right on the runways, closing them instantly. At Fayid, Avihu Ben-Nun rolled in through a hole in the clouds, dropped two bombs, and then two more in front of four MiGs that were rolling out for takeoff. Two of the MiGs blew up instantly, and the other two stopped dead in their tracks as huge craters opened right before them. At the same instant a few miles to the south, Yak Nevo rolled his Super-Mystère into Kabrit. He had spent the past year studying in the United States, but on June 1 he skipped his graduation ceremony, left his family behind, and talked his way onto an El Al flight to Israel. He barely had time for a few refresher flights when the war he had meticulously planned for actually broke out.

Farther north at El 'Arīsh, four Ouragans with no bombs—the Israelis planned to occupy El 'Arīsh that night and to use it as their own frontline airfield, so there was no sense in damaging the runways—blew up the base's antiaircraft batteries with rockets, then came around again, guns blazing, to demolish six MiGs on the ground.

At 7:50, free of the heavy bombs they had lugged in across the desert, the attacking planes doubled back over the same fields to strafe any planes in sight with their guns. Ignoring Egyptian antiaircraft fire, Ronen and his pilots crisscrossed the field, turning MiGs into fireballs with each pass. At Cairo West, Lapidot's formation torched eight Tupolev-16 and one IL-28 bombers, and three MiG-21s. At Fayid, Ben-Nun's Mystères left sixteen MiGs burning on the ground, but narrowly missed a huge Antonov transport that miraculously landed unharmed amidst the commotion.*

The war was now on. At 7:45, just as the first planes went into their bombing dives, Rabin barked into his microphone the code words that sent the IDF Southern Command's tanks and infantry charging at the Sinai fortifications. Rabin still had no way of knowing if his massive gamble had paid off, but at 7:55, the speakers at the IAF command bunker suddenly exploded in a barrage of radio messages as, one by one, the pilots began to report in. As each

---

*The Antonov carried Field Marshal Abdel Hakim Amer, Egypt's chief of staff, and his entire general staff, who had just completed an inspection tour of the Sinai. The Antonov pilot reportedly received numerous decorations for evading Ben-Nun's gunfire.

formation leader gave his call sign, location, and the code letter indicating how well he performed his mission, the small crowd in the bleachers behind Hod drew its breath in shock and disbelief.

It was just the beginning. At 8:00, as if directed by the baton of an invisible conductor, the second strike wave arrived at their targets just as the first wave's planes were about to depart for home. At Inshas, Ronen's Mirages were climbing away just as Yalo Shavit dived in with a Super-Mystère foursome to continue the devastation. Oded Marom arrived at Cairo West a minute after a Vautour formation left for home. Diving at the runway intersection, he spotted several huge Tupolev-16 Soviet bombers at the edge of the field. At the end of the second pass, all five were on fire.

And on it went. Egypt was given no chance to catch its breath. At Abu Suweir, 102 bombs were dropped by twenty-seven planes that swooped in in ten formations, minutes after one another. Similarly hit was Cairo West, home of fifteen heavy Tupolev-16 bombers. At 8:15, the Vautours that had left Ramat David almost an hour earlier reached Beni Suef, sixty miles south of Cairo up the Nile, to find "Egyptian soldiers running from the mess hall to their artillery positions. We switched to strafing and set all their planes on fire. The Tupolev-16s had the best-looking explosions," the mission leader reported later. Turning to leave, his navigator looked back just in time to see ten Tupolev-16 bombers burning below. "The field is all plugged up, planes burning as in a movie; no, much more than that. What a fire, as if huge oil tanks were set ablaze," the navigator later wrote in his diary.[23]

The toll was staggering. By 9:00 A.M., nearly two hundred planes—most of Egypt's bombers and practically its entire Sinai fighter force—had been destroyed. The eleven airfields targeted for the first attack, including the four Sinai bases and the two across the Canal from which Egyptian fighters could reach Israel, were rendered useless.

At the IAF bunker, Rabin watched Hod for signs of I-told-you-so glee. "After all, this was precisely how he predicted events. . . . I was quite prepared to accept such a reaction with perfect humility. But his features were rocklike . . . not a muscle moved," Rabin would note in his memoirs.[24]

Hod's silence lasted for three hours after the first formation lifted off toward Egypt, and then he turned to Rabin and said, "The Egyptian Air Force has ceased to exist." Breaking security, Weizman called his wife from the bunker. "We won the war," he said.[25]

Victory was not coming in cheap. Radio reports of demolished fields and blown-up enemy planes also brought news of losses in planes and men. By midmorning the toll reached five dead, three wounded, and two captured pilots. Eight planes had been destroyed. At Abu Suweir, an Egyptian MiG shot down an Israeli Vautour, whose pilot bailed out and was captured. Jonathan Shachar, commander of a Mystère squadron, blew up a MiG-21 on the Fayid tarmac, but damaged his own plane in the explosion, bailed out in the Sinai, and was rescued only later that night. At Inshas, a Super-Mystère exploded when antiaircraft fire struck its bombload. An Ouragan pilot who shot down a MiG-17 was struck by the ejection seat of the escaping Egyptian pilot, crashed at sea and was taken prisoner. Another Ouragan pilot, who had apparently struck high-tension wires while dive-bombing yet another airfield and might have lost consciousness, was brought down by an Israeli Hawk surface-air missile when he inadvertently attempted to fly home over Israel's super-secret nuclear reactor at Dimona, in the northern Negev.

Hardest hit was Yak Nevo's Super-Mystère's formation. Having destroyed several MiGs and two IL-14 transports at Kabrit, they were returning home across the Sinai when "I suddenly saw two MiGs in the distance, right behind us at six o'clock, about two kilometers back. I called out 'MiGs' and we opened up speed, staying close to the ground,"[26] but flying so low and fast over the sand dunes with the sun in their eyes, two of the pilots crashed and were killed, one instantly, and one later by a roving band of Bedouins that robbed him and slit his throat.

By mid-morning, with Jordan and Syria yet to scramble a single plane, Hod ordered a second round of strikes against Egypt, this time targeting the distant air bases of El Mansūra and Bilbeis northeast of Cairo; Helwân, El Minya, and Luxor up the Nile Valley south of Cairo; and Ghardaka on the west coast of the Red Sea. Two hours and 164 sorties later, 107 more Egyptian planes were gone. Two-thirds of the Egyptian Air Force had already been destroyed, and it was not yet lunchtime.

The war had just begun. "Only one part of the enemy force was destroyed, its air force, and we had yet to engage its armor. But already . . . the oppressive nightmare that hovered over us since our War of Independence suddenly vanished," Dayan would write later.[27] Also at noon, BBC correspondent Michael Elkins had talked IDF censors into letting him report that, after three weeks of impending doom, Israel had just won the war in three hours. The report provided no details and, for the time being, was largely dismissed as Israeli propaganda.

Chapter 18

KEEP IT SIMPLE

At high noon—the day was still June 5, 1967—Ran Ronen led a Mirage formation down the Gulf of Aqaba, 30,000 feet above a breathtaking moonscape of dark peaks and rocky fjords flanking the oily-blue waterway. The Egyptian Sinai was on the right, Jordan and Saudi Arabia to the left. It was Ronen's third mission that morning. Following his early raid on the Inshas near Cairo, he led a second Mirage attack on the Abu Suweir airfield just across the Suez Canal, leaving ten Soviet-built IL-28 bombers burning on the tarmac. With barely enough time to debrief his pilots and make his mission report, he was on his way again.

More than anything, more than the pilots' stamina or their new commander's nerve, the whirlwind air war that erupted that morning was the ultimate test and—should its success hold—confirmation of the metamorphosis that the IAF had undergone since the 1956 war. And of the man who had led it until just a few months ago. Every aspect of the force's appearance, function, and performance on that morning, from the way its pilots had been screened before flight training, to the last detail of the *Moked* plan that they were now following, to the guns carried by their stiletto-shaped Mirages, to the layout of the command bunker from which the operation was run, and even to the very men who issued the commands from that bunker—everything was the product of Weizman's eight years at the IAF controls.

His stamp was everywhere. Virtually every senior officer, from base commanders on up to branch chiefs and to Moti Hod himself at the commander's seat, started out at Ramat David in the early 1950s, during his Camelot years of Air Force North. And the young men who commanded the squadrons and flew the planes that morning had been molded under his command and in his image— aggressive, fast-talking, competent, performance-driven, charismatic, fiercely patriotic.

Few better epitomized this new generation of "Ezer's boys" than Ran Ronen. Blond, blue-eyed, and handsome, Ronen was the most naturally gifted fighter pilot the IAF had known. His bailing out of a Mirage that then landed by itself; his 1966 downing of the Jordanian Hunter in the toughest and longest *mano a mano* dogfight in IAF annals; the story of how, after losing a MiG in the clouds on April 7, 1967, he ambushed it behind another cloud bank and shot it down over Damascus—all these were now the stuff of legend.

It was not just that "little Weizman," as he was often called, could fly. He exuded leadership. He came from an illustrious pioneering farm family, and the fervor of his patriotic oratory was such that "You'd think he invented Zionism single-handedly," a friend once remarked. His wife, too, was one for the books—beautiful, smart, poised, and appropriately named Heruta, Hebrew for liberty. Since taking over the 191 squadron two years earlier, he had whipped it into fever-pitch performance, ruthlessly expelling pilots who did not measure up and seducing promising pilots from other squadrons into requesting transfers to his, much to the chagrin of the other commanders. Since the 191 had Mirages equipped for photo-reconnaissance, Ronen consistently drew more and better assignments for his adventurous pilots. "He was the greatest squadron commander ever, period," says Menahem Shmul, who flew with him at the 191 and is today chief test pilot for the Israel Aircraft Industries.[1]

Three days before the war broke out, when doubt-ridden Rabin toured IAF bases, Moti Hod saw to it that he visited Ronen's squadron. Rabin would later concede that in no small measure it was Ronen's unbounded confidence—Ronen treated Rabin to an air show that included a stunt one-wheel takeoff in a Mirage—that led him to accept Hod's preemptive-strike plan. "Whatever you write about [Ronen] would be true when it comes to professional ability, leadership, and bravery," Moti Hod would tell a reporter. Like Ronen himself, so did his Mirage and his mission plan, even the target he was heading for, epitomize the sweep of the Weizman revolution. Located in a remote lunar landscape 300 miles inside Egyptian territory on the west coast of the Red Sea, Ghardaka was a small and remote fighter strip—only two runways, a small control tower, and a clump of hangars—from which several squadrons of MiGs and combat helicopters controlled the entrances to the gulfs of Aqaba and Suez, and to much of the southern Sinai. It was not only isolated and difficult to find, but to reach it the attacking force would have to come within range of not just Egyptian but also Jordanian and Saudi air patrols. And Ronen had just four Mirages with which to take Ghardaka out.

Shortly after they passed Sharm el Sheikh, the high-flying Mirages dived down, leveling just above the Red Sea's dark-blue waters. The terrain was unfamiliar and difficult to navigate—there were no roads, no harbors or light towers, only rocky islands that looked remarkably alike. Ronen turned west over what he hoped was the right small island and crossed over the rocky coastline into Egypt. If he chose correctly, their target was just one minute away. Spotting a sharp turn in a dry wadi below, ostensibly his mark to begin the attack, he rammed forward his throttles, pulled hard on his stick to throw his plane into a steep climb, and turned to look for his target.

Ghardaka was not only there, but waiting. As if expecting the Israelis, its antiaircraft guns opened fire as soon as the Mirages rose over the rocky ridge to the east. Oblivious to the fire, the Mirages executed a textbook bombing run, hitting the two runways and rendering them unusable, then dashed fast and low to the west, to come around for their three strafing runs. Fortunately, the skies over the base were clear. Anticipating an Israeli attack, Ghardaka's commander had scrambled four MiG-21s to guard the base from above, but because the attackers were expected to arrive from the north—along the shortest route from Israel—the MiGs were now circling and watching over the southern end of the Gulf of Suez. By coming from the east, the Mirages had Ghardaka to themselves, without its fighter cover, for the few minutes it would take the MiGs to get back.

Coming around after dropping his bombs, Ronen found two MiGs that he had spotted earlier on the tarmac, and set them on fire with one burst from his 30-mm guns. In his second pass, he blew up a helicopter. A third pass left three more MiGs burning on the runway. Officially the mission was now over. The Mirages were already at their fuel and ammunition limit. In fact, one of Ronen's pilots had already reported low fuel and was sent home alone.

Ronen was about to gather his remaining pilots when a shrill warning—"break, on your tail"—ripped through his earphones, and he looked back just in time to see a MiG closing in and firing behind him. The MiGs had come back. Warning his two remaining pilots to drop their empty fuel tanks and get ready for air combat, Ronen dived down and shook the MiG with a quick "let him pass" maneuver. As the MiG sailed past—"it was bigger than my Mirage, its wings longer, its body dirty, its silhouette coarse," Ronen noticed—Israeli and Egyptian pilots briefly locked eyes before the startled Egyptian shot on ahead. Ronen rolled in right behind him, fired, and watched it crash into the airfield below.

His crew members were nowhere to be seen, but on the radio one reported closing in on a MiG at the northwest corner of base, and the second following another MiG west of the field. Ronen calculated quickly. Counting the MiG he had just shot down, that made three MiGs. But like the Israelis, Egyptian fighters usually traveled in fours. Where was the fourth MiG?

Swinging west of the field in the direction of his wingman, he noticed three dark specks flying in a row. The center speck seemed smaller and lighter in color. "Wave wings," he called into the microphone. The tiny light plane in the middle waved. So engrossed was the young pilot in chasing his MiG he didn't notice that the fourth MiG had arrived behind him and was about to shoot him down. Ronen shouted a warning and threw his plane into afterburner. As his wingman fired, hit the first MiG and promptly broke off, Ronen squeezed his remaining twenty or so shells at the other. It, too, crashed.

Time was running out. "What's happening with you?" Ronen growled into the mike after failing to spot his last remaining pilot. "Still after him south of the runway," the pilot's disappointed voice came through his headset. Glancing down, Ronen turned cold. Right below him, an Egyptian MiG was coming in for a landing, nose-up, flaps out, and wheels ready to hit the ground. Close behind was the missing Mirage struggling to remain airborne, "maneuvering wildly, helplessly, trying not to overshoot the slowing MiG." So determined was the young pilot to bag his first MiG, that he was now going so low and slow he was more likely to crash into his MiG than to shoot it down.

"Leave him. Right turn low. Full dry engine. Loose flaps. Gather speed," Ronen snapped into the mike. Reluctantly, the young pilot peeled off and regained control of his plane. Below, just as Ronen expected, the MiG touched down and, as its nose wheel dropped into a bomb crater, exploded in a huge smoky mushroom.

Ronen and his remaining pilots were cruising north over the Gulf of Aqaba when the leader of a second Mirage formation from Ronen's own squadron, on his way to help out at Ghardaka, popped up on the radio and asked for guidance. "Ghardaka is finished for the foreseeable future," Ronen announced. The fresh Mirages turned back north, received a new mission heading, and at 1:15 rolled into the Amman airfield in Jordan to destroy its two runways and close it for the remainder of the war.

A remarkable spectacle was now unfolding over the desert country. One moment every airborne Israeli plane was on its way to Egypt. The next, it switched directions in midair to head for Syria or Jordan. Just as Moti Hod had predicted, half the day and most of the Egyptian Air Force were gone before Jordan, Syria, Lebanon, and Iraq had finally figured out what was happening and joined the fighting.

The first Arab attacks began at noon. A dozen Syrian MiGs arrived over the Jordan Valley, then separated into several attack formations. Two went south over the Sea of Galilee. They strafed a hay barn and several chicken houses at Moti Hod's home *kibbutz* of Degania, and then shot up a small military outpost and a dam on the Jordan River before two Israeli Mirages shot them down. Three other MiGs attacked the Megiddo airfield near Ramat David and were shot down by Mirages and ground fire. Two other MiG formations strafed a farming village on the Mediterranean Coast and a convalescent home near Nazareth before getting away.

Jordan entered the war at about the same time. As its artillery batteries at the north end of the West Bank shelled Ramat David, several of its British-built Hunters bombed the Israeli beach resort town of Netanya north of Tel Aviv, then strafed the Kfar Sirkin airfield on their way back, destroying a French-made Nord transport on the ground.

So did Iraq. Uri Even-Nir, deputy commander of the 117 Mirage squadron at Ramat David, was sitting inside his Mirage on the tarmac, waiting for orders, when "right out of the eucalyptus trees and over the fence, right in front of my eyes, three Hunters pulled up, leveled off, and started to roll in. I knew that position and what it meant. There was no way they could miss me. I felt a horrible sense of helplessness."[2] Amichai Gal, his squadron commander, had just landed and was taxiing back to his hangar when he, too, spotted the Hunters rolling in for an attack, seemingly coming straight at him. Yet nothing happened.

The Iraqi pilots had navigated perfectly and pulled up for the attack precisely at the right place. But as they looked down, their target somehow wasn't there. Flailing about briefly, they gave up, continued to the west, and dropped their bombs on several chicken houses in the nearby village of Nahalal, whose roofs made them appear like aircraft hangars.*

At 12:45, with the Egyptian Air Force all but destroyed, Hod ordered the IAF into action over Jordan and Syria. The switch came so quickly—Hod would later admit that in his "wildest dreams" he did not expect to be through with Egypt before nightfall—that IAF Operations actually had trouble picking and feeding new target

---

*The next day, an Iraqi Soviet-built Tupolev-16 bomber that had just dropped three bombs over the coastal resort town of Netanya and was on its way back to Iraq also came over Ramat David but missed it. Only when it had passed the base and the antiaircraft batteries opened up below did its tail gunner realize where he was and open fire. By then it was too late. The bomber was struck by ground fire and then by a missile from a Mirage interceptor. Changing direction, it made for the most visible target around—the freshly painted runways of the nearby Megiddo field, where it found no planes but a fuel dump into which it crashed, killing fourteen Israeli soldiers. According to returning Israeli prisoners from Iraq, the Tupolev-16 had originally meant to bomb Tel Aviv, sixteen miles south of Netanya.

assignments to the squadrons fast enough. For all intents and purposes, the *Moked* offensive was over, along with its meticulous
planning and preparations. Scrambled or diverted to new targets
without adequate briefings or even proper maps, formation leaders
had to find their way by memory or—in the case of Yak Nevo, who
was diverted in midair from the Mafraq airfield in Jordan to Syria's
new Seiqal airfield, where he'd never been—by instinct.

Even with Egypt's fighters out of the picture, the Israeli air
offensive was entering a critical phase. To take out Syria's and
Jordan's frontline airfields now that the surprise was gone, Israeli
pilots who had already logged two or three grueling combat missions that day had to dogfight their way to and from their targets.
Losing the surprise edge was particularly hard on Israel's older
attack planes which, with no fighter cover, often had to contend
with Syria's superior MiG-21s. Yalo Shavit, commander of the 105
Super-Mystère squadron, had just dropped his bombs on a runway
at Seiqal, east of Damascus, when two MiG-21s swooped in behind
his formation. Years of "inferior versus superior plane" dogfight
training, however, came in handy. Shavit turned "belly up and
going down like I was in trouble [and] let him come nose-down after
me. But just as he thought he had me I broke hard, did a barrel roll
and came behind him. He did a few tight turns, but at that low
altitude and speed there was no way he could get away. I shot him
and he crashed right into a hangar."[3]

For the Mirages, too, missions that would have been simple with
adequate preparations and assured surprise were now full of unknown risks and surprises. Two formations from Ronen's squadron, about to take off for the airfields of Inshas in Egypt and Dumeir
in Syria, were abruptly diverted to T-4, a remote Syrian airfield
which, located a hundred miles beyond Damascus, was not only
outside their normal range but did not even appear on their maps.
At the last moment, two maps were located and handed to the
leaders of the first formation. The second formation, already in the
air, had neither maps nor an idea where T-4 was. Breaking regula-
tions and radio silence, one of its pilots climbed high enough to
establish radio contact with the lead formation and ask for directions.

Whether Syrian intelligence monitored that call or not, by the time the first formation reached T-4 the field was already protected by two high-flying MiG-21s. Still, the first Mirage formation managed to sneak into the field unnoticed and drop its bombs, but by the time the Mirages pulled up the MiGs had come down, forcing one of the pilots to abandon his strafing runs to keep them at bay. He shot down a MiG with barely enough time to catch up with his formation, which was already heading home. When the second MiG gave chase, a Mirage pilot named Giora Rom, who had already shot down two MiGs that morning on the Egyptian front, turned back to face it.

What happened then only underscored how crucial both secrecy and precision were for the success of *Moked*, and how easily its Swiss-watch precision could have been disrupted by the slightest lapse in surprise. Rom was just settling on his MiG's tail when the second Mirage formation arrived and rolled into its bombing run, smack through the ongoing air battle. Suddenly surrounded by bomb-laden Mirages, the MiG that Rom was following turned after the leader of the arriving Mirages. Abandoning their precision bombing sweep, both Oded Sagie, the flight leader, and Menahem Shmul, his wingman, kicked their planes into afterburner and went after the MiG. In the confusion, Sagie got on the MiG's tail only to have Shmul cut him off and go for the shot himself. But Shmul's engine suddenly died, and as he flipped over to dive into the field and restart it, the Syrian MiG doubled back after Sagie. Rom, still trying to sort out the mess, finally found himself back behind the MiG, shot it down, and rushed to get back to Israel before his fuel ran out.

Although the commotion lasted no more than a minute, and Shmul managed to restart his engine before crashing into the tarmac with his bomb-load, the strike's carefully orchestrated rhythm had been broken. When Shmul pulled back up, he was out of synchronization with the rest of his formation, so he began his dive at the field alone. Mechanically watching his altimeter, and waiting for it to reach the 3,500-foot mark—the proper altitude for releasing his bombs—he inadvertently glanced at the field and suddenly "realized that the runway in front of me looked way too wide, incredibly too wide." In a flash, he remembered that since T-4 was 2,000 feet above sea level, he was already less than 2,000 feet above the runway, and "going down so fast and so low that all I could do was drop the bombs and get out as fast as I could." As he turned to pull back up, however, he found himself coming behind a MiG that was taxiing out on the ground. He pressed the trigger and began to pull up, but so close was he to the MiG that as it exploded Shmul ran right into the fireball.

Back up over the field, and still unable to see any of his formation members, he went into his strafing run, turning sharp right into "a delicious target—three MiG-21s sitting in a row at the edge of the runway." He was briefly hanging sideways above the field, right wing pointing straight down and his left pointing up, when "something, I still don't know what it was, made me straighten up just for a quick look around. I did it barely in time to avoid a belly collision." Just as he had arrived from one side, his flight leader had come down from another direction in a left-handed dive—right wing up and left wing down—after the same three MiGs. Flying out of sync and unaware of each other, the two planes had arrived over the same spot at the same time, closing belly-to-belly like two hands clapping. Shmul, who "could see and count every rivet on [the other plane's] undercarriage" quickly broke off hard and moved away (he made up for it by staying behind after his formation departed, and shooting up another MiG on the tarmac before heading for home alone).[4]

By midafternoon, the Jordanian Air Force was demolished, as were half of Syria's fighters. At 3:00 P.M., in one of the longest and most dangerous raids of the day, three unescorted Vautours from Ramat David flew clear across Jordan and Syria to attack the Iraqi air base at H-3.* Although attacked by several MiG-21s even before they reached the field, the Vautours managed to destroy six MiGs and three Hunters on the tarmac before leaving. By evening, the Israeli air victory was stunning and complete. "It is . . . late, and all is quiet and peaceful in the Middle East," a Ramat David pilot scribbled in the squadron book, "with not a single enemy plane left anywhere. We are the sole rulers of the skies. Just one day of fighting—and already there is nobody left to stand up to the IAF."[5]

---

*It was the same base from which the Iraqis lobbed Scud missiles into Israel during the 1991 Operation Desert Storm.

The Israelis took heavy casualties. A Mystère pilot was shot down by a Jordanian Hunter. A Super-Mystère was shot down over Syria and its pilot was killed by angry villagers. Seven planes were downed by Syrian ground fire, with only three of their pilots surviving to fall prisoner. Two Mirages were hit during a strafing run over the Damascus airport, one crashing with its pilot and the other barely staying aloft long enough to get back to Israel, where its pilot bailed out. Although only half as many missions were launched at Syria and Jordan as against Egypt, those afternoon missions took as many casualties as the entire massive morning campaign.

The day was not yet over. Through much of the night, their targets lit by flares, Vautours, Super-Mystères, and other attack crews carried out their fifth and sixth missions of the day, demolishing Jordanian artillery and blocking Jordanian Legion advances on Jerusalem. "All of the Jerusalem area was like a fireworks show, with artillery fire and flares," Yalo Shavit recalled.[6] Also that evening, Ran Ronen led his fourth mission of the day, to drop delay-action bombs on Cairo International Airport, where the Egyptians had moved some of their remaining MiGs and heavy bombers. In nearly one thousand missions and at a cost of twenty dead pilots, 240 Israeli fighters and fighter-bombers destroyed nearly 450 enemy planes, most of them on the ground and only 70 in air combat.

With the Arab air power gone, Israel's ground forces had been slugging their way into the Sinai since morning without fear of Arab air attacks. By the end of the first day, General Tal's armor and Col. Rafael Eitan's paratroopers had broken through the heavily defended northern entrances to the Sinai all the way to El 'Arīsh. Farther to the south, Gen. Ariel Sharon's mechanized infantry division broke through the fortified complex of Um Katef and Abu Ageila, the nerve center of the Egyptian Sinai front. On the Jordanian side, as IAF Fouga Magister flight-school trainers rigged with guns and rockets demolished a Jordanian hundred-tank column heading from Jericho to Jerusalem, IDF Central Command armor and infantry broke into the West Bank north and south of Jerusalem. Before dawn, the old fortress of Latrun, at the gateway to Jerusalem, was in Israeli hands.

The war turned into a rout. Early the following morning, with Jerusalem surrounded, Dayan and Weizman drove in a Jeep into the old Hebrew University campus on Mount Scopus, occupied since 1948 by Jordan. Bursting into an old laboratory where one of his uncles once taught chemistry, Weizman was stunned to find that the place had remained untouched for nearly twenty years. "On the table I find a stack of Uncle Moshe's papers. On the blackboard, in white chalk in my uncle's handwriting, the title of his next lecture and the date—1948," he would write later.[7]

By the end of the second day the Egyptian army had begun to retreat from the Sinai, and by midnight so had Jordan's forces from the West Bank. On Wednesday morning, June 7, the third day of the war, Israeli paratroopers broke into the Old City of Jerusalem and reached the Western Wall. At noon, Israeli paratroopers and naval units landed at Sharm el Sheikh and found it empty. On Thursday, as the Jordanian Legion completed its retreat across the Jordan, Israeli sappers blew up the bridges behind it. In the Sinai, wave after wave of Israeli aircraft destroyed the retreating Egyptian convoys, lining the desert roads with burned-out shells of tanks and trucks.

It was toward noon of that day that the most unfortunate mistakes of the war took place. It began when Israeli troops on the Sinai coast near El 'Arīsh reported being shelled from the sea. Israeli torpedo boats rushed to the area and spotted an unidentified ship escaping rapidly toward Port Said, but were unable to catch up with it. Shortly past noon, IAF Control asked two Mirages that had just completed a ground attack mission near El 'Arīsh to check out the ship. "We found a large gray ship, the size of a medium merchant ship, with two U-shaped masts carrying numerous antennas," recalls Gad Eldar,* who led the flight. "We had no idea what it was. We flew in a circle, low and slow. We did not see a single identifying mark or flag except for a huge black number painted on the side. We called in the details, when suddenly the controller's voice changed and he ordered us to get away immediately because, as he said, 'This is a third force.' As we found out later, they thought it was a Soviet war ship."[8]

Around 2:00 in the afternoon two more Mirages were dispatched for a look. They, too, reported that the ship carried no identification

---

*Not his real name.

marks. "No flag?" IAF Operations reportedly asked. When the pilots confirmed the message they received permission to fire, and in three strafing passes struck the ship's center and set it on fire at several points. The Mirages were followed by two Super-Mystères, whose pilots, flying lower and slower, read the letters "C.P.R.S.C." off the side of the ship. Both planes and torpedo boats were then ordered to stop firing.

At 2:23, one of the Israeli boats approached the ship again and demanded identification. "Identify yourself," came the reply—the same reply that the Egyptian destroyer *Ibrahim al Awal* gave during the 1956 war when confronted off the coast of Haifa. Their suspicions aroused, the Israeli sailors consulted their manual and concluded that the ship was the *Al Kussar*, an Egyptian supply ship which the previous night was seen evacuating Palestinian fighters from Gaza. The Israelis resumed firing. The ship took a napalm bomb from one of the Super-Mystères and five torpedoes from the Israeli boats before a large American flag was suddenly unfurled from the side and the fire stopped.

It was the first time the Israelis realized that the ship was American. Although officers of the *Liberty*, an American spy ship, would later testify that a huge American flag was raised over the ship as soon as the first Israeli planes arrived, this is contradicted not only by Israeli pilots and sailors on the scene, but also by Israeli gun-camera footage which showed the *Liberty* under fire—with no flag anywhere to be seen. Subsequent inquiries revealed that the ship was monitoring Israeli and Arab field communications, that neither warring country was notified of its presence there, and that the ship's crew were following orders when they refused to identify themselves to the Israelis. The results were costly—thirty-four American sailors died before the ship finally identified herself (Israel subsequently apologized to the United States for the unintentional attack, and paid compensations to the families of the dead sailors).

On the morning of June 9, with only Syria left unscathed, Dayan decided to settle that account, too, and ordered Gen. Dado Elazar's Northern Command to take the Golan Heights. With just three brigades, some of them already cannibalized for the effort in the south, Elazar's troops charged straight up the cliffs at the northern and central sectors of the heights, and by noon of the next day had seized the rim. It was almost too late to do any good. Although the Syrian army was in retreat, hectic negotiations at the United Nations were almost certain to result in the imposition of a truce by nightfall. With Israel's dead-tired tankists, infantrymen, and paratroopers unable to move fast enough to expand their toehold on the rim of the heights, the Syrians could easily dislodge them with a surprise attack, and certainly could go on shelling Israeli settlements right over their heads.

For a while it seemed that on this, Israel's most troublesome border, the war would end up achieving nothing. Later that afternoon, however, Eliezer "Cheeta" Cohen, now a scrappy helicopter squadron commander, proposed that, instead of ferrying paratroopers only to the edge of the cliffs, he'd carry them as far to the rear of the Golan Heights as the retreating Syrian troops would allow. He did, and by evening, instead of gathering just three miles east of the Sea of Galilee as originally planned, the paratroopers had taken the critical Butmyeh Junction fifteen miles inland from the edge of the heights, and remained there as the truce went into effect that night.

By the end of the week Israel had not only broken the Arab noose but pushed its borders farther back than anyone had ever expected. To the south, the IDF was digging in along the Suez Canal and the Straits of Tiran. In the east, the nearest Jordanian guns were behind the Jordan River. To the north, the Syrians had been pushed so far back that, for the first time in years, children in Galilee villages could sleep in their own rooms aboveground, rather than in underground bomb shelters.

Internationally, where the heretofore unknown IAF had suddenly exploded on the scene with the sort of victory only Hollywood could dream up, the victory was put in charming perspective by Moti Hod who, when pressed by a foreign correspondent for the "secret" of the remarkable victory, shrugged and replied "We try to keep things very simple."

To those in the know, however, there was no question but that the victory was brought about as much by the frontiersman as by the prince. Not only because of his promise of victory, which rallied Rabin on the night of his collapse, and which had now come true, but because of the entire eight years that preceded it. As an unknown senior IDF officer confessed—and was widely quoted for years afterward—"Remember all those crazy things Ezer said he could do? The son of a bitch wasn't kidding."

PART FOUR

THE BLOODYING

Chapter 19

"TEXAS"

In the early morning hours of June 26, 1969, a little-noted drama took place over the Egyptian desert. Maj. Oded Marom and Lt. Iftach Spector, commander and deputy commander of the 101 Mirage squadron out of Hazor, had come looking for Egyptian MiGs that had been taunting Israeli troops on the Suez Canal for days. They spent an hour looking before two MiG-21s finally showed up, but the MiGs kept their distance and only drew the Israelis into wide chase circles leading nowhere. Finally, with their fuel down to 700 liters—IAF rules prohibited remaining across the Canal with less than 750—Marom called the mission off and turned for home.

Spector was about to follow when he noticed the afterburner's flame dying under the tail of the MiG he had been following. "He was sure there was nobody behind him, [and] I felt with my whole being that was The Moment," he recalled later.[1] Without saying a word to Marom or to his IAF controllers, he rolled his Mirage back to the west, and kicked his throttle forward. "How was I to know he was chasing a MiG the other way?" Marom would later bristle at the suggestion that what happened next was somehow his fault.[2]

By the time Spector closed in on his MiG and shot it down, he found himself near Cairo, alone, and with little fuel left. He quickly climbed to 30,000 feet and headed east, so that if his fuel ran out he could glide his fighter across the Canal to an emergency landing in the Sinai. Suddenly, however, distant specks of glistening metal appeared from the north, and soon Spector was staring at four MiG-21s in combat formation bearing down on him. He was trapped, with too little fuel to flee or fight. Marom had already passed the Canal on his way home, and was himself too low on fuel to turn around. If there were other Mirages in the area, they were too far to help. Instinctively, Spector dived to the safety of the desert floor and darted south, away from the MiGs.

By that time, realizing what had happened, his controllers dispatched a couple of Mirages for the rescue. But it would be some time before they could reach him, and meanwhile news of his predicament spread like wildfire. However few on the outside had ever heard of him, in the IAF fighter community everybody had. Two years earlier, on April 11, 1967, the Day of the MiGs, it was Spector who downed the first Syrian fighter over the Golan Heights, and he followed it two months later with two more MiGs during the Six-Day War. Slight of build and boyish, with huge eyes set wide apart, Spector was not only a brilliant flyer with a deadly killer's instinct but a natural leader, a gifted intellect, the kind of "thinking pilot" the IAF cultivated for top leadership positions. Moti Hod had a particular stake in getting him back from behind enemy lines. Twenty-eight years earlier, at the height of the Nazi advance on the Middle East, Spector's father commanded a naval commando team of twenty-two, whose boat disappeared without a trace en route to blowing up the Axis powers' oil refineries near Tripoli, on the Syrian coast north of Lebanon. At that time, it was Moti Hod's father who searched the Lebanese coast and countryside in vain for the missing commandos.

Meanwhile, Spector was alone in the Egyptian desert. With the MiGs in hot pursuit, he was twisting and turning like a jackrabbit among the sand dunes, his fuel rapidly running out. For a brief moment he toyed with a "mad notion to use my remaining 100–200 liters to shoot one of [the MiGs] down," but he quickly abandoned it for an even madder notion. Holding the stick with one hand to keep his buffeting Mirage on course, he pulled out the gun camera cassette and zipped it inside his flight suit. If he lived through it all, the proof of his MiG-kill over Cairo might save him from being court-martialed for disobeying Marom's order to turn back, for remaining behind enemy lines with too little fuel, for running out of fuel, and, the way things seemed, for losing a precious Mirage. It mattered little that the camera made it impossible for him to survive if his Mirage didn't—it would crush his chest if he attempted to punch out through the canopy with it.

He was hurtling above the desert floor, his left hand resting lightly on the throttle, ready to eject the moment his engine began to cough, when he noticed that the MiGs were no longer behind him. From the radio chatter he gathered that other Mirages had arrived, and he threw the plane into one last climb and turned east. But so far south had the MiGs chased him that instead of the narrow Canal, it was the twenty-mile-wide Gulf of Suez that now separated him from the safety of the Israeli-held Sinai. He was flying gingerly over the Gulf's deep-blue waters, "slumping in my cockpit, trying not to touch, not to move a flap, not to create any aerodynamic drag," when his engine died. Instantly, the Mirage began to drop. There was no way of telling where it would crash, into the shark-infested waters below, or against the primordial, yellow-brown mountains on the other side.

Just then, like a desert mirage, a small runway materialized out of the shimmering haze. The 1100-meter, rock-strewn landing strip at Abu Rudeis, normally used by rugged IAF transports and helicopters to land supplies for Israeli ground forces in the lower Sinai, was far too short and too rough for the delicate French fighter, but it was the only one around. Spector aimed his skydiving ninja triangle at its end, dropped his flaps, and slammed into the rocky ground. The Mirage shuddered but came to a safe stop.

Spector's escapade, for which he was disciplined but not court-martialed, epitomized a strange new war that Israel entered almost as soon as it dealt the combined Arab armies one of the most decisive defeats in military history.

No one had expected it. On June 8, 1967, with the Six-Day War half over and Egypt's beaten troops clambering back across the Suez Canal, a mechanic breathlessly rushed up the ladder of a ready-to-roll Mirage on the Hazor tarmac, shouting that Nasser had resigned. The pilot in the cockpit, Yoram Agmon, began to shiver.

"I was so excited, I had hot flashes at the thought of peace talks and all that," he would say later.[3] By the end of the month, however, Nasser had withdrawn his resignation, fired his defense minister and top military commander, and resumed the fighting. In mid-July, Agmon flew his Mirage back across the Canal to where Egyptian SU-15 attack jets were strafing Israeli positions, and shot one of them down. Five more planes were brought down by other Israeli fighters that day. A new war was unmistakably on.

Just three months after its humiliating defeat, the Arab world rallied around Nasser once more, and at a September 1 Arab League conference in Khartoum backed him with money and with a unanimous refusal to recognize, negotiate, or make peace with Israel. Egyptian guns immediately began firing at Israeli ships in the Gulf of Suez, and on October 21 Egyptian missile boats sank the Israeli flagship *Eilat* off the coast of Port Said, killing 47 of its 199-member crew. The Israelis replied in such force—on October 25 their artillery destroyed the Suez and Nasser oil refineries and petrochemical installations near the city of Suez—that the front calmed for a year, but on September 8, 1968, more than one thousand Egyptian guns, mortars, and tanks opened fire once more along the sixty-five-mile front, killing eleven and wounding seventeen Israelis. A second nine-hour artillery barrage on October 26 killed fifteen more Israelis. Israel struck back again. On the night of October 31, Israeli helicopter-borne paratroopers penetrated deep into Egypt and struck Najh Hamadi, a vast and strategic complex of dams, bridges, and power-switching stations 300 miles up the Nile from Cairo, and blew up enough power lines to plunge much of Egypt into darkness. Nasser briefly shut down the war, but on March 3, 1969, turned the artillery on the Canal on again, and this time kept it going for more than a year with virtually no interruption. Israel's new Canal fortifications— dubbed the Barlev Line after Lt. Gen. Chaim Barlev, who replaced Rabin as IDF chief of staff at the end of 1967—were barely in place when 10,000 artillery shells fell on the first day of the new offensive, 35,000 by week's end.

Nasser's new offensive—he called it *Harb al-Istinzaf*, the War of Attrition—was one of two separate wars that grew like a phoenix out of the ashes of the 1967 Arab defeat. From Jordan and Lebanon, the Palestine Liberation Organization launched a massive terror campaign against Israeli settlements, with Jordan and Syria pitching in with artillery cover and logistics support. Unlike the static, World War I–like trench war imposed by Egypt's artillery in the south, in the north and the east the IDF faced a Vietnam-style counterinsurgency campaign. But it was the war in the south that strained and mystified the Israelis. Militarily, it offered no attainable goals for either side. Nasser's recently beaten army had no chance at a victory, while Israel, already straining to get a hold on the Sinai, the West Bank, and the Golan Heights which it just won in one war, could not afford to win another one if it meant taking in more territory. But Nasser was less after a military victory than a new and improved cease-fire agreement. To get it, he had to void the 1967 agreement by going—or at least appearing to be going—to war. This "war about the war," as Dayan dubbed it, was not about winning or losing but about whether or not to have it in the first place. Israel could lose only by scrapping the 1967 cease-fire agreement, and it now clung to it by refusing to be dragged into a fighting war. As Nasser kept upping the ante, Israel kept *pretending* that the carnage on the Canal was routine border violence.

And since keeping the no-war myth meant keeping the IAF out of the fighting, the three-year air war that enveloped and ultimately overshadowed the fighting on the Canal still remains the least reported, known, or understood of all of Israel's military campaigns. To this day, even after downing 137 enemy planes—five of them Russian—and losing twenty-four of their own by the time the fighting ended in the summer of 1970, and even after IDF soldiers received special decorations for active duty beyond the country's borders for that war, the IAF has yet to issue War of Attrition campaign ribbons. For the IAF, the longest, strangest, and in some respects the most important war in its existence officially never took place.

The IAF came out of its Six-Day War victorious, but also bruised and depleted. One pilot in ten was dead or in an Arab prison, and one combat jet in five was destroyed. And while the Soviet Union quickly rearmed the Arabs—Egypt and Syria received 150 new tanks, a hundred heavy guns, and a hundred new combat planes by August of 1967, barely two months after the fighting ended, and far more later—Israel's military reeled under a twin embargo by its main suppliers. France, anxious to repair its commercial ties with the Arabs, canceled all military sales to Israel, including the IAF's paid-for order for fifty new M-5 Mirages (and option for fifty more). The United States likewise suspended delivery of forty-six A-4 Skyhawks due later that year. In early 1968 Israel finally received the Skyhawks, which promptly went into action silencing Jordanian artillery and hunting down PLO terror bands in Jordan and Lebanon, and it got extra mileage out of its aging Super-Mystères by souping them up with Skyhawk engines, doubling their range and life span. But the IAF was running out of frontline fighters. While the Israel Aircraft Industries (IAI) was trying to produce a new fighter from Mirage blueprints that the *Mossad* and IDF Military Intelligence (AMAN) stole in Switzerland,* and while President Lyndon B. Johnson agreed to sell Israel fifty new F-4 Phantoms, it would be five years before Israel would have its home-made Mirages, and the new war would be into its third year by the time the Phantoms arrived.

Until then—actually, for the entire three-year duration of the conflict—the brunt of the air war would be borne by the same three squadrons of aging and war-battered Mirages. And since the Ramat David Mirages had to watch the Syrian front, and Tel Nof's were kept busy over Jordan and in photo-reconnaissance missions over the entire region, for the most part the air war on the Canal had to be carried by the 101 Mirage squadron at Hazor.

Had the war been foreseen, Oded Marom might not have been made the 101's commander. A decade earlier, his IAF Flight School instructors found him too gentle to fly fighters and sent him to fly Vautour bombers, instead. He only briefly flew Mirages with the 101 in the early 1960s before returning to IAF Flight School as an instructor, and it was as a flight instructor on an emergency assignment to the 101 that he led several successful missions during the Six-Day War. By IAF standards, this hardly qualified him to command a squadron, but just as his flight school tour ended, the 101's outgoing commander had to leave in a hurry, his scheduled replacement landed another post, and in the resulting confusion Marom was handed the job.

---

*The project, at the Israel Aircraft Industries complex outside Lod airport, was headed by the IAI's founder, Al Schwimmer, who ran the blockade-running *Yakum Purkan* operation in 1948.

He barely had time to establish a semblance of authority over his wild pack of veteran MiG-killers when the Canal war broke out. Small-framed and baby-faced, with a flair for art and poetry that would later lead to a career as writer and illustrator of children's books, Marom had seen or been through nothing to prepare him for his new assignment. If before the 1967 war a Mirage taking off from Hazor had to break hard to avoid entering Egyptian airspace, now the frontier was hundreds of miles away on the other side of the Sinai desert, "a vast, desolate area with an operational potential of zero, [where] you could not land anywhere or find a place to refuel. You could not even look to your air controller for help," Marom would recall.[4]

He was patrolling near the Canal one day with another Mirage when his air controller popped on the radio to say that two MiGs were just ahead of them, and volunteered to "lead" them to their prey. The two promptly took off in that direction, and with the controller ticking off the remaining miles "it was a vector out of the movies—eight miles, four miles, two miles. Only I couldn't see anything. The controller says 'looking good' and I still cannot see anything. Suddenly, my wingman yells 'Break,' two MiGs are right behind us, and as we break away two missiles pass us on both sides. Two more seconds and we'd be dead." With the IAF's old, under-powered radar unable to tell a MiG from a Mirage at that distance, the operator simply assumed that the closer blips were the Mirages and the others were the MiGs.

In the summer of 1967, to help Marom's gunslingers ride the skies of the vast and increasingly angry southern frontier, IAF Operations repaired the bombed-out runways of the former Egyptian airfield of Bir Gafgafa in the deep Sinai, fifty miles east of the Canal. Marom promptly sent four pilots there with their Mirages and a skeleton maintenance crew, to serve as quick-draw backup for the routine air patrols from the north. As two pilots strapped themselves into their Mirages and went on interception alert, the other two commandeered a stranded Soviet ZIL troop carrier and went scrounging for living amenities. They crossed thirty-five miles of desert until, at the former Egyptian Sinai command complex at Bir el Tamade, "we walked [into] this huge Egyptian sleeping hall, and there were those hundreds of beds, huge beds with thick cotton-stuffed mattresses," recalls Gad Eldar, a slim, cheerful paratrooper turned fighter ace. "We threw four mattresses into the ZIL and took them back. They were so comfortable that for a long time afterward, each time I'd be detailed to Bir Gafgafa, I'd be dreaming about the great sleeps I would have there."[5]

From that point and for the next three years, Bir Gafgafa would be the center and twisted reflection of the strange new air war.* The pilots found themselves in a ghost town. Shut off from the outside by low sandstone mounds, Bir Gafgafa had a pair of bombed-out, sand-swept runways, a few open-air fighter pens with burned-out MiGs still inside, and a small shell-pocked control tower. Under the tower, steps led to a small bunker whose ground-level windows were blown out during the fighting. Clouds of dust whipped through each time a plane took off or landed. Huge flies, drawn by the stench of decaying bodies, swarmed in and out.

Even with thick Egyptian mattresses, sleeping was risky. Egyptian soldiers, left behind after the 1967 fighting, still wandered the desert. Fearing capture but unable to get back home, they crept through Bir Gafgafa's downed fences at night in search of food. "We had to sleep with our guns ready until finally the Piper Cub boys strapped machine guns to their landing gear and went out to search and shoot those who wouldn't surrender," recalls Marom. Abandoned Egyptian ammunition was everywhere, inviting disaster. One bored pilot nearly blew himself up when he emptied several artillery shells, stacked up their macaroni-like gunpowder charge, and touched it off with a match. Two other pilots were firing their handguns at an abandoned Egyptian truck when a huge load of explosives it carried exploded. And because the fighter pens that now housed the Mirages faced the tower, any time a sleepy pilot accidentally squeezed his trigger a barrage of deadly 30-mm explosive shells slammed into the bunker where the other pilots slept.

Unlike the IAF's main bases, which still reflected the peacefulness of the Israeli home front, and where a pilot returning from a frontline mission could be sitting at a Tel Aviv sidewalk café an hour later, at Bir Gafgafa every moment was high noon. "It was easy for us to realize a war was on. At Bir Gafgafa the war *was* on,"

---

*Ironically, it was the same airfield where, on May 22, 1967, Nasser surrounded himself with jovial Egyptian pilots to announce the closure of the Tiran Strait, and in effect triggered the Six-Day War.

recalls Spector. "We scrambled all the time . . . to hold on to the Canal, to reduce our casualties, to hurt the Egyptians, whatever."[6] From dawn to darkness, two Mirages stood ready, pilots strapped in, canopies ready to pull down, technicians ready to disconnect all hoses and cables in a flash. To shave precious seconds off their scramble time, the Mirage crews hooked a monstrous bell from an abandoned Egyptian copper mine to the telephone in the control tower. As soon as IAF Operations rang up the tower and the bell blasted off, the Mirages rolled out. By the time the tower operator read the new orders on the radio the fighters were well on their way to the Canal, and a second pair of fighters had rolled up to the head of the runway.

"It was what set the whole tone and style of the war, this constant and very hot activity at Bir Gafgafa all the time," says Spector. "At first there were many false alarms. You scrambled and waited and nothing happened. Later on you found yourself deeper and deeper in a real war."

For the first two years of the war, the constant scrambling and patrolling kept Egyptian air attacks to a minimum, and actual air engagements were a rarity. But the opening of Nasser's attrition phase in the spring of 1969 changed all that as the Egyptian air offensive grew heavier. It didn't matter that, when they met, the Israelis won every engagement hands down, downing one MiG-21 on March 8, another one a week later, and two more on May 21. The trouble was that the small band of overworked Mirages could not be everywhere at the same time, and in the vast desert spaces from Port Said on the Mediterranean to the Red Sea in the south the Egyptians still determined the time, place, and nature of each engagement. By arriving fast and low, and pulling up only at the last moment, the MiGs could bomb and strafe any sector of the Israeli-held Canal and be gone by the time Bir Gafgafa's Mirages got there.

Battered by mounting air and artillery attacks, Israeli soldiers and field commanders along the Canal began to clamor for air cover. Starting as a faint rumble deep down in the bunkers at the far edges of the Sinai, a question began to bounce from bunkers to command posts and on up the IDF chain. Picking up momentum and volume along the way, the question soon echoed through IDF headquarters in Tel Aviv, was picked up at the Diezengoff Boulevard sidewalk cafés where politicians and journalists hung out, and finally exploded along every city street and around every dining table at the remotest border *kibbutz*.

It went like this: "Where is the Air Force?"

Aside from the fact that Moti Hod was reluctant to get involved in a static war, the IAF was busy taking care of itself. "You must remember that while the Skyhawks were finally arriving, everything else was wearing down, especially the Mirages, and the Phantoms had yet to come," says Yeheskiel Somekh, then chief of IAF Air Section.[7] Even after the three Mirage squadrons began to take turns at the desert base, each squadron sending four Mirages and pilots down there for two weeks at a time, the Bir Gafgafa routine alone was exhausting the IAF's entire fighter force. If that had been a real war, each Mirage squadron would have thirty pilots to draw on, most of them reservists and "emergency assignments" from other posts, at IAF Flight School or IAF headquarters. This time, since Israel's no-war pretense precluded calling in the reserves, the Mirage squadrons had to carry out the war with only standard peacetime strength—a squadron commander and his two deputies, two or three seasoned pilots, and three or four young flyers.

Less strength, actually, since in 1968 some of the very best Mirage pilots were pulled out to command new Skyhawk squadrons, and in early 1969 others were sent to the United States to train on F-4 Phantoms. As a result, when the fighting grew hot and heavy in 1969, no Mirage squadron had more than half a dozen experienced pilots on hand, and since only experienced flyers were allowed at Bir Gafgafa, each time a squadron deployed its four-Mirage team to the desert base it virtually had to shut down. To accomplish their assigned missions, squadron commanders had to fend for themselves. "Sometimes IAF Operations would wake me up at 2:30 A.M. and order me to have eight fighters ready in two hours because one thing or another was about to happen," recalls Marom. "But I didn't have eight fighters. So at 3:30 I would start calling up reservists at home on my own to be on the flight line at 4:30. They would call in sick at El Al or wherever and come to help out, and perhaps shoot themselves a MiG."

To the ground troops, however, none of that hardship mattered. They needed air cover, and they needed it then and there. When

Moti Hod resisted the Greens' pleas for more air support, Ezer Weizman, then chief of IDF Operations, went to work on Hod's colonels, most of them his own protégés from the Camelot days of Air Force North. On May 29, 1969, he got Moshe Dayan and the IAF senior command together at the briefing room of the 109 Skyhawk squadron at Ramat David, apparently hoping to goose Hod into some sort of bombing offensive on the Canal. "Assuming that we want to break the impasse on the Canal once and for all, is the IAF ready to go to war today?" Beni Peled remembers Dayan asking. The Blues stirred uneasily. "Of course we are ready, but we would be in a much better position in August or even December," Hod replied without enthusiasm. It was not the rousing battle cry Dayan expected, and "I remember the spark dying in his one eye; he said, 'All right, you guys, where are the sandwiches?' He had his answer. The IAF was not ready," says Peled.

But Hod had to do something about the marauding MiGs, and on June 17 he sent two Mirages "to leave our calling card in Cairo [with a warning]: If the Egyptians did not stop the fighting on the Canal, other actions would follow."[9] Ostensibly on a photo-reconnaissance mission over Egyptian airfields, the fighters peeled south and triggered a sonic boom over Cairo, popping plate-glass windows, downing power lines and collapsing walls under construction. When the furious and embarrassed Nasser—he was working at his Heliopolis mansion when the Israeli jets boomed overhead—fired his air and air-defense chiefs but refused to downscale the fighting, Hod put the rest of his plan into action. On June 24, the same day on which Gen. Ali Mustafa Baghdadi took over as Egypt's new air force chief, two Mirages from Tel Nof sauntered over the Canal into Egypt, and began to circle aimlessly in plain sight of the Egyptian radar. When two MiG-21s showed up to investigate, the Mirages shot one of them down and returned home. Two days later, another pair of Mirages from Tel Nof shot down a second MiG near the Canal. It was also on that day that Iftach Spector gunned down his own MiG near Cairo, and ran out of fuel on the way back.

The MiG downings began so surreptitiously that, at first, the Egyptians did not even realize that what Hod had begun was an entirely new kind of air campaign. Historically, dogfighting was a sideshow, fighters tangling while escorting or blocking bombing missions, or when meeting by chance. This time Hod sent his pilots to find and destroy MiGs in the air inside Egypt (Israel's no-war strategy precluded attacking Egypt's airfields). Freed from altitude, safety, or border restrictions, "we were supposed to shoot down and humiliate the enemy until it stopped bothering us. It was said at the briefings—'You are expected to bring results,' " recalls Spector.

However lackadaisical it appeared, the campaign carried Hod's unmistakable brand of ruthless pragmatism. "Moti sent in only championship teams, the best pilots from each squadron, usually the squadron commander, his two deputies, and one or two others, no more," says Uri Even-Nir, then commander of the 117 Mirage squadron at Ramat David.[10] Hod also ran each and every battle personally, slouching in his seat at the IAF command bunker—the "Hole"—and, stopwatch in hand, conjuring images of unfolding battles hundreds of miles away. "Moti had a theory—which sounded stupid except that it worked—that whatever didn't happen in the first couple of minutes of battle was not going to happen," says Marom, a frequent flyer on Hod's all-star team. "When he had enough he clicked off the stopwatch, ordered you to 'break contact,' and you had to stop fighting and start back. If you were about to drop a MiG, or had a MiG on your tail, you had another minute or so to wind things up, but then Moti called 'stop battle' and everything had to stop."

At first the Egyptians responded to the intrusions by scrambling more MiGs. "We sent in two Mirages, and they sent in four of their fighters. We sent in four and they sent in eight," recalls Even-Nir. Following a fierce air battle on July 2, in which six Mirages shot down four out of twelve MiG-21s that intercepted them southwest of Suez, the Egyptians began to stay away, but the Israelis quickly came up with new tactics for drawing them back out. One ploy was to send in a lone Mirage, ostensibly on a photo-reconnaissance mission. When the MiGs arrived to intercept it they were jumped by other Mirages that had been cruising behind the hills and below radar level.

Another ploy utilized stealth and deception to turn the war into a huge three-dimensional chess game, played over hundreds of miles of empty spaces. On July 7, Marom was sent on a seemingly routine patrol to Sharm el Sheikh, where MiGs from Ghardaka used to harass Israeli troops when the Mirages were not around. Nothing happened, and when he seemingly turned back for home, Ghardaka's MiGs were back in the air on their way to Sharm el Sheikh. But Marom had not left. He and his wingman had simply dropped below radar level and then switched back. They arrived at Sharm el Sheikh just in time to shoot down two MiG-17s as they prepared to attack Israeli positions below.

By early July, after losing nine MiG-21s in a few days, the Egyptians "realized there was no point scrambling their planes [and] they just stopped coming up," says Somekh. So did the Syrians, after losing seven MiG-21s on July 8, after attempting to intercept Israeli Mirages on a photo-reconnaissance mission. While IAF Operations code-named the new air campaign *Rimonim* (Hebrew for pomegranates or grenades), the Mirage pilots had a better name for it. Borrowing the code name by which their maps defined the chunk of desert over which the dogfighting took place, they called their gunslinging fighter war "Texas."

But "Texas" did not stop Nasser's campaign of attrition. The Egyptian artillery continued to take its daily toll along the Canal—in July alone, thirty-one Israeli soldiers and officers were killed and eighty-one were wounded in the incessant shelling. "The consensus was that the IAF was not doing its share like the rest of the IDF," says David Ivri, then chief of IAF Operations. "Shooting down planes did not help. It did not deter the Egyptian artillery."[11] At Bir Gafgafa in particular, Mirage pilots felt guilty and impotent as they watched the endless procession of body bags and shell-shocked soldiers heading north from the Canal killing grounds. "We couldn't help them. It was terrible," says Gad Eldar.

Eldar was at Bir Gafgafa when, in the course of a three-day artillery barrage, an Egyptian phosphorus shell struck an Israeli troop carrier and burned its occupants, who then had to be carried on foot to the surrounding swamp, where an IAF helicopter nearly sank in the mud trying to evacuate them. "I shall never forget that chopper landing at Bir Gafgafa," says Eldar. "The doctor sat in the middle, with the seven burn victims arranged on the floor around him like dominoes, heads in and bodies going every which way. The side doors were off and twelve stretchers with bodies were strapped against the sides. . . . When the injured walked off, one's skin had shrunk and dried up so badly he moved like a robot."

On the night of July 12, Egyptian commandos crossed the Canal and destroyed two Israeli tanks before they were chased back by the gunners of a third. Stunned at the daring and ease of the Egyptian penetration, Israel's military leadership ordered Hod to move on the Canal. Operation Boxer, launched on Sunday afternoon, July 20—counting on the Apollo moon landing to divert public attention from the Canal fighting—was the biggest and most elaborate IAF operation since the opening of the Six-Day War. Starting at 1:30 P.M., the entire IAF took to the air and, flying low and in radio silence, headed for Egypt. Uri Even-Nir, who flew just ahead of the force, was struck by the utter silence of the frontier as he dived at the critical SA-2 missile battery that guarded the airspace around Port Said, and shot up its fire-control system. Pulling up from the smoking SAM site, Even-Nir "looked down and the entire Canal was exploding, everything blowing up in fire and smoke."

For two hours, in wave after devastating wave, IAF attack planes dropped 159 tons of bombs and 72 napalm canisters on Egypt's massive Canal fortifications. The Egyptians were caught completely off guard. It was three hours before their MiGs scrambled, and while they shot down two Israeli Mirages at a cost of five of their own, they failed to stop the Israeli air offensive. The Skyhawks came back the next day, and the next. At the end of a week, six SA-2 missile batteries and countless antiaircraft positions were destroyed, and seven more Egyptian fighters were shot down.

On the face of it, Operation Boxer achieved on the ground what "Texas" did in the air—it ended any dreams Nasser had of crossing the Canal and gaining a foothold on the other side. It also allowed the Israelis to move at will through Egyptian territory. On September 9, an Israeli armored force crossed the Gulf of Suez under heavy air cover and swept unopposed along the entire western bank of the Gulf, destroying Egyptian army camps, radar stations, and observation posts. When the Egyptian Air Force attempted to strike back two days later, eight of its MiGs were shot down in one afternoon. And on December 26, IAF helicopters crossed the Gulf, picked up and brought home with them an entire Soviet-made radar station.

Yet, like "Texas," Boxer failed to move the Egyptians any closer to stopping the fighting. As they simply repaired the gun batteries, replenished their damaged forces, and kept up the artillery fire, "we had to attack again and again, and gradually we were simply sucked in. Since each time we struck them things grew quiet for a while, the ground forces began to ask for air support again and again, and we had to go on," says Ivri. Instead of knocking the opposition out in one blow—*Zbeng ve'gamarnu* in the favorite Israeli expression—Boxer stretched for days and weeks, turning the IAF's Skyhawk squadrons into no more than a flying artillery.

"We could have gone on like that indefinitely," says Somekh, but "it was pointless. We bombed and bombed, and controlled the area [until] there was nothing more that we could do—but we came no closer to a cease-fire." Like two overtired prizefighters, locked in a stubborn toe-to-toe slugging spree, unable to quit or knock each other out, Israel and Egypt kept punching. The war had become precisely what Nasser set out to make it, a war of attrition, and as the Egyptians showed a seemingly unlimited capacity to take punishment and still keep fighting, by year's end both sides had to up the ante if they wanted to break out of the impasse.

Chapter 20

PHANTOMS

From the start of the conflict that became the War of Attrition, first under Levi Eshkol and then, after his death on February 22, 1969, under Golda Meir, the Israeli government abstained from using its air force inside Egypt. This was partly to maintain the no-war myth, and partly to avoid antagonizing the United States. Israel's new ambassador to the United States, Yitzhak Rabin, saw things differently. If Israel was antagonizing the United States, he thought, it was not by fighting but by not winning. American public pronouncements notwithstanding, he cabled to Jerusalem on September 19, "A man would have to be blind, deaf and dumb not to sense how much the administration favors our military operations." In fact, America's "willingness to supply us with additional arms depends on us stepping up the military activity against Egypt, not reducing it."[1]

The Israeli government balked at the notion of a major air offensive that would shift the war from the Canal to Egypt's interior. As 1970 began, however, several developments combined to change the government's mind. First, in a massive, eight-hour Christmas Day offensive, the IAF demolished a dozen SA-2 missile batteries that Egypt had installed along the Canal, so that a missile-free corridor now led from the Sinai clear into the Egyptian interior. Secondly, on

January 5, 1970, Rabin cabled home that Secretary of State William Rogers was about to pressure Israel to withdraw from the occupied territories, so Israel now had little to lose by moving to wind up the conflict quickly. Finally, on September 5, 1969, the first four Israeli Phantom fighter-bombers had arrived from the United States (with a Mirage foursome from the 101, led by Oded Marom, meeting them on the way and providing escort to Hazor). As more Phantoms arrived through the fall, Israel now had two operational Phantom squadrons, the 221* at Hazor and the 69 at Ramat David. Indeed, on the day following Rabin's telegram, the IDF proposed, Hod agreed, and the Knesset Committee on Security approved a deep-penetration bombing raid against Egypt. The very next day, IAF Phantoms moved unopposed into the Egyptian heartland and blasted two major air bases near Cairo, and a missile training and storage camp thirty miles farther to the south. A week later, the Phantoms sledgehammered the same targets again, and they kept coming back every week to strike at Egyptian bases from Cairo all the way to Najh Hamadi, 300 miles up the Nile. For the first time, Israel possessed a truly strategic weapon, capable not only of dogfighting and short-range ground attacks, but of the kind of massive and deliberate long-range destruction of which victories are ostensibly made.

If the Mirage was a celebration of minimalist French elegance, the F-4 Phantom, America's Cold War interceptor, violated every rule of aesthetics and aerodynamics. It was huge—weighing more than twice the Mirage—and its bent-down tail, bent-up wings, pinched nose, and smoky engines gave it a put-together look. But those same engines also blasted it through the air with such brute force that between December 1959 and April 1962, the Phantom set overall world altitude (98,557 feet) and speed (1,606.51 mph or Mach 2.59) records, and many secondary speed records from 300- and 60-mile closed circuits (1,216.76 and 1,459 mph) to U.S. cross-country runs (2:48 hours from Los Angeles to New York).

More impressively, in spite of its enormous weight and the fact that it took two to fly it—a pilot in front, a navigator in back—the Phantom could turn, run, climb, and fight not only faster than any other fighter around, but slower. Its powerful engines were so stall-

*Not real squadron number.

free that a pilot could throttle it so far back that it virtually stood still in midair—an ultimate dogfighter's advantage. And where the dart-shaped Mirage carried just two infrared missiles and one ton of bombs, the Phantom could truck four infrared Sidewinders, four radar-guided Sparrow missiles, and *seven tons* of bombs for 300 miles—and then get back without having to stop for refueling. For the first time in the modern era, both U.S. armed services adopted the same fighter—there was a navy Phantom that could fold its wings and land on a carrier, an air force Phantom with rigid wings and wide tires for landing on soft asphalt runways, and reconnaissance versions of each.

The Phantoms gave the IAF a fighting edge beyond anything it ever had before. Through the spring, the Phantoms sowed devastation throughout Egypt's military infrastructure. They could go anywhere and do anything, until it seemed only a matter of time before Nasser recognized the futility of his war and called it off. Rabin proved correct in his assessment. With Nasser seemingly on the ropes, the Nixon administration stopped talking about a pullback and allowed Israel to play its hand, while Egypt's allies watched silently from the sidelines. By February, Cairo was a city under siege, blacked out and sand-bagged. Egyptian training bases and bomber squadrons were being evacuated to Libya and the Sudan. "The psychological effect of the bombings was even worse than the physical impact, [especially with] Israel's announcement that her attacks . . . aimed at liberating the Egyptian people from President Nasser," Mohamed Fawzi, Egypt's minister of war at the time, would write later.[*2]

Yet like "Texas" and Boxer before it, *preeha,* the deep-penetration raids, still failed to make Nasser stop the fighting. Some Israelis would later attribute this to the raids' slow pace—one a week—and others to some Egyptian superhuman ability to absorb punishment and keep on fighting. In retrospect, it may have all

---

*In fact, so freely were the Phantoms now moving about Egypt that the only two mishaps in four months of raids were due to pilot errors. On February 12, 1970, as a result of navigation error, one Phantom bombed a civilian metal works at Abu Zabel, thirty miles north of Cairo, instead of the military base next to it, killed seventy civilian workers and wounded a hundred. In a similar accident on April 8, several Egyptian children were killed when their school mistakenly took the bombs intended for a nearby military complex.

been an intelligence failure—both AMAN and *Mossad* apparently failed to grasp how devastating the Phantom strikes really were. In reality, even as many Israelis marveled at his toughness and endurance, Nasser was so close to collapse that escalating the bombing campaign's once-a-week pace might have done the job.

Israeli intelligence also failed to take seriously—or project to their logical conclusion—Nasser's protests that it was against the United States, not Israel, that he was really fighting in the desert. Nasser did both. At the end of January, after lulling the Israelis into self-satisfied calm by giving several foreign press interviews in which he conceded their supremacy in the air, Nasser secretly flew to Moscow and demanded not only more and better weapons, but actual Soviet help in stopping the "Americans." When Communist Party chairman Leonid Brezhnev hesitated, Nasser threatened to tell his people that "the Americans are the masters of the universe" and to resign from his presidency. Brezhnev calmed his prize client and approved for immediate delivery an entire division of SA-3 missile batteries with Soviet operating crews, three Soviet-manned MiG-21 interceptor squadrons, and large numbers of older interceptors, radar warning systems, and advanced jet engines to retrofit Egypt's older MiG-21s.

In effect, Nasser had turned the defense of his country over to the Red Army. He had barely returned to Cairo when massive Soviet shipments began to arrive by sea and air. In March, the three Soviet MiG-21 squadrons took positions around Cairo, Aswan, and Alexandria. On April 18, several MiG-21s intercepted two IAF Phantoms on a reconnaissance mission north of Cairo, and Israeli intelligence monitors heard their pilots speaking in Russian to their controllers. Defense Minister Moshe Dayan took it for a Soviet message to stay out of the Cairo region, and he ordered Hod to suspend the deep-penetration raids and to restrict IAF operations to the Canal area. "We shouldn't expect to behave in Cairo's skies as if it were our own," he said gloomily.[3]

Dayan may have expected a gentlemanly acknowledgment of his concession in the shape of a Soviet agreement to let Israel stay in control of the Canal skies, but the Soviets had something else in mind. Having pushed the IAF back to the Canal, they now went after it with devastating new weapons and tactics which the Israelis only vaguely recognized and had no idea how to counter. Regardless of what Nasser thought or said about American involvement on Israel's side, the fact is that until then the conflict on the Canal was strictly between Egyptians and Israelis. And since the Soviets kept their new role in Egypt secret (not from the American government, which the Soviets went out of their way to keep informed), the public still thought it was Israelis and Egyptians who were slugging it out on the Canal. In reality, however, Nasser's war had now become a global conflict. Instead of Arab armies, Israel was now facing the Evil Empire itself, with its Darth Vader arsenals which even the Americans knew nothing about and would have had trouble coping with.

In early February, dozens of new excavations suddenly appeared around Cairo, Alexandria, and along a strip of desert running a few miles west of the Suez Canal. Although they had no idea what they were, the Israelis promptly bombed and destroyed them. They were mystified when the Egyptians rebuilt or replaced them again and again, at a cost of thousands of civilian workers' lives. Only in March was the puzzle solved, when IAF surveillance flights identified a new type of surface-air missile batteries around Cairo and Alexandria, and noted the similarities between their bunkers and the unidentified construction projects behind the Canal. "For a long time we did not understand the connection between the diggings and missiles," says Yeheskiel Somekh. "We suspected some connection, but we didn't actually *know*."

Like the American Phantom, the SA-2 surface-air missile was a product of the post–World War II search for the ultimate interceptor. First spotted in a 1957 May Day parade in Moscow, just a year before the Phantom's maiden flight, the SA-2 was also huge, ungainly, and deadly. Although weighing more than two tons, it could zip through the air at an incredible three and a half times the speed of sound and deliver nearly three hundred pounds of explosives to a target more than twenty miles away and eleven miles high. Launched and guided by radar, it could be directed to either follow its prey or to compute where it was going and head it off—and it could change course in midair if its target tried to get away. Once it caught up with it, the SA-2 could destroy it by blowing up on impact or simply by exploding near it. During the 1960s, SA-2s anchored the air defenses of the Soviet Union and its allies, from Eastern Europe and Afghanistan to Algeria, China, and Vietnam, where a U.S. Navy attack pilot who ran into an SA-2 barrage later described it as "a bunch of telephone poles with lit ends, all coming right at me."

But the SA-2 was not a plane, and in small doses it was no match for even a mediocre fighter. It had no wings or pilot, and it was so clumsy that it could destroy a target only if it could sneak up on it unnoticed. If the plane it was following banked sharply, the SA-2's primitive tracking system would lose its "lock" and the missile would sail on aimlessly and harmlessly. Also, since the SA-2 was not effective below 3,000 feet or so, a fighter pilot could easily destroy an entire SA-2 battery (six missile launchers) by coming in fast and low and shooting up its radar control unit, thus rendering the entire assembly helpless. In fact, the moment he learned of the new missile batteries near Cairo and Alexandria, Moti Hod promptly "went to Moshe [Dayan] and told him that we didn't have to know they were Russians, and that we should hit them there and then to discourage them a little."[4] Dayan, however, fearing direct confrontation with the Soviets, refused and ordered Hod to keep his Phantoms out of the Cairo region altogether.

But the Israelis underestimated the new Soviet missile threat. Although they generally handed them out to their allies in small numbers, more for effect than effectiveness, Russian missile experts never meant for their dumb, pilotless brutes to duel *mano a mano* with enemy fighters. Once they took personal control of Egypt's air defense, they made three changes that instantly transformed the entire force equation. First, they brought in many more SA-2s and deployed them en masse. This made them far more lethal in the air, since a pilot could dodge one or two missiles, but ultimately would lose speed and altitude and get hit by the third or the fourth. In addition, this made the batteries more secure on the ground, since a plane attacking one battery could get hit by missiles from another battery nearby.

Second, the Soviets plugged the SA-2's low-altitude blind spot by providing the Egyptians with newer SA-3 missiles, which could hit a plane flying as low as 300 feet. Finally, as the IAF surveillance flights discovered in the northeastern section of the Nile Delta, the

Soviets combined the SA-2s and SA-3s with radar-guided anti-aircraft guns—effective against the lowest-flying planes—to form super-batteries that were virtually indestructible from the air.

It was not the SA-2s or even SA-3s, but these missile-and-artillery super-batteries, complete with Russian operators that could play them like deadly video games, that became the Soviets' ultimate weapon in the battle for the Canal. It was a weapon the Israelis could not begin to tackle—unless they did it before the Soviets had their batteries in place. Suddenly, a furious race began along the stretch of bleak, hazy desert behind the Canal, where thousands of Egyptian work crews prepared fortified positions for the new missile batteries in a vast and bloody construction project worthy of the Pharaohs. Day by scorching day, workers kept digging huge holes and trenches in the sand in the shapes of rosettes and tapestries, and lining them with heavy concrete, and day by day Israeli Phantoms and Skyhawks bombed their handiwork back to primordial dust. Thousands of Egyptian workers died in the bombings, only to have thousands more take their place. When working in the daytime proved too hazardous, the Egyptians began to work at night. "No less than 800 or 1,000 missile positions were under construction between the Canal and the Nile Delta, and each time construction would begin anywhere we in the Phantoms would hit it. It became our daily routine. Mornings we'd fly training missions with young pilots, and afternoons we'd be bombing missile batteries in Egypt," recalls Rami Harpaz, one of the Phantom pilots.[5]

The race lasted for three months. By early June, the Phantoms were still masters of the skies; the Soviets had yet to install a single missile battery behind the Canal and were growing frantic. Since the end of World War II, the security of the USSR itself had depended on the same elaborate missile defenses that were now failing to protect Egypt's skies. "If the thick defense system around Cairo was built in the image of the one built around Moscow, was planned by the same generals, contained the same hardware and was manned [by the same] Soviet crews—then the thrust of an Israeli Phantom [to] Cairo meant that an American bomber could reach Moscow," Dan Schueftan, an Israeli military historian, would later write.[6]

The Soviets now changed tactics. On June 15 a delegation of top missile experts arrived in Cairo with new plans of action. On the night of June 23, just as secretly, a small motorized caravan made its way across the Egyptian desert toward the Canal—a few ZIL-157 semitrailer trucks, each carrying a single SA-2 missile, and a radar van. Once at the waterway, the trucks were hidden in the thick greenery on the Canal bank, the missiles were erected and armed, and when two Phantoms streaked overhead at daybreak, the missile operators fired at them like hunters from a duck blind.

They missed. The Israeli pilots spotted the missiles, evaded them easily, and reported their location to IAF Operations. Several minutes later, a second Phantom team arrived and wiped out the battery—missiles, trucks, and radar. Over the next two weeks, several more such attempts at missile-ambushing the Israelis met with similar results. But the duck blinds on the Canal were only a diversion, to keep Israeli attention riveted to the Canal long enough for the Soviets to put the main element of their plan to work.

In the early-afternoon hours of Saturday, June 30, two camera-equipped Israeli Mirages were making a routine north-to-south reconnaissance run eighteen miles west of the Canal when they spotted four SA-2 missiles coming up at them. The problem was not the missiles, which the Mirages easily evaded, but where they came from. Instead of the Canal banks on the Mirages' left, the missiles unexpectedly showed up from the west, from the open desert country between the Canal and Cairo where no missiles were supposed to exist. When the Mirages returned to base and their films were processed, it turned out that overnight the Soviets had moved twelve SA-2, two SA-3, and a number of radar-controlled anti-aircraft gun batteries into the area and set them up in super-battery formation on the sand without bothering to dig bunkers or pour any concrete shelters.

Suddenly, the entire picture changed. "It was the beginning of what we came to call a 'rolling pack,' " says IAF Brig. Gen. Eitan Ben Eliahu, then a Phantom pilot at Hazor. "Until then, there was one missile pack near Cairo, and a pack under construction near the Canal. They were separate. There was no overlapping of their radii of effectiveness. But the new missile pack near Qutmieh was no longer just a few batteries defending each other—this entire new pack was itself defended from the rear by the Cairo pack. If we allowed it to remain, the entire missile system would in effect roll forward toward the Canal, with each new pack defended from behind. In a matter of days, it would be in a position to defend the pack being built along the Canal."[7]

A frantic debate ensued at IAF headquarters. David Ivri, head of IAF Operations, suggested waiting for more surveillance data before doing anything. "When you are not sure where all the batteries are, how many there are, and which are alive or not, there is a risk that if you don't attack all of them at the same time you are vulnerable to fire from those that are not being attacked," he argued.[8] IAF Air Section chief Yeheskiel Somekh, however, feared that "if another night passed they'd be settled and organized and it would be much harder to hit them." He ordered an immediate strike.

In midafternoon, Shmuel Hetz and Avihu Ben-Nun, commanders of the two Phantom squadrons, were rushed to Tel Aviv to get their orders. By the time they returned to their squadrons in Hazor and Ramat David, they had little time to prepare—their Phantoms had to be over their targets by 5:30—and almost no data to give their pilots about how many batteries there were, where exactly they were, or which ones each flight crew should go after. The pilots were already in their cockpits when the newly developed aerial photographs arrived and were handed to them. The photos did not actually show any missile batteries, only gray expanses of featureless desert with pencil-marked X's where the rushed photo interpreters thought they spotted something through their magnifying glasses. It was up to the pilots to locate the photo scenes on their maps, and to match them with the actual locations in the desert.

In reality, even the little information they had was wrong. IAF intelligence analysts, who received their copies of the photos at the same time as the pilots, compared the target markings on the photos with the data they assembled from pilot accounts and found numerous discrepancies. It meant that at least some of the Phantoms might miss their targets and be exposed to missile threat far longer than anticipated. But it was too late to warn the pilots. The first attack wave—six Phantoms from Ramat David and two from Hazor—was already nearing the missile field in radio silence. Besides, warning them would have helped little since their cockpit maps did not match either the photographs or the terrain below. "The fact was that we didn't have good maps for the area between, say, fifty kilometers [30 miles] behind the Canal and Cairo," says Eitan Peled, one of the Phantom pilots in that mission. "Cairo, the Delta, and the Canal were no problem, but there was a map gap precisely in the Qutmieh area. When you flew over it, the wadis in the field didn't match those on our 1:250,000 map, and we did not have 1:100,000 maps. Even the intelligence people who had to mark the targets on the maps had trouble figuring out what was where."[9]

Incredibly, in spite of the map gap and the difficulties of low-altitude navigation or of seeing anything at all in the haze of the setting sun, the strike was remarkably successful. At 5:30 on the dot, the eight Phantoms reached the target area, split right and left, and destroyed five of the missile batteries and damaged two. There was only one close call, when Hetz narrowly escaped being hit by two SA-2 missiles.

On the way back, however, either due to error, as he now claims, or obstinacy, as his colleagues insist, Rami Harpaz did not stay close to the ground but climbed to 10,000 feet for the run home. He was still climbing when the remaining missile batteries began firing. "I saw a strong SA-2 launch at my ten o'clock, and then I saw the missile itself at my seven o'clock, going after me. I waited as long as I could [and] broke. The missile passed by and we breathed easy," Harpaz later recalled. But the sharp breaking slowed him down, and he was traveling at mere 200 knots when a second missile exploded right behind him, shearing off the Phantom's tail and giving Harpaz barely enough time to eject himself and his navigator from the spinning plane. They landed in an Egyptian military compound near Qutmieh, where they were captured and imprisoned by the Egyptians.

At 6:15 that evening, two more Phantoms were dispatched to take out the remaining batteries. With the sun low and the desert draped in thickening haze, the crews had trouble seeing the target or anything else. Yitzhak Pier, the flight leader, was rolling to the right for a better view of the target area when two SA-2 missiles emerged from the haze. He barely had time to ditch his bombs before the first missile exploded underneath his plane, and was just regaining control and turning his plane back toward the Sinai when it was hit by the second missile. The Phantom's right-hand engine caught fire, the cockpit rapidly filled with smoke, and the plane listed to the left and began to spin. Pier pulled the ejection lever, but only managed to pop out his navigator. His spinning plane was just above the desert floor when he manually yanked his canopy open, unbuckled his harness, climbed out of the cockpit and threw himself out of the plane. He was taken prisoner by Egyptian soldiers as soon as he reached the ground.

Yair David, Pier's navigator, managed to escape. A wiry, curly-haired former paratrooper who joined the IAF after an outstanding commando career, David radioed his position to a passing IAF Skyhawk while still parachuting down, then buried his parachute and hid in an old Egyptian foxhole until dark, lying quiet and motionless as men and vehicles searched all around him. At night he activated his radio again, and two hours past midnight a huge IAF CH-53 helicopter picked him up and ran him back through heavy antiaircraft fire.

That made it two downed Phantoms and three captured crewmen in just one day. "For the first time, we started to get a feeling that . . . the real threat was a missile, not a plane," says Ben Eliahu. "All along, we felt that with tenacity and flying skills we could overcome any obstacle. Our entire doctrine, our whole air culture had been based on flying virtuosity. In case of missiles, it meant minimal exposure, precise diving, good timing, cutting-edge performance—all of which we knew inside out. Now, for the first time, it was not enough."

There was more. From the very start, even before any of them first laid eyes on their super-plane, the Phantom crews were under strict secrecy bordering on quarantine. They could not talk to anyone outside their own little circle about their plane or missions, or even admit to anyone on the outside that they flew Phantoms. Even the Mirage pilots who escorted them past the border—and waited for them to return—during the deep-penetration bombing campaign had no idea where the Phantoms went or what they did. Once initiated into this secret order, with its voodoo arts of electronic countermeasures and weapon systems, the Phantom crews, glowing with a mysterious Buck Rogers aura, turned inward and kept to themselves.

Their leader was Shmuel Hetz, who headed the Phantom transition team and now commanded the 221 Phantom squadron at Hazor. Pale, thin, stoop-shouldered, and going bald, "he was the kind of a guy you'd never pay attention to. He actually seemed to shrink into himself in company," recalls Oded Marom, his former commander at the 101 Mirage squadron. "He used to organize folk dances and painting competitions, or bake-offs for the wives. He brought in writers to talk about their latest books, an English teacher, even a relaxation therapist. [But] all that disappeared when you got him into a one-on-one dogfight or argument. Suddenly, you were stunned by the awesome force of his flying or thinking. You could not figure out where such strength came from."[10]

Avihu Ben-Nun, Hetz's deputy on the Phantom transition team and now commander of the 69 Phantom squadron at Ramat David, was his complete opposite. The younger brother of Israel's leading naval hero, he was dark-haired and handsome, cool and calculating, with a promotional flair surpassed only by that of Ran Ronen, his former commander at the 191 Mirage squadron. Both Hetz and Ben-Nun, and their handpicked crews, were fine flyers with an impressive range of expertise—Yitzhak Pier was an outstanding aerial gunner, Rami Harpaz a weapon systems expert, Yoram Agmon a dogfighter and a slick administrator. Together, they made up one of the best and brightest teams the IAF had ever put together.

But also one of the youngest. To make sure that they would stick with the Phantoms for more than a couple of years, Moti Hod abandoned an IAF tradition of letting only veteran commanders bring new cutting-edge planes into the IAF—as Menahem Bar did the Meteor, Beni Peled the Mystère, Yak Nevo the Super-Mystère— in favor of younger officers with less experience than promise. Neither Hetz nor Ben-Nun had commanded squadrons, or saw much combat in frontline fighters (in the 1967 war Hetz flew Ouragans and Ben-Nun Mystères, although both briefly flew Mirages before or after the war, and were superb pilots).

And because they were in training in the United States at the time of the "Texas" and Boxer campaigns, the Phantom crews had even less experience with Soviet missiles than most Mirage and Skyhawk pilots. On November 27, 1969, as he briefed his crews before their first Phantom strike against four Egyptian SA-2 batteries on the Canal, Hetz asked how many had seen missiles in flight. No one had. "We were all virgins before that flight," says Yair David. He witnessed his first SA-2 launch during that mission—"a huge blast, a giant dust mushroom rising from the launch area, and then a smoky ribbon snaking up from the cloud."[11]

By early summer, of course, they knew as much as anyone. They learned not to "spend too much energy dodging missiles that weren't even aimed at us," and in time "could tell which one of us a missile was going after," says Yoram Agmon.[12] Some even came to attribute personality traits to the missiles. "It may not be a plane, and it may have different flight and response characteristics—it is faster, a little less maneuverable, less intelligent since it lacks a pilot's brains—but it still responds to what you do. In fact, you can manipulate it," says Eitan Peled.

But now all that had become irrelevant. Attacking the missile super-batteries, however hastily assembled on the sand without fortified walls to protect them, was no longer a dump-truck bombing run against isolated batteries, or against a bunch of construction crews and their wet-concrete forms in the sand. In just one afternoon, as Pier and Harpaz were shot down, the sheen of invincibility suddenly wore off the Phantoms, and the very exclusivity of the Phantom crews became a liability because their know-how had reached its limit and there was no one they could go to for more. In a normal course of events, experienced Phantom commanders would have moved up to IAF Operations, and experienced Phantom technicians to IAF Technical Requirements. They would be available for advice or to brainstorm a problem. Also, in the normal course of events evolving enemy tactics would be studied by the intelligence community and appropriate countermeasures would be designed by the IAF's own black-arts experts, and then tested and practiced in the squadrons.

But the Phantoms had only just arrived, and even the most experienced of the Phantom crews had first laid eyes on the plane less than a year earlier. In just one day, that handful of young pilots and navigators came up against the most advanced missile-warfare systems in the world, which the Soviets developed in secrecy for decades and which even the Americans knew very little about. IAF

Operations was no help. Oded Marom, now head of IAF Strike Planning and in charge of directing the Phantom missions, knew nothing about missile warfare. To plan the Phantom raids, he simply drew circles on a map to denote the missiles' reach—blue circles for SA-2 missiles, red circles for SA-3s—and then figured out approach and escape routes that would keep the planes out of those circles for as long as possible.

"I worked like a robot. I'd get a risk graph, pick the lowest point on the graph and then play with choices of approach, standoff defenses, number of planes, and so on. The risk was never zero," Marom says. While IAF Operations analysts and enemy-doctrine experts later ran his plans through paper simulations to assess the actual risk, "it was all still very iffy. All our calculations could be confounded by unexpected missile masses and antiaircraft fire. Besides, if a plane was hit, it was not always possible to figure out exactly what it was that hit it."

The Phantom crews' sense of isolation grew as "the instructions we received from headquarters seemed to be drifting farther and farther away from reality," Eitan Peled would say later. "The gap grew between what we in the squadrons knew, and between the ability of the IAF Operations staff to analyze or plan events in the field." Some pilots blamed the mission planners for Pier's downing, because his orders required him to approach his target directly from the Sinai, where the Egyptians expected him, and where the sun was bound to be in his eyes and the desert draped in a thick haze that hid targets and approaching missiles alike.

Slouching for hours on pipe-leg chairs at their squadron briefing rooms, living and reliving each mission, they searched for new tactics. "It became obvious to us, long before IAF Operations realized it, that 18,000 feet was too high a climb before rolling into an attack, because it overexposed us to the missiles. If we only pulled up to 12,000 feet we could reduce the danger. Also, it was not enough to go against a missile battery with just two planes, because they now drew fire from other missile batteries in the area. You needed more planes," says Eilan Peled.

It was not that IAF Operations was oblivious or antagonistic to flyers' ideas. On July 2, their ideas were incorporated into a mission that Peled led in the same area where Pier had been shot down three days earlier. This time he was assigned an approach route from the south, rather than head-on from the east, and he managed to find and bomb his target before any missiles were launched against him. Two days later, in a mission planned jointly by the Phantom crews and IAF planning staff, one Phantom team rushed straight toward the Canal at high altitude, to draw the attention of the Egyptian radar, while the main attacking force swept out over the Mediterranean, crossed the Delta and struck the missiles from the rear. The mission was a success only in the sense that not a single Phantom was hit. Not a single missile battery was destroyed, either.

But not getting hit by a missile hardly mattered when the Soviet missile pack kept rolling toward the Canal. Once there, Soviets would win the war, because the missiles would keep the IAF out, and without the IAF the Greens would also have to break camp and fold back into the rear of the Sinai. There was still a lot more to the war than what happened to the two Phantom squadrons. The Mirages were devastating the Egyptian Air Force in the air—one Mirage pilot logged twenty-two combat missions in just two weeks at Bir Gafgafa—Skyhawks kept up their devastating Boxer bombings along the Canal, Israeli commandos carried out spectacular raids behind enemy lines, and all the while Israeli soldiers were being devastated by the unrelenting Egyptian artillery on the Canal.

In reality, however, all that had become trivial once the Soviets assembled their missile packs near Cairo and began rolling them forward toward the Canal. Just how totally the fate of the war had come to depend on the Phantoms became obvious when Moti Hod decided to debrief the July 4 mission at IAF headquarters in Tel Aviv, and when Dayan, IDF chief of staff Barlev and his deputy, Gen. David Elazar, suddenly showed up to sit in on it.

It was a gloomy meeting. As each Phantom crew gave its report, it was obvious that not a single missile battery had been taken out. Hod dismissed the tired Phantom crews, leaving behind only the two squadron commanders and Menachem Eini, Hetz's navigator and the 221 squadron's weapon systems expert. He asked for ideas about how to proceed. None were forthcoming. The Phantom teams had thrown their best at the rolling pack and failed, and now they had nothing else to offer except more of the same. IAF Operations had no suggestions, either. Moti Hod, who only two months earlier had confidently predicted the demolition of the missiles, was quiet.

It was at that point that Col. Joseph Na'or, the IAF's senior electronics warfare officer, took charge of the meeting. A self-taught iconoclast, a supplies officer with no flying experience, he had worked on his own to develop an electronic warfare system for the IAF, and through sheer charisma, self-assurance, and tenacity had become high priest of the new voodoo technology. "He was our *urim ve'tumim* on the subject, the only one who knew anything about electronic warfare," says Jacob Agasi, who just a week earlier, on June 30, took over IAF Operations.[13]

What Na'or offered was precisely what the sad conclave needed—a miracle. Although few understood the technical details of his presentation, there was no missing its gist—Na'or was in a position to provide an electronic magic show that would confound Egypt's radar and let the Phantoms sail safely into the missile fields and destroy them at their leisure. Eini, who had worked at the IAF Technical Requirements before joining the Phantom transition team, was thrilled. "I did not recall us having such sophisticated electronic warfare capabilities. If we now had them, we must have received them after I left," he would say later.[14] Better yet, Na'or had already set things in motion. Two days earlier Golda Meir had asked Nixon for an emergency shipment of special electronic gear to foil the SA-2s' guidance and targeting system, and on the day of the meeting Nixon approved it.

On the next day, another Phantom was shot down without denting the rolling missile pack. In less than a week, only five missile batteries were destroyed at a cost of three down Phantoms and five imprisoned crewmen. By July 13, the SA-2s were twenty-one miles west of the Canal, and the SA-3 batteries just six miles behind them. Also on July 13, in great secrecy, a number of large crates arrived at Hazor, and inside them the American solution to the missile predicament.

Chapter 21

MISSILES

The crates contained not bombs or rockets, but large and shiny football-shaped aluminum pods. The pods contained not explosives but electronic gear, designed to work on what passed for the missiles' brain, the targeting radar that controlled their firing and flight. The key was the SA-2 battery's narrow radar beam that swept back and forth like a narrow shaft of a flashlight through an eight-degree slice of skies. As it moved, it showed up as two thin white lines sweeping back and forth across two small screens in front of the missile operator. On the directional radar screen, the line was vertical and swept right and left. On the altitude radar screen, the line was horizontal and swept up and down. When the search beam bounced off a target, its location was marked on the two screens by stationary white lines, a vertical line marking the direction of the target from the missile battery, and a horizontal line showing its altitude. The target was at the point where the two lines intersected.

But if the plane that the radar beam struck carried one of those aluminum pods, and if the pod had been switched on, it could pick up and distort the radar beam just enough so by the time it bounced back home it would mark the Phantom's location on the screen not as thin lines but as thick bright bands, covering as much as one quarter of each radar screen. By itself, this was not much, since the missile could still find its target where the two bands intersected. But if several pod-equipped Phantoms approached the battery together, flying just far enough apart so the white bands that they projected onto the radar screen lined up alongside each other, together they would white out the entire screen and shut the radar down.

It was not as simple as all that. To block the directional radar screen, the one with the thin vertical line sweeping right and left, the Phantoms would have to spread out from side to side so that their vertical bands lined up alongside each other across the screen. But that only took care of the directional radar. To similarly white-out the altitude radar, the same planes would also have to spread out vertically, one above the other, so that the horizontal bands they projected also lined up one above the other, from the bottom of the screen all the way up. To "blind" just one battery, then, the Phantoms would have to approach it head-on in the form of a diagonal, say one plane at eleven o'clock and one at five o'clock, and the rest spread out between them.

But the Phantoms were no longer dealing with one battery. The way the Soviets set them up, the missile batteries were now everywhere. To also block out the radar screens of batteries on their right or left, the Phantoms had to spread out not only side to side and up and down, but also front to back, resembling the diagonal of a cube—or a flight of migrating ducks.

Finally, they had to do all that at 18,000 feet, and to stay locked into their precise "pod formation" positions even after the enemy discovered them and the missiles started to fly in their direction. If they stayed in position, the SA-2 batteries' radar screens would stay whited out, and whatever missiles were fired would simply wander away or explode harmlessly in the distance. But if just one plane broke off to dodge a missile—and on this the American technicians who accompanied the pods to Israel were adamant—the radars would instantly lock and the Phantoms would become ducks in a missile shooting gallery.

In reality, the Americans were not all that sure the pods would work. When Rabin had first approached the Pentagon several days earlier he was told that the system had just been developed and was

not considered reliable yet (he actually recommended against ordering the pods).[1] The American technicians in Israel were more posi-
tive about the pods' ability to handle SA-2 missiles, but they made
it clear that the system was never designed to and could not be
counted on to stop the SA-3s. But it is not certain how much of the
reservations really registered. Israelis tend to take American under-
statement with a grain of salt, and they may have figured that while
the system might be imperfect the Americans would not have sent
it over if it didn't work at all. Besides, they had no choice. The
Soviet missiles were almost at the Canal, and the pods were the only
game in town.

The first pod-formation strike was scheduled for July 18. As the
date approached, a conflict bubbled over in the fighter community.
Some of the Phantom pilots, and a few Mirage pilots who got wind
of the scheme, thought the entire premise of the pod formation
tactic deranged. "Coming in high and letting things happen to
us—it was the total opposite of any kind of flying we had ever
done," says Eitan Ben Eliahu.[2] Another Phantom pilot, Yoram
Agmon, "was all for using pods, but only up to a point. I thought
that once a missile was actually approaching we should have been
free to resort to old-fashioned breaks."[3] Iftach Spector, now in
command of the 101 Mirage squadron, blew his stack and accused
Hetz of blindly following an American high-tech siren song by
placing "electronics before physics, when it should be physics
before electronics. The first rule is to come in low so they cannot see
you."[4]

As Hetz's good friend from their Mirage-flying days at the 101,
Spector now assigned himself to escort the Phantoms on their
July 18 mission, but to the last minute he kept hammering at Hetz
to abort or modify the strike. Near the end of the week—the
mission was planned for Saturday—he joined Hetz and one of the
American experts for dinner at a popular Jaffa restaurant. "We had
a real quarrel there," he recalled years later. "We spoke a little
English and a lot of Hebrew. We smiled in English and fought in
Hebrew. We said nice things about the pods in English, but something else again in Hebrew. I kept telling him, we all attacked in
missile fields just three years earlier and we were not hit by even half
a missile, so why not go back to those old methods? Why use the

damned pods, instead of flying like we knew how to fly? Why this
magic? Why these formations? Why this rigidity? Why go in like
sitting ducks? Hetz just laughed and said he had reasons for doing
it that way."

But Hetz, too, must have had misgivings, because when he and
Spector got out of their car at Hazor that night, Hetz lingered. "He
hesitated, and then he told me that he had a dream the night before
about Aki, a good friend of ours who was killed earlier in that war.
I understood immediately. He was telling me that Aki had come to
call him," Spector says. The sense of foreboding seemed to run
clear up the IAF's chain of command. On Friday afternoon, as Hetz
and Eini put the final touches on the "forces and missions" chart
in the squadron mission room, Rafi Harlev, Hazor's commander,
"joined us and we sat and talked a lot about the risks in the
mission," Eini recalls. "Rafi was uneasy about having Hetz and me
fly in the same plane. Of our original Phantom transition group,
Pier, Harpaz, and [Eyal] Ahikar [Harpaz's navigator] had been shot
down, and Rafi worried that between us Hetz and I had accumulated
so much vital information it was not good for us to fly together. But
Hetz and he were very close friends, as was I, so it came down to two
friends against one, not a base commander against two pilots. Rafi
gave in."[5] Actually, Harlev brought the matter up again that night,
when he and his wife showed up for dessert at the Hetz and Eini
families' joint Sabbath dinner, but Hetz clung to the plan.

At 10:45 on Saturday morning, at Hazor and Ramat David, Hetz
and Ben-Nun gave their pilots final briefings. Twenty Phantoms,
nearly one-half of each of the two squadrons, were assigned to the
mission, which made for fairly crowded briefing rooms in both
bases. At Hazor, Hetz was followed by Na'or, who outlined the
massive electronic array that would back up the Phantoms, particularly a flight of specially equipped Skyhawks that would loiter
outside the missile field and jam the main Egyptian radar to keep
it from warning the missile batteries and pointing them in the
direction of the approaching threat. At noon, the Skyhawks took off
first, to take position across from the Egyptian missile front. They
were followed by Phantoms from Ramat David and then from
Hazor, and finally by Mirage escorts. At 12:30, the Phantoms met
close to the Egyptian front, climbed to 18,000 feet, broke into

formations of four, and spread out the width of most of the Canal front, each four Phantoms falling into their staggered migrating-ducks positions. Hetz led the first formation of four, Ben-Nun the second, Eitan Ben Eliahu the third, and so on. "It was peaceful and quiet, almost pastoral," Eitan Peled, who led the second pair in Hetz's formation, would recall. "Visibility was good, just a beautiful Saturday morning flight. Crazy."

As soon as they crossed the Canal into Egypt, the missile field came alive, and the pilots activated their pods. "I remember seeing the explosions of missiles in the air far ahead, and I was sure they were blown up by our pods," says Ben Eliahu. As they came close to the missile fields, their target area, "the place lit up like fire-works. You couldn't see the missile launches, but you saw them approach and explode a hundred or two hundred meters away, apparently, at least in part, due to the pods." In spite of numerous missile launches Ben Eliahu's formation entered right into the heart of the missile field, located and destroyed the two SA-2 batteries assigned to them, and with missiles exploding all around turned and got out safely. At the north end of the attack front, Eitan Peled, too, "never heard any missile locks" as he found and bombed his as-signed target. For a while things seemed to be going just fine all across the field. One missile crossed in front of Hetz as he led his formation into the missile field, but it was far away and it blew up harmlessly in the distance. When Eini called out a warning of a second missile heading toward them, Hetz simply held his position, switched on his radio, and ordered everyone else to do the same.

But that second missile was different. It was smaller and faster, and from the moment they spotted it "we had a missile lock warn-ing, so we knew it must have been an SA-3," Eini would recall. "We kept going straight and level, looking at it all the while, and then it came close to us and exploded." Eini made a mental note that its smoke cloud was shapeless and reddish brown, unlike the SA-2's, which was white and ring-shaped.

Hetz and Eini checked their plane, and although hit it seemed to be fine. "A few warning lights went on, and we lost radio contact with the outside, but there was no fire or loss of hydraulic pressure, and we could still talk with each other. Still, there was no point in going on, so we dropped our bombs and turned to go home, very low and very fast," Eini recalls. They were nearing the Canal when the damaged Phantom suddenly gave in and went out of control. Eini was reaching for the ejection lever, but Hetz beat him to it and Eini was blown out of the cockpit unprepared, like a rag doll. The rushing air knocked him out, and when he came to he was lying on the ground with his arm and leg broken nearly off. With his good hand he pulled out his radio, and he was still talking to a passing Phantom when a truckload of Egyptian troops arrived and took him prisoner.

Hetz never left his Phantom. Three years later, in the wake of the 1973 Yom Kippur War, his remains were discovered, still inside the wreckage of his Phantom on the Egyptian side of the Canal. "Either his canopy did not open and he never got out, or he was getting out just as the plane hit the ground," Eini said after returning from Egypt in a prisoner exchange forty months later.

At the same time that Hetz was hit, a second SA-3 struck Avihu Ben-Nun's Phantom. Ben-Nun managed to bring it to Bir Gafgafa, but barely survived the landing as his plane failed to stop, ran off the runway, broke its front wheel, and plowed a hundred yards in the sand before finally coming to rest.

The mission was not entirely unsuccessful. Of ten targeted batteries, four were destroyed and three damaged, and the loss of one Phantom and its crew would not normally seem out of line. But Hetz was no ordinary pilot, and his death led his colleagues to dub a failure not only the mission but the entire pod-formation tactic, which was immediately nicknamed *putz formation* and abandoned. Although few realized it at the time, Hetz's death signaled the end of the war itself.

"All along, because of the IAF's emphasis on flying virtuosity, every time a pilot was killed the feeling was that, had it been a truly great pilot there, it would not have happened," says Ben Eliahu. "Here, in quick succession, Pier, who was one of our outstanding pilots, was shot down, and then Hetz, who was not only a great pilot but a squadron commander and a superb leader, the ultimate authority in the Phantom community. In a matter of days, we went from absolute superiority in conventional air war, with a kill ratio of one-to-forty, down to a ratio of two-to-four against the missiles. Had it happened in air combat, it would have been a major disaster."

It didn't matter that Eitan Peled blamed the mission planners for rendering the pods less effective by spreading the planes out too far apart, or that David Ivri, who two weeks earlier moved from IAF Operations to command Tel Nof, blamed the Phantom crews themselves for letting their fatigue dictate "solutions not through . . . hard work or tactical personal effort but by getting somebody else's answer," or that Menachem Eini, upon returning from imprisonment in Egypt, blamed Na'or for overstating the electronic promise in the first place. It also didn't matter that "those who believed in physics over electronics only became more set in their opposition to the pods, while those who believed in the pods seized on the fact that it was an SA-3 that killed Hetz, which the pods were never claimed to be effective against," says Agmon. With Hetz gone, the debate itself became irrelevant because, no matter how long it now continued, the war was really over.

That night, Hod called Ran Ronen, who had just completed a two-year stint in command of IAF Flight School and was about to leave with his family for an extended leave abroad, and asked him to take over Hetz's devastated squadron. Ronen arrived at Hazor that night, and although he had never flown in a Phantom, he promised to lead his pilots in battle within a week. But his rousing confidence and legendary reputation did little to ease the hollow feeling. Almost mechanically, the Phantom crews continued to fly across the Canal day after day, to nibble at the edges of the rolling missile pack. To the Mirage pilots who flew cover during those missions, the spectacle of the Phantoms' persistent charges was humbling. "They were getting chewed up, and we'd see it all from above. We'd see them going into the jaws of death with masses of missiles shooting up at them," recalls Even-Nir.[6] By the end of the month, the few experienced Phantom pilots and navigators had grown so exhausted that senior Mirage pilots volunteered to ride in the Phantoms' backseats to give at least the navigators a chance to rest.

On July 30, however, the depression and sense of impotence were temporarily relieved by a moment of euphoria. All through that summer, the Soviet pilots and advisors kept deriding Egyptian MiG pilots for failing to stop the IAF Mirages and Skyhawks. Having fallen time and again into Mirage traps during the "Texas" campaign, the Egyptians had stopped challenging the Israelis and stayed away from them. To the Russians, it was not only cowardice but a blot on Soviet training, tactics, planes, and reputation. At the end of July, Soviet MiG-21 crews took to the field themselves and began to harass IAF Skyhawks during their bombing runs along the Canal. On July 25, a Soviet MiG-21 formation caught up with some Skyhawks, chased them back into the Sinai, and ostensibly managed to hit one in the tail with an air-to-air missile.

Hod may have felt helpless against the Soviet missiles, but the MiG challenge was right up his alley. He ordered Jacob Agasi, his operations chief, to draw up plans for an aerial rumble with the Russians, and began to lobby Dayan and the Greens for permission.

Agasi could have simply told his staff to draw up plans for just one more "Texas"-style ambush, but instead he called in David Porat, a brilliant planner of many "Texas" dogfights who had since been reassigned, and asked him to come back for a last, once-in-a-lifetime mission. "He didn't want to do it, but I told him his name would be on the plan and he finally agreed," says Agasi.[7] By the end of the month, Hod had received his permission, and Porat had completed his plan.

The plan, which was put in motion on July 30, surpassed any aerial ambush the IAF had ever carried out before. First, Avihu Ben-Nun was dispatched with four Phantoms from Ramat David to attack Egyptian ground positions near El Adabiya, six miles south of Suez on the Egyptian side of the Gulf. Only, instead of attacking in normal Phantom fashion, the four planes used tactics which "we knew that the enemy knew were unique to the Skyhawk squadrons," Hod would say later.[8] Like Skyhawks, the Phantoms formed an "Indian circle" above the target, with each pilot in his turn calling out and taking a steep Skyhawk-style dive at the target. On the Egyptian radar, the four circling blips registered as Skyhawks on a routine bombing mission.

Then, while the Phantoms did their Skyhawk routine, four Mirages from Tel Nof were sent into the same area at 20,000 feet, flying straight and level from south to north. Like the Phantoms, however, the Mirages were not what they seemed. Flying so close together that they registered on the Egyptian radar as a single blip, the four fighters appeared as a lone Mirage on a photo-reconnaissance flight. Then, four low-flying Mirages from Ramat David flew into the area so low they didn't even show up on the Egyptian radar, and they kept flying back and forth behind the low mountain ridge east of the Canal. Finally four more Mirages stood ready at the edge of the Bir Gafgafa runway.

So well had Porat manipulated electronic signals and radar perceptions that, in a remarkable sleight of hand, he had literally hidden four Mirages and four Phantoms in the clear steel-blue summer skies over the Egyptian desert, and eight more Mirages nearby. At the controls of these fighters sat the most awesome championship team Moti Hod had yet assembled—among them, the pilots had a combined total of fifty-nine enemy air kills, which by day's end they would jack up to sixty-four.

As Porat expected, the sight of four defenseless Skyhawks and an unarmed camera-carrying Mirage was too much for the Russians, and soon sixteen MiG-21s rushed toward El Adabiya. Four of the MiGs came low, almost hugging the ground. When they were almost underneath the "Skyhawks," their pilots kicked in their afterburners and shot up to attack them from below. At the same time, four other MiGs came in high above the supposed lone Mirage, with eight more MiGs following closely behind. It was precisely what Porat had planned on. The MiGs had just begun climbing up at the "Skyhawks," and swooping down at the "Mirage," when Moti Hod, slouching in his seat at the IAF bunker with his stopwatch in hand, issued the attack order.

Instantly, four things happened. First, the "Skyhawk" Phantoms broke up their "Indian circle" and went into a steep climb, to stay and watch the impending battle from above, and to swoop down on any MiG attempting to leave the scene. Second, the four close-flying Mirages broke apart, dropped their external fuel tanks, and looped around to face the approaching MiGs. Third, as the low-flying MiGs climbed up toward the "Skyhawks," the Ramat David Mirages popped up from behind their mountain ridge and climbed up right alongside and behind them. Finally, Iftach Spector and his Mirage group scrambled from Bir Gafgafa and rushed toward the battle site.

In seconds, everything changed. Instead of surprising four oblivious Skyhawks and a harmless Mirage, the Russians were suddenly surrounded by eight Mirages and shut in from above by the Phantoms. The stunned MiG pilots fell on their Soviet training and tactics and looked to their radar controllers for guidance, but Na'or had set up his magic show and jammed the Egyptian radar altogether, and the Russians were on their own. In the scramble, they also made a fatal mistake and began to dive after the fuel tanks that the Mirages above them had dropped, leaving themselves open to the Mirages that now rolled right in after them, downing two of the MiGs in one pass.

One of the MiG pilots bailed out. Dangling from his parachute and frantically waving other jets away as he coasted down amidst a clutter of MiGs, Mirages, Phantoms, and tumbling fuel tanks of all shapes and sizes, "he may have been the only one who saw the whole battle. In the heat of battle we actually used him as a marker, you know, like 'I am ten kilometers from the parachutist,'" recalls Aviem Sela, Ben-Nun's wingman.[9]

As the Mirages went after their MiGs, four from below and four from above, the Phantoms reached the top of their climb, flopped over, and began to dive after strays. The Soviets fought hard. "They shot from every angle and from every position. It was impossible to catch a MiG without getting yourself sandwiched from the back by another," says Sela. But while the Israelis were reared on precisely this kind of unstructured battle of loose pairs and mostly single combat, to the Russians the experience was traumatic. With their rigid battle formations broken, their plans gone awry, and their controllers unable to provide guidance, all they could do was maneuver violently to get away as one by one the Israelis separated them from the pack for the kill. Sela, finding a MiG behind him, slammed on his air brakes, broke into a flaps-down barrel roll—Yak Nevo's old "let him pass" maneuver—and as the Russian shot on ahead Sela chased it down to 2,000 feet and blew it up with a Sidewinder missile. Ben-Nun went after another MiG, already being chased by a Mirage, and shot it down, too. The battle began and ended so quickly that Spector counted three fireballs during his brief dash in from Bir Gafgafa, and by the time he got there he had barely time to go after the first MiG he saw and shoot it down before the battle was suddenly over.*

Just two minutes into the battle, Moti Hod clicked off his stop-

---

*Actually, he and a second Mirage shot at the MiG at the same time, but neither saw it crash. Six years later, however, during Anwar Sadat's visit to Israel, he confirmed the downing of the fifth MiG and the two pilots were credited with a half-kill each.

watch and ordered his pilots back. As the skies instantly cleared of planes, the three Russian pilots who managed to bail out were still drifting down. The wrecks of five Soviet MiGs lay smoking in the Egyptian desert. That night, victory parties were held not only at Hazor, Ramat David, and Tel Nof—but in every fighter base in Egypt; to the Egyptian pilots, too, the Russians had finally got their comeuppance.

But the dogfighting victory was a passing interlude. The missile fields were where the real war took place, and it was there that the Soviets, just three days after the loss of their five MiGs, got even.

On the morning of August 3, Ran Ronen was returning from his first Phantom mission with Yair David as his navigator when they spotted SA-2 missiles heading toward them from near the Canal. Another pair of Phantoms was scrambled to the area, and when they, too, were shot at, IAF planners triangulated the two missile sightings and figured out where they had come from. Eitan Peled was then ordered to take four Phantoms there and take the battery out.

Employing a new tactic that the Phantom crews had devised, Peled left two Phantoms to circle high overhead and watch for other missiles while he dived with his wingman toward the launch site. They arrived just as the battery was being packed up on trucks and about to leave, and demolished the assembly with four well-placed bombs. As they pulled back up, however, they ran smack into a barrage of six missiles from a second SA-2 ambush. Although he had no bombs left, Peled flew in the direction of the missiles and located the source of the second ambush—again just a few truck-borne missile launchers spread out alongside a highway. The two Phantom pairs now traded places. As Peled and his wingman climbed up to serve as lookouts, the second pair dived at the new target.

But the Russian missile trap was no less intricate than the Israeli fighter ambush over El Adabiya three days earlier. As Yigael Shochat and Ra'anan Ne'eman, the young pilots of the second Phantom pair, dived at the roadside missile battery, they ran into a third ambush—this time of SA-3 missiles—which had so far maintained total electronic silence. Shochat, who flew first, was already too low and going down too fast to do anything. He had just dropped his bombs and started back up when an SA-3 missile exploded at his side in a reddish brown cloud, then a second, and a third. Shochat and his navigator bailed out just before the plane crashed. They reached the ground safely, but the Egyptian soldiers who quickly closed in on them fired as they approached, killing the navigator and shattering Shochat's right knee. He was unconscious when the Egyptians took him to a hospital, where his leg was subsequently amputated.*

Ra'anan Ne'eman, in the second Phantom, had begun his dive when he saw the SA-3s explode near Shochat's Phantom below. Without thinking twice, he jettisoned his bombs and turned to leave, but he, too, was late. A fourth SA-3 exploded to his left and knocked his head so violently against the cockpit wall that he lost consciousness. When he came to seconds later, his left hand was shattered and bleeding, and he saw pieces of flesh scattered all around the cockpit. He ripped off his oxygen mask to avoid heaving into it. "Of all things, I suddenly remembered the story of an American pilot in Vietnam whose hand was shot off by a cannon shell," he would write later. "That American pilot continued to fly, and ultimately bailed out over the ocean and was rescued. I decided that if he did it I would do it. . . . I then remembered watching an old movie about the Battle of Britain, where this old pilot was telling a young one that if he ever flew straight and level for ten seconds he'd get shot down. So I started to break every five."[10]

It all took place in seconds. He was twisting and turning toward the Sinai in his broken-up metal box, trying to work the throttle with his elbow to spare his bleeding hand, when he heard Shochat announce that he was bailing out. He heard several more explosions, and saw a few missiles sailing past him like huge bonfires. Then, just as a piece of metal from Shochat's Phantom came tumbling down past him, he saw two more SA-3 missiles coming straight at him. "Until then I had avoided going down too low, but this time I gambled everything, my life, and went down. I had to keep blinking hard just to focus my blurred vision. At one point I saw what looked like a telephone pole flying alongside me." Then, as suddenly as it

*Shochat has since completed medical school, and served as chief physician for the IAF.

all began, the beeping in his earphones stopped, the missiles were gone, and down below he saw the Suez Canal. A minute later, he was in Israeli airspace, over the Sinai.

Tired, dizzy, and in excruciating pain, he wanted to bail out right there and then, but a thought flashed in his mind that "the sand and flies wouldn't do much for my wounds, and [I] decided to go for Bir Gafgafa." By that time, Eitan Peled had pulled up above, figured out what happened, and urged Ne'eman to let his navigator operate the controls (the Phantom had a set in each cockpit) while he bandaged his shattered hand. That was how they landed at Bir Gafgafa, with Ne'eman operating the stick with his right hand, and the navigator working the throttles from the rear.*

The missile race was over. For weeks, United Nations and American diplomats had been working to bring about a cease-fire. Now both Egypt and Israel agreed to stop the fighting. "We shot down five Russians, they shot down five of our Phantoms, so I guess both sides felt they could accept the cease-fire without losing face," Hod would note later. The cease-fire went into effect on August 7, 1970. Under its terms, the lines of confrontation were to be frozen, with the Soviet missiles remaining behind the thirty-kilometer line west of the Canal. That same night, however, in clear violation of the agreement, the missiles were moved closer to the water. Israel protested to the Americans and the United Nations, but did nothing. Neither Israel, the UN or the Americans did anything in the following days, when the missiles were brought right up to the Canal and began to multiply rapidly, from sixteen batteries on August 7, only one of them inside the thirty-kilometer line, to fifty by the middle of October, forty of them within a strip running thirteen to twenty-one kilometers from the Canal. Some sixteen of them were SA-3 batteries operated by Russians.

In truth, the handful of Mirage and Phantom crews who carried the brunt of the endless war had reached their breaking point.

---

*Three of Ne'eman's fingers were subsequently amputated. When Prime Minister Golda Meir visited him in the hospital and asked him what she could do for him, he said he wanted to go back to flying. Meir looked at Hod, who nodded his agreement, and a year later Ra'anan was flying Phantoms again.

"When the cease-fire was declared we thanked God," says Even-Nir. "I never thought such a thing would happen, but we were at Bir Gafgafa one night, and IAF Operations called down and wanted us to scramble. I told them 'Dear friends, scramble from the North because we have no strength left.' "

"We were fighting a centipede—you hit it here, and two more legs grow in its place. You hit there and it keeps growing. We were fighting an enemy that seemed not only irrational but with unlimited resources. It was like trying to empty an ocean with a bucket," says Oded Marom. "By the middle of the summer we were like marathon runners, hoping to just be around at the finish. We then ended the fighting saying that the missiles wouldn't move an inch toward the Canal, but they moved, grew, multiplied, and came right up to the water line—they couldn't get any closer—and then we did nothing."[11]

In the summer of 1971 the missile density and aggressiveness got to a point where the IAF actually gave up its high-altitude Mirage and Phantom surveillance flights, and began using a World War II–era Boeing Stratocruiser transport with a special long-range camera shooting obliquely from its window, to photograph in a slant from deep inside the Sinai. On September 17, an Egyptian SA-2 missile shot the Stratocruiser, too, down. Of its crew of eight, only one mechanic survived by climbing up the inside walls of the tumbling and spinning plane until he reached a window, and threw himself out.

This time the IAF had to do something, and on that same day Hod approached the IDF General Staff with a plan that seemed worthy of an avenging Buck Rogers. The United States had just provided Israel with Shrike air-ground, antiradiation missiles, capable of homing in on precisely the sort of electronic signals with which the missile batteries located their targets and directed their missiles. As Hod presented it, a force of Phantoms would fire Shrikes at seven missile batteries across the Canal without themselves venturing into missile range. Then, as the Phantoms turned back to return home, the small Shrikes would slither into the heart of Egypt's missile fields, sniff out the SA-2 radars with their nose-cone antennas, follow the scent to its source, and crash into the batteries' radar-control units.

In reality, the missiles had little chance of inflicting any damage. Once launched, the small Shrikes could not be guided or controlled. Unless they found active SA-2 radar signals to home in on, they would meander aimlessly and explode somewhere in the Egyptian desert. Since SA-2 radars were ordinarily switched off, to be turned on only by impending threat, the missile batteries had to be teased into switching on their radars if the Shrikes were to do their job.

But the proposed operation, code-named Toaster, called for no decoy flights and no intrusion into enemy territory. It was certain to be "a wasted effort," as Beni Peled, who had recently been appointed chief of IAF Air Section, told Moshe Dayan when he came to IAF headquarters to find out more about the plan. Peled estimated that, at most, a few missile batteries might be temporarily disabled. "Are you finished? Sit down," Hod said. The next day, Eitan Peled led his Phantoms "to the outer reaches of the [Egyptian] missile field, and we fired the Shrikes from as far as possible. Since the Egyptians had no reason to switch on their radar, we fired the missiles to the skies in the general direction of the target, and that was that. The missiles went God knows where, and if there was damage, it was minimal."

Operation Toaster's chief accomplishment lay in being "safe, since no great damage was anticipated, and limited—even if everything worked out, there would still not be enough damage to prompt the Egyptians to renew the fighting. In reality, [the notion of damaging the missiles with the Shrikes] was an illusion which could not even be presented with a straight face," says Ben Eliahu.

To the ever pragmatic Hod, however, who saw no point in sacrificing more Phantoms to the angry Russian missile gods, the operation was perfect. It calmed the Greens and pleased the politicians, and it left Hod free for what really had to be done. Before all else, the IAF had to develop an answer to the missile threat. "We had to develop new tactics, new ways of combining diversion, suppression, and attack. We needed stand-off weapons and homing ordnance. Such things take years to acquire and implement," Hod would say later. So long as he could not defeat the missiles cleanly and totally, buying more time was good enough.

Chapter 22

JUDGMENT DAY

In May 1973, Moti Hod retired as the most adulated and accomplished wartime commander the IAF had known. The man who seven years earlier seemed too colorless and weak to follow in Ezer Weizman's huge footprints led the IAF to a spectacular victory in the Six-Day War, and held off the massive Egyptian and Soviet offensive of the War of Attrition. In thousands of combat missions the IAF destroyed hundreds of enemy planes, many of them in air battles that Hod conducted himself. And while waging those wars Hod also managed to switch the IAF from French to American— and Israeli-built—weapons systems.

By contrast, his successor, although clearly one of the force's brightest and most accomplished stars, was an enigma. Even when he practically created and ran the IAF's French-era jet fighter force in the 1950s—selecting and ferrying the Ouragans and Mystères to Israel, commanding their first squadrons, developing their flight and combat doctrines, and leading the Mystères in their first war— Beni Peled was never part of the Weizman-Hod warrior fraternity. Chubby, bookish, belligerently argumentative, and forever immersed in technical literature, he disdained most fighter pilots as know-nothing playboys, and had only contempt for those who held up the IAF for apartments or university scholarships, calling them "mercenaries [who] could not tell a job from a high calling" (he himself signed up for life when his initial service term was up).[1]

Even more important, it was Peled's passion for organization and technology that set him apart from his stick-and-throttle contemporaries. In 1958, instead of elbowing his way up the narrowing command pyramid as the IAF's leading squadron commander, he took an extended leave to—of all things—study engineering. To most of his colleagues, it made him, underneath his fighter-jock veneer, a nerd. Menahem Bar, by then commander of Ramat David, predicted that Peled would end up at some meaningless technical post if he ever returned to active IAF service. Moti Hod warned him that "if you leave the operational track for four years they'll forget who you are." Halfway through his studies, Peled discovered that Weizman indeed planned to give him a technical appointment when he got back; he threatened to leave the IAF, and Weizman agreed to return him to the command loop at the end of his studies.

He almost did not make it back. He was hunting jackrabbits in the fall of 1961 when he accidentally shot himself in the chest. The bullet severed an artery, and tore into the circuit of nerves that controlled his right arm. He was rushed home, and then to a hospital in Haifa, and was unconscious for hours. He began his fourth year of engineering studies with an artery transplant operation, followed by months of difficult and painful therapy for his paralyzed right arm. Yet such was his drive and focused brilliance that he still completed his studies on schedule, received his engineering degree, returned to active duty, and was soon flying again.

His arrogance and argumentative belligerence did not soften while he was away—"If you didn't have an engineering degree he treated you as if you were an idiot and a moron," says Oded Marom.[2] "It was up to you to prove that you were not." Peled's estrangement from the flying ranks grew as for the next decade he bounced from one top-secret, high-tech assignment to another. While his arm recovered he ran IAF Technical Requirements, and then oversaw the secret development of an unmanned surveillance drone. In 1964 Weizman appointed him commander of Hazor, but almost immediately assigned him to draft the acquisition plans that would transition the IAF from French- to American-based hardware, and then took him to Washington to help lobby for Skyhawks and Phantoms. He commanded Hazor during the Six-Day War, after which Moti Hod appointed him head of IAF Air Section, but in March of 1969, just as the War of Attrition was reaching its critical phase, Hod sent him to head two more secret projects, the development of a new Israeli fighter from the stolen Mirage blueprints and of a newer generation yet of surveillance drones.

Peled's reputation as a technical genius, and his absence from the IAF command bunker during most of the War of Attrition, caused misgivings when Hod picked him as the next commander of the IAF. For the rank and file and for many junior officers, the appointment was a mystery. Between the Technion and his assorted top-secret projects, Peled had been away for much of fifteen years. Nearly two decades had passed since his glory days with the Meteors, Ouragans, and Mystères, when many of the present-generation of flyers were still in grammar school. Peled had never shot down a MiG. His one great war story involved his getting shot and bailing out over Sharm el Sheikh in 1956—and then being so fat he almost could not be lifted into the Piper Cub that came to get him. "We knew him only as someone who used to be big and did great things once, but who was now out of it," says Giora Furman, who became Peled's first chief of IAF Operations.[3]

There was something else. If Peled's passion for technology seemed eccentric, his preoccupation with organizational charts and systems seemed downright bizarre. To a force that prided itself on swaggering informality and improvisational brilliance, Peled's furious insistence that thirteen years of Weizman and Hod management left the IAF in utter chaos appeared absurd if not sacrilegious. "Delegation of responsibilities was intolerable. Instead of organized hierarchy, I found . . . a Byzantine court where titles meant nothing," Peled would recall. "It was like walking into a palace and finding the horses stabled in the dance hall. Joseph Na'or was the pope of electronic warfare, but IAF Technical Requirements had no idea what he was doing because he was talking directly with Hod. The whole place was one big jam session." Na'or in particular drew Peled's wrath. "One day a genius shows up, and right away he is in charge of all electronic warfare for the entire IAF, and the IAF command listens to him as if he were Rasputin?"[4]

In early 1973, Hod brought Peled to headquarters as chief of IAF
Air Section, and was clearly grooming him as his successor. But
instead of using the time to bond with the senior command staff
Peled antagonized everybody by launching a ruthless restructuring
drive that smacked less of reform than a purge. He had just begun
it when, on May 10, 1973, his appointment came through and he
took command of the IAF. Joseph Na'or promptly retired. Others
grumbled and stayed, but made no secret of their reservations. Of
those who played along, not all were quite sure what he was trying
to do and where things were heading.

He was barely three months on the job, isolated and just getting
a handle on things, when he was awakened at four-thirty one Saturday morning to take an urgent telephone call from Lt. Gen. David
Elazar, the IDF's new chief of staff. In just over twelve hours, Elazar
said, at six in the evening to be exact, Israel would be attacked by
the combined armies of Egypt and Syria. Worse yet, the IDF was
totally unprepared to stop such an attack. It had only skeleton crews
manning its border outposts to north and south, no reservists on
call, and not enough time to rush tanks and artillery to the front to
make a stand. Unless the IAF could stop them, fifteen Arab divisions would pour into the Sinai and the Golan Heights in a matter
of hours.

"How long will it take to prepare a preemptive strike, and where
should it be?" Elazar asked.

"Syria, with the surface-air missiles as first target," Peled replied. Ever since the War of Attrition had ended, when the Egyptians all but drove the IAF out of the Canal area by setting up their
missile batteries almost at the water line, it was clear that attacking
under an umbrella of missiles to neutralize the IAF had become a
tenet of Arab military doctrine. Before the IAF could stop any tanks
and enemy troops, it first had to take out the missiles. Peled told
Elazar the IAF would be ready to carry out the mission by eleven-
thirty that morning.

"Start rolling," Elazar said, and rushed to an emergency meeting
with Israel's shaken government, which would have to approve the
orders. Peled himself called IAF Operations and ordered immediate
activation of Operation *Dougman V*, an elaborate multiprong strike
on twenty-five-odd batteries of SA-2, SA-3, and SA-6 missiles that

in the preceding weeks the Syrians had moved close to the Golan Heights. He then rushed into his car and drove to the IAF compound in Tel Aviv, to personally command the operation from the "Hole."

But the attack on the Syrian missiles did not take place. At 6:00 in the morning, heavy clouds materialized over the Golan Heights, and since the operation required low-altitude flying and visual identification of the missile batteries, many of them small and mobile SA-6As, Peled had to call it off. Instead, at 6:45, he activated an alternative plan to knock out Syrian airfields behind the Golan Heights, where visibility was fine, to deprive the attacking Syrians of air cover. Although the sudden change entailed a massive and time-consuming reconfiguration of the entire force—new mission orders had to be dusted off and updated, squadrons reassigned, planes rearmed, pilots rebriefed—the well-oiled IAF machinery smoothly switched leads in mid-course, and was ready to launch the attack just before noon, only half an hour later than the original strike date.

But that attack, too, never took place. At the Israeli government emergency meeting, Dayan persuaded Golda Meir that however imminent the Arab threat was, a preemptive strike would paint Israel, not the Arabs, as the aggressor, and would alienate the United States precisely when Israel needed its help most. Instead of striking first, Dayan advised warning Egypt and Syria to cancel their attack plans immediately and, should they attack anyhow, letting the IDF take the initial blow and then rally for a counteroffensive. With great misgivings, Meir agreed to let the Arabs attack first. Elazar, who pushed for a preemptive strike and for immediate and full call-up of the reserves, was overridden on both points. Shortly before noon, he left the meeting and told Peled to call off the airfield strike, and to prepare to defend the country against the Arab invasion.

Peled, however, was certain he did not have until six in the evening to get ready. As he saw it, since the Arabs would not attack without air support, "the latest they could launch their aircraft and still get something done before dark was at three in the afternoon." Just before noon, he ordered IAF Operations to send three reconnaissance flights over the Egyptian and Syrian fronts at 2:00. At

1:30, Gad Eldar, the Mirage dogfighter who that morning was rushed back from a weekend assignment in Bir Gafgafa to man the strike-planning desk at IAF Operations, walked down to the "Hole" and began briefing Peled on the reconnaissance operation that was about to take place.

As Eldar later recalled, Peled was already sitting in his central command seat, facing the big table on which the forthcoming operation would be simulated as it took place. To Peled's right sat Giora Furman, head of IAF Operations, and to his left Rafi Harlev, chief of IAF Intelligence. To Harlev's left was a glass window, on the other side of which was the IAF Intelligence command desk. "We were still talking when I look to my left and see the intelligence guy in the window talking to Rafi [Harlev], who turns pale and tells Beni [Peled], 'Sir, Egyptian and Syrian planes are in the air.' "[5]

It was now two minutes before 2:00. Peled instantly canceled the reconnaissance missions and ordered his entire fighter-bomber force scrambled to defend the nation's skies. But the orders were barely out of his mouth when air-raid sirens went off throughout the country. The war had begun.

To hear the Israelis tell it, the war broke out suddenly and unexpectedly. In reality, it was nothing of the kind. In the three years of relative calm that followed the end of the War of Attrition, Anwar el-Sadat, Egypt's president since the death of Nasser on September 28, 1970, and Hafez al-Assad of Syria never hid their intent to avenge their 1967 defeat—or to keep up with the PLO, which in the early 1970s seized the hearts and minds of the Arab world with a spectacular international terror war of airline hijacking, bombings, and assassinations against Israel and its allies. By the fall of 1971, Lt. Gen. Saad el-Shazly, Egypt's new chief of staff, had a massive plan in place for crossing the Canal in strength, destroying the Barlev Line, and seizing back some or all of the Sinai. In November of 1972, Sadat promised war with Israel in six months to a year.

Israel, too, prepared for war, beefing up fortifications along the Suez Canal and the Golan Heights, and developing new battle plans that anticipated every combination of Arab forces and tactics.

Massive arms deliveries from the United States and Europe doubled the size of Israel's tank force, bolstered its navy with a fleet of deadly Israeli-designed missile boats, and added several squadrons of U.S.-built Phantoms, Skyhawks, and C-130 Hercules transports to the IAF (which also took delivery of a squadron of Israeli-made Nesher [Eagle] jet fighters, built from the Mirage blueprints stolen in Switzerland five years earlier). This hardly matched the Soviet buildup of the Syrian and Egyptian military, but it kept the Arab advantage at three-to-one in troops, tanks, ships and fighter-bombers, and nearly six-to-one in artillery.

More important, both sides were preparing for the same kind of war. First, since the Egyptian soldier was at his best when performing by rote, Shazly had launched a series of massive rehearsals for crossing the Canal, demolishing Israeli-style sand fortifications with powerful water jets, and seizing road crossings and fortified bunkers. Since these rehearsals took place across the Canal in full view of Israeli troops and intelligence observers, not the smallest detail remained secret.

Second, both Shazly and the Israelis agreed that the Egyptian Air Force was no match for the IAF, and that any Egyptian offensive would have to take place under a massive surface-air missile umbrella to protect the invasion forces from IAF strikes (it would leave the rest of Egypt to the mercy of the IAF). The 150 surface-air batteries that Egypt had in place by early 1973 (a third of them just behind the Canal), and the smaller missile fields that Syria set up just opposite the Golan Heights, were at the heart of both the Arab attack and the Israeli defense plans. Three years after losing five Phantoms to Egyptian missiles in the summer of 1970, the IAF had ostensibly figured out a way to knock out the missiles, and the new Israeli defense doctrine now called for the IAF to do just that in a massive preemptive strike at the first sign of an Arab move.

Where Arabs and Israelis differed, however, was in what they thought of each other. While the Egyptians were so sure of a ferocious Israeli response that they overdesigned their attack plan and prepared to take casualties by the tens of thousands at the hands of the avenging Israelis, Israel so underestimated Egypt's ability and will to fight that in January, in response to Sadat's threat to hit Israel with "the most cruel war in all of history, a war before which even the American bombing of North Vietnam would pale,"[6] IDF chief of staff Elazar merely noted that "in the context of the 1973 balance of power, Egypt has no chance whatsoever of accomplishing any significant military goal [against Israel]."[7]

Much of that assurance radiated from Gen. Eliahu Zeira, Israel's handsome, brilliant and arrogant chief of IDF Military Intelligence (AMAN). In the spring, when Egypt announced plans to hold another series of war games at the Canal in April, and the foreign press and some foreign intelligence agencies warned that Sadat really was planning to attack Israel around May 15—and if not then, then in October—Zeira dismissed the warnings out of hand and assured Elazar that if and when the Arabs decided to go to war, he would personally make sure that Elazar knew at least one week before it happened.

The IDF had no reason to doubt Zeira. Each time Shazly had staged his Canal-crossing games in 1971 and 1972, Zeira had told the IDF command not to worry, and indeed, each time, the Arabs ended their war games by folding up their tents and stealing back home across the desert. Still, Zeira's latest assessment was disputed by the *Mossad*, Israel's equivalent of the CIA, and Elazar himself had grown so uneasy that he disregarded Zeira's assurances, mobilized his forces at the Sinai and called in the reserves against a possible Egyptian invasion. In June, however, the Egyptian forces once again packed up and went home just as Zeira had predicted. By summer's end Zeira's reputation was such that even as Shazly huddled with senior Egyptian and Syrian planners in September to finalize his attack plans, the IDF calmly began to rotate its top command, and announced a three-month reduction in the mandatory service term of its conscripts.

On September 13, the tensions that had been building up since the start of the year exploded on the northern front when sixteen Syrian MiGs jumped four Israeli Phantoms photographing military installations in northern Syria. The massive air battle that followed claimed twelve MiGs and one Israeli Mirage. Ironically, it also provided the ultimate cover for the Arab attack. As Egypt and Syria went on the alert and began to move men, tanks, and missiles to the front, Zeira dismissed it as mere saber-rattling. So convinced was he of an Arab bluff, and so dominant in Israel's intelligence community, that when Syria moved three divisions to the front and spread twenty-five missile batteries along the Israeli frontier, so that the entire Golan Heights airspace was now within missile range, Israel's defenses were nonchalantly beefed up with just one reduced-strength tank battalion, and one artillery battery (one additional artillery battalion was placed on alert).

On October 1, Egypt announced its intent to begin a new round of war games on the Canal, but Zeira still insisted that Sadat had "no intent to go to war." On Friday morning, October 5, as 900 Syrian tanks and 140 artillery batteries lined up along Israel's northern borders, ten Egyptian divisions got in place to the south, and Soviet advisors' families were spotted being airlifted out of Egypt, Zeira again rated the outbreak of war at "very improbable."[8]

Still uneasy, Elazar placed the IAF on alert, canceled all leaves of senior IDF officers, and ordered 177 more tanks and 11 artillery batteries to the Golan Heights. This still left the Israelis greatly outgunned, twenty-to-one in artillery pieces, but so completely was Zeira's limited-Syrian-retaliation scenario accepted that at 2:30 that Friday afternoon, when Beni Peled and his senior staff met with IAF attack squadron commanders, the only item on the agenda was the *Dougman V* plan for destroying the Syrian missiles.

Shazly had three reasons for choosing the next day, October 6, to start his war for the liberation of the Sinai. First, the Suez Canal tide would be at its highest, making the crossing easier. Second, the day coincided with the tenth day of the holy month of Ramadan, when in the year A.D. 624 the prophet Mohammed and his troops scored their first *jihad* victory in the battle of Bader (Shazly even code-named the operation Bader).

Third and most important, October 6 was Yom Kippur, the Day of Atonement. The most sacred date in the Jewish calendar, it is a day of fasting and praying for divine forgiveness. At the end of the day, God is believed to inscribe every Jew in the Book of Life or in the Book of Death, and the verdict is sealed at sundown. Observant Jews spend the entire day at their synagogues in prayer, but even secular Israelis stay close to home and synagogue, as if to avert divine wrath.

At no other time of the year do Jewish families turn so inwardly. At sunset on Yom Kippur Eve, from the tenements of Beersheba in the Negev and Qiryat Shemona in Galilee, to the plush seaside villas of Herzliyya, Jewish families light twenty-four-hour memorial candles and sit down for an early supper. Shops and factories, radio and television stations, restaurants, theaters, and most traffic shut down for "that awesome day." As darkness falls, tables are hastily cleared and much of the nation crowds into synagogues for the recitation of the *Col Nidré* cantor's chant, which is then virtually the only sound heard in the entire country. Following evening prayers, the entire nation turns in early in anticipation of the hard fast day ahead.

It was on that kind of night in 1973 that the telephone rang at AMAN's headquarters in Tel Aviv and a critically placed agent delivered the report that finally persuaded Zeira that the Arab attack was indeed imminent. To a nation suddenly jolted out of sober reflection to the reality of an impending war, the enormity and timing of the Arab attack assumed apocalyptic dimensions. As men rushed home from synagogues to pick up their army gear and join their military units, two words from the prayer books they left behind would haunt them in the days and weeks to come—*Yom Ha'Deen*, Hebrew for Judgment Day.

At precisely two in the afternoon, 2,000 Egyptian guns opened withering fire along the entire Canal front, and hundreds of Egyptian tanks rushed up the high ramps on their side of the Canal, lowered their guns, and fired point-blank into the Israeli fortifications on the other side. Fifteen minutes after the attack opened, 8,000 crack Egyptian assault troops crossed the Canal and passed unseen among the fortifications. Some stopped after 200 yards and dug in. Others proceeded to mine the access roads to the fortifications, and to set up antitank ambushes for the anticipated Israeli reinforcements. Only 436 Israeli soldiers, most of them reservists and many of them immigrants with little military experience, manned the twenty fortifications along the Barlev Line. As devastating artillery and tank fire kept them pinned down—an estimated 3,000 tons of exploding ordnance in less than an hour—thousands of Egyptian troops began a crossing so massive that they appeared like swarms of locusts. Of the one Israeli tank division in the area, only three tanks were actually at the front, the other 227 kept as reserves back in the Eastern Sinai. It would be hours, in some cases days, before reinforcements could be brought to bear on the enemy.

By that time, the entire Israeli frontline, with the exception of a single fort at the north of the Canal, would collapse.

In the north, because of the proximity of the Syrian frontier to Israeli population centers in Galilee, Maj. Gen. Yitzhak Hofi, commander of IDF Northern Command, had demanded and received limited reinforcement in the preceding days. But even so, the 1,500 Syrian tanks that hit the Israeli lines under massive air and artillery cover were opposed by only 170 Israeli tanks and 60 assorted pieces of artillery, most of which would be wiped out by morning. Here, too, it would take at least a day before ground help could arrive.

There remained the IAF, of course, but to do what? All along, every IDF scenario and contingency plan was based on two assumptions. One, the Arabs would attack under an umbrella of surface-air missiles to keep the IAF off their backs. Two, the IAF would have enough advance warning to beat the Arabs to the punch by taking out the missiles first. The assumptions were sound. As expected, the Arabs attacked under a heavy missile cover, and in reality Israel had more than enough warning. But the warnings were ignored, and once the war began, volleys of SA-2, SA-3, SA-6, and SA-7 shoulder missiles were keeping Peled's fighters from getting anywhere near where they were needed most.

Like the rest of the Israeli military, the IAF was caught unprepared. Although Beni Peled had warned for weeks that the Arabs meant business, few in the IAF, from his senior staff down to the pilots in the squadrons, shared his alarm. In the first place, their air victory three weeks earlier, when twelve Syrian MiGs were shot down at the cost of just one Israeli Mirage, bolstered their disdain for Arab war-making ability. Second, Rafi Harlev, chief of IAF Intelligence, accepted Zeira's no-war assurances and formally or informally passed the message on down through the grapevine. Even as they prepared to hit Syria's missiles and airfields on Saturday morning, few of the pilots believed that the mission would take place at all, or that anything more than a day or two of routine fighting was in the offing, culminating in another decisive Israeli victory.

But this lack of preparedness was only a matter of attitude. Like the Greens, the IAF was surprised by the sudden attack, as 240 Egyptian fighter-bombers suddenly crossed into the Sinai to strike

Israeli airfields, missile batteries, and command posts, and as Syrian MiGs drove deep into Galilee. Unlike the Greens, however, the IAF did not have to worry about getting its planes to the flight line from miles away. Although enemy planes were already approaching when Peled scrambled his fighters—many of them were still carrying bombs that first had to be dumped at sea—the Arab attack was blocked in minutes and decimated by nightfall. In fact, the Mirage and Phantom flight crews were seemingly relieved to forget for a while about the missiles and concentrate on precisely the sort of helter-skelter dogfighting where they functioned at their spectacular best.

Nowhere did they perform more spectacularly than at Iftach Spector's new 171* Phantom squadron, formed a year earlier at the new desert air base of Hazerim. Already a legendary fighter-thinker with ten downed enemy MiGs to his credit—sixteen by the time he would retire from active service ten years later—Spector had his pick of young pilots who volunteered once they heard he was forming his own squadron, and the unique quality of his men and leadership became apparent from the moment war broke out and IAF control called frantically at two in the afternoon to say that "your base is about to be attacked, prepare for air defense."[9]

Spector was settling in his Phantom in preparation for takeoff when his deputy, Shlomo Egozi, made a quick judgment call and came on the air with striking calm, not even bothering with code names. "Spector, nobody is attacking us. Can you wait a couple of minutes to have the bombs taken off your plane?" When Spector told him to go ahead, Egozi scrambled four Phantoms to secure the base and warned them not to dump their bombs ("we were a new squadron, and still short on supplies and ordnance," Spector would say later). Then, after Spector and his four Phantoms were rearmed and took off to defend Bir Gafgafa in the Sinai, he let the first four come down to have their bombs unloaded, too.

But it was in the air that the squadron scored most spectacularly that day. As the IAF's southernmost fighter squadron, the 171 kept two Phantoms at the tiny Ophir airfield at Sharm el Sheikh, to watch out for MiGs from Ghardaka that periodically threatened the

---

*Not real squadron number.

small Israeli navy Red Sea flotilla, and the surface-air Hawk missile batteries guarding the strategic Red Sea straits. On that day, the Ophir shift fell to two of the squadron's youngest and least experienced pilots—Danni Brown had just completed IAF Flight School, while Josh Elon had flown Phantoms for only four months.* At two in the afternoon, they were strapped in their Phantoms when the IAF controller alerted them that "numerous fighter formations are heading toward you at low altitude," but ordered them to stay put until further notice.

Danni Brown felt uneasy. For one thing, he'd been in a war before. Having washed out of IAF Flight School in the early 1960s, he was a tank commander during the Six-Day War, before reentering IAF Flight School and this time finishing with honors. Disregarding orders, he slammed his throttle into afterburner and took off, with Josh Elon following. They were still climbing to the northeast when more than two dozen Egyptian MiG-17s and MiG-21s swept in from the south and began bombing the small airfield and the surface-air Hawk missile battery north of it. The two rookies split up, Elon taking the west end of the base and Brown staying east of it, and each swept down alone into the MiG pack.

There were MiGs everywhere. Spotting a MiG-17 diving to bomb Ophir's runway, Brown went after it, couldn't get a missile lock, came around again and this time blew it up with a single missile shot. As he pulled up, he saw two MiG-17s diving at the Hawk missile battery and went after them, but his plane suddenly acted sluggish and the MiGs pulled away easily. Still keeping the MiGs in sight, Brown quickly checked his plane to find out that one of his engines had flamed out during the shooting. He restarted it and went after the same two MiGs again, this time shooting one of them down, then turning and destroying a third MiG-17 that was going for a communications station near Ophir. Finally, after chasing a pair of MiG-21s, missing, and ending up flying awkwardly on his back, he saw a MiG-17 streaking in front of him and instinctively fired. The MiG went down—Brown's fourth in less than half an hour. By the time he straightened up and climbed to look over the battlefield, the sky had suddenly cleared and the two Phantoms

*Not their real names.

were alone over the base. With the three MiGs that Josh Elon shot down on his side of the field, it made seven kills—one-fourth of the entire attacking force.

The MiG attacks throughout the Sinai were only one part of the Egyptian air offensive. As darkness approached, dozens of low-flying Egyptian helicopters, each carrying a full commando platoon, swept into the Sinai, to land behind Israeli lines, set up antitank ambushes, blow up facilities, and disrupt all movement and communications. Shlomo Egozi, Spector's deputy at the 171 squadron, had reached the Canal just before dark on his first mission that day when the IAF controller directed him to the Gulf of Suez, where dozens of Egyptian helicopters were seen crossing into the Sinai. The slow and agile helicopters tried to blend into the darkening terrain and hide in the canyons leading away from the Gulf, but Egozi and Dubi Yoffe, his young wingman, downed seven of them before breaking off at nightfall. The seventh had almost escaped into a narrow canyon, but Egozi put his engines into full after-burner, went above the helicopter, and suddenly turned nose up. The downward blast from the Phantom's powerful tailpipes smashed the chopper into the canyon floor.

Spector had just landed in the dark after a fruitless mission over Bir Gafgafa when he was told that Brown and Elon had shot down seven MiGs at Ophir. "Nonsense, just a stupid rumor," he said in disbelief. A few minutes later, the IAF controller announced that Egozi and his wingman had shot down seven helicopters. "I told him to stick them together with [Brown's] MiGs. I didn't believe a word of it until I saw the film from the gun cameras later that night," Spector would say later.

At other times or other wars, the IAF's performance that day would have turned the course of battle. Some thirty-seven Egyptian and five Syrian planes were shot down, no targets inside Israel were seriously hit, the damaged runways at Bir Gafgafa and Ophir were quickly repaired, and along with six more Egyptian helicopters that were shot down by two Phantoms from Hazor, a full two-thirds of the 1,700-commando force which the Egyptians tried to put down in the Sinai was wiped out. Within hours of the beginning of hostilities, the IAF easily reestablished air superiority, and had Peled been ordered to flatten Cairo or Damascus, bomb the Aswan

Dam, or lob a single rocket through Sadat's bedroom window, he could have done so easily and without serious opposition.

This war, however, was different. In past wars, knocking Arab air forces out of the picture meant automatic victory. This time, it was almost irrelevant. With two exceptions, the entire airspace of the Arab world was open to Israeli air attacks, but those two exceptions made all the difference. The IAF could go anywhere except near the Golan Heights and the Suez fronts, where it was needed most. As they had begun to do three years earlier, the Soviet missiles successfully redefined the nature of modern war. By relying on massive missile power to keep the air over the battle zone free of Israeli fighters, and by gambling that Israel would be morally and politically unable to unleash its air power against civilian populations, Egypt and Syria might as well have left their air forces home.

Which was why, by the end of the first day, all the IAF's spectacular victories in the air had done nothing to halt the Egyptian and Syrian advance on the ground. Although a few Phantoms were sent out that night to toss bombs in the approximate direction of the Egyptian bridges on the Canal, by midnight more than seven Egyptian infantry brigades and 300 tanks had crossed the Canal. In the north, Syrian tanks had broken through Israeli defenses and were on their way down to the Jordan Valley. The IAF could do nothing about it.

The shining hope of the Israeli military machine had seemingly let it down. Moshe Dayan articulated the national disappointment when, in a subsequent autobiography,[10] he pointed out that unlike the Greens, who were caught by the Arab invasion literally with their pants down, "when the war broke out the IAF was the only force that was mobilized to its full strength. At noon on Yom Kippur, 75 percent of its manpower was already mobilized, and the active portion of the force even before that." The implication was that the IAF had no excuse for failing to peel off the enemy missile cover before the fighting got out of hand.

But Dayan's remarks were also blatantly self-serving—several months earlier, he himself assured Peled that in any future conflict with the Arabs, the IAF could take its time and go after the missiles first, a commitment that Dayan broke by allowing Israel to absorb the Arab first strike. Still, to a force raised on Weizman's unsparing

"Don't complain, don't explain" dictum, the fact remained that for the first time in nearly two decades, Israel was being attacked and the IAF could do nothing about it. Having assumed the mantle as the nation's premier guardian—not to mention the main consumer of its national defense resources—the IAF had failed its mission.

That was how the country would see it, and the Greens who were now taking the worst beating, and even the IAF flight crews themselves as they watched the carnage on the Canal from a distance without being able to break through the walls of missiles that protected the Arabs forces.

But the war had only just begun. As IAF Phantoms, Skyhawks, and Mirages played catch-as-catch-can with enemy tanks at the edge of the missile fields, IAF Operations planners worked feverishly into the night on a plan that would devastate the Arab missiles and change the course of the war just as the *Moked* strike did in the first three hours of the Six-Day War in 1967. Sometime past midnight, they issued a flurry of secret orders that gave each fighter and attack squadron its mission orders. By the time dawn broke, the first formations of Phantoms and shotgun-riding Mirages rolled out from Ramat David, Tel Nof, and Hazor and headed south. The end of the sudden and messy war seemed finally at hand.

Chapter 23

OPERATZIOT

No single image so haunted the IAF fighter community in the early 1970s as that of Shmuel Hetz being plucked out of the sky by an SA-3 missile on July 18, 1970. More than anything, it was that image that fueled the feverish quest for a missile cure, that consumed and dominated the force through and beyond the decade. The quest began on the day the War of Attrition ended, and quickly enveloped the entire force. At his magic shop, Joseph Na'or combed through foreign literature, particularly U.S. military surplus catalogs, and began to collect mounds of electronic discards that he assembled into home-made missile-zapping hardware. At IAF Intelligence, must-have lists were drawn up and rushed over to *Mossad* and AMAN, which mobilized their assets around the world. At IAF Operations, a new plan called *Srita* was developed in case the Egyptians attempted a Canal crossing under their missile umbrella before the IAF had figured out a way for properly taking care of the missiles (it called for Phantoms and Skyhawks to toss bombs at the bridges on the Canal from a distance, without venturing into missile range).

By now the SA-2s were no problem, and even handling the SA-3 missiles was relatively easy, since Na'or soon had enough junked

American hardware to build a jamming system that could confound the SA-3s the way that the American pods confounded the SA-2s in the summer of 1970. The problem was that the new SA-6 missiles were so new that their electronic behavior or even what they looked like was a mystery. What was known was that the SA-6s were far smaller than the SA-2s or SA-3s, that each SA-6 battery consisted of no more than three missiles mounted on a half-track, and that they could be moved around the battlefield quickly and easily as in a shell game. Also, the SA-6's two-phase engine made it virtually invisible in the air, since the initial rocket launch with its telltale smoky contrails lasted only six seconds, after which a clean-burning ramjet engine kicked in. Not until the summer of 1972, in a hazardous mission led by Aviem Sela, did two Phantoms from Ramat David manage to bring back detailed photographs of five Syrian SA-6 batteries located between the Golan Heights and Damascus.

As new information was assembled, it was funneled to IAF Operations and from there to the squadrons, where it was worked up into new attack and evasion tactics. But there the quest for protection against missiles split and proceeded along two different, even contradictory trajectories. The split grew out of Shmuel Hetz's fateful pod-formation strike in the summer of 1970, and from the "physics" versus "electronics" arguments that Iftach Spector and Hetz began in the days just before Hetz was killed.

Iftach Spector, particularly since taking over the 171 Phantom squadron at Hazerim, once again pushed "physics." Using a dummy-missile field that Ariel Sharon, then head of IDF Southern Command, built for the IAF in the Sinai, Spector and his pilots, stopwatches running, worked incessantly on getting to the missiles so fast and low that their fire-control radars wouldn't even detect the approaching Phantoms. Speed, stealth, minimum radar exposure, and pilots' improvisation were everything. Instead of flying straight and level into harm's way with the pods broadcasting, Spector's pilots slithered in at ground level, using only sticks and throttles under total electronic silence. When they reached their targets, they quickly climbed up, struck, and bounced back to the ground to get away. Different combinations of speed, direction, and bombing altitude and angles were tried, to shave off a second here, two seconds there.

To make up for insufficient intelligence or lack of electronic guidance, Spector developed a missile-hunting technique which he called "hunt." His pilots went out in teams, each consisting of "decoy" Phantoms that flew high to tease the batteries and spot missile launches, and "hunter" Phantoms that came from below at their targets. Although the Phantoms now carried more sophisticated American jamming pods that could disrupt both SA-2 and SA-3 missiles, Spector had his pilots switch them off, so their telltale beams would not announce the Phantoms' approach. Only at the last moment, when enemy missiles were already in the air, could the pods be switched on for protection.

In the spring of 1973, Spector codified his "hunt" doctrine by gathering leading pilots from all IAF fighter and attack squadrons for an intense antimissile warfare workshop at his squadron. At the end, each participant was to impart his newly acquired skills to the rest of his squadron members. The course, however, ended in July, just three months before Yom Kippur. By the time war broke out, only Spector's own squadron had mastered the new tactics.

In marked contrast, from his new post as head of IAF Strike Planning at IAF Operations, Avihu Ben-Nun relied on huge and intricate attack formations, backed by massive electronic support systems, to overwhelm rather than finesse missile defenses—a frontal tank attack to Spector's commando strike. Like many young officers of his generation, Ben-Nun was awed by the *Moked* airfield-attack plan that brought the dramatic victory in 1967. Indeed, the plan he unveiled at the end of 1972 for eliminating the Egyptian missiles, code-named *Tagar*, was bigger and more complex than anything the IAF had ever attempted. Using hundreds of planes in several attack waves, weaving in and out with the split-second timing of a Swiss watch, *Tagar* intended to systematically peel off Egypt's missile defenses layer by layer until there was nothing left.

On paper—which was the only way the plan could be presented, analyzed, and debated—*Tagar* was awesome. It began with an aerial strike against the antiaircraft gun batteries that guarded the missiles against low-flying planes. The entire Canal front was lined with "exit towers," tall markers carrying huge numbers. Low-flying Phantoms charged toward their assigned markers at designated speeds and directions, then pulled up at precisely dictated angles and power. At predetermined altitudes, each plane released its bombs and looped back toward home, while the bombs continued to fly across the sky as if hurled by giant slingshots, to devastate their targets deep inside Egypt.

Next, dozens of refueled and rearmed Phantoms, backed by Skyhawks and Super-Mystères carrying elaborate electronic jamming and deception systems, zeroed in on the missiles' radar control units, their "eyes and ears." Not all Phantoms carried the same ordnance. Some came in high and carried small Shrike antiradiation missiles, which would home in on any enemy radar that came to life. Others came in low with giant regular or cluster bombs. This combination checkmated the Egyptians by forcing them to either "shut off the radar, which would let us attack with regular bombs, or switch the radar on and get hit by the Shrikes," says Eitan Peled, veteran of numerous antimissile attacks in 1970, and one of *Tagar*'s planners.[1]

Finally, with the radars destroyed, waves of Skyhawks safely swept in to destroy the missiles themselves. The entire operation could take anywhere from a few hours to a couple of days. In early 1973, a second antimissile plan, code-named *Dougman V*, was developed to counter the growing missile buildup on the Syrian front.

To Spector, the plans were an offense. Deriding Ben-Nun's "Swiss watch" schemes as *"operatziot,"* Spector argued that they were too massive, complex, and rigid, like doing battle by bureaucracy. So little leeway was built into the plans, he argued, that if one plane was late or off course, it threw everything and everybody off. Every cog and spring of the "Swiss watch" was so closely meshed to the others that unless everything worked perfectly, everything had to fail. It gave the IAF no better than a heads-or-tails odds of success.

"As interceptor pilots, we were used to having a wingman leave a flight leader to get something done. We called it '*Modia ve'-holech*' (Notify and leave)," Spector would say later. "But in those *operatziot* you could not simply notify and leave, because you would be tampering with a huge formation. . . . I felt the *operatziot* in a sense closed us up, turned us into Arab pilots or Russian pilots [while] I wanted us to be Jewish pilots."[2]

Spector was not the only one to criticize Ben-Nun's approach. So did Beni Peled, although for different reasons. Peled had nothing against electronics or organizational complexity, but to his engineer's mind, trained on worst-case scenarios, Ben-Nun's plans seemed based on an assumption that everything would work out perfectly—perfect weather, perfect intelligence, perfect surprise. Peled also objected to IAF Operations' underlying assumption that the missiles could be attacked only by planes, as opposed to say, tank or commando strikes, and that only Phantoms could do the job. "When I took command, everybody knew my intentions to demolish all those [*Moked*-like] plans," Peled says.

On May 13, 1973, three days after he took command, Peled put his reservations on record when Dayan and Elazar dropped in at his bunker to find out how the IAF planned to handle the Arab missiles if war broke out. Peled sat quietly as IAF Operations officers put on an impressive presentation of *Tagar* and *Dougman V*, but he grew uneasy as the guests seemed relieved that the IAF once again assumed responsibility for the outcome of the next war.

"There are vast differences between carrying out these plans when we are the initiators, and between carrying them out in response to enemy attack," Peled warned them. That was particularly true in the case of *Dougman V*, the plan to take out the Syrian missiles on the Golan Heights. Whipped out in a rush along the general outlines of *Tagar*, *Dougman V* differed in one critical aspect—the prevalence of mobile SA-6 missiles on the Syrian front precluded the kind of elaborate foreplay that assured the success of *Tagar* in the south. There could be no last-minute reconnaissance flights to determine precisely where the missile batteries were, or artillery-suppressing slingshot attacks to pave the way for the bombers. Since any Israeli movement would spook the Syrians into shuffling their missiles, *Dougman V* had to come straight "out of the blue." In fact, the mission planners used those very words, in English, to describe their concept and tactics. Put another way, *Dougman V* was at best a gamble on the missiles being where they were the last time anybody looked, whenever that was.

To have any chance of success, Peled told Dayan and Elazar, the IAF had to have everything just right. It needed at least forty-eight hours of advance warning so it could attack under as perfect as possible flying conditions. And it had to attack first to maintain surprise. Finally, since either *Tagar* or *Dougman V* would require every flyable vehicle the IAF had, the Greens had to have it understood that, until the missiles were wiped out, they could have no air support—whether it took two hours or two days.

"Beni, my friend," Peled would recall Dayan telling him at the end of the meeting, "do you really think that if we knew we were going to be attacked we'd let the IAF sit quietly? Of course we would be the initiators." Thus five months before war actually broke out, the blueprint for victory seemed clear and reassuring. If the missiles were the new wrinkle on the old military balance, *Tagar* and *Dougman V* effectively ironed them out.

But Zeira's intelligence failure, and the Israeli government's decision to let the Arabs strike first, destroyed that blueprint. The advance notice shrank from forty-eight to eight hours on the morning of Yom Kippur, and then to nothing as weather and government objections precluded an IAF first strike altogether. And instead of having a few hours or days to itself to handle the missiles during the first hours of the Arab offensive, the IAF first had to defend the national airspace against Arab fighters, bombers, and commando-bearing helicopters. Only at the end of the first day did Peled get around to doing anything about the missiles, sending a few Phantoms in the dark to toss bombs slingshot style in the direction of the Egyptian missiles and Canal-crossing positions. The Phantoms were not expected to accomplish much, and they didn't. Something far more drastic had to be done.

The trouble was, with the exception of *Tagar* and *Dougman V*, the IAF had no way of dealing with the missiles, and both plans were predicated on conditions that may have no longer existed. Still, the two plans were all there was. Thus on the first evening of the war, when reports from the north suggested that the Syrian advance into the Golan Heights had been checked on the ground, Peled accepted IAF Operations' assessment that the Egyptians had not yet had the time to move their heavily fortified missile batteries, and their recommendation to launch *Tagar* the following morning.

Actually, as the first day of the war drew to a close, few in or out of the Israeli military felt particularly alarmed by the sudden war. Practically all Israelis, from civilians in bomb shelters to uniformed personnel everywhere, although kept in the dark by total radio silence, matter-of-factly anticipated an Israeli counteroffensive the following day. Few doubted that, once faced with the Greens on the ground and the Blues in the air, the Arab offensive would collapse. The IAF in particular, after a spectacular first-day harvest of Arab MiGs, bombers, helicopters, and a couple of guided missiles (which Israeli Mirage pilots chased and shot down before they reached Tel Aviv), had no reason to be worried. Angry, perhaps, for not being allowed to attack first, but not worried.

Indeed, as *Tagar* began the next morning and the first wave of Phantoms charged toward their markers at the western edge of the Sinai, the end of the war seemed in sight. At seven o'clock, on time, the Phantoms reached their markers, slammed into afterburn to pull up, then slung their bombs at the antiaircraft gun batteries that guarded the missiles. At the same time, other Phantoms and Mirages attacked Egyptian airfields around the Canal and in the Nile Delta, shattering their runways and preventing their MiGs from interfering with the counteroffensive. Although the Egyptians had plenty of time to prepare—and should have anticipated such a counterattack—the Israelis ran into little opposition. The Phantom crews were elated as they thundered back to their bases to rearm, refuel, and get back down to the Canal to knock out the missile batteries.

It was not to be. Even as the Phantoms were still charging toward their targets, the operation had been canceled. At six that morning, a shaken Moshe Dayan telephoned Beni Peled from IDF Northern Command with an apocalyptic message—"the Third Temple is in danger." Contrary to the previous night's impressions, the Syrian attack had not been blocked. Instead, a full Syrian armored division broke through Israeli defenses during the night, rolled over the lone Israeli tank brigade that stood in its way, and was now inside the southern sector of the Golan Heights, halfway down to the Jordan River. Unless Peled immediately moved his entire force to the north to block the Syrian advance, Dayan warned, Syrian tanks would soon cross into Israel.

Dayan's "Third Temple" warning was not a coded message. It was a cry of anguish echoing innermost Jewish fears. The first Jewish Temple, built by King Solomon in 940 B.C., was destroyed

354 years later by the Babylonians, in 586 B.C. The Second Temple, built in 538 B.C. on the ruins of the first, was destroyed by the Romans 600 years later. Following each destruction, the country was sacked and its entire Jewish population forced into exile, the first lasting fifty years, the second for nearly nineteen hundred.

Now, after barely twenty-five years of restored Jewish statehood, Dayan was raising the specter of another biblical-scale devastation. Peled's protestation that Operation *Tagar* was in progress in the south, and that once the Egyptian missiles were taken out the IAF would be in a much better position to help the ground forces in the north, paled before Dayan's doomsday warning. "The Sinai is sand. Here are homes," Dayan dismissed his objections tersely. There was no middle ground, no room for disagreement. In any other country, such talk of national annihilation would be dismissed as an exaggerated figure of speech. In Israel, thirty years after the Nazi Holocaust, it was a real possibility with ample historic precedent. Dayan's telephone call, bypassing military channels that required him to work through IDF chief of staff Elazar, placed the responsibility for the lives of the outnumbered tank crews on the Golan Heights—if not the survival of the first Jewish state in two millennia—squarely on Peled's shoulders.

"I did not even bring up [the May 13, 1973, meeting with Dayan and Elazar]," Peled would later say. "This is not a perfect world. Things change." His awesome burden was visible as, at six-thirty, he walked into the IAF bunker and "in a manner that did not invite any discussion, ordered *Tagar* stopped and the entire IAF activity moved to the north," recalls Amos Amir, a former Phantom squadron commander who was at the bunker learning the ropes in preparation for taking over IAF Operations.[3]

If Golda Meir's decision to stand by and let the Arabs attack first was the second most momentous decision in Israel's history, after Ben-Gurion's decision to declare statehood on the eve of the 1948 Arab invasion, Peled's order to call off *Tagar* came close behind. His staff was stunned. Giora Furman, chief of IAF Operations, exploded with rage. Not only would the cancellation of *Tagar* hand the Sinai to the Egyptians, but the Golan Heights was too tiny an area to waste the entire IAF on in the first place. By sending a few more Skyhawks to deal with the Syrian tanks, the IAF could still keep *Tagar* going as planned and win the war. Furman's misgivings were shared by virtually everyone on Peled's senior staff.

But none of the young colonels had heard Dayan's anguished warnings. They had no idea whether things on the Golan Heights were or were not as bad as Dayan said they were—or worse. None had the responsibility for the survival of the "Third Temple" thrust upon them. All they really knew was that the opportunity to carry out the plan in which they had invested their time and effort for the past three years was being snatched away, probably because Peled did not put up a sufficient fight on the plan's behalf.

But it was Peled's judgment call. "I'm sure Peled thought that if the ground forces [on the Golan Heights] could hold on a little bit longer it would have been different, but I also think that he was persuaded at that moment that there was no little bit left . . . that the IDF did not have two more hours to hold on, and he decided to go there," says Yoram Agmon, then commander of the Ramat David Phantom squadron.[4]

Brusquely cutting off any debate, Peled ordered all available Skyhawks to the Syrian front, to stop the Syrian tanks from reaching the Jordan River. He then gave IAF Operations five hours to launch *Dougman V* at the Syrian missiles. "What happened was that . . . we had a so-called labor agreement about how the IAF would function during a war and under what conditions. [But] we had the agreement with the IDF and with the government of Israel, when in reality we should have had it with the enemy," Peled would sarcastically reflect later on the turmoil in the bunker. "Since the enemy was not party to the agreement, it took several senior IAF staff members some time to grasp it, that's all."

The day before, when Moti Hod reported for duty at the IAF bunker, Peled sent him to the Syrian front, to serve as air advisor to the chief of IDF Northern Command. Hod was there when Dayan read his "Third Temple" warning to Peled over the telephone. "Tell him to send in Skyhawks in fours, one after the other, so the Syrians could not lift their heads," Hod urged Dayan to tell Peled.[5] Now Peled placed a squadron of Skyhawks from Ramat David directly under Hod's command. The Syrian tanks had already started down the basalt-strewn Gamala Grade, sloping down to the Sea of Galilee from the ancient fortress-mound of Gamala, site of a desperate Jewish last stand against the Romans two millennia earlier. For the rest of the day, with Hod directing them from his observation bunker, the Skyhawks held off the Syrian attack until Israeli tank reinforcements arrived that afternoon and began to push the Syrians back. Although some Syrian tanks came within four miles of the Jordan River that day, it was as far as they would get during the entire war. Not one enemy tank would cross the Jordan River into Israel.

At eleven-thirty, without surprise or current intelligence, the *Dougman V* strike against the Syrian missiles began under the worst possible conditions. The Syrians were on the move, and it was a virtual certainty that so were the missiles. But there was no way of finding out where they were, and just flying and looking over the front, now bristling with antiaircraft guns on hair-trigger alert, would be suicidal. Worse yet, the quick shift from south to north meant that helicopters, transports, and Skyhawks carrying crucial electronic jamming and deception gear could not be brought back up in time to cover the operation. Phantom crews returning from Egypt had no time to be properly briefed. Iftach Spector had just landed after an early morning raid on the Beni Suef airfield, seventy miles up the Nile from Cairo, when he found out that *Dougman V* was about to begin. Promptly assigning himself to lead his squadron's portion of the operation, he was walking back to his plane when he suddenly stopped and turned toward his deputy. "Remind me what *Dougman V* is all about, won't you?" he asked.

Taking off from Hazerim, Hazor, Tel Nof, and Ramat David, some fifty Phantoms headed out to sea, turned back, spread out in attack formations, and charged into the wall of frenzied antiaircraft fire that hovered like fireworks over the advancing Syrian forces. The Phantoms covered the front in geographical order, the Ramat David Phantoms at the north sector, Tel Nof's and Hazor's at the center, and Spector's squadron from Hazerim in the south.

Eitan Peled's formation, six Phantoms from Hazor, got the worst of it. Plowing single file into what—until the day before—was the seam between two Syrian troop concentrations, they found themselves instead flying smack over the Syrian advance force, which virtually exploded with barrages of gunfire and SA-7 "Strella" shoulder missiles. Zigzagging madly, Peled, who flew first, got through this wall of fire intact, but two of the four Phantoms behind him were shot down, and two more from the second foursome of his squadron at his right. The survivors of that murderous gauntlet arrived at their target area, six miles behind the Syrian line, only to find the missiles gone. As they pulled up and rolled down toward where the batteries were supposed to be, all they could see was empty dugouts everywhere, but no missiles except for those being fired at them. There was nothing to do but return to base, with nothing to show for the four Phantoms they lost going in.

The other squadrons did only a little better. In the north, leading a formation of Ramat David Phantoms, Ehud Henkin also began his dive only to realize that his target was not there. But then he spotted the missile battery a short distance away. Henkin was in a bind. Under the strict "Swiss watch" rules of *Dougman V*, he was not allowed the slightest deviation from the attack plan, and a second pass over a target was specifically prohibited. But the missiles were there. Instead of pulling back up and clearing out, Henkin changed direction halfway through his dive. Pulling the giant Phantom into a tight high-G turn, he managed to come over the target and release his bombs. But that was all he could do. Already going too fast and low to either pull back up or bail out, his Phantom slammed into the rocky terrain and exploded at virtually the same time that his bombs struck the missile battery. Henkin and his navigator were killed instantly.

Ironically, a second, younger Ramat David Phantom pilot named Yehuda Palit* was also in mid-dive when he spotted a missile battery at a different location. As there was only slight antiaircraft fire from below, he ignored his standing orders, came around again and destroyed the battery before heading back for home.

Farther to the south, sixteen Phantoms from Tel Nof also failed to find any targets, and lost one Phantom to ground fire before turning back. Only Spector's squadron came out unscathed. Although he was already in his plane when he looked at his mission orders and maps, Spector immediately demanded and received permission to change his attack route. "From personal experience I knew that in its rear the enemy was never on alert, and therefore

*Not his real name.

never presented a threat. During all those years along the Suez Canal, the danger was between the water line and perhaps ten or twenty kilometers on the other side. Behind that, in Egypt's exposed belly, you could fly quietly. I used to cross that belt very fast, then cut down speed, save fuel, and I was never hit and never lost a plane," Spector would say later. Now, instead of charging head-on at the southernmost flank of the rolling Syrian forces, he went around it, taking his formation due east into Jordan, then circling north to arrive at his target from the rear, unexpected and undetected. His formation found no missiles either where they were supposed to be, but they avoided the Syrian antiaircraft fire entirely, and did not lose a single plane.

Dougman V's failure was total. Six Phantoms were lost and their crews killed or captured, but only two out of more than thirty missile batteries were destroyed or damaged. What made it worse was the feeling, both at IAF Operations and in some of the squadrons, that had they stuck to Operation *Tagar,* the Egyptian missile system would have been destroyed by sundown, and Egypt would be out of the war. Certainly there was no disputing the fact that halfway through the second day of the war, the IAF had already lost thirty-five planes without so much as nicking the massive missile packs across the Canal and on the Golan Heights.

Peled's colonels did not give up. In the hope that *Dougman V* had disoriented the Syrians even if it did not destroy their missiles, Avihu Ben-Nun now put forward a plan to throw every available Phantom, Mirage, and Skyhawk back into the same area to seek out and destroy the remaining batteries before they could be repositioned. In retrospect, he was probably right. According to Yoram Agmon, commander of the Ramat David Phantom squadron at the time, none of the Israeli Phantoms at the *Dougman V* operation was shot down by SA-6 missiles, apparently because the SA-6 batteries were on the move. It might indeed have been possible to go back and take them out before they became operational.

But from the start of the war Dayan had objected to the IAF's even trying to hit the missiles once it lost the initial edge. For two days now, he'd been pushing for sending the IAF against the invading Arabs regardless of casualties. "In my opinion, the Air Force must give up on attacking missile batteries now and do everything possible to prevent the passage of Egyptian tanks into the Sinai, even if it means losing planes. If the Air Force keeps concentrating on the missile batteries and fails, we lose both ways," he would later describe his thinking.[6] Now the IDF command came around and Ben-Nun's plan was rejected. "Drop it," Peled told his staff. "From now on we go around the missiles when we can, through them when we must."

At two that afternoon, with *Dougman V* barely over, Peled joined an IDF high command assessment meeting on the worsening situation. The change of mood from the night before could not have been more extreme. Twenty-four hours into the fighting, even as reserve tank and infantry units began arriving at the front, the Israeli lines were in shambles. In the north, Syrian commandos captured critical Israeli positions on Mount Hermon, Israel's vital communications and observation stronghold, and Syrian tanks were all over the Golan Heights. In the south, the first Egyptian attack wave demolished Israel's line of fortifications along the Canal. Nineteen out of the twenty forts were either wiped out, abandoned, or had surrendered. However valiantly and well their defenders fought, the sheer magnitude of the Egyptian offense made their resistance futile. IAF Skyhawks and the few IDF tanks in the area managed to destroy sizable numbers of Egyptian tanks, but so many more kept pouring into the Sinai that it made little difference.

By the end of the day, entire Egyptian tank, infantry, and commando divisions had completed the crossing on schedule and seized the entire east bank of the Canal. Nearly a hundred Israeli tanks, one-third of the entire tank force in the Sinai, were destroyed, many of them just as they reached the front, before they had a chance to take cover or figure out what was happening.

All along, confident that it was only a matter of time before they could rally and "throw" the Egyptians back over the waterway, the IDF command had asked the IAF to refrain from destroying the Egyptian bridges. The Greens were actually hoping to use the enemy's own bridges for their counteroffensive. But traffic across the bridges was still moving in only one direction, and "throwing" the Egyptians back seemed less and less likely. Conjuring up frightening images of hundreds of millions of Arabs, backed by the full might of the Soviet Union, closing in on Israel with her limited human resources and rapidly dwindling tank and fighter-bomber reserves, Dayan now pressed for abandoning the Canal front altogether, and pulling back to a second defense line at the Mitla and Gidi passes in Central Sinai.

"Is it an advise or a command, Sir, because if it is an advise I am rejecting it," Gen. Samuel Gonen, commander of the Suez front, responded in shock. But bravado alone could not change the fact that, with the Egyptian missiles still in place, Dayan seemed to be right in insisting that the Egyptian bridges—or for that matter the entire front—were beyond the reach of the IAF and therefore indefensible. Dayan was about to leave for a cabinet meeting, where he was expected to have little trouble pushing through a pullback order, when Beni Peled said "Excuse me for a moment," and walked out of the room.

Rushing back to his own IAF bunker, he ordered an immediate all-out attack on the bridges. Within minutes, running under, around, but mostly through the missile umbrella, IAF Skyhawks and Phantoms began to seek out and bomb the bridges. Dayan was still at the IDF bunker when Peled called to report that two of the bridges had been taken out, and at four-thirty he reached Elazar at Golda Meir's office and reported that seven—one-half—of the Egyptian bridges had been bombed and that the operation was still continuing. "Come over and I'll give you a kiss," Elazar replied, then turned to give Meir and her cabinet their first good news of the day. The pullback proposal was put off for the time being. Dayan acidly pointed out that "this is not the [Tel Aviv] Yarkon Bridge you are talking about, but strings of rafts and pontoons which the Egyptians can easily repair at night,"[7] but the sense of impending doom had been relieved.

Out on the Canal, however, dozens of Phantom and Skyhawk pilots weaving their way through missile barrages made their own discovery. The problem was not demolishing the bridges, or even dodging the missiles. The problem was that nobody seemed to know where anything was. For the second time that day, Iftach Spector had to change his mission orders to protect his pilots. Instead of sending them straight to where IAF Operations suspected that the bridges were and risk getting shot down only to find out there was nothing there to bomb, he devised a way of taking a peek first.

Instead of going in in attack formations, he spread each formation out along a section of the Canal, and had them come in low, pull up quickly and loop right back—while looking to their right at the Canal just below them. If they saw nothing, they would regroup, move several miles up the Canal, and repeat the routine. If they spotted a bridge, they'd note its precise location, pull back, then return in attack formation to take it out.

For the second time that day, Spector brought his squadron back without a single loss. His own formation looped around twice, under heavy antiaircraft gun and missile fire, before they found their bridge and destroyed it. But instead of bringing relief, the successful attack only deepened the sense of bewilderment that enveloped the squadrons at the end of the war's second day. The day before, setbacks could be blamed on the government's decision to let the Arabs strike first. But now, for the second time that day, IAF Operations sent the Phantoms into harm's way unprepared and without basic battlefield intelligence. In fact, squadrons who followed mission orders to the letter suffered the heaviest casualties. Some, like Spector, kept their crews safe only by changing every mission order they received.

But the missions were not about staying alive. They were about stopping the enemy and relieving the pressure on the battered ground troops on the Canal front, and there the IAF was still accomplishing nothing. On the morning of October 8, the third day of the war, the two Israeli armored divisions on the Canal front counterattacked, aiming to roll back the Egyptian advance, and perhaps even to cross the Canal and shift the fighting to the Egyptian rear. But short of nibbling at the Egyptian tanks at the edges of the missile fields, the IAF could provide no significant close-air support, and the tank offensive was decimated by the Egyptian armor and by masses of shoulder-launched antitank missiles that Egyptian troops fired with abandon.

Never in its history was the IAF bigger and stronger—and never more helpless in carrying out its share of the war's burden. "The IAF gets the biggest share of the military budget precisely to stop such attacks, and in 1973 it didn't do it," an Israeli professor who went through the war as a frontline medic would later say, speaking for many Greens who survived the war. Neither the pilots in the cockpits nor the colonels at IAF Operations had to be told all this. They did not have to tune in on the Greens' radio frequency to learn of their desperate need of support. All they had to do was roll down their windows, so audible was the cry from the Canal sands in the south to the basalt ridges of the Golan in the north—"Where is the Air Force?"

Chapter 24

LEGACIES

Where *was* the Air Force?

The question was devastating precisely because everybody knew the Air Force was right there and trying its best; because what the question really meant was "what *happened* to the Air Force?" It meant that the IAF was worse than absent—it was ineffectual. It almost did not matter how many MiGs were shot down, or how quickly and brilliantly air superiority was established over most of the region. It was also no use blaming the government for keeping the IAF from launching a preemptive strike against the Syrians—or preventing it now from carrying the war to Egypt's rear with devastating interdiction and strategic bombings.*

*Since bad weather precluded an attack on the Syrian missiles just before the war began, it is still not clear that a preemptive attack on Syrian airfields would have materially altered the initial success of the Egyptian and Syrian offensive. But there is no question that, since Shazly's missile-umbrella strategy left his entire country—indeed the entire Middle East—undefended, IAF Phantoms could have gone anywhere in Egypt's soft belly, from Cairo to the Aswan Dam, and made her war costlier if not downright impossible to sustain. Starting on October 9, the IAF did just that on the Syrian front. Responding to Syria's launching of surface-surface missiles at Ramat David and nearby towns, IAF Phantoms bombed the headquarters of the Syrian army and air force in Damascus, fuel depots and power stations in the city of Homs to the north, and Syrian armor concentrations at the Syrian rear. Strategic bombings of

What mattered was that, for the first time in its existence, the IAF wasn't there where the threat to the nation's survival was at its worst—on the field of battle. And to those in the know, mostly inside the IAF, it also mattered that the IAF wasn't there not just because of some Soviet missiles, but mostly because of three long-festering historic failures of its own, failures that the missiles had not created but only aggravated and exposed. Failures that—like computer viruses programmed to lie dormant for months or years and then come alive on a given date—kicked in as if on cue at the worst possible time, and paralyzed the entire system.

The failures were not new, mysterious, or unexpected. Everybody knew they were there. But almost everybody thought they wouldn't matter, that everything would be all right.

The first failure concerned the crucial matter of battlefield intelligence. Two weeks into the war, a stack of black-and-white aerial photographs arrived at Beni Peled's desk, date-stamped October 6 and 7, the first and second days of the war, and showing the Egyptian bridges over the Suez Canal. As photographed from 30,000 feet, each bridge appeared as the thin waist of an old-fashioned hourglass, with two dark blobs ballooning on each side. Upon closer inspection, the blobs turned out to be masses of Egyptian tanks and infantry, one mass funneling into each bridge from the west, and the other spilling back out on the Sinai side, like a genie out of a bottle.

The photos were startling in clarity and detail. With them, missiles or no missiles, IAF Phantoms could have devastated the Egyptian invasion across the Canal in a matter of hours by first knocking out the flimsy bridges, then strafing and demolishing the trapped Egyptian forces with cluster bombs. Yet although Peled's own pilots had snapped the shots, his own technicians developed the films and his own interpreters examined the prints, neither Peled nor anyone at IAF Operations ever saw the photos until days later, when it was too late to do anything with them.

More incredible yet, this was no error or oversight. When Iftach

airfields, fuel depots and other noncivilian targets kept up until the war ended two weeks later. They not only devastated Syria's fuel and power infrastructure, but slowed her momentum on the Golan Heights enough to let the Israelis rally and push the Syrian forces back toward Damascus.

Spector pulled up to attack a Syrian airfield only to discover that instead of two parallel runways, as the aerial photo in his mission file showed, the airfield had three pairs of runways forming a triangle, that was an oversight. IAF Intelligence knew about the new runways, but someone had neglected to update the files. Such things happen. But the bridge photos were something else again. There, Peled did not get the pictures because in the Byzantine system of Israeli military intelligence, they were considered none of his business.

History could not have picked a worse time to catch up, but that was precisely what happened. Just as Israel began the fifth and potentially the most disastrous war of its existence, that was the moment in which the ragged chickens of—all things—the old Remez-Yadin debates of 1949 chose to come home to roost. In those debates, Remez—and every IAF commander after him—demanded the authority and resources to generate the required intelligence for the IAF's own operations. Yadin—and every chief of IDF Staff that followed—considered the IAF a support arm like the artillery, and insisted that the Greens would tell it where and when to strike, and provide it with all that it needed to do the job. The Greens won, and AMAN's monopoly over the collection and processing of all military intelligence—including the power to decide who needed to see what and when—was almost total. There was one exception. Since the IAF took the aerial photos that AMAN used, and since some target classes, like enemy airfields or surface-air missile batteries, primarily concerned the IAF, an arrangement was worked out by which the IAF took and developed the photos, IAF photo interpreters quickly went through them and pulled out anything dealing strictly with IAF business, and everything else was then rushed to AMAN's massive intelligence workshops for processing and distribution at the Greens' discretion.

It was by the dictates of the system, then, that when IAF interpreters ran across the photos of the Egyptian bridges they went right on past them. Since Egyptian troops and tanks did not fall under the heading of IAF business, the pictures of the crossing points were sent on to AMAN, and from there to the ground forces at the front, where they got lost in the shuffle until days later.

The bridge pictures not only epitomized the intelligence failure, but concerned the second failure, as well, which had to do with the procedures for delivering air support to ground forces. For had IDF Southern Command received the photos and decided to ask for air strikes on the bridges, that request would most likely have been lost in another, even more labyrinthine section of the Blues-Greens working arrangement. According to that arrangement, an infantry or tank field commander in need of air support had to pass his request—accompanied by the necessary intelligence on enemy strength, location, and so on—to IDF Artillery, where it ran up the chain of command until it became an item on the agenda of the IDF General Staff, where its relative priority was assessed against dozens or hundreds of similar requests from other field units. If it made it through there, it was finally routed to IAF Operations, where it would again be weighed against other claims for planes and air crews, and where the necessary mission orders would finally be drafted and transmitted to the squadrons—which carried them out the following morning.

The process was not only slow—downright useless in the case of liquid and fast-changing battles—but inherently flawed. "I knew as far back as 1966 that . . . what the ground forces know about their own situation was barely enough to run their own battles. What they could glean out of it to give me was not worth the paper it was written on," says Peled. "Yet the entire system worked on the premise that the ground forces knew what was going on. But to change it was tantamount to reforming a church which believed in the virgin birth. I couldn't just gather everybody and say 'From this day on we think different. Mary was *not* a virgin.' I couldn't do it while also running an air force and fighting a war. So we suffered, and did the best we could."[1]

Finally there was the IAF's own historic disdain—the lasting legacy of Air Force North—to the whole matter of ground support. While IAF centralized doctrine required all air operations, including close air support, to be directed and controlled from the "Hole" underneath Tel Aviv, there was no machinery in place for carrying out extensive and systematic ground-support operations.

In the fall of 1973, IAF Strike Planning Branch at IAF Operations had half a dozen sections but only two section heads, with practically no staff. On the day the war broke out, both section heads had been on the job only a few weeks, and physically at their posts less than a day. Eitan Ben Eliahu, a Phantom pilot who arrived in September to head the strategic bombing and antimissile desks, was on vacation until October 5. Gad Eldar, a Mirage pilot who arrived in August to run the photo-reconnaissance, ground support, and special operations sections, was back with his old squadron at Bir Gafgafa on air intercept alert on Yom Kippur morning.

When Eldar was finally rushed back to Tel Aviv from Bir Gafgafa and had to start scrambling reconnaissance and then air-ground support missions, he did not even have a properly equipped underground office with established staff and work routines. At the last moment, he was shuttled to a small room with a desk at the IDF Artillery's small warren of rooms underneath the IAF's bunker, where he "did not have enough room for my mission-planning team, so we actually had to do some of the planning in our regular offices upstairs," he recalls.[2] Work routines were so primitive that "each mission order had to be handwritten in quadruplicate, with the carbon papers inserted by hand. Through the first part of the war my hands were always black with carbon. The orders were then rushed upstairs for approval and then to the teleprinters for dispatch to the squadrons. When the teleprinters turned out to be too slow, we started reading the orders to the squadrons over the telephone." The improvised setup was so primitive that Eldar did not even know that Yeheskiel Somekh, a retired IAF general who reported for duty at the start of the war, was also running a similar air-ground mission center from his own little room somewhere nearby.

How could the IAF exist for twenty-five years and fight at least four wars without the basic machinery for receiving field intelligence, communicating with the Greens, or dispatching ground-support missions? That, too, was the legacy of the "Have jet, will travel" Air Force North, for the fact is that until the fall of 1973, none of those problems mattered. With total and unbroken Israeli control of the region's skies, IAF pilots could go anywhere to find their own targets or to locate ground units in trouble, and in the process they could report and comment on the goings-on below with the authority and comprehensiveness of radio sports announcers. In every past war, IAF squadrons had used their own pilots' observations to assemble "living maps" of the front that were far more detailed and accurate than anything AMAN could provide, while IDF senior commanders routinely trooped to the IAF bunker underneath Tel Aviv to find out what things were like at the front.

Whatever formal working arrangements the Blues and the Greens had on paper, in time of war the IAF was not only Israel's flying sword and shield but also its eyes and ears, its main source of battlefield intelligence.

It was here that Shazly's missile umbrella had its most devastating effect. By themselves, the missiles would have made the IAF's work more difficult but not impossible. With proper target data— like the aerial photos of the bridges—IAF Phantoms or Skyhawks could still slip in low and undetected, pull up quickly at the right places, bomb their targets, and dive back to the safety of the ground for the flight back home. Throughout the war the IAF logged hundreds of successful strikes against missile-defended airfields and radar installations with minimal casualties. Missiles or no missiles, once the location of a target and its defenses was established, it was as good as destroyed.

But with the missiles keeping its planes from going sight-seeing over the battlefields, the IAF for the first time in its existence had to depend on its formal intelligence and air-ground arrangement with the Greens. It wasn't that the system suddenly failed—it had failed in every past war, only this time it mattered. Shazly's missiles, which were only meant to protect his invasion force by taking the edge off Israel's formidable war machine, ended up blinding it altogether.

It was this blindness that threw the IAF into a tailspin, from IAF Operations at the top, where some colonels were so affected by the collapse of their "Swiss watch" doctrines that they had to be relieved of their duties or go back to their squadrons to fly for a while and get their bearings back, all the way to the squadrons, where air crews were so torn between desire and inability to help the beleaguered troops on the Canal that they turned with fury against the overworked and unprepared mission planners.

Indeed, next to the troops on the Canal, it was the air and ground crews who bore the brunt of the crisis, as mission orders arrived without sufficient intelligence, target definition, or clear objectives—and kept changing from one minute to the next. "Nights were mechanics' nightmares," says Spector. "IAF Operations would send instructions for arming the planes early evening, then new orders would come at midnight and the planes would have to be refitted all over again, and then new changes would come at two in the morning. Each time, the mechanics had to be waked up to do everything once more. After a while I just ordered all mission orders coming at night to be filed away. At two I'd wake up, look at the latest orders, change them as I saw fit, and decide what we should do. That way the mechanics could at least eat and get some sleep. It was the only way I had of protecting my pilots and mechanics from burning out."[3] At the end of the war, Spector spoke for many when he wrote in his squadron book that the real enemy was not the Arabs, but the mission planners at IAF Operations.

So elemental were these crises that, to pull its share in this war, the IAF not only had to switch priorities but to literally reinvent itself in mid-fighting to perform missions it had ignored if not resisted for years. It was ironic but entirely in character that in the one area where substantial progress had been made before the war, it occurred almost by chance and against solid resistance.

Back in 1965, after completing the *Moked* airfield-strike plan, Rafi Sivron, the Akim Tamiroff look-alike, ignored Moti Hod's advice and dropped out of active service to study economics at the Hebrew University in Jerusalem. When he returned three years later, Hod made him do penance by training navigators at IAF Flight School for three years—"I considered retiring, but I was married with three children, times were tough, and I could not afford to be proud," Sivron says—before putting him in charge of IAF Combined Operations, which handled such joint Blues-Greens operations as parachute drops or airborne commando missions. Although close air support was not part of his job, his close work with the Greens caused him to look into the matter. "In all my years in the IAF I was never so alarmed and frightened about a subject as I was about this. The IAF was simply unable to provide support to ground troops. It never could," he now says.[4]

His appointment came fortuitously just as Beni Peled, as head of IAF Air Section, began his reorganization purges. Peled instantly grasped the scope and significance of Sivron's concerns. With his support, Sivron set his spreadsheet-mind to work and in 1972 had the outline of a solution. Simply put, Sivron's idea was for IAF Operations to "hand over" the required fighter-bomber formations to the field theater commander to use as he saw fit, thereby eliminating the command bureaucracy on both the Blue and Green sides. With the field commander—working through an expert on-the-spot IAF liaison—talking directly to the flight leader in the air, close-air support could be delivered in real time instead of a day later.

But his notion flew in the face of the IAF's basic doctrine of central control. According to Sivron, "Moti Hod nearly threw me out of his office. He said, 'You are taking control away from me, you've gone crazy.' He totally failed to understand not only my plan but the very problem. On the other hand, Beni Peled . . . understood the problem and the solution, and in fact began to assign communications resources—radio frequencies, telephone lines, instruments, vehicles—to [Sivron's project], contrary to [Hod's] existing policy."

Peled was not in command long enough to put the new system to work before the war broke out, but he did ship Sivron to the northern front to start implementing his ideas on the spot (ironically with the help of Moti Hod, who volunteered for duty and was appointed air advisor to IDF northern command). Sivron's concept promptly proved its worth by twice saving the day, literally. The first time was on the second day of the war, when Hod himself used it to direct a squadron of Ramat David Skyhawks to hold off the Syrian tanks on the Gamala Grade above the Jordan River until Israeli armor reinforcements arrived.

The second time came ten miles uphill and two days later, two days in which two developments took place. First, starting at the bottom of the Gamala Grade and slugging their way up the heights, three Israeli armored brigades and one mechanized brigade had begun the tedious and bloody chore of pushing the Syrians back. By the morning of October 9, they had rolled the Syrians back to their main concentration at the critical Khushniye-Butmyeh salient, but there their advance stopped. With the Syrians not only outnumbering the Israelis but also controlling the terrain after capturing Tel Fares, a cone-shaped dormant volcano that towered over the entire area and gave the Syrians both a fire advantage and a full view of

Israeli movements, the Israelis were stuck. At Moti Hod's urging, Gen. Yitzhak Hofi, chief of IDF Northern Command, asked for an air strike on the Syrian defenses, but the IAF had no planes available and the tank battle at Tel Fares turned static.

The second thing that happened during those two days was that the Syrians had begun lobbing surface-surface Frog missiles at Ramat David and nearby civilian targets. This persuaded the Israeli government to approve Beni Peled's proposals for strategic aerial bombings inside Syria, to damage its military capabilities and at the same time to dissuade Jordan from entering the war. On the morning of October 9, eight Phantoms from Tel Nof swept out to sea, swung north into Lebanon and headed for Damascus. Although running into heavy clouds and drifting off course, at the last minute they managed to find Damascus through an opening in the clouds and dived in to destroy the Syrian army command complex and a nearby Soviet Cultural Center. On their way back, one of the Phantoms was shot down by Syrian ground fire, its pilot killed and navigator captured.*

A second formation of eight Phantoms from Hazerim, however, commanded by Iftach Spector, never made it to Damascus. Running into a heavy cloud cover that seemed to grow thicker and taller the farther east they flew, Spector was more than halfway to Damascus when he aborted the mission and called IAF Operations to say that he was heading back. Not having another target for him in the area, IAF Operations recalled the appeals for help from IDF Northern Command, and called Rafi Sivron at his command post across the Jordan from the Golan Heights, and asked if he could use Spector's formation.

Sivron could not have asked for a better project-validation opportunity. Calling IDF Northern Command on one telephone to ask for proposed targets—"You're heaven-sent. There's a Syrian tank column heading toward us and in ten minutes we have a good chance of being decimated," he recalls being told[5]—he called Spector on

---

*According to returning Israeli POWs, the Syrians were mystified if not downright spooked by the fact that a section of their headquarters where the Israelis were held had escaped damage. They later questioned the POWs on how Israel knew where they were held, and how the Israeli attackers pinpointed their bombing to avoid hitting the POWs' quarters.

the radio and asked for his estimated arrival time. "Five minutes, but I don't have a map of the area in question," Spector replied. It was precisely that predicament, where neither Blues nor Greens had any idea where the other was, that Sivron had elaborately thought out in the preceding months. "I directed the [planes] to a spot all the pilots knew, Kibbutz Ein Gev on the northeast shore of the Sea of Galilee, and from there I gave them directions and distances to the target," Sivron recalls.[6]

"Whoever directed us in the air was a legend, a real professional," one of the pilots in Spector's formation recalled. "He brought us to the target outstandingly . . . the highway is here, Tel Fares is there, our forces are south of this road and the Syrians are north of that road . . . he gave us targets, figured out what was there, calculated the distances and directions. . . . I had never received better directions in war."[7]

The Phantom strike—fifty-six tons of bombs were dropped on the advancing Syrian armor in just two minutes—decided the battle for control of the Golan Heights. "I was stunned by the intensity of the strike and the effect it had," recalls Gen. Joseph Peled, who commanded one of the Israeli armored brigades. "The Air Force may not have ended the battle, but it took the pressure off of us significantly. . . . One thing is certain, that battle with the Syrians would have been ten times tougher, and we would have paid with far more casualties and damaged tanks, were it not for that air strike."[8] That afternoon, the Israeli tanks seized control of the area around Tel Fares. An Israeli soldier with a rifle and a bag full of grenades scaled the dead volcano on foot and destroyed the Syrian tank that perched on top of it and demolished any vehicle that tried to get up the narrow and twisting road to the top. By the following day, the Syrians had been pushed beyond the 1967 cease-fire "purple line" and out of the Golan Heights.

But it was impossible to change the IAF's entire air-ground support system and start "handing out" squadrons to field commanders who did not know the first thing about using air power in such a way. Fortunately, a routine personnel shift on the fourth day of the war brought about another—also unplanned and unexpected—revolutionary improvement in the IAF's ability to deliver badly needed ground support to the Greens: Gad Eldar, dazed by three days of constant work underground, was allowed to return to his squadron to do some flying, while Oded Marom, his former commander at the 101 Mirage squadron, was called back to replace him at IAF Strike Planning Branch.

Although so many IAF staff officers were switching back and forth between the "Hole" and their squadrons that IAF Operations had come to resemble a game of musical chairs, in no other case did simply trading places so affect the course of the air war. That Eldar was far more effective in a Mirage cockpit than behind a desk was no secret, as he soon proved by shooting down twelve enemy planes in the next two weeks—four of them in a single battle, three in another. By the end of the war, when added to the six air kills he had accumulated before, it made him the IAF's leading ace with a total of eighteen kills (Spector, with sixteen, would be third.)

But it was Marom's arrival at IAF Strike Planning Branch that had the most impact on the conduct of the air war. Recently appointed head of IAF Training, Marom with the baby face and booming voice had reported to his old 101 Mirage squadron the moment war broke out, and shot down three enemy planes before, on the fourth day of the war, he was hit in the eye by a fragment from his third air kill, and was ordered back to IAF Operations. Like Eldar and Somekh before him, he, too, was given a desk and a telephone in the catacombs underneath the IAF complex in north Tel Aviv, and vaguely told to do what he could to support the ground forces. It wasn't much of a setup. His telephone was so old that "if I wanted to call someone I had to have an operator get him,"[9] and the "office" was a cavernous widening in a dark, wet passage. To go anywhere, he had to carry a flashlight and hop from one concrete block to another to avoid stepping in a puddle. A kitchen on the other side of a plywood wall caused the air to reek with the smell of fried eggs.

Unlike his predecessors, however, Marom quickly began to modify and embellish his work space. At his insistence, "they sent me a secretary, and a day later two sergeants to help draw maps," and finally, after much screaming and table pounding, his single telephone line was replaced by four—connecting him directly to the IDF's main bunker and to its three regional commands. When IAF work crews also put up plywood partitions around him in the shape of a large room, he really went to work. First, he placed a desk and a telephone against each of the four walls. One telephone—his own—was connected to the Greens' bunker. The other three desks each had a direct telephone link to one of the three IDF regional commands—north, south, and center. Behind each desk, Marom hung a large map of the corresponding theater of operations, so that from his own desk he could view each map and get an instant picture of the fighting without having to go elsewhere.

Finally, at each desk he assembled a planning team that consisted of representatives from the appropriate Greens command, IAF Control, IAF Communications, IAF Operations, and IAF Intelligence (he later added an electronic warfare expert). By the second week of the war, the four desks were not only dispatching hundreds of planes each day to ground-support missions north and south, but were collecting information—from the Greens in the field through one telephone system, from returning pilots through another—to assemble the first reliable "living maps" since the start of the war.

For the first time since the war began, ground-support missions were scrambled fast, well, and in huge numbers. Things worked particularly well in the north, where Marom let Sivron work directly with the chief of air operations of Ramat David, "borrowing" planes as he needed them to support the troops on the Golan Heights. "I became their rubber stamp, writing up orders after the fact for things they had already carried out on their own, just to keep them from going to jail for working without authorization," Marom now says. The plywood room, which Marom christened "Center for Air Support," became so central to the war that it was there, not at the IAF's main bunker, that Blues and Greens, reservists, politicians, and reporters, flocked to see what was happening at the front. Traffic got so heavy—thirty to forty visitors at a time— that Marom finally threw a fit until a military police guard was installed at the door to keep nonessential visitors away.

Not everything, however, could be fixed on the run—least of all the missiles. Short of dodging missiles or attacking isolated batteries, the IAF had not targeted any missile systems since the failure of *Dougman V,* or figured out new ways of doing that. In the north, matters more or less took care of themselves when the Syrians quickly expended their entire stocks of SA-6 missiles, and the

Soviets then prudently refused to ship them more. Evading the remaining SA-2s and SA-3s presented little problem, and from the second week of the war on the IAF had little trouble carrying out operations on the Golan Heights and over Syria. By October 10 the two IDF armored divisions on the scene pushed the Syrians out of most of the Golan Heights, and by October 13 were deep inside Syrian territory, beating back combined Syrian and Iraqi counterattacks and placing Damascus within artillery range. With their missile cover worn off, the Syrians threw their air force into a frantic effort to stop the Israeli advance, but after eleven attack planes and nine interceptors were shot down on October 12 (nine of them by Phantoms from Ramat David), and nearly as many the following day, their fighters stopped coming and Syria was effectively out of the fighting.

The southern front, however, was something else again. Huge Egyptian armor and infantry forces were dug in, fortified and bristling with massive antitank artillery and missiles along the entire length of the Sinai side of the Canal, shielded against air attacks by thick missile packs behind the waterway. As soon as they secured their bridgeheads and holdings on the Canal bank, the Second and Third Egyptian armies—the former controlling the northern section of the Canal from Port Said to the Great Bitter Lake, the latter from the Little Bitter Lake to the Gulf of Suez—were now striking out to expand their holdings. The attacks were devastating. Chinese-style tidal waves of men and machines, saturating the air ahead of them with shoulder-launched antitank weapons, kept washing again and again against the Israeli defenses, which were wearing down under the assault.

A week after the war began, time was running out. Of the three military options before the Israeli command—attacking along the entire front to push the Egyptians back across the Canal, crossing the waterway en force to envelop the Egyptian expeditionary forces, or holding out in place until a cease-fire—the first was suicidal and the third could not be banked on for long, not at the going rate of attrition. While Soviet airlifts were replenishing Arab losses in planes, missiles, and ordnance, Israel's appeals to the United States for replenishment met with more sympathy than action. The Pentagon agreed to provide new Phantoms and Skyhawks, but would send only two Phantoms per day by air, and Skyhawks by boat. For a while, the Israeli government considered accepting a cease-fire in place, in effect surrendering the western Sinai to Egypt, but Egypt rejected the option and kept up the offensive.

On October 14, however, three factors combined to turn the course of the war. First, affairs in the north were so well in hand that the IAF—and major units of the Greens—could switch their activity back to the southern front. Second, a massive Egyptian offensive along the Canal was beat back so decisively by dug-in Israeli tanks that the shell-shocked Israeli government gave serious thought to Elazar's proposal for an all-out Canal crossing, to envelop the Egyptian invasion forces from behind and force them to surrender or be destroyed.

Finally, to help Elazar push through his attack plan, on October 12 Peled let it be known that IAF losses had been so heavy that it was fast approaching its "red line," and that if the attack were postponed by even a day or two he might not be able to provide the necessary air support. Technically, he lied, as the IAF was still comfortably away from its "red line." "I did not tell the truth, but in fact a long delay would have brought us to our 'red line,'" he now says, pointing out that the number of serviceable planes was indeed dropping steadily.[10]

On the afternoon of October 15, an IDF armored division commanded by Ariel Sharon struck fast and hard at the area where the Suez Canal runs into the Great Bitter Lake—the "seam" between the Second Egyptian Army to the north, and the Third Army to the south, and passed a paratrooper brigade in rubber boats to the west side of the waterway. In three days, two Israeli divisions followed across even as the Egyptians furiously threw every available infantry, armor, and air unit into a frantic effort to close the breach.

Before the Greens could complete their envelopment of the Egyptian armies, however, they first had to carry out a new—to them—and critical mission. From the start of the crossing, even while doing all it could to protect the crossing forces from Egyptian air strikes—Egyptian airfields were attacked daily, and dozens of Egyptian fighters were downed—the Air Force did little to assist them on the ground. The Greens took horrendous casualties. Several frontline tank units had lost their commanders several times over in the devastating Egyptian fire. Close-air support would have made all the difference, but two weeks into the war the Egyptian missile packs still cast giant shadows over the entire front, from Port Said down to the Gulf of Suez, keeping the IAF out. To win the war the Greens had to envelop and decimate the Egyptian ground forces, but they could not do it without air support, and to get it they first had to help destroy the missiles. Getting rid of the missiles had become everybody's business.

On October 18, special armor and paratrooper assault units from the Israeli crossing force fanned out in the vast desert country behind the Egyptian Third Army to destroy the broadly deployed missile batteries on the ground. By the time the war would end a week later, just one Israeli tank division would destroy thirty-four batteries—nearly one-half of the entire Egyptian missile strength behind the Canal. At the same time, while Israeli Mirages and Neshers fended off a desperate last-ditch Egyptian air attack, shooting down twenty-five Egyptian planes in a few hours, IAF Phantoms began a systematic assault against the remaining missile systems, starting at the north sector of the Canal behind the Second Egyptian Army, and working their way south.

At first, convinced that operations *Tagar* and *Dougman V* had not so much failed as been botched up, the colonels at IAF Operations attempted to resurrect their "Swiss watch" *operatziot*, although on a smaller scale, with a massive and elaborate Phantom attack against fifteen missile batteries near al-Qantara, between Port Said and Ismailiya. The attack was poorly planned. The main force arrived from the north over swampy flatlands and was easily picked up by the Egyptian radar. Shrike-carrying Phantoms that were meant to pick off any missile battery that came to life arrived from the east with the sun and haze in their eyes, and could not pinpoint the locations of the missile launches. While six Egyptian missile batteries were destroyed, six Phantoms were also shot down in the process.

It was the war's last *operatzia*. Under pressure from frustrated squadron commanders, Amos Amir, new chief of IAF Operations, began to assign targets to individual squadrons and to free them to plan their own attacks. For the first time, Iftach Spector got to implement the "hunt" antimissile tactics he developed before the

war, while at the Phantom squadron at Hazor, Eitan Ben Eliahu and
Eitan Peled, both veterans of the Phantom-missile wars at the end
of the War of Attrition, worked out elegant schemes for using
anti-radar Shrike missiles to manipulate enemy missile systems into
shutting down or activating their radars. In just four days, more
than forty out of seventy missile batteries along the Canal were
destroyed by the Phantoms at no losses, this in addition to a similar
number demolished by the Israeli ground units.*

By October 22, the missile threat along the Canal had been lifted,
the envelopment of the Egyptian Third Army was complete, and
the IAF moved in furiously to beat it into surrender. For the next
two days, the Egyptians scrambled every available plane in a desperate attempt to avert defeat, but wherever they went, they were met
by Israeli Mirages. On the morning of October 24, Egypt and Syria
agreed to a UN-arranged cease-fire.

That afternoon, the last day of the war, Gad Eldar led a four-
Mirage team from Hazor to relieve four Neshers in a routine day's-
end patrol over the Canal, when the air controller suddenly ordered
the Neshers to the west, where other Israeli Mirages had been
jumped by a large flight of MiGs.

"What about us?" Eldar asked.[11]

"Get off this frequency and resume your patrol," the controller said.

"We are going to battle and we are staying on the frequency,"
Eldar announced and turned to the west, where two explosions in
the air and several on the grounds pinpointed the fight area. As they
approached they found four Mirages holding off a large number of
MiGs. Eldar picked two MiGs, took off after them and hit one with
a heat-seeking missile. When the plane kept flying, trailing a thin
column of smoke behind it, Eldar closed in to finish it off with guns
when its pilot ejected himself and the plane went down.

As Eldar broke off and looked around, another pair of MiGs
streaked below. He dived after them, blew up one with another
missile, stalled and restarted his engine, closed on a third MiG and
after a few sharp turns shot it down with his guns before the battle
ended, as suddenly as it began.

---

*The discrepancy in missile counts may be due to multiple strikes against the same
batteries, mistaken identification, or faulty intelligence in the first place, especially
concerning batteries added or moved during the war.

"Suddenly the skies cleared up. No MiGs, no nothing," he recalls. "I still had plenty of fuel, 2,000 liters, 90 shells in each gun (and my belly fuel tank that I never got around to drop), so I asked the controller for additional targets but there were none." As it was, his foursome shot down seven MiGs, as did a second Mirage foursome from Bir Gafgafa (altogether, sixteen MiGs were reported shot down during this, the last air battle of the war, although the IAF formally recognized only eleven, including Eldar's three.) The war was over.

The cease-fire that went into effect that morning was followed by American-arranged troop-separation agreements with Egypt on January 18, 1974, and with Syria four months later. Israel not only won the war, but won it so decisively and under such adverse conditions as to dispel any Arab hopes of ever dislodging the Jewish state from the Middle East by force. Four years after trying and failing to reclaim the Sinai by force, Sadat was handed it by a magnanimous Menachem Begin, then prime minister of Israel, as part of the historic Camp David Israel-Egypt peace treaty.

For the Air Force, however, at the time and for a long while afterward, the flurry of MiG kills on the Egyptian and Syrian fronts in the last days of the war made no more difference than the MiG turkey-shoot on the first day. In that sense, it almost did not matter that Israel won the war and held on to the Sinai and the Golan Heights, or that a postwar, government-appointed Israeli commission of inquiry placed the full blame for the Yom Kippur fiasco on the Greens (particularly on IDF chief of staff Elazar and AMAN's chief Ze'ira).

To the Air Force, the war that truly mattered was not over, and certainly it had not been won. For the next decade, it would live— and work to break out from—under the shadow of that unfinished war. If the spirit of the Six-Day War was captured by the anonymous reference to "those crazy things Ezer [Weizman] said he could do," for the Air Force the essence of the Yom Kippur War was captured by Ezer Weizman's own brief phrase at the end of the autobiography he published two years later.

"In this war," he said, "the missile bent the wing of the airplane— that is a fact."[12]

EPILOGUE

A FOREIGN FORCE, BUT FRIENDLY

Shortly before midnight on June 3, 1982, Israel's ambassador to Britain, Shlomo Argov, stepped out of London's Dorchester Hotel and into a Palestinian machine-gun ambush that left him badly wounded and paralyzed. The next day, IAF fighter-bombers demolished Beirut's soccer stadium, whose bleachers hid huge PLO armament vaults. The PLO responded by shelling civilian settlements in Galilee, IDF artillery fired back, and on Sunday, June 6, massive Israeli armored and mechanized-infantry forces crossed into Lebanon and began rolling up PLO bases, camps, and compounds away from the border.

Since Operation Peace for Galilee ostensibly aimed only at evicting the PLO from a forty-mile safety zone north of the Israeli border, the Syrians, who occupied parts of Lebanon and had a mutual defense pact with the PLO, at first remained on the sidelines and let the Israelis play their hand. But the Israeli troops did not pause at the forty-mile line. Led by Defense Minister Ariel Sharon and IDF Chief of Staff Rafael Eitan, they kept on going, to Beirut, to wipe out the PLO from Lebanon and to install a Christian-dominated Lebanese government. As their armored columns swept up Lebanon's central mountain ranges—and the Bekaa Valley between them, they ran into Syrian forces who reluctantly joined in the fighting.

Syria's entry into the Lebanon conflict changed the situation. Until that point, Syria's nineteen batteries of surface-air missiles in the Bekaa Valley, more than half of them deadly SA-6s, had been shut down, allowing the IAF to provide the Greens with all the close-air support they needed against the PLO. But now the Syrian command switched them on, spreading a missile umbrella over most of southern Lebanon and putting it out of bounds for the IAF. Before they could take Beirut, the Israelis first had to take out the missiles.

And so it was that on Wednesday, June 9, 1982, twelve years after Shmuel Hetz was shot down by an Egyptian SA-3 over the Suez Canal and nine years after six Israeli Phantoms were downed over Syria while hunting for those same SA-6 batteries that the IAF took up once more its unfinished war against the missiles.

This time, to use the logic of Ezer Weizman's famous metaphor after the 1973 war, it was the "plane that bent the missile." Seventeen of nineteen missile batteries were demolished in the initial assault alone, and twenty-nine Syrian MiG-21 and MiG-23 fighters that attempted to defend the missiles were shot down by Israeli interceptors. The next day, the IAF destroyed the remaining batteries, and four more that the Syrians brought in as backup (two weeks later, IAF planes also destroyed three batteries of advanced SA-8 missiles that the Soviets rushed to the Bekaa after the Israeli attack). By the time a cease-fire went into effect on June 12, the entire Syrian missile system in Lebanon lay in ruins, and eighty Syrian jets had been shot down. IAF losses amounted to no more than one A-4 Skyhawk and two helicopters, downed by Syrian ground fire.

The battle of the Bekaa was a seminal event in several important ways. It concluded Israel's twelve-year war against the missiles so decisively as to demolish the Soviet missile-defense doctrine itself. It also marked the physical and emotional rehabilitation of the IAF from the trauma of the 1973 war. Finally, more than any event before or since, it marked the completion of the third-century saga of the making of the Israeli Air Force. For it was only during the decade following the Yom Kippur War that the IAF truly became the do-anything, go-anywhere wonder machine it had all along claimed to be. It was during those crucial years that, like two tectonic plates jerked together by an earthquake, the IAF's abilities snapped forward to fully catch up with its promise.

The first clue to that transformation came three years after the war. Up until that point, the IAF's reputation was still so low that, on the night of June 29, 1976, Beni Peled was virtually laughed at by the Greens when he proposed to fly as many as twelve hundred paratroopers for 2,000 miles—at night over hostile terrain—to rescue the ninety-seven passengers of Tel Aviv-to-Paris Air France Flight 139, which Palestinian terrorists had hijacked to Uganda two days earlier. IDF Chief of Staff Mordechai "Mota" Gur dismissed Peled's proposal out of hand in favor of an Israeli navy plan for a naval commando rescue strike from Lake Victoria. Yitzhak Rabin, who had become Israel's prime minister two years earlier following Golda Meir's resignation, at first also thought Peled's plan was unworkable.

All that changed five days later, after Defense Minister Shimon Peres brought them around to approve Peled's plan. The result was Operation Thunderbolt, the most spectacular hostage-rescue mission in history. At sunset on July 3, the eve of America's bicentennial celebration and, as far as the rest of the world believed, of Israel's capitulation to the terrorists' demands, four IAF Lockheed C-130 Hercules transports, three of them packed with commandos and one with extra fuel and refueling gear, flew 1,000 miles to the south along the centerline of the Red Sea, then banked right and flew for another thousand miles into the heart of darkest Africa, most of the way through heavy storm clouds that threatened to scatter the formation and sabotage the entire mission.

The C-130s were followed south by two IAF Boeing 707s. One, converted to an emergency hospital, flew to Nairobi, Kenya, to handle and evacuate casualties should anything go wrong. The other, a sophisticated airborne command and control center with Beni Peled himself at the controls, circled over the Red Sea to monitor the operation, and to bounce radio signals from Entebbe to Tel Aviv and back, enabling Rabin or Peres to talk directly to any one of the commandos on the ground.

At no time had the Air Force operated so far from home, unless one counted Al Schwimmer's Operation *Yakum Purkan* twenty-eight years earlier. The C-130s arrived at Entebbe airport only seconds off their eleven o'clock deadline, which allowed the lead plane to steal into Entebbe unnoticed in the jet wash of an arriving British Airways jet. Once on the ground, the heavy plane unloaded its commando troops with their camouflage—a black Mercedes identical to the one driven by Uganda's president Idi Amin, and two four-wheel Land Rovers of the kind used by Amin's bodyguards—and swung around to wait for the rescued passengers. Within minutes, the rest of the transports also landed and regurgitated their armed passengers, who fanned out throughout the airport on their precisely described and well-rehearsed missions.

Just eighteen minutes after the first Israeli commandos burst out of the lead plane and headed for the air terminal where the hostages were kept, six terrorists and twenty Ugandan soldiers were dead, eleven Ugandan MiGs were destroyed on the ground to keep them from interfering with the rescue, and the dazed passengers of Air France 139 were brought on board for the ride home. By midnight, less than an hour after arriving at Entebbe, the entire Thunderbolt force was on its way back. Its sole casualty, besides three hostages who got caught in the cross fire, and an elderly passenger who had been evacuated to an Ugandan hospital a day earlier and was subsequently executed by Amin's guards, was Jonathan "Yoni" Netanyahu, commander of the commando strike force, who was killed by a single shot from an Ugandan soldier.*

Entebbe was more than an Israeli rescue operation. Reaching so far, and so devastatingly, beyond Israel's borders, it set the tone and style for the free world's war on international terrorism. Five years after Entebbe, the IAF struck another spectacular blow at an even greater global menace—nuclear proliferation. Sometime during the summer of 1981, Saddam Hussein's Osirak nuclear power plant near Baghdad was scheduled to go operational—enabling Iraq to produce weapons-grade plutonium to use against Israel. It did not

---

*Older brother of Benjamin Netanyahu, Israel's deputy foreign minister in Yitzhak Shamir's Likud government.

matter that it could be months or years before Saddam actually accomplished all or any of that. Once the reactor was "hot-fueled" with uranium, an Israeli attack would raise a radioactive cloud and cause massive civilian casualties in Baghdad. To Menachem Begin, who took over as Israel's prime minister four years earlier on a tidal wave of Israeli disgust with Labor's lack of accountability for the Yom Kippur War, the choice was clear. Israel could attack immediately and risk international criticism, or it could do nothing and risk a second Jewish Holocaust.

At four in the afternoon of June 7, eight IAF F-16 Fighting Falcons, each loaded with three external fuel tanks and two bombs weighing 2,000 pounds each, secretly lifted off from a desert air base near Eilat and, hugging the rocky desert terrain, flew east with six F-15 Eagles riding shotgun at their flanks and rear. It was the most hazardous and the longest combat mission the IAF had undertaken to date. Unlike most targets in neighboring Egypt, Syria, Jordan, or Lebanon, Osirak was hard to get to. Situated between the Tigris and Euphrates less than 100 miles this side of Iran, it lay 635 miles from Israel, at the very end of the F-16s' range even with the extra fuel they carried.* To get there, the planes had to fly the entire way in enemy—Saudi and Jordanian—airspace, and since the Saudis possessed U.S.-made Airborne Warning and Control System (AWACS) planes that could spot air movements almost anywhere in the Middle East, they had to fly at ground level, where fuel consumption was highest, navigation most difficult, and air currents over the hot terrain so violent that the slightest pilot's error or lapse in concentration during the long flight could send his plane smashing into the desert floor.

Finally, Iraq's war with Iran was at its height, and every MiG, antiaircraft gun and surface-air missile battery in the country was likely to be on hair-trigger alert. Especially around Osirak, Iraq's prime military installation, which the Iranians had already tried to

---

*The Israelis had begun planning a strike against Osirak back in 1979, using Phantoms and Skyhawks that had to be refueled once or twice during the mission, over enemy territory. Following the toppling of the shah of Iran by the Khomeini revolution, the U.S. government canceled a massive sale of F-16s to Iran, and in 1980 used those planes to fill Israel's order ahead of schedule. The F-16s had the range to fly to Baghdad and back without refueling.

destroy and failed. Even fully armed, fourteen fuel-short Israeli fighters were no match for the inferno of MiGs, SA-6 missiles, and artillery fire that the Iraqis would unleash in their direction once they were spotted heading for Fortress Baghdad. Their only protection was secrecy, stealth (IAF markings were painted over), and meticulous planning.

At 5:35 in the afternoon, right on schedule, the planes pulled up and, two-by-two, rolled into the target, dropping their bombs right at the center of the huge concrete dome that housed the Iraqi reactor's cooling-water pool. The first two bombs broke through the thick dome, and the others blasted their way all the way down to the reactor's innermost underground chambers. Only one bomb missed the dome, destroying instead an adjacent neutron guide chamber. In less than two minutes, the reactor, and with it much of Iraq's nuclear potential, lay in utter ruins. The Iraqi surprise was total. No MiGs scrambled. Antiaircraft fire began when the attack was all but over, and was so ineffectual that none of the planes was damaged. In fact, until Israel announced the success of the mission later that day, the Iraqis had no clue who it was that hit the reactor.

Four years after Osirak, the IAF pulled another spectacular coup by sending, on October 1, 1985, ten F-15s twice as far to destroy the PLO headquarters at the resort beach of Hammam Lif in Tunisia, 1,280 miles away. Flying almost the entire length of the Mediterranean, undetected by friend or foe even as they stopped for midair refueling from IAF Boeing 707 tankers, the F-15s found and destroyed with surgical precision several PLO command buildings, causing only minimal damage to the surrounding beach bungalows and yacht docks.

What made these operations significant was not only the perfection of their execution—in the telling, all are remarkably anticlimactic, lacking the surprises, glitches, or close calls of which legends are made—but also the fact that they took place under three different IAF commanders and three different Israeli administrations. Entebbe was Beni Peled's operation, under the Labor government of

Yitzhak Rabin as prime minister, Shimon Peres as defense minister, and Mota Gur as IDF chief of staff. David Ivri, who was Peled's deputy during the 1973 war and succeeded him in 1979, commanded the IAF during the Iraqi raid and the battle of the Bekaa Valley, with the Likud's Begin as prime minister, Sharon as defense minister, and Eitan as IDF chief of staff. The destruction of the PLO facilities in Tunisia was ordered by Amos Lapidot, the IAF's most lackluster commander ever, under a Labor-Likud coalition headed by Peres as prime minister, Rabin as defense minister, and Lt. Gen. Moshe Levi as IDF chief of staff.

It was as though the IAF, which until the Yom Kippur War tended to be only as good, daring, or competent as its commander at that moment, had suddenly turned bionic. Plug in the requirements, goals, and mission parameters, and it would take care of the rest, irrespective of who issued the orders or punched in the data. "A foreign force, but friendly," the awed Greens had come to call it.

It is this systemic excellence, the fruit of his brilliant and Herodian reconstruction of the IAF after the Yom Kippur War, that is the final legacy of Beni Peled's stormy years in command of the IAF. No one before or since has been so uniquely suited for such a crucial mission, not only because of his technical expertise, awesome intellect, and infatuation with organizational charts and chains of command, but also because of his argumentative, unsparing lack of sentiment for traditions and dogmas.

From the moment the war ended, Peled channeled his pilots' fury into a bruising no-holds-barred debriefing series about every aspect of the war, then read and reread the avalanche of complaints, accusations, and recommendations that they produced and turned it into bricks and mortar for his reconstruction. No one else could have so effectively and productively plowed through such a melange of fact, opinion, and fulmination, ranging from engineering and tactics all the way to cultural philosophy (one paper, by Eitan Ben Eliahu, who planned many of the antimissile campaigns of the war, actually analyzed a pilot's need to attribute humanlike traits to surface-air missiles).

Just keeping it all in perspective was a challenge of the first order. Iftach Spector, whose devastating criticism of IAF Operations' mis-

sion planners epitomized the postwar mood in the squadrons, recalls how Peled patiently persuaded him to withdraw his report.
"He told me this story," Spector says: "Sometime far in the future,
visitors from another planet are going through what is left of Planet
Earth. They stumble upon a film vault, and suddenly there it all is,
in reel after reel—what life was like, how Earth's inhabitants
looked, spoke, worked, played, ran their affairs. Now the visitors
understand everything about our civilization—except why it was
called *Looney Tunes*.*"

"I understood what he meant," Spector says. "I was not wrong,
but what I saw was only a small part of the entire picture."

The entire picture, of course, as Peled had warned before the war,
was that in critical areas the IAF of the 1970s had advanced little
since the halcyon days of Air Force North of the 1950s. However
impressive its centralized control system looked in peacetime, at
wartime that elaborate command machinery broke down and the
squadrons were left on their own. Having spent a quarter of a
century developing a field force of white-heat brilliance, the IAF did
not provide it with a command of matching depth and sophistication. By the 1970s, it was running Star Wars fighting teams from a
World War II command bunker with World War II tools.

Even before the debriefings ended, Peled and his deputy, David
Ivri, began to redesign and rebuild the force, often assigning the
worst critics to implement their most extreme suggestions (like
sending Spector to IAF Training Command, to develop and implement new air combat tactics, including the flight-leadership con-
cepts that were at the heart of his anti-*operatziot* tirades before and
during the war).

The reconstruction took place behind a veil of secrecy that still
stands today. Only occasional glimpses appear from time to time to
outline its incredible scope. When asked about a helicopter full of
troops that crashed during night exercises on his watch, killing
everyone on board, Peled only shook his head sadly and noted that
"if we didn't train to land in the dark, we would have never made
it to Entebbe." And after the raid on the PLO headquarters in

---

*Peled actually used the term "Mickey Mouse," the Israeli catchall name for all Disney
cartoons.

Tunisia, six years after he left office, it came out that for years he had been sending his pilots far out over the Mediterranean to practice long-distance navigation and precision rendezvous and refueling techniques.

Nowhere did all aspects of the Peled reconstruction come together as completely as in the quest for a magic antimissile bullet. "It was the one topic that, during my two years as the head of IAF Operations after the war, occupied us out of all proportion to anything else," says Amos Amir, who took over IAF Operations halfway through the Yom Kippur War.[1] The quest gave focus and purpose to every phase of IAF development, from reforming the intelligence system—"it was not enough for somebody in IDF Southern Command to know where a missile battery was; the person at IAF Operations who sat down, wrote the mission order, and then directed the planes to their targets had to know precisely where the missiles were at any given instant," says Amir—to exotic if not esoteric research into new weaponry and battlefield management tools, conducted in or out of the Air Force.

In 1967, an American aerospace engineer named Al Ellis, a specialist in autopilot systems, was recruited by Al Schwimmer's Israel Aircraft Industries to work on the Kfir, Israel's ultimate version of the Mirage. It was not Ellis's first time in Israel. A World War II veteran (he won the Purple Heart at Okinawa) and ardent Zionist, he was among the foreign volunteers who helped win the 1948 war. Back in Israel for the second time, Ellis built himself a beach house north of Tel Aviv and launched a small model-airplane business on the side with three Air Force friends. The business failed, but it gave him an idea for a remote-controlled model plane that would fly over enemy installations with a video camera, and beam back live TV footage.

The IAF was not interested at first, but after the Yom Kippur War, Tadiran, a leading Israeli electronics company, hired Ellis and his buddies to develop the idea. Five months later, on an old airstrip, an IAF evaluation team watched as a prototype drone carrying a small Sony home-video camera scooted off the runway, disappeared in the hazy air, then beamed back to a makeshift panel a perfect TV picture of a lone bicycle rider pedaling down a side road.

This time the IAF grabbed it, and by the late 1970s dozens of mini-RPVs (remotely piloted vehicles) were already at work, mostly in Israel's antiterrorist war on the Lebanon front. Hovering just low enough to evade radar and high enough to be invisible to ground gunners, they provided live TV coverage so accurate that Israeli operators, controlling their tiny drones with joysticks from miles away, could watch enemy gun crews take lunch breaks, or follow a car carrying a PLO commander through the hills and into Beirut's casbah. In 1979, one of the little drones actually scored an air kill—a Syrian MiG-21 in Lebanon tried to shoot it down, but the drone's operator manipulated it so deftly that it not only escaped the MiG, but caused it to crash.

At the same time that Al Ellis was building his small drones, an unlikely expert was tinkering with the IAF's digital brain. Menachem Goldman* was a brilliant ultrareligious *yeshiva* student who, bored with liturgical studies, took up washing machine repair and then computer programming. He ended up working with advanced computers at the Weizmann Institute when Aviem Sela, chief of IAF Strike Planning at Beni Peled's IAF Operations, came for help in developing computerized control of great numbers of planes and weapons in increasingly sophisticated and time-sensitive missions. The applied mathematics experts he consulted thought it would take years to develop such a system. Goldman, a blackclad ultra-orthodox Jew who packed special Kosher meals and broke away every few hours to face Jerusalem and pray, gave Sela the outline of a solution after just one month, an entire preliminary system in three, and a final working version in six. It proved so efficient and revolutionary that even the ever-skeptical and challenging Peled was won over, and in 1976 awarded Goldman the annual Air Force prize.

Finally, "what we really needed was a doctrine that pulled all those things together," says Amir. "There came a day, which I still remember with utmost clarity, when I took the heads of IAF Strike Planning and IAF Control down to the 'Hole.' I asked them to do

---

*Not his real name.

just that, to come up with a way of getting all target and other relevant information to one center. That was the basis on which, for years afterward, we built and elaborated. In time, we added computers, sophisticated communication systems, means of transmitting pictures in real time, and so on. But at the heart of it all was still this basic idea—true centralized control of the entire force."

By the time he left the IAF command in the fall of 1977, Peled had remade the IAF in his own image, from structures and weaponry—he was among the early developers of the Kfir, and oversaw the selection of the American F-15s and F-16s as the IAF's latest generation of frontline fighters—to the next commander.

Slow, quiet, and lacking the flash and charisma of Weizman, Hod, or even Peled, Ivri was a competent enough pilot, but he had never shot down a MiG or commanded a squadron in battle. He had flown an Ouragan in the 1956 war and commanded IAF Flight School in 1967, and only filled in as a Mirage pilot in the Six-Day War. He spent the next two wars mostly at IAF headquarters—the War of Attrition as chief of IAF Operations, and the Yom Kippur War as Peled's chief of IAF Air Section. The closest he came to shooting down a MiG was in the late 1950s, but ended up downing his own Super-Mystère by getting into a spin and then—as he freely admitted afterward, earning points for honesty—pushing the wrong pedal and crashing his plane instead of saving it. When asked to contribute a most-memorable combat story to an IAF magazine anthology, the best he could recall was circling over a downed pilot on the Golan Heights on the last day of the Six-Day War, and protecting him until the rescue helicopter arrived.[2]

Yet Ivri was also solid, bright, organized, and a superb manager, and he so complemented the explosive and high-flying Peled that it was their partnership, like that of Weizman and Hod in Ramat David two decades earlier, that defined the course and nature of the IAF in the 1980s, if not for the rest of the century. Appointed by Peled to head a task force on the lessons of the Yom Kippur War, Ivri translated some of Peled's big-picture revolutions into feasible work plans, scuttled those he deemed too wild or unrealistic, and ran interference during Peled's scorched-earth interludes with his commands. In 1975, Peled sent him to the Technion, where Ivri earned an aeronautical engineering degree in just two years and came back in time to ensure orderly transition and undisrupted continuation of Peled's reconstruction.

For a while, it seemed as though they had come around too late, that their ultimate legacy would be the shutting down of the IAF. Just a month after Peled handed Ivri the command, Sadat flew to Israel to proclaim "no more war" between Jew and Arab. In 1979, thirty-one years after King Faruk sent the Egyptian army north to help wipe out the Jewish state at its birth, Israel and Egypt concluded a peace treaty, Israel handed back the Sinai, and Ivri's main task became the rolling back of the IAF from the vast desert spaces into a suddenly tiny Israel and—if Sadat's and Begin's peace campaign pulled in other Arabs and Palestinians—into mothballs.

But no other Arab state immediately joined the peace parade, and the Palestinians, rejecting the autonomy offered them under the Camp David formula, escalated their guerrilla and terror campaign against Israel. Instead of leading the Arab world toward reconciliation, Sadat was assassinated by Moslem fanatics for making peace with Israel—ironically during a military parade marking the anniversary of the Yom Kippur War—and on June 7, 1981, just before returning it to Egypt, Ivri used one of the Sinai air bases one last time to launch the raid on Saddam Hussein's Osirak nuclear reactor.

It would take ten more years, the collapse of the Soviet Union, and an American victory over Iraq in 1991 before Syria, Jordan, Lebanon, and the Palestinians would sit down to talk peace with Israel. It was during that twilight era between war and peace that, on June 9, 1982, with Israeli ground troops moving on Beirut, Ivri gave Aviem Sela, his chief of IAF Operations, the go-ahead, and the unfinished war that had haunted the IAF for so long was finally and decisively won.

Israel still guards closely the details of what happened at the Bekaa Valley, so what follows is probably, but perhaps not entirely, accurate. It is safe to assume that American-made Hawkeye command and control planes were used to jam Syrian radar and communications systems, and to monitor Syrian aircraft movements for miles around. And it is a matter of public record—including Syrian accounts of the battle—that swarms of Al Ellis's little drones, made by Tadiran and the Israel Aircraft Industries, buzzed unnoticed over the Bekaa and beamed back video images of every missile battery and its operating crew.

Back in Israel, powerful IAF computers, programmed by Menachem Goldman, digested the billions of bits of incoming data into an instant picture of the battle scene and zipped it through modems, high-speed transmission lines, and powerful printers to the field units.

Next, attack planes carrying special Israeli-made pods dubbed "Samson," and small drones code-named Delilah, moved into the Bekaa, emitting electronic signals that made them register as attacking aircraft on the Syrian missile radar. As missile batteries came alive and began to fire, their radar frequencies were monitored, beamed back home, and plugged into the guidance systems of sophisticated radiation-homing missiles—both airborne and ground-launched—that were fired so fast as to demolish the batteries' control systems before the Syrians could shut them down.

Finally, with the batteries blinded and helpless and with the tiny drones still circling overhead to provide a play-by-play account of the unfolding destruction, flights of Phantoms and Kfirs dropped masses of hard, guided and cluster bombs that ripped missiles and launchers to shreds. All the while, Israeli fighters overhead, guided by airborne controllers who kept track of every single plane in the air—Israeli or Arab—used radar-guided missiles to down scores of Syrian fighters from such great distances they could not even see them. Only when the Syrians threw so many aircraft into a desperate effort to save the missiles that not all could be shot down from far away, did young Israeli F-15 and F-16 pilots get a chance— probably their last—to dogfight with MiGs and use guns for the kill.

The destruction of the missiles took place thirty-four years to the week after Modi Alon shot down two Egyptian bombers over Tel Aviv in 1948, and only fifteen since Moti Hod scrambled his entire force against Egypt in 1967. But the Israeli Air Force that won the

battle of the Bekaa already belongs to another era, and probably in
another book, were it not for the fact that Beni Peled, the man who
brought it to this new age and completed its making, had himself
begun at the start of the previous one, as a young Messerschmitt
mechanic at the Red Squadron.

AUTHOR'S NOTE

This book began with a red herring which Tony Cantafio, Northrop Corporation's vice president for Public Communications, threw at me ten years ago. I was grilling him about Northrop's top-secret Stealth bomber. "Do you realize that one of the greatest untold aviation stories ever is sitting right in your own backyard? Why don't you do the Israel Air Force story?" he said, trying to divert my attention from the confidential Stealth project. Unwittingly, he became responsible for this book and for the ten aggravating and fascinating years that went into it.

Early thanks also go to Lou Lenart, the former Messerschmitt pilot, whose enthusiasm and generosity with time and connections were crucial in getting me started, especially in locating the rest of the 1948 volunteers and in opening important doors in Israel. He has since retired to Tel Aviv, where his apartment overlooks the spot where he landed in his Norseman forty-four years ago, on the eve of Israel's statehood.

It was also Lou who, over a hot beef brisket lunch at a Los Angeles Hungarian restaurant, introduced me to Moti Hod, who was visiting California as a private businessman. By then I was well into the project and close to sensory overload from attacking it from all directions at once. Hod cut right through it. "Start from the beginning, talk to all the Air Force chiefs in chronological order starting with Remez, and when you come to my period I'll talk to you," he said. I did, and when the time came so did he, readily, repeatedly, and at great length. His support had as much to do with my book as with the solidarity of men of the land. Having lost my father around that time, and my only brother ten years earlier on the Golan Heights in the Yom Kippur War, I had taken over the running of our family farm in the Galilee foothills. As I flew over from California for weeks at a time to plant, harvest, and squeeze Air Force interviews into free evenings or rainy days, Hod approvingly made this fact known to anyone he knew I planned to see.

This is a good place to explain some special problems I faced from the start. In the first place, I never served in the IAF—nor ever wanted to. The closest I came to air combat was as a child during the 1948 war, when a small Arab plane came over my farming village, and a neighbor took my father's shotgun and fired up at it. Although our village lay a few miles from Ramat David, I never desired to fly. When time came to enlist, only one man out of my graduating class of sixty-five at the Kadoorie Agricultural High School (cradle of the *Palmach*, and Yitzhak Rabin's alma mater) joined the Air Force, the rest of us opting for settling as soldier-farmers on the angry frontiers. But with few exceptions, the first question from anyone I had spoken with was, "Did you serve in the Air Force?" and when I answered in the negative a certain curtain dropped between us, never to be lifted.

Second, like most young Israelis of my generation, I knew very little about the IAF beyond standard mythologies and grapevine stories. We vaguely knew that Modi Alon shot down two Dakotas over Tel Aviv in 1948, and we took it for granted that the Air Force REALLY began only with Ezer Weizman. Of course, most of what I thought I knew was wrong, which meant that I had to start my research from scratch. Israeli military histories habitually omit the vital part that the foreign volunteers played in the 1948 air war, and the secretive IAF seldom gives out anything beyond glowing and heavily sanitized wartime success accounts.

It was not about to change with me. "If not a single word ever appears in print about the Air Force I would be a happy man," I was told by an IAF security man who came to look me over after I petitioned for research access. Yoram Agmon, the Phantom pilot, admitted to me that as Air Force attaché at the Israeli embassy in Washington at the time I began my research, he had advised his superiors against cooperating with me.

Finally, I was an Israeli who lived abroad, and who was not writing an officially sanctioned history. "You are a *Yored** and you write for money. Why should I help you?" Amos Lapidot, IAF commander in the mid-1980s, asked me flat out, and denied me any access to information. He might not have been so harsh had he not been bogged down in a major scandal. It was during his watch—and apparently with his approval—that Aviem Sela, then on a study leave in the United States, became involved with Jonathan Pollard, the United States Navy intelligence expert who passed secret data to Israel about Arab terrorist, tactical, and nuclear preparations. When the affair blew up with Pollard's arrest and ultimate imprisonment for life, Lapidot made things worse by promoting Sela to the command of Tel Nof. Under furious American threats of suspending critical arms sales to the Air Force, Sela left Tel Nof, and ultimately retired from active service. Lapidot himself retired not long after we spoke, at the expiration of his IAF command term.

Lapidot's successor, Avihu Ben-Nun, was slightly more forthcoming, but only as far as telling the retired Air Force officers I was trying to interview that he had no objection to them talking to me. He, too, might have been more helpful, except that his senior acquisitions officer, Brig. Gen. Rami Dotan, had just been charged with a multimillion-dollar bribery and corruption scheme involving major IAF procurement in the United States. Although the offenses occurred before Ben-Nun assumed IAF command and in no way involved him, the charges were made during his term, and his initial refusal to believe them—he instinctively stood by his comrade-in-arms—came to haunt him when the charges were proven and Dotan was convicted and sent to prison.

*Meaning, literally, "descender," this is a derogatory term for an Israeli who lives outside the country. In contrast, an immigrant who "goes up" to Israel is an *Oleh*, or "ascender."

Given all that, I was probably lucky to have as many people help me as I did. It will take too long to thank each and every one of them. The list of interviews in the Sources section acknowledges many, while others were thanked in person because they could not and cannot be named. A few individuals, however, were particularly helpful in repeatedly opening their homes—and personal logbooks and archives—to me, and must be acknowledged. All former IAF commanders were most cooperative, cordial, and patient, and made time for me in their busy civilian pursuits. Aharon Remez, who lives in Jerusalem and is an accomplished sculptor, is president of the Lapid Movement for Transmitting the Lessons of the Holocaust. Dan Tolkowsky is a leading high-tech venture capitalist. Ezer Weizman, who had served as Israel's defense minister and played an active part in the Camp David peace talks between Israel and Egypt, recently retired from the Knesset and is a candidate for Israel's presidency, the post once held by his uncle Chaim Weizmann. Moti Hod heads Israel Aircraft Industries. Beni Peled runs a small skunkworks-style military R & D company, and is a director of three of Israel's leading high-tech companies. David Ivri is director general of the Israel Defense Ministry.

Aharon Yoeli, now an El Al pilot, was helpful in bringing to life the early jet era of the 1950s. Shaya Gazit, who flies for Israel's domestic airline, Arkia, provided valuable instruction in several critical areas, particularly concerning the evolution of the IAF's flight-training system. Jacob Agasi, also an El Al pilot, gave me crucial insight into the 1950s, and into the air-combat aspects of the War of Attrition. Yak Nevo, who ran a large wood-carving shop at the time I spoke with him and died unexpectedly two years ago, patiently took me through the fine points of his dogfighting techniques. Rafi Sivron briefed me in detail about the air-ground support system he developed on the eve of the 1973 war, and both he and Nevo spent hours tracing the evolution of their landmark *Moked* airfield-strike plan.

One of the problems in tracking the history of an organization as complex and ego-driven as the IAF has to do with a revisionism that, consciously or subconsciously, constantly takes place. I owe particular thanks to Eli Eyal, Moshe Peled, and Tsahik Yavneh, the veteran *Palmach* pilots, who alerted me to Menahem Bar's unique and critical early contributions, largely omitted from most IAF histories and anthologies today. Bar, who recently retired from El Al but is still a formidable international gliding competitor, proved most forthcoming and cooperative, and sat through several lengthy interviews at his farmhouse near Ramat David.

Of the younger generation of IAF pilots, I owe special thanks to Gad Eldar, an El Al pilot and holder of the world's unofficial record for jet-era air kills. Eldar—he still flies F-16s, so his real name cannot be used—went out of his way to convince Avihu Ben-Nun to allow still-active IAF veterans like himself to talk to me. It was only when that official sanction was issued that I came to meet with Oded Marom, Iftach Spector, Eitan Peled, Eitan Ben-Eliahu, Yoram Agmon, and many others of their era. Another IAF insider who encouraged and guided me informally even when he could not do so officially was Ido Ambar, the former transport pilot who planned the Entebbe rescue flight in 1976, and was head of IAF History Branch when I met him.

Nat Sobel, my agent, was steadfast in his support and wise in his counsel from the moment he received my proposal letter a decade ago. I am grateful to the late great Harold Hayes and to Andrew Olstein, my editors at *California* magazine, who ran my story on Operation *Yakum Purkan* and the California origins of the IAF ("The Secret Birth of the Israeli Air Force," August 1986). It was the enthusiastic public response to that piece that kept me going. Fred Jordan, my editor at Pantheon Books, was particularly supportive as we got into the homestretch and it seemed as if nothing would ever be finished right. And then, of course, there is my family, both in California and in Israel, who tolerated my long absences, frantic efforts to sustain existence on both sides of the globe, and seeming proclivity for impossible projects.

Ehud Yonay
Los Angeles, 1992

NOTES

INTRODUCTION: A LINE OF BLOOD AND FIRE

1. *Abba Eban: An Autobiography* (New York: Random House, 1977), 99.
2. Uri Milstein, *The War of Independence—The First Month* (Hebrew) (Tel Aviv: Zmora, Bitan, Publishers, 1989), 41.

CHAPTER 1. DEAD RECKONING

1. Lou Lenart, in an interview with the author, Oct. 17, 1982.
2. Coleman Goldstein, in an interview with the author, Oct. 17, 1984.

CHAPTER 2. THE NEW BRUNSWICK WARNING

1. Leonard Slater. *The Pledge* (New York: Simon & Schuster, 1970), 100.
2. Aharon Remez, in an interview with the author, Apr. 1, 1983.
3. Michael Bar-Zohar. *Ben Gurion* (Hebrew, abridged edition) (Tel Aviv: Israel Ministry of Defense and Magal Publishing, 1986), 255.

CHAPTER 3. THE CZECH KNIVES

1. Lou Lenart, in an interview with the author, Oct. 21, 1982.
2. G. Rivlin and Dr. E. Orren, eds., *The War of Independence, Ben-*

Gurion's Diary (Hebrew) (Tel Aviv: Israel Defense Ministry Publishing, 1982), 2:427.
3. Ezer Weizman, in an interview with the author, July 23, 1986.
4. Lou Lenart, in an interview with the author, Oct. 21, 1982.
5. Aharon Remez, in an interview with the author, Apr. 1, 1983.

CHAPTER 4. THE BANANA GROVE

1. Aaron Finkel, in an interview with the author (undated).
2. Sid Antin, in an interview with the author, July 14, 1986.
3. Aharon Remez, in an interview with the author, Apr. 12, 1983.
4. Chaim Herzog, *The Arab Israeli Wars* (London: Arms & Armour Press, 1982), 88.

CHAPTER 5. THE RED SQUADRON

1. Jacob Klivansky, *Ish Kenafayim Be'Israel* (Hebrew) (Tel Aviv: Am Oved Publishing, 1950, 98. (A memorial biography of Modi Alon.)
2. Aaron Finkel, in an interview with the author (undated).
3. Leon Nomis, in an interview with the author, May 31, 1986.
4. Sid Cohen, in an interview with the author, Dec. 15, 1985.
5. Ezer Weizman, in an interview with the author, July 23, 1986.
6. Sid Antin, in an interview with the author, July 14, 1986.
7. Rudy Augarten, in an interview with the author, May 29, 1986.
8. Aharon Remez, in an interview with the author, June 24, 1986.

CHAPTER 6. BLOODYING THE RAF

1. Denny Wilson, in an interview with the author, July 14, 1986.
2. George Lichter, in an interview with the author, Dec. 17, 1982.
3. Aaron Finkel, in an interview with the author (undated).
4. Lichter interview.
5. Chalmers "Slick" Goodlin, in an interview with the author, Sept. 19, 1986.
6. Sid Cohen, in an interview with the author, Dec. 15, 1985.
7. Denny Wilson, in an interview with the author, July 14, 1986. Also Moti Hod, Apr. 13, 1983.
8. Rudy Augarten, in an interview with the author, May 29, 1986.
9. Aharon Remez, in an interview with the author, Apr. 12, 1983.

CHAPTER 7. THE PRINCE

1. Dani Shapira, in an interview with the author, Oct. 14, 1985.
2. Meir Roof, in an interview with the author, Dec. 19, 1985.

3. Ezer Weizman with Dov Goldstein, *Le'cha Sha'maim, Le'cha Eretz* (autobiography, Hebrew) (Tel Aviv: Maariv, 1975), 15. Also published in English as *On Eagles' Wings* (New York: Macmillan, 1976.)
4. Weizman, 18.
5. Boris Senior, in an interview with the author, June 21, 1986. Also see Weizman, 42.
6. Aaron Finkel, in an interview with the author (undated).
7. Bill Kaiser in an interview with the author, Dec. 16, 1986.
8. Weizman, 81.
9. George Lichter, in an interview with the author, Dec. 22, 1982.
10. Eli Eyal, in an interview with the author, Apr. 11, 1983.
11. Roof interview.
12. Eyal interview.
13. Moti Hod, in an interview with the author, Dec. 16, 1985.
14. Grisha Bar On, in an interview with the author, Dec. 14, 1985.
15. Ezer Weizman, in an interview with the author, July 28, 1987.
16. Weizman, 78.
17. Harry Axelrod, in an interview with the author, Dec. 24, 1982.
18. Ezer Weizman, in an interview with the author, July 27, 1986.
19. Kaiser interview.
20. Harry Barak, in an interview with the author, Apr. 17, 1988.

CHAPTER 8. THE FARMER

1. Moshe Peled, in an interview with the author, Oct. 6, 1985.
2. Ze'ev Liron, in an interview with the author, Jan. 26, 1988.
3. Menahem Bar, in an interview with the author, Oct. 13, 1985.
4. Aharon Yoeli, in an interview with the author, Oct. 16, 1985.
5. Rudy Augarten, Yoash Tsiddon, and Ze'ev Liron in interviews with the author. Also, Maj. Itzhak Shteigman, *From the War of Independence to Operation Kadesh* (Hebrew, unclassified) (Tel Aviv: Israel Defense Forces, The Air Force, IAF History Branch, 1990), 41–44. Also Uri Milstein, *The History of the Israel Paratroopers* (Hebrew) (Tel Aviv: Schalgi Ltd. Publishing House, Ltd. 1985), Chap. 7.
6. Adam Tsivoni, in an interview with the author, Dec. 17, 1985.
7. Harry Barak, in an interview with the author, Dec. 12, 1985.
8. Moti Hod, in an interview with the author, Dec. 16, 1985.

CHAPTER 9. THE BLUES AND THE GREENS

1. Yoav Gelber, *The Emergence of a Jewish Army* (Hebrew) (Jerusalem: Yad Izhak Ben-Zvi Institute, 1986), 369.

2. Aharon Remez, in an interview with the author, Apr. 1, 1983.

3. Abbreviated Remez testimony, 1981, in IAF Archives, File 54(6).

4. Gelber, 371.

5. *Ma'ariv*, October 23, 1970.

6. Gelber, 372; David Ben-Gurion, "On the Structure of the Army and Its Direction," Oct. 27, 1949. IDF Archives, File 215/79/90.

7. Remez, in a letter to Yadin (Hebrew), Dec. 12, 1949, IDF Archives 215/79/51.

8. Remez, in a letter to Ben-Gurion, Jan. 18, 1950, IAF Archives, File 54(1).

9. Remez, in letters to his father, David Remez, Dec. 3–15, 1950, IAF Archives, File 54(1).

10. Shaya Gazit, in an interview with the author, Apr. 16, 1986.

11. Ze'ev Schiff, *The Israel Air Force* (Hebrew), vol. 3 of *The IDF and Its Arms—Encyclopedia for Military and Security* (Hebrew) (Tel Aviv: Revivim Publishing, 1981), 48.

12. Mordecai Laor, *Laskov* (Hebrew) (Tel Aviv: Israel Defense Ministry Publishing, 1988), 229.

13. IAF Commander report, Gen. Chaim Laskov, Sept. 2, 1951, IAF Archives, File 54(2).

14. Minutes of IDF General Staff meeting for Jan. 20, 1952, IDF Archives, File 54(1).

15. Moti Hod, in an interview with the author, Dec. 16, 1985.

16. Dan Tolkowsky, in an interview with the author, Jan. 27, 1988.

17. Harry Barak, in an interview with the author, Dec. 12, 1985.

18. Minutes of IDF General Staff meeting, Feb. 23, 1953, IAF Archives, 54(2):11.

19. Minutes, 20.

20. Minutes, 21.

21. Dan Tolkowsky, in an interview with the author, Dec. 24, 1985.

22. Michael Bar-Zohar, *Ben-Gurion* (Hebrew, abridged edition) (Tel Aviv: Israel Ministry of Defense and Magal Publishing, 1986), 364. Also Uri Milstein, *The History of the Israel Paratroopers* (Hebrew) (Tel Aviv: Schalgi Ltd Publishing House, 1985), 225.

CHAPTER 10. THE BLACK SPITFIRE

1. Maj. Itzhak Shteigman, *Operation "Kadesh"* (Hebrew, classified), (Tel Aviv: Israel Defense Forces, The Air Force, IAF History Branch, 1986), 42. Also in *The First Jet Squadron*, (Hebrew, classified) (Ramat David: Squadron 117, 1982), 3.

2. Aharon Yoeli, in an interview with the author, Oct. 16, 1985.

3. Avraham Yoffe's logbook.
4. Menahem Bar, in an interview with the author, Oct. 13, 1985.
5. Yalo Shavit, in an interview with the author, Apr. 20, 1983.
6. Beni Peled, in an interview with the author, Apr. 7, 1985.
7. Yitzhak "Tsahik" Yavneh, in an interview with the author, Dec. 16, 1985.
8. Ezer Weizman with Dov Goldstein, *Le'cha Sha'maim, Le'cha Eretz* (Hebrew) (Tel Aviv: Ma'ariv Publishing, 1975), 124. Also published in English as *On Eagles' Wings* (New York: Macmillan, 1976).
9. Weizman, 123.
10. Weizman, 124.
11. Weizman, 125.
12. Jacob Agasi, in an interview with the author, May 17, 1989.
13. Yoeli interview. Also see *The First Jet Squadron*, 7.
14. Weizman, 126.
15. Eli Eyal, in an interview with the author, Apr. 11, 1983.
16. Weizman, 147.

CHAPTER 11. FRENCH SHUTTLE

1. Harry Axelrod, in an interview with the author, Dec. 22, 1982.
2. Beni Peled, in an interview with the author, Apr. 7, 1985.
3. Col. (ret.) Benjamin Kagan, *Hem Himri'u Ba'alata* (Hebrew) (Tel Aviv: Davar Publishing, 1960), 260. According to Kagan, who headed the negotiations, Saab's change of mind was probably because a major shareholder was a bank with many obligations in Egypt, and Saab's management feared economic retaliation by Egypt.
4. Ezer Weizman with Dov Goldstein, *Le'cha Sha'maim, Le'cha Eretz* (Hebrew) (Tel Aviv: Ma'ariv Publishing, 1975), 138. Also published in English as *On Eagles' Wings* (New York: Macmillan, 1976).
5. Kagan, 263.
6. Kagan, 265–66.
7. Tolkowsky's letter to Dayan, IDF Archives, File 753–56/178.
8. Weizman, 138.
9. Maj. Itzhak Shteigman, *Operation "Kadesh"* (Hebrew, classified) (Tel Aviv: Israel Defense Forces, The Air Force, IAF History Branch, 1986).
10. Aharon Yoeli and Yoash Tsiddon in interviews with the author. Also see Shteigman, *"Kadesh,"* 58, and Tzvika Vered, ed. *The First Jet Squadron* (Hebrew, classified) (Ramat David: Squadron 117, 1982), 12.
11. Shteigman, *"Kadesh,"* 50.

12. Michael Bar-Zohar, *Ben-Gurion* (Hebrew, abridged edition) (Tel Aviv: Israel Ministry of Defense and Magal Publishing, 1986), 406.
13. Tolkowsky, in a letter to Moshe Dayan, cited in *"Kadesh,"* 292.
14. Moti Hod, in an interview with the author, Dec. 24, 1985.
15. Eli Eyal, in an interview with the author, Apr. 11, 1983.
16. Joseph Tsuk, in an interview with the author, June 22, 1986.
17. *The First Fighter Squadron,* a diary (Hebrew, classified) (Hazor: Squadron 101, 1973) 65.
18. Shaya Gazit, in an interview with the author, Dec. 24, 1986.
19. *20 La'Tayeset, 1948–68* (Hebrew, classified) (Hazor: Squadron 101, 1968), 66.
20. Shteigman, *"Kadesh,"* 357–64.

CHAPTER 12. KADESH

1. Moti Hod, in an interview with the author, Dec. 24, 1985.
2. Harry Barak, in an interview with the author, Apr. 17, 1988.
3. Dani Shapira, in an interview with the author, Feb. 1, 1988.
4. Ezer Weizman with Dov Goldstein, *Le'cha Sha'maim, Le'cha Eretz* (Hebrew) (Tel Aviv: Ma'ariv Publishing, 1975), 154. Also published in English as *On Eagles' Wings,* (New York: Macmillan, 1976).
5. Joseph Tsuk, in an interview with the author, June 2, 1986.
6. Ran Ronen, in an interview with the author, Apr. 14, 1983.
7. Itzhak Shteigman, Maj. *Operation "Kadesh"* (Hebrew, classified) (Tel Aviv: IAF History Branch, Israel Defense Ministry, Tel Aviv, 1986), 195.
8. Michael Bar-Zohar, *Ben-Gurion* (Hebrew, abridged edition) (Tel Aviv: Israel Ministry of Defense Publishing, 1986), 421–45.
9. Shteigman, *"Kadesh,"* 88.
10. *Abba Eban: An Autobiography.* (New York: Random House, 1977), 210.
11. Yoash Tsiddon, in an interview with the author, Oct. 26, 1987. Also in Tsiddon's recently declassified account (Hebrew, unpublished) of Operation Rooster. Also in *In Day, Night and Fog* (Hebrew, classified) (Tel Nof: Squadron 191, 1981), 15.
12. Tsuk interview. Also see *The First Fighter Squadron,* a diary (Hebrew, classified) (Hazor: Squadron 101, 1973), 71.
13. Shaya Gazit, in an interview with the author, Dec. 24, 1986.
14. Yak Nevo, in an interview with the author, July 26, 1987.
15. Aharon Yoeli, in an interview with the author, Oct. 16, 1985. Also in *The First Jet Squadron* (Hebrew, classified) (Ramat David: Squadron 117, 1982), 18.

16. Menahem Bar, in an interview with the author, Oct. 13, 1985.

17. Shteigman, *"Kadesh,"* 150.

18. Ibid, 198; *The First Fighter Squadron,* 73.

19. Shteigman, *"Kadesh,"* 179.

20. Jacob Agasi, in an interview with the author, May 17, 1989.

21. Dan Tolkowsky, in an interview with the author, July 20, 1986.

CHAPTER 13. MIRAGE

1. Shlomo Lahat in an interview with the author, Feb. 6, 1988.

2. Lahat interview; also several entries in Ben-Gurion's Diary, especially October 27, 1954, July 14, 1956, and July 29, 1956. According to Lahat, he turned down at least one attempt by the Greens to dump Tolkowsky and have him take over as chief of the IAF. In fact, when talks began on joint military action with France, Lahat was personally invited to attend the planning meetings, while Tolkowsky was kept out of the loop. According to Lahat, he kept Tolkowsky apprised of all that was happening even though the Greens "strongly suggested" keeping Tolkowsky in the dark.

3. Ezer Weizman with Dov Goldstein, *Le'cha Sha'maim, Le'cha Eretz* (autobiography; Hebrew), (Tel Aviv: Ma'ariv, 1975), 187. This account is missing from *On Eagles' Wings,* the English version of the book (New York: Macmillan, 1976).

4. Weizman, 188.

5. Lou Lenart, in an interview with the author, Oct. 24, 1984.

6. Menahem Bar, in an interview with the author, Dec. 22, 1985.

7. Lahat interview.

8. Lahat interview.

9. Ezer Weizman (Jan. 25, 1988), Moti Hod (Nov. 9, 1986) and Aharon Yoeli (Oct. 16, 1985), in interviews with the author.

10. Yak Nevo, in an interview with the author, Feb. 3, 1988.

11. Shaya Gazit interview, July 14, 1987.

12. Rachel Shaked, in an interview with the author, undated.

13. Zehava Gazit, in an interview with the author, July 14, 1987.

14. Ezer Weizman (Jan. 25, 1988) and Dani Shapira (Feb. 1, 1988), in interviews with the author.

CHAPTER 14. REBELS

1. Shlomo Lahat, in an interview with the author, Feb. 6, 1988.

2. Ezer Weizman, in an interview with the author, Jan. 25, 1988.

3. Shaya Gazit, in an interview with the author, July 14, 1987.

4. Yoash Tsiddon, in an interview with the author, Oct. 26, 1987.

5. *The First Fighter Squadron, a diary* (Hebrew, classified) (Hazor: Squadron 101, 1973), 100. Also in Murray Rubinstein and Richard Goldman, *Shield of David: An Illustrated History of the Israeli Air Force* (Englewood Cliffs, N.J.: Prentice-Hall, 1978), 82.
6. Dani Shapira, in an interview with the author, Feb. 1, 1988.
7. Ezer Weizman with Dov Goldstein, *Le'cha Sha'maim, Le'cha Eretz* (Hebrew) (Tel Aviv: Ma'ariv, 1975), 234. Also published in English as *On Eagles' Wings* (New York: Macmillan, 1976.)
8. Menahem Bar, in an interview with the author, Oct. 13, 1985.
9. Rudy Augarten, interview with the author, May 29, 1986.
10. Dan Tolkowsky, in an interview with the author, Jan. 27, 1988.
11. Zehava Gazit, in an interview with the author, July 14, 1987.
12. Weizman, 179; Shaya Gazit, in an interview with the author, Apr. 16, 1986.
13. Eliezer "Cheetah" Cohen, in an interview with the author, Feb. 3, 1988.
14. Ezer Weizman, in an interview with the author, Jan. 31, 1988.

CHAPTER 15. *MOKED*

1. Yak Nevo, in an interview with the author, Dec. 12, 1985.
2. Aharon Yoeli, in an interview with the author, Oct. 16, 1985.
3. *"Air Combat"* (Hebrew, top secret), IAF Training Command, July 1958. As in most manuals of military doctrine, this one did not carry an author's byline, although Nevo's sole authorship was never in dispute.
4. Moti Hod, in an interview with the author, Dec. 24, 1985.
5. Yak Nevo, in an interview with the author, Oct. 24, 1987.
6. Maj. Jacob Nevo, *Specific vs. Versatile Planes for the Israel Air Force for the Next 5–7 Years* (Hebrew, classified), IAF Staff Paper, Nov. 8, 1961.
7. Ezer Weizman, in an interview with the author, July 21, 1987.
8. Rafi Sivron, in an interview with the author, Oct. 21, 1987.
9. Aharon Yoeli, in an interview with the author, July 27, 1987.
10. Rafi Sivron, in an interview with the author, Feb. 2, 1988.
11. Yoash Tsiddon, in an interview with the author, Oct. 26, 1987.
12. Shlomo Lahat, in an interview with the author, Feb. 6, 1988.

CHAPTER 16. THE FRONTIERSMAN

1. George Lichter, in an interview with the author, Dec. 22, 1982.
2. Menahem Bar, in an interview with the author, Oct. 13, 1985.

3. Aharon Yoeli, in an interview with the author, Oct. 16, 1985.

4. Dan Tolkowsky, in an interview with the author, Jan. 27, 1988.

5. Ezer Weizman, in an interview with the author, July 21, 1987.

6. Ezer Weizman with Dov Goldstein, *Le'cha Sha'maim, Le'cha Eretz* (Hebrew), (Tel Aviv: Ma'ariv Publishing, 1975), 238. Also published in English as *On Eagles' Wings* (New York: Macmillan, 1976).

7. Yak Nevo, in an interview with the author, Oct. 24, 1987.

8. Moti Hod, in an interview with the author, Nov. 9, 1986.

9. Yoram Agmon, in an interview with the author, July 28, 1988.

10. *In Day, Night, and Fog* (Hebrew, classified) (Tel Nof: Squadron 191, 1981), 48.

11. Rafi Harlev, in an interview with the author, Apr. 25, 1988.

12. Shabtai Gilboa, in an interview with the author, Apr. 20, 1988.

13. Hod interview.

CHAPTER 17. THREE HOURS IN JUNE

1. Ezer Weizman with Dov Goldstein, *Le'cha Sha'maim, Le'cha Eretz* (Hebrew) (Tel Aviv: Ma'ariv, 1975), 258. Also published in English as *On Eagles' Wings* (New York: Macmillan, 1976.)

2. *Abba Eban: An Autobiography* (New York: Random House, 1977), 333.

3. Yitzhak Rabin, *The Rabin Memoirs* (Boston: Little, Brown, 1979), 73.

4. Rabin, 76.

5. Rabin, 76.

6. Moshe Dayan, *Avnei Derech* (Hebrew, Yediot Aharonot, second edition) (Jerusalem: Edanim Publishers and Tel Aviv: Dvir Publishing House, 1982), 399. Also published in English as *Story of My Life* (New York: Knopf, 1976).

7. Rabin, 82.

8. Weizman, 259.

9. Weizman, 264.

10. Rafi Harlev, in an interview with the author, Apr. 25, 1988.

11. Moti Hod, in an interview with the author, Jan. 31, 1988.

12. Weizman, 261.

13. Dayan, 429.

14. Shabtai Gilboa, in an interview with the author, Apr. 20, 1988.

15. Ran Ronen, *"Ne'filat Ha'nesher"* (Hebrew), an article in *Ye'diot Ah'ronot*, Tel Aviv, Oct. 31, 1986, 32. Also see Merav Halperin and Aharon Lapidot, *G Suit, Pages in the Logbook of the Israeli Air Force* (Hebrew) (Tel Aviv: Israel Defense Ministry, 1987), 32.

16. Oded Marom, in an interview with the author, July 25, 1988. Also in Halperin and Lapidot, 27.

17. Amichai Gal (not his real name), in an interview with the author, Aug. 2, 1988.
18. Halperin and Lapidot, 29.
19. Rafi Harlev, in an interview with the author, Apr. 25, 1988.
20. Weizman, 266.
21. Weizman, 267.
22. Dayan, 435.
23. *Israel Air Force* magazine, December 1967, 87.
24. Rabin, 104.
25. Weizman, 269.
26. Yak Nevo, in an interview with the author, Feb. 3, 1988.
27. Dayan, 433.

CHAPTER 18. KEEP IT SIMPLE

1. Menahem Shmul, in an interview with the author, Apr. 2, 1988.
2. Uri Even-Nir, in an interview with the author, July 28, 1988.
3. Yalo Shavit, in an interview with the author, July 16, 1987.
4. Menahem Shmul, in an interview with the author, Apr. 24, 1988.
5. Tzvika Vered, ed. *The First Jet Squadron* (Hebrew, classified) (Ramat David: Squadron 117, 1982), 45.
6. Yalo Shavit, in an interview with the author, July 16, 1987.
7. Ezer Weizman with Dov Goldstein, *Le'cha Sha'maim, Le'cha Eretz* (autobiography, Hebrew) (Tel Aviv: Ma'ariv, 1975), 284. Also published in English as *On Eagles' Wings* (New York: Macmillan, 1976).
8. Gad Eldar (not his real name), in an interview with the author, Nov. 20, 1988.

CHAPTER 19. "TEXAS"

1. *The First Fighter Squadron, a diary* (Hebrew, classified) (Hazor: Squadron 101, 1973), 141.
2. Oded Marom, in an interview with the author, July 25, 1988.
3. Yoram Agmon, in an interview with the author, July 28, 1988.
4. Marom interview.
5. Gad Eldar (not his real name), in an interview with the author, Dec. 20, 1988.
6. Iftach Spector, in an interview with the author, Apr. 21, 1988.
7. Yeheskiel Somekh, in an interview with the author, July 27, 1988.
8. Beni Peled, in an interview with the author, July 21, 1988.
9. Moti Hod, in an interview with the author, July 17, 1987.

10. Uri Even-Nir, in an interview with the author, July 28, 1988.
11. David Ivri, in an interview with the author, May 7, 1989.

CHAPTER 20. PHANTOMS

1. Yitzhak Rabin, *The Rabin Memoirs* (Boston: Little, Brown, 1979), 151.
2. Mohamed Fawzi, *The Three-Year War* (Arabic), quoted in Dan Schueftan's *"Attrition"* (Hebrew) (Tel Aviv: Israel Defense Ministry, 1989), 250.
3. Ze'ev Schiff, *The Israel Air Force* (Hebrew). Volume III in *The IDF and Its Arms—Encyclopedia for Military and Security* (Hebrew) (Tel Aviv: Revivim Publishing, 1981), 140.
4. Moti Hod, in an interview with the author, July 17, 1987.
5. Rami Harpaz, in an interview with the author, Aug. 3, 1988.
6. Dan Schueftan, "From the Six-Day War to the War of Attrition" (Hebrew), *Ma'arachot* 257 (August 1977): 8.
7. Eitan Ben Eliahu, in an interview with the author, Apr. 30, 1989.
8. David Ivri, in an interview with the author, May 7, 1989.
9. Eitan Peled, in an interview with the author, May 8, 1989.
10. Oded Marom, in an interview with the author, July 25, 1988.
11. Yair David, in an interview with the author, Aug. 4, 1988.
12. Yoram Agmon, in an interview with the author, July 28, 1988.
13. Jacob Agasi, in an interview with the author, May 17, 1989.
14. Menachem Eini, in an interview with the author, Aug. 1, 1988.

CHAPTER 21. MISSILES

1. Yitzhak Rabin, in an interview with the author, July 31, 1988.
2. Eitan Ben Eliahu, in an interview with the author, Apr. 30, 1989.
3. Yoram Agmon, in an interview with the author, July 28, 1988.
4. Iftach Spector, in interviews with the author, Apr. 21, 1988, and Nov. 22, 1988.
5. Menachem Eini, in an interview with the author, Aug. 1, 1988.
6. Uri Even-Nir, in an interview with the author, July 28, 1988.
7. Jacob Agasi, in an interview with the author, May 17, 1989.
8. Moti Hod, in an interview with the author, July 20, 1987.
9. Merav Halperin and Aharon Lapidot, *G Suit, Pages in the Logbook of the Israeli Air Force* (Hebrew) (Tel Aviv: 1987) Israel Defense Ministry, 70.
10. *The One and Only 221, 1969–1982* (Hebrew, classified) (Hazor, Squadron 221, 1982).
11. Oded Marom, in an interview with the author, July 25, 1988.

CHAPTER 22. JUDGMENT DAY

1. Beni Peled, in an interview with the author, Apr. 7, 1985.
2. Oded Marom, in an interview with the author, Nov. 27, 1988.
3. Giora Furman, in an interview with the author, Nov. 17, 1988.
4. Beni Peled, in an interview with the author, Apr. 19, 1988.
5. Gad Eldar (not his real name), in an interview with the author, Nov. 21, 1988.
6. Shlomo Nakdimon, *Low Probability* (Hebrew) (Tel Aviv: Revivim Publishing, Yediot Aharonot edition, 1982), 22.
7. Nakdimon, 23.
8. Nakdimon, 61.
9. Iftach Spector, in an interview with the author, Nov. 22, 1988.
10. Moshe Dayan, *Avnei Derech* (2nd Hebrew edition) (Jerusalem and Tel Aviv: Edanim Publishers with Dvir Publishing House, 1982), 593. Also published in English as *Story of My Life* (New York: William Morrow, 1976).

CHAPTER 23. *OPERATZIOT*

1. Eitan Peled, in an interview with the author, May 15, 1989.
2. Iftach Spector, in an interview with the author, Nov. 28, 1988.
3. Amos Amir, in an interview with the author, Nov. 28, 1988.
4. Yoram Agmon, in an interview with the author, Nov. 28, 1988.
5. Moshe Dayan, *Avnei Derech* (2nd Hebrew edition) (Jerusalem and Tel Aviv: Edanim Publishers with Dvir Publishing House, 1982), 596. Also appeared in English as *Story of My Life* (New York: William Morrow, 1976).
6. Dayan, 594.
7. Dayan, 601.

CHAPTER 24. LEGACIES

1. Beni Peled, in an interview with the author, July 21, 1988.
2. Gad Eldar (not his real name), in an interview with the author, Nov. 21, 1988.
3. Iftach Spector, in an interview with the author, Nov. 22, 1988.
4. Rafi Sivron, in an interview with the author, Apr. 26, 1988.
5. Sivron interview.
6. *Israel Air Force* magazine (Hebrew), February 1984, 18.
7. Ibid., 18.
8. Ibid., 20.
9. Oded Marom, in an interview with the author, Nov. 27, 1988.

10. Beni Peled, in an interview with the author, Nov. 20, 1990.
11. Gad Eldar (not his real name), in a handwritten manuscript (Hebrew, unpublished), describing his eighteen air kills.
12. Ezer Weizman with Dov Goldstein, *Le'cha Sha'maim, Le'cha Eretz* (autobiography, Hebrew) (Tel Aviv: Ma'ariv, 1975), 329. Also published in English as *On Eagles' Wings* (New York: Macmillan, 1976).

EPILOGUE: A FOREIGN FORCE, BUT FRIENDLY

1. Brig. Gen. Amos Amir, in an interview with the author, Nov. 21, 1991.
2. Merav Halperin and Aharon Lapidot, *G Suit, Pages in the Logbook of the Israeli Air Force* (Hebrew) (Tel Aviv: Israel Defense Ministry, 1987), 46.

SOURCES

I. GENERAL BIBLIOGRAPHY

Abba Eban: An Autobiography. New York: Random House, 1977.

Amir, Israel. *Unpaved Road*. Autobiography, Hebrew. Tel Aviv: Israel Ministry of Defense Publishing, 1988.

Avneri, Aryeh. *Ha'Mahaluma*. Hebrew. Tel Aviv: Revivim, 1983.

Bartov, Hanoch. *Daddo—48 Years and 20 More Days*. Gen. David Elazar biography, Hebrew. Tel Aviv: Ma'ariv Book Guild, 1978.

Bar-Zohar, Michael. *Ben Gurion*. Hebrew, abridged edition. Tel Aviv: Israel Ministry of Defense and Magal Publishing, 1986.

Ben-Porat, E., E. Haber, and Z. Schiff. *Entebbe Flight 139*. Hebrew. Tel Aviv: Zmora Bitan Publishing, 1990.

Cohen, Eliezer "Cheetah," and Zvi Lavi. *The Sky Is Not the Limit*. Autobiography, Hebrew. Tel Aviv: Ma'ariv Book Guild, 1990.

Dayan, Moshe. *Avnei Derech*. Autobiography, Hebrew, Yediot Aharonot second edition. Jerusalem: Edanim Publishers, and Tel Aviv: Dvir Publishing House, 1982. Also published in English as *Story of My Life* (New York: Knopf, 1976.)

Eitan, Maj. Gen. (ret.) Rafael "Raful." *A Soldier's Story*. Autobiography, Hebrew. Tel Aviv: Ma'ariv Library, 1985.

Gelber, Yoav. *The Emergence of a Jewish Army, the Veterans of the British Army in the IDF*. Hebrew. Jerusalem: Yad Izhak Ben-Zvi Institute, 1986.

Gunston, Bill. *An Illustrated Guide to the Israeli Air Force.* New York: Arco Publishing, 1982.

——. *Modern Fighters and Attack Aircraft.* New York: Prentice-Hall Press, 1987.

Haber, Eitan. *Today War Will Break Out.* Hebrew. Tel Aviv: Edanim Publishers, 1987.

Halperin, Merav, and Aharon Lapidot. *G Suit, Pages in the Logbook of the Israeli Air Force.* Hebrew. Tel Aviv: Israel Defense Ministry, 1987.

Heikal, Mohamed H. *Cutting the Lion's Tail.* New York: Arbor House, 1987.

Herzog, Chaim. *The Arab-Israeli Wars.* London: Arms and Armour Press, 1982.

Kagan (ret.), Col. Benjamin. *Hem Himri'u Ba'alata.* Hebrew. Tel Aviv: Davar Publishing.

Mardor, Munia. *Strictly Illegal.* Hebrew. Tel Aviv: Ma'arachot Publishing, 1957.

Mason, Francis K. *Phantom—A Legend in Its Own Time.* Osceola, Wis.: Motorbooks International, 1984.

McKinnon, Dan. *Bulls-eye One Reactor.* San Diego: House of Hits, 1987.

Meir, Golda. *My Life.* New York: G.P. Putnam's Sons, 1975.

Members, *Kfar Yehoshua in Its Jubilee (1927–1977).* Hebrew. Tel Aviv: Sifryiat Ha'Poalim Publishing, 1982.

Mersky, Peter B., and Norman Polmar. *The Naval Air War in Vietnam.* Annapolis: Nautical and Aviation Publishing Company of America, 1981.

Milstein, Uri. *The War of Independence.* Vol. 1. *The Roots of the Struggle.* Hebrew. Tel Aviv: Zmora Bitan Publishing, 1989.

——. *The War of Independence.* Vol. 2. *The First Month.* Hebrew. Tel Aviv: Zmora Bitan Publishing, 1989.

——. *The War of Independence.* Vol. 3. *The First Invasion.* Hebrew. Tel Aviv: Zmora Bitan Publishing, 1989.

——. *The History of the Israel Paratroopers.* Hebrew. Tel Aviv: Schalgi Ltd Publishing House, 1985.

Nakdimon, Shlomo. *Low Probability.* Hebrew. Tel Aviv: Revivim Publishing, Yediot Aharonot Edition, 1982.

Neuner, Ithamar. *Six O'Clock Position, As Usual.* Hebrew. Tel Aviv: Kineret Publishing, 1990.

Nordeen, Lon O., Jr. *Air Warfare in the Missile Age.* Washington, D.C.: Smithsonian Institution Press, 1985.

Rabin, Yitzhak. *The Rabin Memoirs.* Boston: Little, Brown, 1979.

Rivlin, G., and Dr. E. Orren, eds. *The War of Independence, Ben Gurion's Diary.* Hebrew. Tel Aviv: Israel Ministry of Defense Publishing, 1982.

Rubinstein, Murray, and Richard Goldman. *Shield of David, An Illustrated History of the Israeli Air Force.* Englewood Cliffs, N.J.: Prentice-Hall, 1978.

Schiff, Ze'ev. *The Israel Air Force.* Hebrew. Vol. 3 in *The IDF and Its Arms—Encyclopedia for Military and Security.* Hebrew. Tel Aviv: Revivim Publishing, 1981.

———. *Phantom Over the Nile.* Hebrew. Haifa: Shikmona Publishing Company Ltd., 1970.

——— and Ehud Ya'ari. *Israel's Lebanon War.* New York: Simon & Schuster, 1984.

Schueftan, Dan. *Attrition—Egypt's Post–War Political Strategy 1967–1970.* Hebrew. Tel Aviv: Ministry of Defense, 1989.

el Shazly, Lt. Gen Saad. *The Crossing of the Suez.* Hebrew edition. Tel Aviv: Ma'archot Publishing, Israel Defense Ministry, 1987.

Shteigman, Maj. Itzhak. *Operation "Kadesh."* Hebrew, classified. Tel Aviv: Israel Defense Forces, The Air Force, IAF History Branch, 1986.

———. *From the War of Independence to Operation Kadesh.* Hebrew, unclassified. Tel Aviv: Israel Defense Forces, The Air Force, IAF History Branch, 1990.

Slater, Leonard. *The Pledge.* New York: Simon & Schuster, 1970.

Steven, Stewart. *The Spymasters of Israel.* New York: Macmillan Publishing Company, 1980.

Taylor, Michael J. H. *Missiles of the World.* New York: Charles Scribner's Sons, 1980.

Waddell, Col. Dewey, et al., eds. *Air War—Vietnam.* New York: Arno Press, 1978.

Wallach, Col. Jehuda, Moshe Lissak, and Shimon Shamir. *Carta's Atlas of Israel.* Hebrew. Jerusalem: Carta, 1980.

Weizman, Ezer, with Dov Goldstein. *Le'cha Sha'maim, Le'cha Eretz.* Autobiography, Hebrew. Tel Aviv: Ma'ariv, 1975. Also published in English as *On Eagles' Wings.* New York: Macmillan, 1976.

2. IAF PUBLICATIONS AND MANUSCRIPTS

The Air Force in the "Yom Kippur War." Tel Aviv: Israel Ministry of Defense Publishing, Israel Air Force, IAF History Branch, 1975.

The First Fighter Squadron, a diary. Hebrew, classified. Hazor: Squadron 101, 1973.

Meir, Amitai, ed. *In Day, Night and Fog.* Hebrew, classified. Tel Nof: Squadron 191, 1981.

The One and Only 221: 1969–1982. Hebrew, classified. Hazor: Squadron 221, 1982.

Squadron Pilots Recall the Six Day War. Hebrew, untitled, unpublished, classified. Tel Nof: Squadron 191, 1968.

20 La'Tayeset (1948–1968). Hebrew, classified. Hazor: Squadron 101, 1968.

Vered, Tzvika, ed. *The First Jet Squadron.* Hebrew, classified. Ramat David: Squadron 117, 1982.

3. INTERVIEWS

Jacob Agasi, May 17, 1989.

Yoram Agmon, July 28, 1988; Nov. 28, 1988.

Ido Ambar, May 8, 1989.

Amos Amir, Nov. 28, 1988; Nov. 21, 1991.

Sidney Antin, July 14, 1986.

Rudy Augarten, May 29, 1986.

Harry Axelrod, Dec. 24, 1982.

Gera "Grisha" Bar On (Braun), Dec. 14, 1985.

Menachem Bar (Bernstein), Oct. 13, 1985; Dec. 22, 1985.

Harry Barak (Krasenstein), Dec. 12, 1985; April 17, 1988.

Eitan Ben-Eliahu, April 30, 1989; May 3, 1989.

Adi Bnaya, July 26, 1988.

Eliezer "Cheetah" Cohen, Feb. 3, 1988.

Sid Cohen, Dec. 15, 1985.

Maurice Commanday, Oct. 11, 1982.

Yair David, Aug. 4, 1988.

Menahem Eini, Aug. 1, 1988.

Gad Eldar (not real name), Nov. 20–21, 1988.

Al Ellis, Jan. 4, 1982.

Gideon Elrom, Dec. 19, 1985; Oct. 25, 1987.

Uri Even-Nir, July 28, 1988.

Achikar Eyal, July 26, 1988.

Eli Eyal, April 11, 1983.

Aaron "Red" Finkel, undated.

Giora Furman, April 25, 1988; Nov. 17, 1988.

Amichai Gal (not real name), Aug. 2, 1988.

Yeshayahu "Shaya" Gazit (Schwartzman), Dec. 16 and 24, 1985; April 16, 1986; Dec. 24, 1986; July 14, 1987; Feb. 2, 1988.

Shabtai "Gromek" Gilbo'a, April 20, 1988.

Coleman Goldstein, Oct. 24, 1984.

Chalmers "Slick" Goodlin, Sept. 19, 1986.

Norik Har'el, Aug. 22, 1982.

Raphael Harlev, April 25, 1988.

Rami Harpaz, Aug. 3, 1988.

Moti Hod (Fine), April 13, 1983; Dec. 16 and 24, 1985; Nov. 9, 1986; July 17 and 20, 1987; Jan. 31, 1988; May 6 and 8, 1990.

Penina Hod, Jan. 26, 1988.

David Ivri, May 7, 1989; May 15, 1990.

Julius Ahron "Bill" Kaiser, Dec. 16, 1986.

Yehuda Koren, July 26, 1988.

Shlomo Lahat (Landau), Feb. 6, 1988.

Lou Lenart, Oct. 17 and 21, 1982; Oct. 24, 1984.

George Lichter, Dec. 17 and 22, 1982.

Ze'ev Liron (Londoner), April 19, 1986; Jan. 26, 1988; Feb. 2, 1988.

Oded Marom, April 25, 1988; Aug. 1, 1988; Nov. 27, 1988.

Joseph Na'or, undated.

Jacob "Yak" Nevo (Milner), Dec. 12, 1985; July 9 and 26, 1987; Feb. 3, 1988.

Leo Nomis, May 31, 1986.

Benjamin "Beni" Peled (Feldman), April 7, 1985; April 19, 1988; July 21, 1988.

Eitan Peled, May 8 and 15, 1989.

Moshe Peled (Weidenfeld), Oct. 6, 1985; Dec. 23, 1985.

Yitzhak Rabin, July 31, 1988.

Aharon Remez, April 1 and 12, 1983; June 24, 1986.

Ran Ronen (Pecker), April 14, 1983.

Meir Roof, Dec. 19, 1985.

Yohanan Rosner, July 24, 1988.

Boris Senior, June 21, 1986.

Uri Shahar, Nov. 29, 1988.

Danny Shapira, Oct. 14, 1985; Feb. 1, 1988.

Aharon "Yalo" Shavit (Yalovsky), April 20, 1983; Oct. 17, 1985; July 16 and 22, 1987.

Menahem Shmul, April 24, 1988.

Rafi Sivron, Oct. 21, 1987; Feb. 2 and 3, 1988; April 26, 1988.

Yeheskiel Somekh, July 27, 1988.

Iftach Spector, April 21, 1988; Nov. 22, 1988.

Dan Tolkowsky, Dec. 24, 1985; July 20, 1986; Nov. 19, 1986; Jan. 27, 1988.

Yoash Tsiddon (Chato), Oct. 26, 1987.

Adam Tsivoni, Dec. 17, 1985.

Joseph Tsuk, June 22, 1986.

Ezer Weizman, April 21 and 26, 1983; July 23, 1986; July 21 and 28, 1987; Jan. 25 and 31, 1988.

Denny Wilson, July 14, 1986.

Tsahik Yavneh, Dec. 16, 1985.

Aharon Yoeli, Oct. 16, 1985; July 27, 1987.

MEDITERRANEAN
SEA

Homs •

Tripoli •

BEKAA VALLEY

Dumeir •

Beirut ⊙

LEBANON

Damascus ⊙

▲ MT. HERMON

GOLAN
HEIGHTS ←

ISRAEL

TEL FARES

SEA OF
GALILEE

GAMALA GRADE

Haifa •

Galilee •

Ramat
David • • Nazareth

Mafraq •

WEST
BANK

• Tel
Aviv

⊙ Amman

Tel Nof •

Jerusalem
⊙

Hazor •

DEAD
SEA

GAZA
STRIP

THE NORTHERN FRONT

T-4 ■

Khabrat es Seigal

SYRIA

IRAQ

H-3 ■

JORDAN

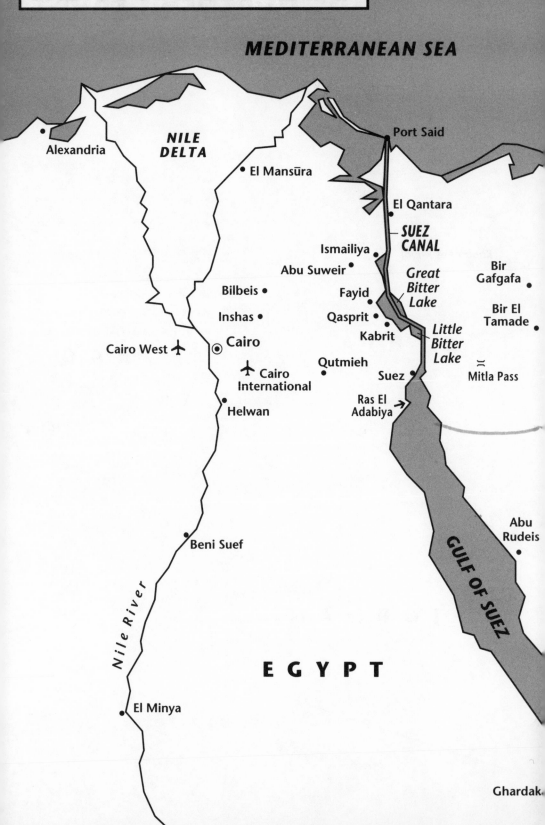

THE SOUTHERN FRONT

MEDITERRANEAN SEA

Alexandria

NILE DELTA

El Mansūra

Port Said

El Qantara

SUEZ CANAL

Ismailiya

Abu Suweir

Great Bitter Lake

Bir Gafgafa

Bilbeis

Fayid

Inshas

Qasprit

Bir El Tamade

Cairo West ✈

⊙ Cairo

Kabrit

Little Bitter Lake

✈ Cairo International

Qutmieh

Mitla Pass

Suez

Helwan

Ras El Adabiya →

Beni Suef

Abu Rudeis

GULF OF SUEZ

Nile River

E G Y P T

El Minya

Ghardak

INDEX

A-4 Skyhawk aircraft, IAF, 266,
    270, 274, 309, 313, 323, 326,
    358
  in War of Attrition, 282, 286,
    295, 298, 299
  in Yom Kippur War, 331, 335,
    346–47, 351–52
Abu Rudeis airstrip (Israel), 263
Abu Suweir air base (Egypt), 159n,
    171
  in Six-Day War, 236, 237, 240,
    243, 245
Afghanistan, 281
Agasi, Jacob, 130, 133–36, 189,
    291, 299
Agmon, Yoram, 218–19, 220,
    263–64, 287, 288, 294, 298,
    331, 334
Agronsky, Martin, 161
Ahikar, Eyal, 295
Airborne Warning and Control
    System (AWACS) aircraft,
    Saudi, 361

"Air Combat" (Nevo), 205
air-launched missiles, see missiles,
    air-launched
Air Ministry, British, 69
Air Transport Command, 71
al-Fattah, xin
Algeria, 142, 160, 281
Al Kussar, 256
Al Mazzah air base (Egypt), 159n
Alon, Joe, 122, 132, 190n
Alon, Mina, 50, 55–56
Alon, Modi, 24–25, 32, 34–35, 39,
    43, 49–50, 51, 53, 54,
    55–57, 72, 84, 127, 144, 370
Altalena, 39
AMAN (IDF Military Intelligence),
    162, 225, 266, 279, 314, 316,
    323, 341, 344, 345
Amer, Abd el Hakim, 161, 162,
    163n, 241n
Amin, Idi, 360
Amir, Amos, 330, 353, 365,
    366–67

Amman airfield (Jordan), 249
Andrews, Stanley, 41
Anglo-Egyptian Treaty (1936), 66
Anson bombers, *Haganah*, 8, 9
Antin, Sidney, 36–37, 43, 55–56
Antonov transports, EAF, 241
Arab-Israeli wars, *see* 1948 War;
    Sinai campaign; Six-Day
    War; War of Attrition; Yom
    Kippur War
Arab League, x, 28, 264
Arab Legion, Jordanian, 27, 30, 153
Arab Liberation Army, xiii, 37, 39,
    44, 59
Arafat, Yasser, xi*n*
Arazi, Yehuda, 7, 23–24
Argov, Shlomo, 357
Ariav, Omri, 130, 134–36
Army of Salvation, xi, xiii
Assad, Hafez al-, 225*n*, 312
AT-6 Harvard trainers, Syrian, xiii
Augarten, Rudy, 37, 43, 57, 61, 63,
    69, 71, 72, 87, 88, 92, 95,
    96, 97
Auster aircraft, *Haganah*, 21
Avidan, Shimon, 31, 33
AWACS (Airborne Warning and
    Control System) aircraft,
    Saudi, 361
Axelrod, Harry, 83, 84, 115, 137
Azzam Pasha, Abdul Rahman, x, 28

B-17 Flying Fortress bombers,
    Haganah, 7
B-17 Flying Fortress bombers, IAF,
    109, 159, 193
    in 1948 War, 41, 43, 44, 54, 57
    in Sinai campaign, 171, 173
B-25 bombers, *Haganah*, 7
B-26 Marauder bombers, 190, 207
Bader, Operation, 315
Baghdadi, Ali Mustafa, 271

Balfour, Arthur James, 75–76
Balfour Declaration, 75–76
Bar, Menahem, 102, 108, 119, 121,
    137, 138, 139, 146–47, 148,
    149–50, 171, 181, 197, 200,
    202, 215, 287, 308
    background of, 90–91
    Hod opposed by, 86–87, 88, 92,
        192
    jet training and, 123, 125–26
    105 squadron innovations of,
        92–95, 100–101, 124
    117 squadron formed by, 122
    at RAF training school, 98–99,
        100
    training methods of, 93–95,
        98–101
    Weizman and, 133–35
    Yoeli on, 123–24
Barak, Harry, 87, 111, 157
Barbarosa, Operation, 201
Bareket, Yeshayahu, 238, 239
Bari airfield (Italy), 9
Barker, Evelyn, 77–78
Barlev, Chaim, 264, 290
Barlev Line, 264, 312, 316
Bar On, Grisha, 79, 81, 84, 85–86,
    87, 88
Bar-On, Mordechai, 168
BBC, 244
Beaufighter dive-bombers, IAF,
    54–55, 59
Begin, Menachem, 39, 70, 231, 361,
    363
    Camp David treaty and, 355, 368
Beit Daras airfield (Israel), 32–33
Bekaa, battle of, 358, 363, 368–70
Ben Eliahu, Eitan, 283–84, 286,
    294, 296, 297, 306, 343, 354,
    363
Ben-Gurion, David, 14, 16, 18, 19,
    21, 23, 24, 28, 70, 108, 110,
    112, 113, 114, 116, 121, 126,

142, 143, 145, 146, 151n, 152, 154, 180, 181, 188, 229, 231
air doctrine and, 45–46
IAF-IDF relationship and, 102–6
Israeli statehood announced by, 27, 330
Mapam and, 38–39
MiG incident and, 183
Operation Dust Bowl and, 47–48
retirement of, 117
Sinai campaign and, 158, 160, 169, 171
White Paper and, 15
Beni Suef airfield (Egypt), 332
Ben-Nun, Avihu, 238, 241, 284–85, 287, 295, 296, 297, 299, 301, 325–27, 334–35
Ben Porat, Pinya, 24–25, 27
Berg, Joseph, 66n
Bernadotte af Wisborg, Count Folke, 47
Bernstein, Penny, 90
Bernstein, Yitzhak, 90
Bilbeis air base (Egypt), 243
Biram, Dr., 107
Bir El Tamade air base (Egypt), 236
Bir Gafgafa airstrip (Egypt), 236
Bir Gafgafa airstrip (Israeli-occupied), 267–69, 270, 273, 290, 300, 304, 318, 320
Black Arrow, Operation, 143
Black September, xin
Black Sheep Squadron, U.S., 37
Bloch, Lionel, 42, 43
Boeing 707 aircraft, IAF, 359, 362
Bourgès-Maunoury, Maurice, 146, 152
Boxer, Operation, 274–75, 278, 287
Boyington, Pappy, 37
Brezhnev, Leonid, 279

Brindisi airfield (Italy), 3–5, 9, 147, 150, 151
Brown, Danni (pseudonym), 319, 320
BT-13 trainers, Haganah, 29

C-46 Commando transports, Haganah, 6, 7, 8, 24, 29
C-46 Commando transports, IAF, 46, 47, 54, 57
C-47 Dakota aircraft, EAF, xix
  in 1948 War, 34–35
C-47 Dakota aircraft, IAF, 109, 145
  in 1948 War, 41, 54
  in Sinai campaign, 155–57, 161, 167, 174
C-54 Skymaster aircraft, 29
C-54 Skymaster aircraft, IAF, 46
C-130 Hercules transports, IAF, 313, 359–60
Cairo East air base (Egypt), 171
Cairo International Airport, 254
Cairo West air base (Egypt), 158, 159n, 171
  in Six-Day War, 236, 237, 240–41, 242
Camp David treaty, 355, 368
Canada, 140
Canberra aircraft, RAF, 171
Central Intelligence Agency (CIA), 53, 314
České Budějovice air base (Czechoslovakia), 25, 29, 63
CH-53 helicopters, IAF, 286
Chevra Kadisha, 226
China, People's Republic of, 281
Churchill, Winston, 69
Chuvakhin, Dmitri, 225n
Cohen, Eddie, 4, 9–10, 24, 32
Cohen, Eliezer "Cheetah," 198, 257
Cohen, Joe, 79, 87
Cohen, Sid, 37, 42–43, 51, 56, 61, 63, 68–69, 71, 72

"Command and Staff Structure"
     (Laskov), 113
Command Order 63, 112, 114
Command Order 81, 104–5
Commando transports, *see* C-46
     Commando transports
Constellation aircraft, *Haganah*, 7
Constellation aircraft, IAF, 149
Cordage operation plan, 153
Costa, Joel, 97–98, 108
Czechoslovakia, 53, 145*n*
   IAF equipped and trained by,
     24–26
Czechoslovakian Air Force, 120

Dakota aircraft, *see* C-47 Dakota
     aircraft
Dangott, Cesar, 71, 72
David, Yair, 286, 288, 302
Dayan, Moshe, 86, 112–13, 135,
     139, 140–41, 144, 145–46,
     151*n*, 152, 178–79, 180,
     231, 233, 238, 239, 254–55,
     256, 265, 271, 279, 281, 290,
     299, 306
   IAF criticized by, 321
   Makleff replaced by, 117
   missile offensive opposed by,
     334–35
   Peled's meeting with, 327–28,
     330
   preemptive strike opposed by,
     311
   pullback proposed by, 336
   on Rabin, 229
   Sinai campaign and, 160, 165,
     167, 171, 174
   on Six-Day War victory, 244
   "Third Temple" warning of,
     329–31
   Weizman and, 84–85
Dayan, Ruth, 84
Dayan, Shmuel, 135

DC-6 aircraft, U.S., 190
Dean, Patrick, 154
Defense Department, U.S., 293,
     351–52
Defense Ministry, Israeli, 39, 139
de Gaulle, Charles, 187
Delilah drones, 369
Desert Storm, Operation, 253*n*
DH Dragon Rapide light
     transports, *Haganah*, 20
DH Tiger Moth biplanes,
     Haganah, 20, 21
Dori, Jacob, 102, 104
Dougman V, Operation, 331,
     332–34, 350, 353
Dougman V operation plan,
     310–11, 315, 326, 327–28
Douhet, Giulio, 201
Doyle, Jack, 57
Dragon Rapide light transports,
     Haganah, 20
Dulles, John Foster, 152, 161
Dumeir airfield (Syria), 251
Dust Bowl, Operation, 47–48, 117,
     155

Eagle (F-15) fighters, IAF, 361–62,
     367, 369
Eban, Abba, 37, 96*n*, 161, 229
Eden, Anthony, 153
Egozi, Shlomo, 318, 320
Egozi, Yeshayahu, 165, 169
Egypt, xix, 61, 66, 76*n*, 109, 110,
     129, 141, 187, 210, 211, 220,
     225, 230, 232, 254, 321, 329,
     334, 361
   Camp David treaty and, 355, 368
   Czechoslovakia and, 145*n*
   Great Britain and, 142
   1948 armistice signed by, 70
   Six-Day War aftermath and, 265
   Soviet arms deal of, 145–46
   Suez Canal nationalized by, 148

Yemen and, 224
see also specific wars
Egyptian air bases:
Abu Suweir, 159*n*, 171
in Six-Day War, 236, 237, 240, 243, 245
Al Mazzah, 159*n*
Beni Suef, 332
Bilbeis, 243
Bir El Tamade, 236
Bir Gafgafa, 236
Cairo East, 171
Cairo International Airport, 254
Cairo West, 158, 159*n*, 171
in Six-Day War, 236, 237, 240–41, 242
El 'Arīsh, 131, 182–83, 210
in 1948 War, 30–31, 40, 41–42, 52, 54, 57–58
in Sinai campaign, 169, 170
in Six-Day War, 241, 254, 255
El Mansūra, 243
El Minya, 243
Fayid, 159*n*, 161
in Six-Day War, 236, 237–38, 241
Ghardaka, 243, 247–49, 318–19
Helwân, 243
Inshas, 159*n*, 171, 240, 242, 243, 251
Kabrit, 159*n*, 161, 171
in Six-Day War, 241, 243
Luxor, 159*n*, 243
Qasprit, 159*n*, 161
Egyptian Air Force (EAF), 142, 232, 250, 290, 313
Egyptian Air Force (EAF) aircraft:
Antonov transports, 241
C-47 Dakota aircraft, xiii
in 1948 War, 34–35
F-8 Meteor fighters, 109, 110, 121, 159*n*, 169, 170
G-55 Fiat fighters, 57

Hawker Fury fighters, 130–31
helicopters, 320
IL-14 transports, 162–63, 243
IL-28 bombers, 145, 158, 159*n*, 171, 241, 245
MiG fighters, 148, 159*n*, 169–70, 171, 190, 318–19
in Six-Day War, 241, 243
in War of Attrition, 267, 269, 271, 274
in Yom Kippur War, 354–55
MiG-15 fighters, 145, 146, 164–66, 205
MiG-17 fighters, 145, 183, 219, 243, 273, 319–20
MiG-19 fighters, 180
MiG-21 fighters, 187
in Six-Day War, 240, 241, 242, 247–48, 249
in War of Attrition, 261–63, 271, 272, 279, 298–301
in Yom Kippur War, 319–20
Spitfire fighters, xiii
in 1948 War, 27–28, 30–32, 34, 41–43, 55, 57, 61, 62, 65, 201
SU-15 attack jets, 264
Tupolev-16 bombers, 241, 242
Vampire fighters, 109, 110, 121, 143–44, 145, 159*n*, 164, 169
Egyptian military units:
First Armored Brigade, 166
Palestinian Brigade, 143
Second Armored Brigade, 30
Second Army, 351, 352, 353
Second Brigade, 164
Third Army, 351, 352, 353, 354
890 Paratroopers Battalion, IDF, 128, 143*n*, 157
Eilat, 264
Eini, Menachem, 290, 291, 295, 296–97, 298
Eisenberg, David, 214

Eisenberg, Dinah, 214
Eisenhower, Dwight D., 146, 161
Eitan, Rafael, 157, 169, 254, 357, 363
El Al airline, 71, 128, 188
El 'Arīsh air base (Egypt), 131, 182–83, 210
  in 1948 War, 30–31, 40, 41–42, 52, 54, 57–58
  in Sinai campaign, 169, 170
  in Six-Day War, 241, 254, 255
Elazar, David "Dado," 222, 256, 290, 310, 311, 314, 315, 327–28, 330, 336, 352, 355
Eldar, Gad (pseudonym), 255, 267–68, 273, 311–12, 343, 348–49, 354–55
El-Hamma incidents, 95–98
Elkins, Michael, 244
Ellis, Al, 365–66, 369
El Mansūra air base (Egypt), 243
El Minya air base (Egypt), 243
Elon, Josh (pseudonym), 319, 320
Elrom, Gideon, 181
Enola Gay, 186
Entebbe mission, 359–60, 363, 364
Eshel, Joshua, 19–20
Eshel, Moshe, 170
Eshkol, Levi, 151n, 217, 222, 225, 226, 229, 230, 231, 238, 276
Etkes, Jonathan, 173
Even-Nir, Uri, 250, 272, 274, 298, 305
Exodus (Uris), 49
Eyal, Eli, 133, 147
Ezion Block, xii, 21, 27, 130

F-4 Phantom fighters, IAF, 266, 270, 277–78, 309, 313, 314, 323, 324, 325–26, 369
  in War of Attrition, 278–91, 293–303

  in Yom Kippur War, 318–20, 322, 328, 329, 332, 333, 337, 347–48, 351–52, 353, 354
F-8 Meteor fighters, EAF, 109, 110, 121, 159n, 169, 170
F-8 Meteor fighters, IAF, 112, 132, 133, 139, 140, 141, 143–44, 148, 162, 171, 198, 202–3
  in Sinai campaign, 155–57, 159, 161, 165
  in Six-Day War, 236
F-8 Meteor fighters, Syrian, 109, 121
F-8 Meteor trainers, IAF, 121–25, 130
F-15 Eagle fighters, IAF, 361–62, 367, 369
F-16 Fighting Falcon fighters, IAF, 361–62, 367, 369
F-86 Sabrejet fighters, 139–40, 146, 151
F-104 Star Fighters, 186
Factor, Max, 6
Faruk I, King of Egypt, 43
Fawzi, Mohamed, 278
Fayid air base (Egypt), 159n, 161
  in Six-Day War, 236, 237–38, 241
Feisal, Prince of Saudi Arabia, 76n
Feldman, Cy, 79, 82, 88
Felix, Otto, 23–24
Fiat G-55 fighters, EAF, 57
Fighting Falcon (F-16) fighters, IAF, 361–62, 367, 369
Fine, Chaim-Moshe, 214
Fine, Joseph, 214–15
Fine, Menucha, 214–15
Fine, Mordechai, see Hod, Moti
Fine, Yocheved, 214
Finkel, Aaron, 36–37, 50, 51, 52, 56, 60, 63, 72, 78
First Armored Brigade, Egyptian, 166

Flying Fortress bombers, *see* B-17
    Flying Fortress bombers
Flynt, Mitchell, 37, 72
Fouga Magister trainers, IAF, 198,
    254
France, 110, 123, 139, 140, 141,
    144, 145, 146, 147
    Foreign Office of, 187
    Great Britain and, 153–54
    Israeli military treaty with,
        148–54
    Sinai campaign and, 160–61,
        166, 171–72, 174
    Six-Day War aftermath and, 266
French Air Force, 140, 148, 149,
    185, 187
Frog surface-to-surface missiles,
    Syrian, 347
Furman, Giora, 208, 309, 312,
    330–31
Fury fighters, EAF, 130–31
Fury fighters, Iraqi, xix

G-55 Fiat fighters, EAF, 57
Gal, Amichai (pseudonym), 237,
    240, 250
Gazit, Yeshayahu "Shaya," 106,
    108–9, 110, 111, 149, 150,
    151, 159, 168, 184, 185,
    188–89, 209, 215, 216
    computers and, 200
    as Flight School commander,
        193–97
    Weizman's confrontations with,
        197–200
Gazit, Zehava, 185, 195
Gelber, Yoav, 102
Ghardaka air base (Egypt), 243,
    247–49, 318–19
Gilboa, Shabtai, 222–23, 224, 234
Givati Brigade, 30, 31, 55
Glubb Pasha, John Bagot, 153

Golan Heights, 311, 315, 330, 351,
    355
    Six-Day War and, 256–57
    Tel Fares battle and, 346–48
Goldman, Menachem (pseudonym),
    366, 369
Goldstein, Coleman, 4–5, 8–12, 147
Gonen, Samuel, 336
Goodlin, Chalmers "Slick," 66–67,
    71
Great Britain, xiii, 15, 98, 109, 112,
    121, 139, 160
    Egypt and, 142
    Franco-Israeli treaty and, 153–54
    Jordan and, 153
    Palestine and, ix–xi, 75–76
    reconnaissance episodes and,
        66–69
    Sinai campaign and, 160–61,
        166, 171–72, 174
    UN and, 61
Gur, Mordechai "Mota," 359, 363

H-3 air base (Iraq), 253
HaCohen, David, 17
Haganah, xiii–xiv, 7, 8, 18, 22,
    23–24, 44, 76–77, 80, 107,
    108, 120
    IAF and, 13–16, 19–20
    see also Palmach
Haganah Air Service, 10, 13,
    19–21, 27, 44, 78, 90, 91,
    94, 115
    Squadron A, 20
Haganah Air Service aircraft:
    Anson bombers, 8, 9
    Auster aircraft, 21
    B-17 Flying Fortress bombers, 7
    B-25 bombers, 7
    BT-13 trainers, 29
    C-46 Commando transports, 6, 7,
        8, 24, 29

Haganah Air Service (*cont'd*)
Constellation aircraft, 7
DH Dragon Rapide light
transports, 20
DH Tiger Moth biplanes, 20, 21
Messerschmitt fighters "Czech
Knives," 23, 24, 25–27,
29–30
Norseman aircraft, 3–5, 8–12,
27, 147
P-47 Thunderbolt aircraft, 7
P-51 Mustang fighters, 7, 24
Piper Cub aircraft, 20
RWD aircraft, 20
Taylorcraft light trainers, 20
Haifa Flight Club, 77, 121, 193
Harb al-Istinzaf, see War of
Attrition
Harlev, Rafi, 222, 223, 224, 227,
231, 233–34, 238, 239, 295,
312, 317
Harpaz, Rami, 282, 285, 287, 288,
295
Harvard aircraft, IAF, 96, 145, 159,
170, 198
Harvard aircraft, Syrian, xiii, 42
Hataf attack tactic, 239–40
Hawker Fury fighters, EAF, 130–31
Hawker Fury fighters, Iraqi, xiii
Hawkeye aircraft, IAF, 368–69
Hawk surface-air missiles, Israeli,
319
Hazerim air base (Israel), 324, 332,
347
Hazor air base (Israel), 108, 109,
124, 141, 143, 153, 208,
220*n*, 308, 309
in 1948 War, 59, 67, 68
101 Squadron moved to, 146–51
in Sinai campaign, 156, 163, 168,
170
in Six-Day War, 235, 236, 237
training at, 71

in War of Attrition, 267, 277,
284, 295
in Yom Kippur War, 322, 332,
354
helicopters, Egyptian, 320
Helwân air base (Egypt), 243
Henkin, Ehud, 333
Hercules transports, IAF, 313,
359–60
Herzl, Theodor, 14
Herzliyya air base (Israel), 40,
41–43, 55, 59, 60
Herzog, Chaim, 48
Hetz, Shmuel, 284–85, 287, 290,
294–98, 323, 324, 358
Hitler, Adolf, xi, 15
Hod, Moti, 63, 70, 71, 81, 82–83,
84, 86, 87, 92, 98, 99, 100,
111, 122, 134, 135–36, 138,
146–47, 148, 149–50, 156,
157, 159, 169, 173, 179, 200,
205, 206, 227, 230, 231,
246–47, 257, 298, 304*n*,
305, 306, 345, 346, 347, 367,
370
background of, 214–15
Hunter air battle and, 220–21
MiG incident and, 182–83
MiG kills and, 218–19, 221–22,
223
Palmach opposition to, 86–87,
88, 92, 192
Peled's replacement of, 307–10
Six-Day War and, 232–33, 238,
239, 242–43
Soviet pilot ambush and,
299–302
Spector and, 262
"Third Temple" warning and,
331–32
War of Attrition and, 270–72,
277, 279, 281, 287, 290–91
Weizman replaced by, 216–19

Weizman's relationship with, 82–83, 192–93, 215–20, 224, 239
Hod, Pninah, 216
Hofi, Yitzhak, 317, 347
Holocaust, 330
Horev, Operation, 65–66
House of Commons, British, 69
Hoz, Dov, 17
hunt combat technique, 325, 354–55
Hunter aircraft, Jordanian, 220–21, 250, 253, 254
Hussein, King of Jordan, 153
Hussein, Saddam, 360–61, 368
Husseini, Abdel Kader al-, xi, xii
Husseini, Faisal, xi*n*
Husseini, Haj Amin al-, xi

Ibrahim al Awal, 256
IL-14 transports, EAF, 162–63, 243
IL-28 bombers, EAF, 145, 158, 159*n*, 171, 241, 245
Independence Day Air Crews Ball, 184, 185
Inshas air base (Egypt), 159*n*, 171, 240, 242, 243, 251
Intifada, xvii*n*
Iran, 361
Iran-Iraq War, 361
Iraq, xiii, 109, 226, 249, 250, 253, 362
  H-3 air base of, 253
  Israeli bombing of, 360–61
  1948 War and, 33–34, 37, 50
  in Yom Kippur War, 351
Iraqi aircraft:
  Hawker Fury fighters, xiii
  MiG fighters, 362
  MiG-21 fighters, 220*n*, 253
  Tupolev-16 bombers, 250*n*
  Vampire fighters, 109, 121
Iraq Suedan fortress, 58–59

Irgun Ze'vai Le'umi (IZL), 14–15, 39, 77–78
Israel Aircraft Industries (IAI), 246, 266, 365, 369
Israel Aviation Club, 90
Israeli air bases:
  Abu Rudeis (Israeli-occupied), 263
  Beit Daras, 32–33
  Bir Gafgafa (Israeli-occupied), 267–69, 270, 273, 290, 300, 304, 318, 320
  Hazerim, 324, 332, 347
  Hazor, 108, 109, 124, 141, 143, 153, 208, 220*n*, 308, 309
    in 1948 War, 59, 67, 68
    101 Squadron moved to, 146–51
    in Sinai campaign, 156, 163, 168, 170
    in Six-Day War, 235, 236, 237
    training at, 71
    in War of Attrition, 267, 277, 284, 295
    in Yom Kippur War, 322, 332, 354
  Herzliyya, 40, 41–43, 55, 59, 60
  Kfar Sirkin, 250
  Lod, 20, 149
  Megiddo, 249–50
  Ophir airfield (Israeli-occupied), 318, 319
  Ramat David (Air Force North), 72, 77, 108, 109, 118, 119, 141, 146, 151, 152, 156, 162, 181, 200, 202, 208, 216, 223, 266, 324, 342, 343
    Bar's innovations and, 91–95, 99–101
    El-Hamma incidents and, 95–98
    as IAF birthplace, 120
    in 1948 War, 40–41, 54, 68

Israeli air bases (cont'd)
　　in Six-Day War, 235, 236, 237,
　　　250, 253
　　training at, 79–88, 120–26
　　in War of Attrition, 277, 284,
　　　295, 299–300
　　Weizman and organization of,
　　　127–36
　　in Yom Kippur War, 322, 332,
　　　333, 346, 350, 351
　Ruhama, 47
　Sedeh Dov, 20
　Tel Aviv, 27–28
　Tel Nof, 153, 208, 266
　　in 1948 War, 29–30, 31, 40,
　　　46, 54, 65
　　in Sinai campaign, 155, 162
　　in Six-Day War, 235, 239
　　in War of Attrition, 271, 299
　　in Yom Kippur War, 322, 332,
　　　347
　　see also Israeli Air Force
　　branches, Flight School
Israeli Air Force (IAF):
　air doctrine and, 45–46, 93,
　　117–18
　basic missions of, 206
　character of, 120–21
　command and control system of,
　　166–68
　computerization of, 200, 366
　Egyptian Air Force compared
　　with, 159n
　fighter doctrine of, 120
　first jet kills by, 143–44
　first mission of, 31–33
　foreign volunteers and, 70–72,
　　79n
　Gazit–Weizman conflict and,
　　197–200
　insignia of, 110–11
　intelligence failure of, 340–41
　Iraqi MiG defector and, 220n

jet program in, 102, 122–25
Jewish war veterans in, 37
Laskov–Makleff rivalry and,
　107–8, 112–14
mission orders and, 344–45
morale and, 129
"physics" vs. "electronics"
　argument in, 324
pilot drain of, 180–81
Six-Day War aftermath and,
　265–66
training methods of, 93–94,
　98–101, 122–25
Israeli Air Force (IAF) aircraft:
　A-4 Skyhawk aircraft, 266, 270,
　　274, 309, 313, 323, 326, 358
　　in War of Attrition, 282, 286,
　　　295, 298, 299
　　in Yom Kippur War, 331, 335,
　　　346–47, 351–52
　B-17 Flying Fortress bombers,
　　109, 159, 193
　　in 1948 War, 41, 43, 44, 54, 57
　　in Sinai campaign, 171, 173
　Beaufighter dive-bombers, 54–55,
　　59
　Boeing 707 aircraft, 359, 362
　C-46 Commando transports, 46,
　　47, 54, 57
　C-47 Dakota aircraft, 109, 145
　　in 1948 War, 41, 54
　　in Sinai campaign, 155–57,
　　　161, 167, 174
　C-54 Skymaster aircraft, 46
　C-130 Hercules transports, 313,
　　359–60
　CH-53 helicopters, 286
　Constellation aircraft, 149
　F-4 Phantom fighters, 266, 270,
　　277–78, 309, 313, 314, 323,
　　324, 325–26, 369
　　in War of Attrition, 278–91,
　　　293–303

in Yom Kippur War, 318–20,
    322, 328, 329, 332, 333, 337,
    347–48, 351–52, 353, 354
F-8 Meteor fighters, 112, 132,
    133, 139, 140, 141, 143–44,
    148, 162, 171, 198, 202–3
    in Sinai campaign, 155–57,
        159, 161, 165
    in Six-Day War, 236
F-8 Meteor trainers, 121–25, 130
F-15 Eagle fighters, IAF, 361–62,
    367, 369
F-16 Fighting Falcon fighters,
    361–62, 367, 369
Fouga Magister trainers, 198, 254
Harvard dive-bombers, 170
Hawkeye aircraft, 368–69
Kfir aircraft, 365, 367, 369
M-5 Mirage aircraft, 266
Messerschmitt fighters "Czech
    Knives," 37, 63, 193, 201
    in 1948 War, 30, 31–35,
        39–44, 46, 52–55, 57, 61,
        68, 118
Mirage fighters, 185–87, 189–90,
    207, 209, 220–21, 223, 246,
    247, 278, 314, 317
    in Six-Day War, 232, 235, 236,
        237, 239, 240–41, 242, 245,
        249–56
    in War of Attrition, 261–64,
        271, 273, 274, 277, 283, 286,
        294, 295, 298, 299–301
    in water wars, 219
    in Yom Kippur War, 322, 329,
        349, 354–55
Mosquito fighter-bombers,
    109–10, 133–34, 144–45,
    146, 158, 159, 171, 173, 178,
    180, 193
Mystère IV fighters, 146–47, 148,
    150–51, 182, 184, 193, 204,
    209, 223, 308

in Sinai campaign, 156, 159,
    161–62, 165–66, 170, 171,
    173
in Six-Day War, 235, 236,
    237–38, 254
in water wars, 218
Nesher fighters, 313, 354
NF-13 Meteor night fighters, 162
Nord transports, 149, 250
Norseman aircraft, 41
Ouragan attack jets, 140–41, 145,
    146, 148, 189, 204, 209, 308
    in Sinai campaign, 156–57,
        159, 165, 168–70, 171–72
    in Six-Day War, 235, 236, 241,
        243
P-51 Mustang fighters, 61,
    68–69, 93, 99, 100, 110,
    135, 138, 146, 152, 157, 178
    capabilities of, 124–25
    in El-Hamma incidents, 95–96
    in Omer operation plan, 145
    in Sinai campaign, 159, 170,
        173
Piper Cub aircraft, 131, 144,
    164–65, 172–74
Spitfire fighters, 63, 84, 85, 90,
    93, 108, 109, 110, 128,
    131–32, 193
    British reconnaissance missions
        and, 67–68
    in El-Hamma incidents, 95–98
    in 1948 War, 53, 54–55, 57,
        58, 61, 62, 67–68
    in Operation Shashlik, 85
    transport of, 63–65
Stearman trainers, 159, 198
Stratocruiser transports, 305
Super-Mystère fighters, 180, 189,
    197, 205–6, 266, 326
    in Six-Day War, 235, 236, 241,
        242, 243, 251, 254, 256
    in water wars, 218

Israeli Air Force (*cont'd*)
  T-6 Harvard trainers, 96, 145,
      159, 198
  Vautour aircraft, 180, 189, 194,
      209, 223
    in Six-Day War, 235, 236, 242,
        243, 253, 254
    in water wars, 218
Israeli Air Force (IAF) branches:
  Air Section, 162, 178–80,
      192–93, 200, 211, 216, 309,
      345
  Air Staff College, 110, 206
  Combined Operations, 345
  Communications, 350
  Control, 167–68, 350
  Flight School, 92, 106, 159,
      193–200, 266
  Intelligence, 105, 200, 211, 312,
      324, 350
  Strike Planning, 289, 325, 342,
      349, 366
  Supplies, 199, 211
  Technical Requirements, 200,
      211–12, 291, 308, 309
  Training Command, 200,
      209–10, 216, 349, 364
Israeli Air Force (IAF) Operations,
      97, 145, 178, 200, 208, 209,
      211, 284, 298, 330, 363–64,
      365
  in Six-Day War, 223, 256
  in War of Attrition, 267, 269,
      289, 290
  Weizman as head of, 86
  in Yom Kippur War, 310, 311,
      312, 322, 324, 328, 329, 331,
      336, 340, 342, 345, 346, 350,
      353
Israeli Air Force (IAF) units:
  69 Squadron (Phantoms), 277,
      287
  101 (Red) Squadron, 109, 111,
      130, 184, 193, 221

  anti-Hod rebellion in, 86–87
  decline of, 87–88, 124
  El-Hamma incidents and
      (Mustangs), 95–96
  jet aircraft conversion of, 146
  Mirages of, 240, 261, 266, 277,
      294, 349
  Mustangs of, 99, 135, 138
  Mystères of, 146, 147, 148,
      159, 166, 171, 181
  in 1948 War (Messerschmitts;
      Spitfires), 39–40, 41–43,
      49–59, 60–72
  105 Squadron and, 92–93
  in Sinai campaign (Mystères),
      161–62, 171
  training of, 81–84, 99–100
  Weizman in command of,
      79–83
104 Squadron (Harvards), 170
105 Operational Training Unit,
    88, 92, 99, 100, 108
105 Squadron, 138
  Bar's innovations and, 92–95,
      100–101, 124
  El-Hamma incidents and
      (Spitfires), 95–98
  Mustangs of, 170
  Spitfires of, 109, 128
  Super-Mystères of, 251
109 Squadron (Mosquitos), 109,
    158
110 Squadron (Mosquitos), 173
113 Squadron (Ouragans), 141,
    147
116 Squadron (Mustangs), 157
117 Squadron, 236
  Meteors of, 119, 121, 122, 133,
      139, 143, 151, 155, 162, 202
  Mirages of, 250, 272
Phantoms of, 318–19, 320, 324
191 Squadron (fictitious number)
  Meteors of, 162
  Mirages of, 219, 246

221 Squadron (Phantoms; fictitious number), 277, 287, 290
transport squadron, 41–42
Israeli Defense Force (IDF), 144
air doctrine and, 45–46
Haganah command of, 44
IAF's relationship with, 102–7, 111–14, 117–18
Palmach and, 38–39
Zeira and, 314
Israeli Defense Forces (IDF) branches:
Central Command, 254, 350
General Staff, 44, 45, 110, 111–12, 113, 342
Intelligence, *see* AMAN
Northern Command, 96–97, 128, 256, 329, 346, 347, 350
Operations, 158
Planning, 142
Southern Command, 167, 241, 342, 350
Training Command, 107, 108, 116
Israeli Defense Forces (IDF) units:
Ninth Infantry Reserve Brigade, 172–73, 174
Thirty-eighth Infantry and Armor Division, 166, 169
202nd Paratroopers Brigade, 157, 164, 172
890 Paratroopers Battalion, 128, 143n, 157
Israel statehood declaration, 27
Italy, 110
Ivri, David, 273, 275, 298, 363, 364–65, 367–68

J-29 interceptors, 139
Jewish Brigade, British, 107
Jewish National Fund, 90

Johnson, Lyndon B., 230, 266
Jordan, 109, 154, 161, 211, 220, 222, 226, 232, 334, 347, 361, 368
Great Britain and, 153
1948 War and, 30, 34, 37, 54, 55, 61
Six-Day War and, 243, 249, 250–53, 254, 255
terrorist raids from, 141–42, 152
War of Attrition and, 264–65, 266
Jordanian air bases:
Amman, 249
Mafraq, 251
Jordanian aircraft:
Hunter aircraft, 220–21, 250, 253, 254
Vampire fighters, 109, 121
Jordanian Air Force, 253
Jordanian Legion, xii, 152, 254, 255

Kabrit air base (Egypt), 159n, 161, 171
in Six-Day War, 241, 243
Kadesh operation plans, 158, 160–61
see also Sinai campaign
Kaiser, Bill, 79, 83–84, 85, 86, 88
Kebab, Operation, 85, 91–92
Kenya, 359
Kerkorian, Kirk, 62
Kfar Sirkin airfield (Israel), 250
Kfir aircraft, IAF, 365, 367, 369
Khartoum conference, 264
Khomeini, Ayatollah Ruhollah, 361n
King David Hotel bombing, 77–78
Kislev, Shmuel, 238, 239
Kittyhawk fighters, 22
Knesset Committee on Security, 277
Kollek, Teddy, 177

Labor Party, 14–15, 361, 362–63
Lahat, Shlomo, 150–51, 162, 189,
    194, 213
  Weizman's rivalry with, 177–82,
    188
Lapidot, Amos, 184, 240–41, 363
Laskov, Chaim, 107–14, 115, 116,
    121, 127, 158, 166–67, 169,
    178, 179, 180, 182, 183, 187,
    195, 197, 207, 213
Lavon, Pinchas, 117, 142
Lebanon, xiii, 70, 218, 249, 347,
    361, 366, 368
  Bekaa battle in, 358, 363, 368–70
  Israeli invasion of, 357–58
  in 1948 War, 61
  War of Attrition and, 264–65
Lenart, Lou, 4, 24, 25, 26, 34, 35,
    41, 42, 46, 51, 52, 71, 147,
    181
  IAF's first mission and, 31–32
  Operation Yakum Purkan and,
    5–11
"let him pass" maneuver, 204–5,
    301
Levi, Moshe, 363
Liberty, 256
Libya, 278
Lichter, George, 62–63, 64, 65, 71,
    80, 82, 193, 215
Likud Party, 363
Liron, Ze'ev, 91, 92, 94, 96, 97,
    200, 210, 211
Lloyd George, David, 75
Lod airport (Israel), 20, 149
Luftwaffe, 201
Luxor air base (Egypt), 159n, 243

M-5 Mirage aircraft, IAF, 266
McElroy, John, 66–67
Mafraq airfield (Jordan), 243, 251
Magee, Chris, 37, 52
Magister trainers, IAF, 198, 254

Makleff, Mordechai, 107–8, 112–14,
    116, 117, 121, 178
Mann, Morris, 42, 56
Mapam (United Labor Party),
    38–39
Marauder (B-26) bombers, 190, 207
Margo, Cecil, 45–46, 57, 93, 102
Marom, Oded, 237, 242, 261, 263,
    266–68, 270, 272–73, 277,
    287, 305, 308, 349–50
Martin, H. B. "Mickey," 131
Megiddo airfield (Israel), 249–50
Meir, Golda, 336, 359
  Eshkol replaced by, 276
  Ne'eman and, 304n
  Nixon and, 291
  preemptive strike decision of,
    311–30
Melnizki, Moshe, 170
Messerschmitt fighters "Czech
    Knives," Haganah, 23, 24,
    25–27, 29–30
Messerschmitt fighters "Czech
    Knives," IAF, 37, 63, 193,
    201
  in 1948 War, 30, 31–35, 39–44,
    46, 52–55, 57, 61, 68, 118
Meteor fighters, see F-8 Meteor
    fighters
Meteor night fighters, IAF, 162
MiG fighters, EAF, 148, 159n,
    169–70, 171, 190, 318–19
  in Six-Day War, 241, 243
  in War of Attrition, 267, 269,
    271, 274
  in Yom Kippur War, 354–55
MiG fighters, Iraqi, 362
MiG fighters, Syrian, 159n, 249–50,
    314, 317, 318, 369
MiG fighters, Ugandan, 360
MiG-15 fighters, 139
MiG-15 fighters, EAF, 145, 146,
    164–66, 205

MiG-17 fighters, EAF, 145, 183, 219, 243, 273, 319–20
MiG-17 fighters, Syrian, 190
MiG-19 fighters, EAF, 180
MiG-21 fighters, EAF, 187
  in Six-Day War, 240, 241, 242, 247–48, 249
  in War of Attrition, 261–63, 271, 272, 279, 298–301
  in Yom Kippur War, 319–20
MiG-21 fighters, Iraqi, 220n, 253
MiG-21 fighters, Syrian, 218–19, 221, 251, 252, 253, 273, 358, 366
MiG-23 fighters, Syrian, 358
MiG-25 Foxbat fighters, 186
Mirage aircraft, 186–87, 189–91, 278
Mirage fighters, IAF, 185–87, 189–90, 207, 209, 220–21, 223, 246, 247, 278, 314, 317
  in Six-Day War, 232, 235, 236, 237, 239, 240–41, 242, 245, 249–56
  in War of Attrition, 261–64, 271, 273, 274, 277, 283, 286, 294, 295, 298, 299–301
  in water wars, 219
  in Yom Kippur War, 322, 329, 349, 354–55
missiles, air-launched, 186, 278, 299, 354
  Shrike, 305–6, 326, 353, 354
  Sidewinder, 278, 301
  Sparrow, 278
missiles, surface-air, see SA missiles
missiles, surface-surface, 347
Mitla battle, 169–70
Mohammed Reza Shah Pahlavi, 361n
Moked operation plan, 202–13, 216–17, 227, 252
  manual on, 210–11

Nevo and, 206–8
Sivron and, 208–9, 212
timing of, 212–13
Tsiddon's reservations about, 212
see also Six-Day War
Mollet, Guy, 146
Mont-de-Marson air base (France), 140, 150
Mosquito fighter-bombers, IAF, 109–10, 133–34, 144–45, 146, 158, 159, 171, 173, 178, 180, 193
Mosquito fighter-bombers, RAF, 69–70
Mossad, 220n, 314, 323
  Mirage blueprints stolen by, 266
  Phantom raid and, 279
Munich Olympics massacre, xin
Musketeer, Operation, 171–74
Musketeer operation plan, 153–54, 160
Mustang fighters, see P-51 Mustang fighters
Mystère II fighters, 139–41, 144
Mystère IV fighters, 139–41, 149
Mystère IV fighters, IAF, 146–47, 148, 150–51, 182, 184, 193, 204, 209, 223, 308
  in Sinai campaign, 156, 159, 161–62, 165–66, 170, 171, 173
  in Six-Day War, 235, 236, 237–38, 254
  in water wars, 218

Nabulsi, Suleiman, 153
Na'or, Joseph, 291, 295, 298, 301, 309, 310, 323–24
Nasser, Gamal Abdel, 129, 143, 145, 149, 153, 226, 230, 231
  Brezhnev and, 279
  death of, 312
  military coup of, 142

Nasser, Gamal Abdel (*cont'd*)
　resignation of, 263–64
　Sinai campaign and, 160, 166,
　　174
　Suez Canal nationalized by, 148
　UN and, 225
　War of Attrition and, 264–65,
　　268*n*, 269, 271, 273–75,
　　278–80
Nathanson, Phillip, 142
National Religious Party, 230
Ne'eman, Ra'anan, 302–4
Ne'eman, Yuval, 142
Negev Brigade, 47, 55
Neguib, Mohammed, 142
Nesher fighters, IAF, 313, 354
Netanyahu, Benjamin, 360*n*
Netanyahu, Jonathan, 360
Nevo, Jacob "Yak," 122, 130, 156,
　　165, 170, 181, 183–84, 197,
　　200–212, 216–17, 219–20,
　　251, 287, 301
　attack doctrine of, 206–8
　"let him pass" maneuver of,
　　204–5, 220–21
　Sivron and, 208–9, 212
　Six-Day War and, 241, 243
　as theorist, 205–6
NF-13 Meteor night fighters, IAF,
　　162
1948 War, 23–72
　Operation Dust Bowl in, 47–48,
　　117, 155
　Operation Horev in, 65–66
　Operation Yoav in, 54–57
Ninth Infantry Reserve Brigade,
　　IDF, 172–73, 174
Nixon, Richard M., 278, 291
Nomis, Leon, 37, 51, 52
Nord transports, IAF, 149, 250
Norseman aircraft, *Haganah*, 3–5,
　　8–12, 27, 147
Norseman aircraft, IAF, 41

North Atlantic Treaty Organization
　　(NATO), 148, 208

Omer operation plan, 145
On Eagles' Wings (Weizman), 80
101 Commando Unit, 117, 128,
　　143*n*
101 (Red) Squadron, 109, 111, 130,
　　184, 193, 221
　anti-Hod rebellion in, 86–87
　decline of, 87–88, 124
　El-Hamma incidents and
　　(Mustangs), 95–96
　jet aircraft conversion of, 146
　Mirages of, 240, 261, 266, 277,
　　294, 349
　Mustangs of, 99, 135, 138
　Mystères of, 146, 147, 148, 159,
　　166, 171, 181
　in 1948 War (Messerschmitts;
　　Spitfires), 39–40, 41–43,
　　49–59, 60–72
　105 Squadron and, 92–93
　in Sinai campaign (Mystères),
　　161–62, 171
　training of, 81–84, 99–100
　Weizman in command of, 79–83
104 Squadron (Harvards), 170
105 Operational Training Unit, 88,
　　92, 99, 100, 108
105 Squadron, 138
　Bar's innovations and, 92–95,
　　100–101, 124
　El-Hamma incidents and
　　(Spitfires), 95–98
　Mustangs of, 170
　Spitfires of, 109, 128
　Super-Mystères of, 251
109 Squadron (Mosquitos), 109, 158
110 Squadron (Mosquitos), 173
113 Squadron (Ouragans), 141, 147
116 Squadron (Mustangs), 157
117 Squadron, 236

Meteors of, 119, 121, 122, 133,
    139, 143, 151, 155, 162, 202
Mirages of, 250, 272
Phantoms of, 318–19, 320, 324
191 Squadron (fictitious number):
Meteors of, 162
Mirages of, 219, 246
Ophir airfield (Israeli-occupied),
    318, 319
Osirak nuclear plant bombing,
    360–62, 368
Ouragan attack jets, IAF, 140–41,
    145, 146, 148, 189, 204, 209,
    308
  in Sinai campaign, 156–57, 159,
    165, 168–70, 171–72
  in Six-Day War, 235, 236, 241,
    243

P-40 Kittyhawk fighters, 22
P-47 Thunderbolt aircraft,
    Haganah, 7
P-51 Mustang fighters, *Haganah*, 7,
    24
P-51 Mustang fighters, IAF, 61,
    68–69, 93, 99, 100, 110,
    135, 138, 145, 146, 152, 157,
    178
  capabilities of, 124–25
  in El-Hamma incidents, 95–96
  in Sinai campaign, 159, 170, 173
Palestine:
  Balfour Declaration and, 75–76
  Jewish settlers in, xi–xii
  Ottoman administration in,
    89–90
  partition of, ix–x
Palestine Arab Higher Committee,
    x
Palestine Liberation Army, 225
Palestine Liberation Organization
    (PLO), xi*n*, 312
  Lebanon invasion and, 357–58

Tunisia bombing and, 362
War of Attrition and, 264–65
Palestinian Brigade, Egyptian, 143
Palit, Yehuda (pseudonym), 333
Palmach, 14, 20, 38–39
  Flight Platoon of, 16, 20, 90, 98,
    120, 121
  Hod opposed by, 86–87, 88, 92,
    192
Peace for Galilee, Operation, 357
Peake, Wayne, 68–69, 147
Peled, Beni, 96, 122, 123, 140, 141,
    146, 147, 148–51, 156, 161,
    165, 173, 192, 200, 204, 215,
    271, 287, 306, 321, 335, 340,
    341, 342, 347, 352, 370
  background of, 137–38
  on Bar, 126
  Dayan's meeting with, 327–28,
    330
  Dayan's "Third Temple"
    warning to, 329–31
  Entebbe rescue and, 359, 362
  Hod replaced by, 307–10
  IAF reconstructed by, 345–46,
    363–65, 366–68
  Suez bridges and, 336
  Tagar and, 327–28, 330–31
  Yom Kippur War and, 310–12,
    315, 317, 318
Peled, Bertha, 137
Peled, Eitan, 285, 288, 289,
    296–98, 302, 304, 326,
    332–33, 354
Peled, Joseph, 348
Peled, Moshe, 87
Peleg, Dov, 86
Peres, Shimon, 125, 139, 141, 151*n*,
    152, 359, 363
Phantom fighters, *see* F-4 Phantom
    fighters, IAF
Pier, Yitzhak, 285–86, 287, 288,
    289–90, 295, 297

Pineau, Christian, 146, 154
Piper Cub aircraft, *Haganah*, 20
Piper Cub aircraft, IAF, 131, 144, 164–65, 172–74
Pitchett, Leonard, 58–59
"pod formation," 293–98, 324, 325
Podgorny, Nicolai, 225*n*
Pomeranz, Bill, 41–42, 50–51, 55, 61, 64
Pomeranz, Sam, 53, 63, 64
Porat, David, 299, 300
Powers, Gary, 158, 190*n*
Preeha raids, 278

Qasprit air base (Egypt), 159*n*, 161

Rabin, Yitzhak, 49, 213, 222–25, 226, 238, 239, 241, 242–43, 246–47, 258, 362–63
Barlev's replacement of, 264
Entebbe mission and, 359
nervous collapse of, 230–31
pods and, 293–94
Moked plan as viewed by, 232–33
War of Attrition and, 276–77, 278
Weizman on, 228–29
Rakir, Shalom, 99, 100
Ramat David air base (Air Force North) (Israel), 72, 77, 108, 109, 118, 119, 141, 146, 151, 152, 156, 162, 181, 200, 202, 208, 216, 223, 266, 324, 342, 343
Bar's innovations and, 91–95, 99–101
El-Hamma incidents and, 95–98
as IAF birthplace, 120
in 1948 War, 40–41, 54, 68
in Six-Day War, 235, 236, 237, 250, 253
training at, 79–88, 120–26
in War of Attrition, 277, 284, 295, 299–300
Weizman and organization of, 127–36
in Yom Kippur War, 322, 332, 333, 346, 350, 351
Ramla command, 109, 110, 121, 150, 162
Sinai campaign and, 166–68
RB-57A spy planes, U.S., 190
Red Sea flotilla, 318
Red Squadron, *see* 101 Squadron
Remez, Aharon, 10, 20–22, 24, 27–28, 30–31, 33, 34–35, 39, 40, 42, 47, 54, 55, 56, 57, 70–71, 72, 80, 86, 98, 109, 111, 112, 113, 114, 115, 121, 179, 201
air force proposed by, 19
appointed IAF commander, 46
IAF–IDF relationship and, 102–6
Pritchett and, 58–59
RAF experience of, 16–18
Yadin's conflicts with, 44–46, 103–6, 341
Remez, David, 16
remote-controlled aircraft, 365–66
Rimonim (Texas), Operation, 270–74, 278, 287, 298
Rogers, William, 277
Rom, Giora, 252
Rommel, Erwin, 15, 37
Ronen, Heruta, 246
Ronen, Ran, 159, 190, 287, 302
Hetz replaced by, 298
Hunter air battle and, 219–21
in Six-Day War, 235–37, 239, 240, 241, 242, 245–49, 251, 254
Weizman's poem and, 191
Roof, Meir, 81

Rooster mission, 162–63
Royal Air Force, British, 111, 114, 194
  Bar and, 98–99
  intervention plans of, 153
  Peled and, 138–39
  reconnaissance episodes and, 66–69
  Remez's experience in, 16–18
Rubenfeld, Milton, 4–5, 9, 24, 33–34
Rudnick, Eleanor, 177
Ruhama air strip (Israel), 47
RWD aircraft, *Haganah*, 20

SA (surface-air) missiles:
  Egyptian, 276–306, 313, 317, 321, 328, 334, 344, 353, 358, 365
  Israeli, 319
  Syrian, 310, 317, 321, 331, 334, 339n, 358, 365
SA-2 missiles, 280–81, 292–94, 305–6, 323–24, 325
SA-2 missiles, Egyptian, 274
  in War of Attrition, 276, 280–91, 292–94, 296, 302, 305–6
  in Yom Kippur War, 317
SA-2 missiles, Syrian, 310–11, 317, 351
SA-3 missiles, 323–24, 325
SA-3 missiles, Egyptian:
  in War of Attrition, 279, 281–91, 294, 296–98, 302–4
  in Yom Kippur War, 317
SA-3 missiles, Syrian, 310–11, 317, 351
SA-6 missiles, Iraqi, 362
SA-6 missiles, Syrian, 310–11, 317, 324, 327, 334, 350–51, 358
SA-7 Strella missiles, Syrian, 317, 332

SA-8 missiles, Syrian, 358
Sabrejet (F-86) fighters, 139–40, 146, 151
Sadat, Anwar el-, 70, 312, 313, 314, 315, 355
  Israel visit of, 301n, 368
Sagie, Oded, 252
Salameh, Ali Hassan, xin
Salameh, Hassan, xi
"Samson" pods, 369
Saudi Arabia, 143, 361
Schueftan, Dan, 282
Schwartz, Re'uma, 84, 86
Schwimmer, Adolph "Al," 7–8, 13, 20, 22, 37, 38, 41, 53, 68, 71, 93, 177, 266n, 360, 365
Scotland Yard, 78
Second Armored Brigade, Egyptian, 30
Second Army, Egyptian, 351, 352, 353
Second Brigade, Egyptian, 164
Sedeh Dov airfield (Israel), 20
Seiqal airfield (Syria), 251
Sela, Aviem, 301, 366, 368
Senior, Boris, 22, 53, 77, 78
sevev (turnaround), 125, 126
Shachar, Jonathan, 243
Shaked, Rachel, 185
Shamir, Shlomo, 106–7, 108, 121, 179, 360n
Shapira, Dani, 63, 70, 71, 76, 77, 122, 156, 158, 173, 185–86, 187, 190, 191, 193, 217, 220n
Shapira, Moshe Chaim, 230
Sharett, Moshe, 79, 117, 141, 142, 143n, 144
Sharon, Ariel, 117, 128, 143, 144, 157, 164, 166, 169, 172, 254, 324, 352, 357, 363
Shashlik, Operation, 85, 91–92
Shavit, Aharon "Yalo," 125, 128,

Shavit (*cont'd*)
    129, 131, 134, 161–62, 169,
    242, 251, 254
Shazly, Saad el-, 312, 313, 314, 315
Shertok, Moshe, 17
Shmul, Menahem, 246, 252–53
Shochat, Yigael, 302–3
Shrike air-ground missiles, IAF,
    305–6, 326, 353, 354
Shuftykeit incident, 68–69, 147
Sidewinder missiles, 278, 301
Silverman, Mrs. Sol, 8
Sinai campaign, 155–75, 201, 205
    Ben-Gurion and, 158, 160, 169,
        171
    British and French intervention
        in, 160–61, 166, 171–72,
        174
    Dayan and, 160, 165, 167, 171,
        174
    Egyptian response in, 157, 160,
        163, 164–65, 166, 174
    Israeli control and
        communications system in,
        167–68
    Kadesh operation plan and, 158,
        160–61
    Mitla battle in, 169–70
    Operation Musketeer in, 171–74
    Tolkowsky and, 157–63, 165–68,
        171, 174, 179
    UN cease-fire in, 174
    U.S. and, 161
    Weizman and, 158–59, 168–69
Sivron, Rafi, 208, 209, 210, 211,
    212, 216–17, 231, 233, 236,
    345–48, 350
Six-Day War (Operation *Moked*),
    235–57, 262, 263, 268n,
    274, 322, 345
    activation of, 232–34
    aftermath of, 265–66
    Arab response to, 249–50

Dayan on success of, 244
desert and, 238
first strike in, 239–42
Ghardaka strike in, 247–49
Golan Heights and, 256–57
Hod and, 232–33, 238, 239,
    242–43
Jordan and, 243, 249, 250–53,
    254, 255
Liberty attack and, 255–57
Nevo and, 241, 243
Rabin's doubts about, 232–33
radio silence and, 238–39
Ronen's missions in, 235–37,
    239, 240, 241, 242, 245–49,
    251, 254
second strike in, 242–43
Syria and, 243, 249, 250–52, 254,
    256–57
69 Squadron (Phantoms), 277, 287
617 "Dam Busters" Squadron,
    British, 131
Skyhawk aircraft, *see* A-4 Skyhawk
    aircraft, IAF
Skymaster aircraft, *see* C-54
    Skymaster aircraft
Somekh, Yeheskiel, 173, 270, 273,
    275, 280, 284, 343, 349
Soviet Union, 313, 335, 351, 358
    Arabs rearmed by, 265
    collapse of, 368
    Egyptian arms deal of, 145–46
    Israel recognized by, 27
    rolling pack innovation of,
        283–84, 288, 290
    War of Attrition and, 279–84
    war warning of, 225n
Sparrow missiles, 278
Spector, Iftach, 261–63, 271, 272,
    324, 340–41, 345, 347–48,
    349
    on Bir Gafgafa operations,
        268–69

Dougman V and, 333–34
hunt technique developed by, 325, 354–55
mission planners criticized by, 363–64
pod strike opposed by, 294–95
Soviet pilot ambush and, 300, 301
Suez bridges and, 337–38
Tagar plan criticized by, 326–27
Yom Kippur War and, 318, 320
Spitfire fighters, EAF, xiii
in 1948 War, 27–28, 30–32, 34, 41–43, 55, 57, 61, 62, 65, 201
Spitfire fighters, IAF, 63, 84, 90, 93, 108, 109, 110, 128, 131–32, 193
British reconnaissance missions and, 67–68
in El-Hamma incidents, 95–98
in 1948 War, 53, 54–55, 57, 58, 61, 62, 67–68
in Operation *Shashlik*, 85
transport of, 63–65
Squadron A, *Haganah*, 20
Srita operation plan, 323
Star Fighters, 186
State Department, U.S., 96n, 140, 161
Stearman trainers, IAF, 159, 198
Stern Gang, 47–48
Stratocruiser transports, IAF, 305
SU-15 attack jets, EAF, 264
Sudan, 278
Super-Mystère fighters, IAF, 180, 189, 197, 205–6, 266, 326
in Six-Day War, 235, 236, 241, 242, 243, 251, 254, 256
in water wars, 218
surface-air missiles, *see* SA missiles
surface-surface missiles, 347

Sweden, 110, 123, 139
Switzerland, 266, 313
Syria, xix, 70, 109, 143, 148, 153, 161, 211, 220, 222–24, 225, 226, 228, 232, 332, 361
Bekaa Valley battle and, 368–70
El-Hamma incidents and, 95–98, 96n
Golan Heights and, 256–57
Lebanon conflict and, 357–58
in 1948 War, 41, 42, 43, 61
Six-Day War and, 243, 249, 250–53, 254, 256–57
War of Attrition and, 265, 266
water wars and, 218–19
see also Yom Kippur War
Syrian air bases:
Dumeir, 251
Seiqal, 251
T-4, 251–53
Syrian aircraft:
AT-6 Harvard trainers, xiii
F-8 Meteor fighters, 109, 121
MiG fighters, 159n, 249–50, 314, 317, 318, 369
MiG-17 fighters, 190
MiG-21 fighters, 218–19, 221, 251, 252, 253, 273, 358, 366
MiG-23 fighters, 358
T-6 Harvard trainers, 42

T-4 airfield (Syria), 251–53
T-6 Harvard trainers, IAF, 96, 145, 159, 198
T-6 Harvard trainers, Syrian, 42
Tagar, Operation, 329–31, 334, 353
Tagar operation plan, 325–29
Tal, Israel "Talik," 222, 254
Taylorcraft light trainers, *Haganah*, 20
Tel Aviv airfield (Israel), 27–28
Tel Nof air base (Israel), 153, 208, 266

Tel Nof air base (Israel) (cont'd)
    in 1948 War, 29–30, 31, 40, 46,
        54, 65
    in Sinai campaign, 155, 162
    in Six-Day War, 235, 239
    in War of Attrition, 271, 299
    in Yom Kippur War, 322, 332,
        347
    see also Israeli Air Force
        branches, Flight School
Tempest fighters, RAF, 68
Ten-Day Campaign, 43–44
terrorism, 359–60
Texas (Rimonium) air campaign,
    270–74, 278, 287, 298
Thant, U, 225
Third Army, Egyptian, 351, 352,
    353, 354
"Third Temple" warning, 329–32
Thirty-eighth Infantry and Armor
    Division, IDF, 166, 169
Thunderbolt, Operation, 359–60
Thunderbolt aircraft, U.S., 7
Tiger Moth biplanes, Haganah, 20,
    21
Toaster, Operation, 306
Tolkowsky, Dan, 111, 112, 121,
    122, 127, 135, 139, 140–41,
    144, 145–46, 147, 149, 151,
    178, 180, 181, 182, 189, 197,
    201, 213, 216
    appointed IAF commander,
        114–18
    Gazit appointed by, 193–96
    Rooster mission and, 162–63
    Sinai campaign and, 157–63,
        165–68, 171, 174, 179
Trans-Jordan, xiii
Tsiddon, Yoash, 96–98, 143,
    162–63, 189, 200, 211,
    212
Tsivoni, Adam, 99
Tsuk, Joseph, 147, 159, 165–66,
    170

Tunisia, 362, 364–65
Tupolev-16 bombers, EAF, 241,
    242
Tupolev-16 bombers, Iraqi, 250n
202nd Paratroopers Brigade, IDF,
    157, 164, 172
208 Squadron, RAF, 67n
221 Squadron (Phantoms; fictitious
    number), 277, 287, 290
Tzur, Zvi, 187

U-2 spy planes, U.S., 190n
Uganda, 359–60
United Arab Republic, 159n
United Labor Party (Mapam),
    38–39
United Nations, 35, 37, 39, 42, 53,
    62, 66, 69, 70, 141
    Bernadotte proposal and, 47
    El-Hamma incidents and, 95,
        96n, 98
    Great Britain and, 61
    Nasser and, 225
    Palestine partition and, ix–x, 15
    Sinai campaign cease-fire and,
        174
    War of Attrition and, 304–5
    Yom Kippur War cease-fire and,
        354–55
United States, 53, 148, 226, 233,
    279–80, 311, 313, 351–52
    arms embargo by, 7, 13
    El-Hamma incidents and, 96n
    Israel recognized by, 27
    Khomeini revolution and, 361n
    Liberty attack and, 256
    Shrike missiles of, 305–6
    Sinai campaign and, 161
    Six-Day War aftermath and, 266
    spy planes of, 190
    War of Attrition and, 276–77,
        304
    Yom Kippur War and, 351, 352
Uris, Leon, 49

Valiant aircraft, RAF, 171
Vampire fighters, EAF, 109, 110,
    121, 143–44, 145, 159n,
    164, 169
Vampire fighters, Iraqi, 109, 121
Vampire fighters, Jordanian, 109,
    121
Vautour aircraft, IAF, 180, 189,
    194, 209, 223
  in Six-Day War, 235, 236, 242,
    243, 253, 254
  in water wars, 218
Vickman, Robert, 41–42, 43
Vietnam, 281

War of Attrition, 264–85, 292–305,
    307, 309, 312, 323
  air cover and, 269–70
  Bir Gafgafa operations and,
    268–69
  deep-penetration raid in, 276–77
  Hod and, 270–72, 277, 279, 281,
    287, 290–91
  Jordan and, 264–65
  Lebanon and, 264–65
  Nasser and, 264–65, 268n, 269,
    271, 273–75, 278–80
  Operation Boxer and, 274–75,
    278, 287
  Phantom-missile race in, 282–83
  PLO and, 264–65
  Porat plan in, 299–300
  Rabin and, 276–77, 278
  rolling pack missiles in, 273–74
  Soviet missile trap in, 302–4
  Soviet pilots in, 298–304
  Soviet weapons and tactics in,
    279–84
  Syria and, 265
  Texas air campaign and, 270–74
  UN cease-fire in, 304–5
  U.S. and, 276–77, 304
wars, see 1948 War; Sinai
    campaign; Six-Day War;
    War of Attrition; Yom
    Kippur War
Weather Service, U.S., 190n
Weizman, Ezer, 10–11, 24–25, 28,
    32, 33–34, 51, 55, 56, 61,
    68, 69, 72, 84–86, 92, 98,
    106, 107, 110, 111, 119, 121,
    137, 139, 141, 146, 147, 148,
    149, 150–51, 196, 201, 206,
    208, 210, 212, 233, 246,
    254–55, 258, 271, 307, 308,
    309, 321, 355, 358, 367
  aerobatics team and, 135–36
  air combat and, 219–20
  background of, 76–78
  Bar and, 133–35
  Gazit's confrontations with,
    197–200
  Hod described by, 239
  Hod's relationship with, 82–83,
    192–93, 215–20, 224, 239
  IAF and mystique of, 127–33
  IAF tenure of, 182, 184–89
  Irgun and, 77–78
  Lahat's rivalry with, 177–82, 188
  Mirage aircraft and, 186–87, 191
  Nevo on, 219–20
  Nevo's doctrine opposed by, 207
  101 Squadron command and,
    79–83
  personal Spitfire of, 131–32
  poem by, 191
  public view of, 217–18
  on Rabin, 228–29
  Rabin's nervous collapse and,
    230–31
  Sinai campaign and, 158–59,
    168–69
  Six-Day War and, 238, 239, 243
Weizman, Yael, 107
Weizman, Yechiel, 75, 76, 77
Weizmann, Chaim, 56, 75, 76
White Paper, 15

Wilson, Denny, 61, 70
World War II, 15, 16, 28, 118, 201

Yadin, Yigael, 21, 24, 31, 39, 57,
    58, 102, 110, 111, 113, 116
  El-Hamma incidents and, 95
  IAF–IDF relationship and,
    103–6, 341
  Remez's conflicts with, 44–46,
    103–6, 341
  resignation of, 112
  Six-Day War and, 238
Yakum Purkan, Operation,
    xiii–xiv, 3–12, 29, 35, 37,
    71, 177, 266n, 360
Yates, Sidney, 161
Yavneh, Yitzhak "Tsahik," 127–28,
    135
Yeager, Chuck, 66n
yemei krav (battle days), 126
Yemen, 224
Yiftach Brigade, 47, 55
Yoav, Operation, 54–57
Yoeli, Aharon, 94, 122, 123–24,
    130–31, 132, 134, 143, 144,
    151, 155–56, 170, 182–83,
    189, 195, 205, 209, 216
Yoffe, Abraham, 172
Yoffe, Avraham, 86, 122, 192, 199
Yoffe, Dubi, 320
Yom Kippur War, 297, 310–55,
    359, 361, 363, 365, 367, 368
  air superiority in, 320–21
  air support failure in, 342–43,
    344, 345

air war in, 317–19
Egypt and, 310, 311, 313,
    314–15, 339, 351–55
envelopment campaign in,
    352–54
ground support in, 344, 345,
    348–49
IAF's failure in, 321–22, 337–40
intelligence failure in, 340–42,
    344
Marom and, 349–50
onset of, 310–17
Operation Dougman V in, 331,
    332–34, 350, 353
Operation Tagar and, 329–31,
    334, 353
Peled and, 310–12, 315, 317, 318
southern front in, 334–36, 351
Suez bridges and, 336–37,
    341–42
Syria and, 310, 311, 313, 314–15,
    339n–40n, 347, 351,
    354–55, 368–70
Tel Fares air strike and, 346–48
"Third Temple" warning and,
    329–32
UN cease-fire in, 354–55
U.S. and, 351, 352
Zeira's failure in, 314–15, 317,
    328
Žatec air base (Czechoslovakia),
    29–30
Zeira, Eliahu, 314–17, 328, 355
ZIL trucks, Egyptian, 267–68, 283
Zimmerman, Tev, 34
Zionism, 14

About the Author

Israeli-born Ehud Yonay is an award-winning West Coast investigative reporter whose articles have appeared in many publications nation-wide. His 1983 "Top Guns" story about U.S. Navy fighter pilots was made into the movie *Top Gun*. It also led to the nine years of research into the history and making of the Israeli Air Force, which resulted in this book. Yonay divides his time between his West Coast residence and his family olive farm in northern Israel.